CW01649802

Interface Criticism

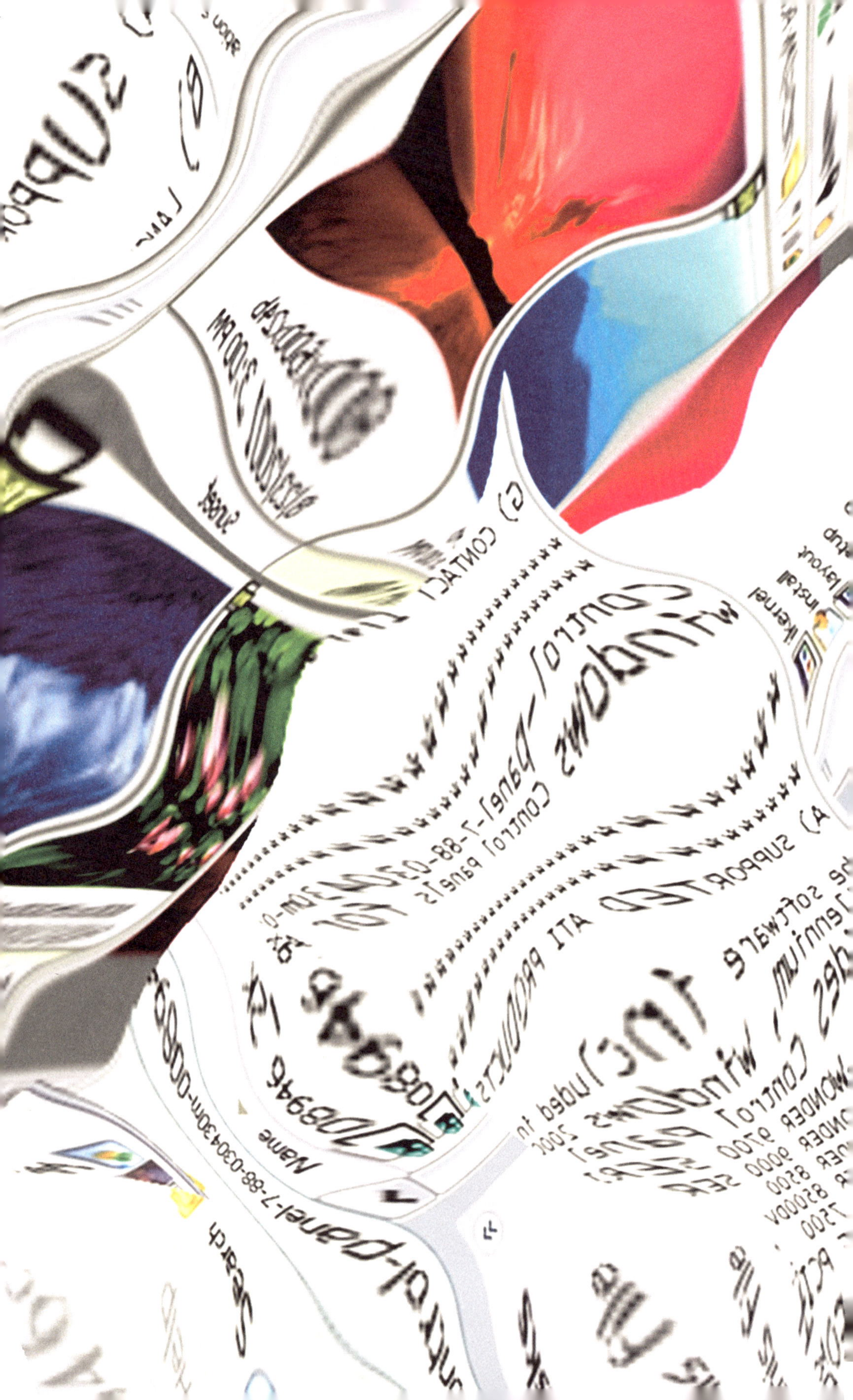

EDITED BY CHRISTIAN ULRIK ANDERSEN
& SØREN BRO POLD

Interface Criticism

Aesthetics Beyond Buttons

AARHUS UNIVERSITY PRESS

Interface Criticism
Acta Jutlandica. Humanities Series 2011/1

Cover design: Carl-H.K. Zakrisson, Polytype
Cover illustration: Alexei Shulgin
Design: Carl-H.K. Zakrisson, Polytype
Printed by Narayana Press, Gylling
Printed in Denmark 2011

ISSN 0065-1354 (Acta Jutlandica)
ISSN 0901-0556 (Humanities Series 1)
ISBN 9788779345041

Aarhus University Press
Aarhus
Langelandsgade 177
8200 Aarhus N

Copenhagen
Tuborgvej 164
2400 Copenhagen NV
www.unipress.dk
Fax 89 42 53 80

International distributors:
Gazelle Book Services Ltd.
White Cross Mills
Hightown, Lancaster, LA1 4XS
United Kingdom
www.gazellebookservices.co.uk

The David Brown Book Company
Box 511
Oakville, CT 06779
USA
www.oxbowbooks.com

Published with the financial support of
The Aarhus University Research Foundation
Novo Nordisk Fonden

Research supported by
The Danish Council for Independent Research, Humanities
Center for Digital Urban Living (The Danish Council for Strategic Research, KINO, grant number 2128-07-0011)
Digital Aesthetics Research Center

Interface Criticism
Aesthetics Beyond Buttons*

BY CHRISTIAN ULRIK ANDERSEN
& SØREN BRO POLD

The human computer interface has been a growing part of our culture for decades. First came the early experiments with computer graphics and games in the 1960s, then the commercial introduction of graphical user interfaces in the mid-1980s, and today computer interfaces take a myriad forms and are constantly met both at work and in our private lives. Wherever we go, we find physical interfaces such as the mouse, keyboards, controllers, touch screens, microphones and cameras; we see visual interfaces such as desktop metaphors and computer game worlds; we hear audible interfaces such as sounds signalling the state of a machine, the start-up of an operating system, an incoming text message, or more sophisticated audio interfaces as in audio based games and sound art. The range of interfaces is expanding to meet the needs of different technologies, uses, cultures and contexts: mobile, networked, ubiquitous or embedded in the environment and architecture. Some interfaces may even be designed to be invisible and imperceptible such as those used in surveillance and tracking technologies. No matter how or where, the interface is a dominant cultural form providing a way to mediate between humans and machines and between culture and data, affecting the way we perceive cultural activities and perform them in public and private.

Interfaces are designed with specific purposes, some very narrow and technically determined as technical protocols, others more application and end user oriented such as interfaces for reading, seeing, listening, communication and experience. Until recently, it has been common practice to discuss interfaces primarily from an

* Thanks to Claire Neesham for language correction.

engineering perspective, as something that should be optimised to offer seamless functionality. This approach has led to the 'what-you-see-is-what-you-get'-text editors and the emphasis on user-friendly and transparent design. The main idea is that the computer should blend smoothly into our homes and environments as something we do not have to deal with consciously.

Simultaneous with the development of the interface, and often in a critical dialogue with this, a digital aesthetics has developed. Even as early as the 1960s, different digital art forms and early computer games were starting to explore the emerging formal languages and new aesthetics of the computer in which it was designed to be experienced; therefore transparency and seamless functionality were not the goal. For many years this meant an apparent antagonism between digital art and interface design. As interface design becomes more diverse, however, it affects cultural practices in new ways, and the antagonism between art and design is thus beginning to dissolve with current developments in design and technology. Business communication has discovered experience oriented design, and computers, smart phones and gadgets are prime fashion objects and culturally coded. Furthermore, in the reign of Web 2.0, the economy of interfaces is changing from a traditional production mode based on employed software developers to being more network oriented and user driven (with the side effect of providing free labour) while still restricting and containing their work. Simultaneously, programmers are becoming culturally and politically aware and engage in the free software movement. Even certain forms of digital art are starting to enter the mainstream both commercially and institutionally. This development calls for a new discussion of the role of digital art and aesthetics within an interface culture where art is increasingly intermingling – though not coinciding – with design.

This book aims to offer a much needed perspective on the role of artistic practices and aesthetic theory within interface culture. As editors of the book, we see interface criticism as an appropriate paradigm for a critical discussion of the computer and how it relates to art and culture today. In the contributions to the book we find a discussion of both developments: how interfaces are related to culture, and how art has developed around interfaces, often undermining common conceptions of the interface. But, before we begin our discussion, we need to define *interface* and describe what we mean by *interface criticism* as *aesthetics beyond buttons*.

Our conception of the *interface* is not restricted to the well-known graphical user interface between humans and computers, e.g. the WIMP (Windows, Icons, Menus, Pointers) interfaces that have become popular and standardised on personal computers the last twenty-five years. As described by Florian Cramer in this volume, the term interface indicates many different contact points and exchanges between different programs and data layers in a computer, between different machines (e.g. in a network), between humans and machines (such as graphical user interfaces), and as a mediator between humans (e.g. in net culture, interface culture and the public sphere). Some interfaces seem more or less mechanical – such as the USB interface that most of us know as a plug, but which is in fact an interface that specifies how communication between devices is established – while others are more clearly directed towards human understanding and cultural traditions such as interfaces for computer games or digital art. All interfaces, however, are designs that combine – and translate – signs and signals. As such, the interface is at the core of the computer. It is not possible to 'unveil' the computer through a deconstruction of the interface. The code behind the interface is just another interface in the layered 'mise en abîme' architecture of the computer. The functioning of the interface, its designed juxtaposing of human signs and machine signals, is therefore essential to the functioning of the computer.

The question of *interface aesthetics* is intrinsically linked to our perception of the interface. If it is not possible to fully 'unveil' the 'mise en abîme' of the interface we can, however, elucidate how interfaces can embed choices, conduct, languages, and ultimately values, worldviews and aesthetics into technical infrastructures. The word aesthetics derives from the Greek 'aisthesis' that means sense perception, and today we perceive our environment through interfaces. Aesthetic theory consequently needs to develop a critical vocabulary towards computers and interfaces, an *interface criticism*, and this book aims to be one such contribution. An aesthetic aspect of the interface is usually subordinated to a functionalistic dimension (e.g. the use of buttons for actions) or even a stylistic dimension (interfaces may look good or feel good). Conversely, in this book interface aesthetics will be developed as a critical investigation of interfaces, what they mean for – and how they function in – contemporary culture.

With the subtitle *Aesthetics Beyond Buttons* we want to point to the working in, between, behind and beyond the interfaces: the mediation and computation in and between the various layers and actors in and around interfaces. We do not subscribe to the idea of transcending the interface, nor do we believe that there is an essential core of the computer, but rather that its meaning and functioning lie in the interface's combination of signals and signs, computation and medium, executive buttons and alluring metaphors. There is no essential truth hidden in the code and no privileged vantage point for finding such a truth, but instead interfaces and interfacing with its layers of mediation and computation open up spaces for criticism: A criticism that draws upon recent theoretical developments such as code criticism, media aesthetics, software criticism, and media archaeology as well as more established theoretical traditions within aesthetics.

Consequently, our investigation of the interface does not stop at the computer's surface but goes beyond the buttons and reaches 'back' into history, and 'through' to the human senses and perception, 'behind' the concept of the interface, 'down' into the machine, 'out' into society and culture. This book is subsequently divided into five sections that overlap in many ways, but which also can be seen as five dimensions in interface criticism: displays and history, sensation and perception, representation and computation, software and code, culture and politics.

BACK: Displays and history. When looking at a computer, we see not only its hardware but also its representation as texts and images displayed on a screen. Perceived as screens and display mechanisms, computer interfaces are not new but belong to a long and continuous tradition of media displays dating back to the 19th century and even further. This book section will examine the screen in relation to both the historical development of a screen-mediated public sphere and an archaeology of video art and installations that represent cybernetic activities. Both of these historical perspectives lead to corrections of contemporary understandings of displays.

Currently, interfaces are spreading into the urban public space as both small portable devices and big architectural screens. In his "Monumental Attractions: An Archaeology of Public Media Displays", ERKKI HUHTAMO depicts a thought-provoking and often forgotten history of public media displays. Even in the 19th century signboards, billboards, various projection forms as well as an audiovisual extension of the telephone were used for attracting people's attention by displaying news and advertisements in the city landscape. Acknowledgement of the past not only helps us frame contemporary urban interfaces, it also enables us to challenge the visual historian Jonathan Crary's hypothesis of modern media spectatorship as an interiorised and privatised mode of experience. Rather than separating the viewer from the surroundings, one needs to understand the experience of urban displays as rooted in a milieu of noises, competing imagery and other distractive elements of the modern landscape.

While Erkki Huhtamo goes back to the 19th century's public displays, BODIL MARIE STAVNING THOMSEN goes back to the video art scene of the 1960s in order to investigate changes in how we perceive and construct the imagery of interfaces. In "The Haptic Interface – On signal transmissions and events", she explores the history behind the outspoken use of different forms of haptic imagery in reality TV, direct news broadcasting and documentary film formats. She argues that among others Nam June Paik and Les Levine were the forerunners of a new media immediacy now associated with the real-time imagery of surveillance cameras and webcams.

THROUGH: Sensation and perception. The appearance and cultural diffusion of interfaces affect the way the world is perceived and sensed. Based on human input, the computer processes and presents an output that is often the starting point for new human input into the computer, and so on. As such, the human-computer interface is an input/output device where humans exist in a symbiosis with the cybernetic system of the computer. In a time where our relationship with the world often depends on an interface (the steering of a car is run by a computer, knowledge is accessed through a web browser, play takes place in a computer game, etc.), our sense perception is influenced by the interface. This book section will discuss this influence and how it is articulated in contemporary net and software art.

In the development of and discourses around interfaces there has always been a strong urge to bypass representation and 'jack' directly in to the human brain, consciousness, perceptions and feelings. In her article "The interface at the skin", LONE KOEFOED HANSEN looks at how two contemporary experimental dresses made by Philips within the field of wearable computing subscribe to the concept of 'ideal communication'. In her article, she explains how this particular type of communication is linked to the paranormal phenomena of mind reading and telepathy and argues that sensor based wearable computing is the newest example of a technological development implicitly or explicitly aiming at manifesting two utopian parameters of communication: immediacy and instantaneity. Though clearly utopian, this manifestation has served as a way to brand Philips and thus, paradoxically, enters into the more traditional communication circuit of public relations.

SØREN BRO POLD's article "Interface Perception – The Cybernetic Mentality and Its Critics: Ubermorgen.com" presents a model for a cultural understanding of the cybernetic feedback loop between human and computer. Using the example of the artist group Ubermorgen.com, he furthermore discusses how cybernetic loops influence both our culture and not least our perception and mentality. Ubermorgen.com explores ways to stage a criticism from within the cybernetic system, attacking both its function and its representation. Using inverted cybernetic strategies the group addresses the cultural role of Google while also examining how entering a cybernetic loop may create new mental illnesses.

BEHIND: Representation and computation. The concept of the interface carries strong connotations towards the graphic human-computer interface with menus, icons, etc. The computer interface is often seen as a screenbased aesthetic representation of the functionality of the computer. As such, interfaces are translating the computational processes into soothing, well-known or 'user-friendly' visuals and metaphors as known from much commercial software, subsequently disguising the computer as something well known. This common understanding of the interface and its aesthetics as surface, aestheticisation and consequently a hiding of the computational processes are criticised in this section of the book, and it is argued that we need to subject our understanding of interfaces and how we co-exist with computational processes through them to critical scrutiny. As a result, an interface criticism should include a criticism of the concept of the interface as a crucial concern and point of departure.

In a critical evaluation of both the interface and aesthetics, FLORIAN CRAMER's "What Is Interface Aesthetics, or What Could It Be (Not)?" discusses the graphical user interface as an aesthetic choice separating users from programmers and favouring beautiful transparency over the sublime opacity of the hidden programming interface. However, interfaces can be much more than just human-computer user interfaces (e.g. an interface between components in the hardware or between hardware and software). Discussing interface aesthetics, we need to get past the classic Kantian dichotomy of the beautiful versus the sublime. Digital artistic practice has often been biased towards the latter, but we need to address all dimensions of interfaces and not stay on the visual surface. Therefore, Cramer argues that interface aesthetics should not be developed as a stable perspective but as a critical paradigm within media theories and computer science, embracing aesthetics as a way to critically analyse technology.

Also DRAGANA ANTIC and MATTHEW FULLER argue that we need to look in other directions than the classic graphical user interface to fully understand what is currently happening with the concept. In their article "The Computation of Space", they propose to think about the question of computation and interface with specific reference to the production of space. With embedded and ubiquitous computing we move beyond the classic screenbased interface towards interpellating computation into multiple kinds of devices and processes. As the interface becomes increasingly co-extensive with what it handles, the authors reflect on the nature of the interface and argue for a need to also consider computation, spatial design and experience. Consequently, computation becomes an important material in architecture and urban space.

DOWN: Software and code. In continuation of the previous section's outline of what lies behind the computer interface conceptually, this section of the book moves beyond an interface aesthetics only concerned with what can be seen, heard or felt, down into the software and code and towards a hermeneutics of suspicion, critically addressing how interfaces function and are understood, also in relation to what they hide behind the screen. Focusing on the interface's duality of medium and computational functionality, this section highlights how the interface leads to new kinds of aesthetic practices that in turn redefine our understanding of the interface. Both within musical software, software art and gaming we find practices that explicitly deal with the creative, artistic vigour of code and software and critically address how interfaces function and are understood.

In his article "Means-End of Software", GEOFF COX investigates the concealed processes of code and software as grounds for artistic and cultural practices. In contrast to common practices where the software functions as a tool, a means to an end, alienating the user from the production process and the workings of the software, he indicates that the production and workings of code can become an artwork in itself. Building on both Hannah Arendt and Giorgio Agamben's philosophical understandings of labour and with references to political theory, free software production and the free labour of Web 2.0, he further argues that the incomplete understanding of software and how it works not only takes place on a technical level but also on a general, societal and economic level. In fact, artistic practices, such as the 'live coding' music scene, hold a unique potential for criticising the false distinctions of means and ends and instead describe a mediality that breaks down the distinction between the means and ends, a way of being in the interface or 'interfacing' as an active process.

With a focus on the musicological perspective on interfaces, live coding and other musical interfaces are also discussed in the article "Poesis of Human-Computer Interaction: Music, Materiality and Live Coding" by MORTEN BREINBJERG. The computer is commonly used either as a tool for editing existing music or as an 'intelligent' machine capable of creating music on its own. However, analysing two contemporary musical software practices, ixi software and live coding, Morten Breinbjerg highlights a contemporary musical practice where the computer is used unconventionally. Here, music is not generated by the computer or controlled by humans but appears as the outcome of a complex relationship between human and computer. Such musical practices not only reflect how the relationship between human and computer challenges our perception of music but also the cultural role of technology.

Turning towards games, CHRISTIAN ULRIK ANDERSEN in "Writerly Gaming: Political Gaming" continues the exploration of aesthetic practices that deal with the coded aspects of interfaces and highlights how they are used for political purposes. A ludic activity is political when the player assumes authorship of the underlying coded dynamics of the game and starts challenging prevailing meanings and control mechanisms. Building this aesthetics of production on both Roland Barthes' concept of the writerly and Jacques Rancière's concept of the literary, he analyses different areas where playing becomes 'writing' and the realisation of other political realities – by consumers creating games on the Internet, hackers developing alternative game expressions or artists using games as interventions in urban settings.

OUT: Culture and politics. Having discussed the historical, perceptional, conceptual and software oriented dimensions of interface aesthetics and criticism, the book's last section focuses on the cultural and political impact of the interface. As a defining contemporary medium, the interface has wide-ranging cultural and political consequences, which are often overlooked or disguised as technical questions and consequently 'black-boxed' and kept out of public political debate. However, artists struggle with re-opening the 'black boxes' and creating alternatives that consciously appear on the cultural and political stages.

The Internet has often been considered a new and important space of social practice. In his article "The Net Interface and the Public Sphere", HENRIK KAARE NIELSEN deals with the Internet as a public sphere. Drawing on Oskar Negt and Alexander Kluge's critical dialogue with Jürgen Habermas in the 1970s, he qualifies the concept and characterises the public sphere in late modernity as relying both on the institutions of a parliamentary democracy (a bourgeois public sphere), oppositional movements (a proletarian public sphere) and the industries of consciousness (a public sphere of production). Before any political decision can gain democratic legitimacy the bourgeois and the proletarian public spheres must interact. In this 'democratic public sphere' the Internet opens up new possibilities, but Henrik Kaare Nielsen also points to how a commercialised space and the public sphere of production pose certain challenges.

In "Is There Really Only One Word For It? Software Vocabularies in the Expanded Field of Interface Aesthetics", JACOB LILLEMOSE takes a closer look at the public sphere of production and its paradigms of images, signs and statements. In particular, he analyses the user interfaces of operating systems, including the popular consumer operating system Windows Vista and Daniel Garcia Andujar's Linux based, artistic operating system *X-Devian – The New Technologies to the People System*. Reading the statements, signs and images of the two systems he expands the field of interface criticism. Not only the software itself (with its use of e.g. metaphors) but also the discourses around software, as found in marketing and media coverage, communicate cultural meaning. The consumer not only engages with a tool but is also staged as a subject who can realise highly different worlds. In contrast to Windows Vista's promised sublime, problem free and transparent interaction with a computer aimed at the non-critical consumer, *X-Devian* stages a critical exploration of the operating system as a cultural phenomenon. Andujar's work thus demonstrates how software art can form alternatives to standardised options of tool use.

With "Transparent World – Minoritarian Tactics in the Age of Transparency", INKE ARNS enters the cultural and political discussion by investigating a crucial concept of interface culture that has also been an issue in many of the articles in this book: transparency. With references to Michel Foucault and Gilles Deleuze, she argues that transparency has shifted meaning with the change from a disciplinary society to the flexible modulations of a society of control. Transparency has gradually shifted from meaning *visibility*, clarity and controllability (e.g. in relation to the combat against corruption), to meaning *invisibility* as in relation to transparent interfaces that conceal their coded performativity (such as those discussed in the section above). She discusses a number of artistic strategies (by artists such as Jim Jarmusch, Michelle Terran, Manu Luksch, Marko Peljhan, 01001...org and Hasan Elahi) that are trying to restore the IT based notion of transparency to its original meaning of clearness and controllability through visibility.

The book closes with an artistic contribution from CHRISTOPHE BRUNO. "Collective Hallucination and Capitalism 2.0" is an essay about how Web 2.0 strategies and control of the marketplace of the gaze lead to a paradigm shift evidenced in the 2007 French presidential elections. The essay is based on the idea that reality turned out to be even more absurd than the artist's own critical net art to the extent that his whole artistic practice had suddenly become obsolete. Christophe Bruno shockingly discovers parallels and similarities between some of his own artworks (e.g. *Fascinum* and *Google Adwords Happening*) and strategies employed by the two candidates: Ségolène Royal's website Segosphere.net and Nicolas Sarkozy's buying the adword 'Racaille' (scum) on Google in order to promote his tough-on-crime politics.

This book sets out to offer a critical investigation of an important cultural form – rather than to provide a design manual or a manifesto for a new art form. The book's five sections outline important dimensions that pave the way for further critical discussions of the interface based on aesthetic theories and artistic practices. Simultaneously, the book develops interface criticism as a theoretical framework for discussing art and aesthetics within our interface culture.

In total, the articles cover a wide range of aesthetic expressions – including urban screens, wearable interfaces, performances, games, net art, software art, and sound art. Also, many of them convey how cultures evolve as practices of e.g. open source or live coding. Though different in perspective, all these articles have in common that they critically investigate the aesthetics of interfaces in ways that transcend the iconic surface of the graphical user interface and go beyond the buttons.

BACK: Displays and History

ERKKI HUHTAMO
Monumental Attractions: Toward An Archaeology of Public Media Interfaces

BODIL MARIE STAVNING THOMSEN
The Haptic Interface: On Signal Transmissions and Events

Monumental Attractions
Toward An Archaeology of Public Media Interfaces

BY ERKKI HUHTAMO

In his article "Géricault, the Panorama, and Sites of Reality in the Early Nineteenth Century," Jonathan Crary uses *Southwark Fair*, a well-known 18th century engraving based on a painting by William Hogarth (1733), to pinpoint an early symptom of the process that led to the formation of the modern spectator. In the carnivalesque chaos of the fair, he notes a detail that contrasts with everything else: two people peering into a peep-show box. While the "disorder of the carnival," to follow Crary's logic, "overturns a distinction between spectator and performer," the "immobile and absorbed figures, interfacing with the window of the peep show" represent an interiorised and privatised mode of experience. Some decades later, as Crary claims referring to Walter Benjamin, something similar manifested itself in the bourgeois reading subject immersed in a novel and, eventually, in various modes of media spectatorship. The "dominant form of visual culture" that gradually came into existence was characterised by "the relative separation of a viewer from a milieu of distraction and the detachment of an image from a larger background."

This interpretation could be criticised on several grounds. As a visual scholar, Crary pays no attention to the effects of the surrounding soundscape. However, noises and voices must have worked against visual immersion into the contents of the peep-show box, anchoring the peeper into the (invisible) present. Physical tactility also played a role, as contemporary engravings and paintings demonstrate. The peepers often touched each other, and could even be harassed from behind their backs (Huhtamo). Focusing on a detail, Crary misses the big picture: the symptomatic meaning of *other* forms of visuality, including banners and signboards. As Jacob Larwood and John Camden Hotten pointed out in their classic *The*

History of Signboards (1866), the use of public signboards goes back to classical antiquity or earlier. Inns, gobbler's workshops and other businesses had used them for centuries as indexical informational signs. The banners used at the Southwark Fair had a more emphatic character, pointing to titillating experiences for sale.[1] They could be characterised as *attractors* representing *attractions* (and sometimes functioning as attractions in their own right).

The discourse on attractions within media culture was introduced by Tom Gunning and André Gaudreault in the early 1980s (Gunning "An Aesthetic of Astonishment..."; Gunning "The Cinema of Attraction..."). Discussing the aesthetics of early film, they identified a tendency toward exhibitionism and visual shocks in order to affect the viewer emotionally. Instead of telling stories that would 'suture' the spectator into a narrative world, the 'cinema of attractions' addressed the spectator directly and displayed curious sights as if it had been a live performance. The origins of such strategies point to the fairground and the variety show, where the early film found both inspiration and a home. However, it could also be argued that the cinema of attractions was an outcome of a much broader and older phenomenon, a 'culture of attractions' as depicted by Hogarth. At the fair, the visitor was constantly bombarded by impulses competing for his/her attention (and purse). Banners, supported by the cries of the barkers, pointed metonymically to pleasures that were kept out of sight and beyond reach – behind closed doors or inside peep-show boxes – until a transaction, mediated by a coin, occurred.

In the 19th century, the culture of attractions came to characterise the evolving urban environment in many ways. Its impact grew in pace with the strengthening of the capitalist economy, manifesting itself in posters, billboards, electric signs and the sensationalist front pages of fiercely competing newspapers at the newsstand (later, revolutionaries used such attractors as well). Walter Benjamin saw such visual extravaganzas as hieroglyphs and image-writing by which the bulging capitalist society expressed its ideals and desires, constituting the subjects roaming the city streets as consumers obsessively looking for new treats and pleasures.[2] It could therefore be claimed that the banners and signboards promoting wax museums, theatre troupes and curiosities of all kinds at the Southwark Fair were as important for the future of media culture as the intimate pleasures inside the peep-show box. Contrary to Crary's interpretation, media culture does not exist only in interior spaces; it has never been segregated from outdoor 'milieus of distraction.'

Public displays seem to constitute a different mode of spectatorship than the one Crary considers the 'dominant form of visual culture.' Yet, they can and should be read as media interfaces that constitute their own peculiar modes of spectatorship. Still, in spite of their ubiquity in contemporary urban spaces, public screens and other visual attractors have until recently remained peripheral as a topic of study.[3] Both cinema and television studies and new media research have largely ignored them. Until the pop-influenced writings of the *Archigram* group (1961-), Guy Debord's *Society of the Spectacle* (1967), and Robert Venturi's, Denise Scott Brown's and Steven Izenour's postmodern classic *Learning from Las Vegas* (1972) appeared, public urban displays were largely missing from architectural and urban theory as well. The spokespeople of modernist architecture were aware of the impact of advertising on modern society; Le Corbusier even wrote that the poster is "the modern fresco, and its place is in the street" (Le Corbusier quoted in Colomina 217).[4] Constructivism, Bauhaus and artist-designers like Alexandr Rodchenko, László Moholy-Nagy, Friedrich Kiesler and Herbert Bayer were all interested in messages of attractions placed in outdoor spaces. Still, modernist architectural theorists often either left public urban displays out from their writings or erased them from the utopias they advocated.

The analysis of public displays as media interfaces can profit from explorations of their historical becoming, a topic that has been left almost completely untouched until now. To further such a goal, this article develops an archaeology of public displays, excavating their formative stages from trade signs, banners and broadsides to billboards and early dynamic displays.

From signboards to placards and billboards

Painted or carved wall inscriptions were used to attract attention already in ancient Rome. Romans also used signboards to identify craftsmen's workshops and various services. Similar practices existed in medieval Europe, although more decisive evidence is only available from the 16th century onwards. Metal emblems with symbolic objects or coats-of-arms suspended from a rod protruding from the front of a house were widely used as means of identification; before the adoption of house numbering they also served as address indicators. The habit of posting printed bills on doors and walls made more varied linguistic messages possible. It began in the late 15th century in the wake of the Gutenbergian revolution. As communities grew and the hold of capitalism became stronger, the role of public advertising gained importance. Signboards developed into vehicles for distinguishing between *similar* competing products and services, which was related to the introduction of other forms, such as printed trade cards and newspaper advertisements.

Strategies of persuasion gained force over the seemingly neutral notices that announced services. As we have already seen, fairs, carnivals and other public gatherings played a role in this development. Market stalls for touring theatre troupes, circuses and other entertainments had large painted banners as attractors and previews of the show's content. The notorious father of humbug P.T. Barnum adopted this practice, displaying large banners of the curiosities he was exhibiting at the American Museum (New York) on the facade facing Broadway, the busiest thoroughfare of the city.

Printed attractions in outdoor spaces became widespread in the early 19th century. Advertising broadsides promoting products and popular spectacles were posted on any available surfaces from fences to walls and even doors. This did not only have to do with the growth of metropolitan cities like London and Paris, or the intensifying competition in the capitalist economy, but also with other issues, such as heavy taxation of paid advertisements in newspapers. Advertising in public spaces was a cheaper channel and could reach a wider audience. The first half of the 19th century was the wild period as the histories of advertising testify (Elliott 164-7; Schuwer 62-3; Sampson). Billposters obeyed no rules, using any available surfaces. Layer upon layer they pasted their broadsides on walls that were often already covered. They competed and even physically fought with each other, paying little attention to the official edicts to control the situation. The cityscape turned into a constantly metamorphosing, tension-filled patchwork of overlapping textual and visual messages.

It would be tempting to say that posted broadsides functioned as proto-screens, but this might be to go too far. As an information interface, the definition of the screen should incorporate a separation between hardware and software. It should function both as a frame and a gateway through which messages are transmitted and retrieved. In a limited sense such conditions appeared, when after decades of bill-posting anarchy, enterprises began to acquire rights to use certain surfaces and rent them out for advertisers. Advertising space was rationally divided into framed lots, and these were cultivated by companies who had bought rights to use them. The newly organised adscape was realised early on at railway stations. The constant flow of passers-by made them attractive; passengers could be forced to see placards from the train as well. The word 'billboard' was adopted in the United States, reflecting a similar institutional and commercial development.[5] Catherine Gudis has aptly summarised its significance, saying, "Like the buildings rising in growing metropolises, billboards contributed to the accretion of commercial centers and formalized the incursion of pictures and texts to the public sphere" (19).

Although billboards represented an effort to tame (and frame) the wild advertising, they did not manage to dampen criticism against

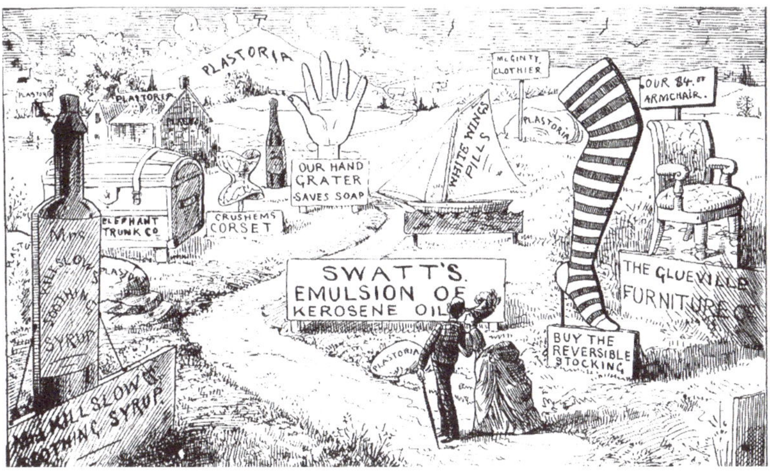

ILL. I: Fantasy about advertisements turned into a 'second nature.' 19th century, source unknown.

its harmful effects. On the contrary, a heated and long-lasting public debate ensued. The tension became even more intense when the introduction of the automobile encouraged advertisers to erect billboards not just in the cities but by the roadsides. They were frequently accused of blocking access to scenic landscapes. This issue did not escape the attention of satirical cartoonists. A cartoon titled "Go Prepared if you Wish to Enjoy American Scenery" (1925) depicts a car parked by a roadside flanked by billboards.[6] The passengers are forced to enjoy the scenic view from the top of long ladders leaning against them. The fight against "rubbish, weeds, and billboards" was declared a "crusade" (Woodruff 345). Taking it literally, the pioneer feminist Frances Power Cobbe attacked billboards with a "pot of paint and a long-handled brush on her rural drives in order to deface defacements," setting an example for the 'adbusters' and critical street artists of later times (Turner 124).

The advent of dynamic displays

By the end of the 19th century, the billboard had become ubiquitous. Billboards were criticised by cultural reformists, and modernist architectural critics were calling for a city cleaned of ornamentation, historicist references and non-functional(ist) features. As usual, Oscar Wilde went against the current when he praised street advertising for bringing "colour into the drab monotony of the English streets" (quoted in Elliott 165). Whatever attitude one adopted, the billboard could not be ignored. And yet, considering it a screen in the media-cultural sense would not be correct. A billboard could suggest a narrative, but it was not a medium for sequential presentations. No matter how gigantic, it was a frozen printed image. It began to move and evolve only in the dreams and fantasies of consumer culture as Busby Berkeley's extravagant "Optical Illusion" sequence in the Warner Bros musical *Dames* (1934) suggested.[7] The billboard was really a huge emblem meant to imprint an idea – the trademark – into the minds of the passers-by.

In the late 19th century, new dynamic elements were added to the urban adscape. Soon after it was invented, electric light was applied to street lighting, leading to an "electric landscape" that "sprang up in patches" (Nye 32). Particularly in the United States, electricity became associated with symbolic values. Extravagant electric light spectacles became a staple of world's fairs. In New York, the Broadway became known as the Great White Way, referring to the electric advertisements and illuminated shop windows that turned the street into a luminous attraction. "The transparent posters on which electricity wrote advertising texts with letters of fire," as Jules Verne characterised them, had qualities lacking from normal billboards (197).[8] Not only did they lengthen the time passers-by were exposed to their messages; animations could be produced by switching the illuminated parts rhythmically on and off. A particularly complex sign was erected on the roof of the Hotel Normandie in New York. It was seven stories high and had twenty thousand light bulbs, depicting an illuminated Roman chariot race. A reporter found it "more perfect and natural in its movement than the finest colored cinematograph picture" (Jones quoted in Nye 52).

Although electricity made spectacular light effects an everyday experience, they were not without predecessors. For centuries, fireworks had been used to illuminate architectural structures to celebrate royal births and weddings as well as war victories.[9] As George Plimpton explained, "machines" (also known as "temples") were used for this purpose already in the seventeenth century. They were "elaborate ornamental structures, usually in the form of buildings, which were decorated with paintings, usually of allegorical figures, flowers, and lamps which were cut out in silhouette to glow from behind" (34-5). There was a relationship between such extravaganzas and the late 19th century electric illuminations of bridges, buildings, statues and other elements of the urban environment (Marvin). According to Carolyn Marvin, the transformation of the traditional effects from the era of fire to that of electricity was "very gradual" (153). Many classical motives, including fountains of fire, were translated into the "vocabulary of electric light effects" (164, 167).

Magic lantern projections – in reality and imagination

Magic lantern projections were another way of introducing dynamic images to the public environment. The magic lantern was originally only suitable for darkened interior spaces, because the available light sources were weak and the projected images dim (Rossell). Dramatic improvements in lighting technology, in particular the oxy-hydrogen limelight ('calcium light') and the electric arc-light, made pro-

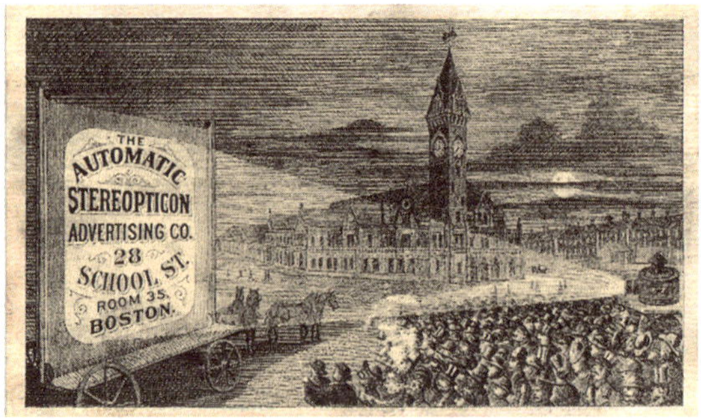

ILL. 2: Trade card for The Automatic Stereopticon Advertising Company, Boston, depicting a commercial outdoor magic lantern projection. Undated (c. 1860s), author's collection.

jections in public outdoor spaces possible. According to Wolfgang Schievelbusch, arc-lights were used as early as the 1840s to illuminate public monuments in Paris (54-5).[10] The idea of projecting not just a beam of light but pictures and texts as well followed as a logical step. An intermediate form was the use of searchlights on night-time river cruises to point out scenes from the darkness of the riverbanks. An enthusiastic participant remembered that "the magic shaft of the search-light swung from point to point *making pictures* of which the details were more clearly shown than they could be by day" (R.A.S. 9).[11]

In the United States (where the magic lantern was often known as the stereopticon) slides were projected outdoors on screens, blank walls and even public monuments since the 1860s.[12] In Boston an enterprise named The Automatic Stereopticon Advertising Company promised that "the Automatic Stereopticon Advertiser Works All Night," displaying "Your Advertisement to Wondering Crowds" (see Figure 2).[13] The illustration on its trade card depicts a large magic lantern on a scaffolding in a town square, projecting the company's name and address on a screen erected on a horse-drawn cart. Although it is night-time, a large crowd of spectators is present (or so the promoter wants us to believe). Commercial outdoor projections became a well-established tradition, although their full extent is not yet known. Later in the century the well-known American soap manufacturer Benjamin T. Babbitt advertised his free touring "Magnificent Stereopticon Exhibition and Musical Entertainment using the Oxyhydrogen or Calcium Light," which was shown after dark at some well-known street corner.[14] The views were claimed to be of "a greater size than the largest Panorama," and the "Magnificent

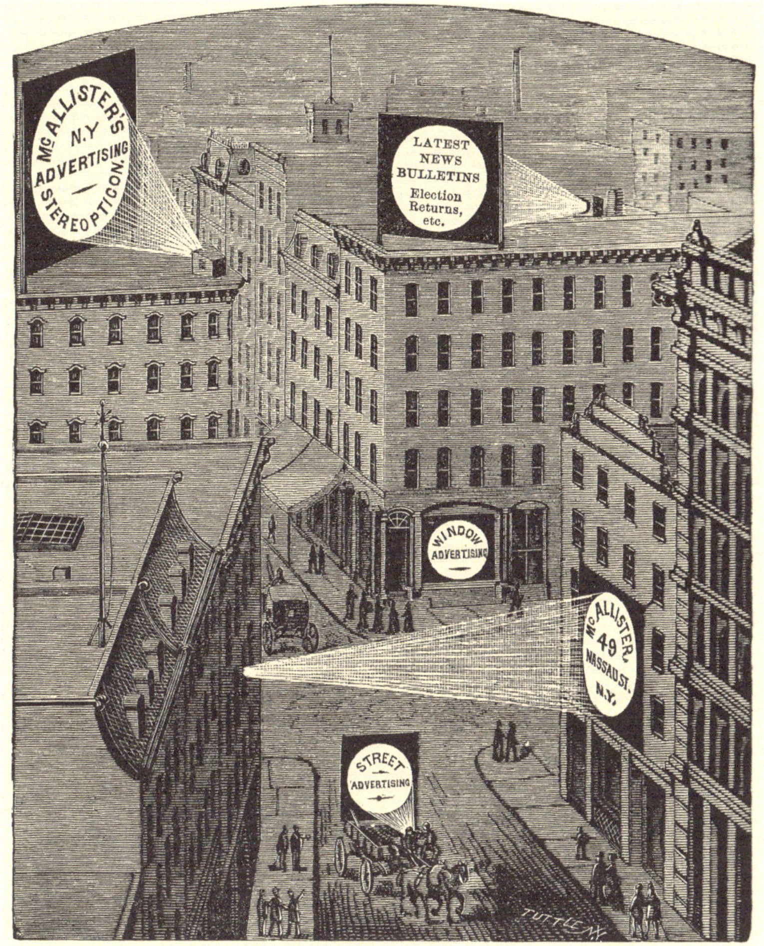

ILL. 3: **Five ways of projecting slides in outdoors spaces with 'advertising stereopticons' (McAllister 35), author's collection.**

Horses and Wagons used for transportation" provided additional "pleasure to thousands."

In 1904, the magic lantern manufacturer T. H. McAllister described five modes of projecting slides in outdoors spaces with its "advertising stereopticons": on walls, shop windows, screens mounted on moving horse-drawn carts and screens erected on the roof, either by using front or rear projection (35). McAllister recommended roof projections for displaying "latest news bulletins" or "election returns," applications which were no longer novelties. On November 24, 1866,

Harper's Weekly published a full page illustration demonstrating the presentation of election returns by means of a magic lantern outside the New York *Tribune's* office building.[15] Similar reports appeared frequently over the years.[16] The information technology was simple: Statistical data about the progress of the ballot count was scribbled on blank lantern slides coated with emulsion as soon as new information was received and beamed to the screen.[17] Although the telegraph (and later the telephone) was used in the news-gathering, a short time-lag was unavoidable. Still, the use of visual media for such purposes anticipated today's election-night broadcasts on television.

In 1896 *The Century Magazine* published a lively report about the spectacle:

> The crowd [...] gathers early in City Hall Park and Newspaper Square to read the messages written upon glass "slides," and magnified upon broad screens outside the buildings by means of a stereopticon. At first these bulletins are vague and partial, but toward midnight they increase in breadth and importance. At intervals the operator presents a summing up like this: "418 districts out of a total of 600 in Ohio give John Smith, Dem., 117,926, and James Brown, Rep., 180,460.", or: "Georgia elects the whole Democratic ticket by an estimated plurality of 20,000." When he has nothing to report the operator displays a portrait of a candidate, or an impromptu cartoon, exhibiting in comical allegory the success of his man, or his side, and the disconfiture of the other fellow. Of late a favorite bit of fun has been to throw upon the screen a question like this: "What's the matter with Cleveland?" Promptly comes the answer from ten thousand throats: "He's all right!" Then shines out: "Who's all right?" And the windows rattle with the acclamation: "C-l-e-v-e-l-a-n-d!"
> ("Election Day in New York" 12)

The information about audience interaction is interesting; an election night was a special festive occasion. Still, most accounts about public projections emphasise the relative passivity of the onlookers, which was reflected in discursive form in satirical cartoons about public figures as outdoor lanternists. On September 19, 1888, *Puck's* front page had President Coolidge projecting his idea of the income tax reform against the dome of the Capitol. *Judge* depicted the notorious newspaper publisher Joseph Pulitzer with a magic lantern, presenting an economic-political commentary from the balcony of his newspaper building to a crowd on the street.[18] In all these cases public projections turned the passer-by, at least momentarily, into a member of an audience. Instead of just casting passing glances, like the ones addressed to billboards and sky-signs, pedestrians were encouraged to stop and stare at the presentation. Although the crowd must have functioned as a distractive factor that beside its perpetual agitation also produced noise, certain elements of indoor spectacles were transferred outdoors (like in the drive-in movie theatres of the next century).

Before declaring such outdoor projections as an unprecedented novelty, one should note that they had been *metaphorically* anticipated much earlier by paintings and engravings depicting magic lantern projections, sometimes in broad daylight! Imagination preceded technological development, ignoring its limitations. In Jean Friedrich August Schall's *La lanterne magique de l'amour* (c. 1810), a cupid is projecting an image for young lovers in a park, using the pedestal of an Amor statue as the screen (Robinson 4-5, Fig. 122B). Even more interestingly, during the Napoleonic Wars British cartoonists represented the threat of French invasion as a kind of phantasmagoria, a ghost projection. George Woodward, for example, depicted in *A New Phantasmagoria for John Bull* (1805), Napoleon and Josephine approaching over the British Channel as rear-projected ghosts.[19] Likewise, in a print by Thomas Rowlandson, John Bull (the personification of the British people) uses his 'magic lanthorn' to project a political slide across the Channel on the rocks of Calais (Rowlandson). Following the French and the American revolutions, a growing need was felt to discuss political and ideological issues in public and to witness the events of the world as they were happening. Before the electric telegraph began to provide newsfeeds for newspapers and photographers to map the globe into its own likeness, visual media had already attempted to satisfy the thirst to see.

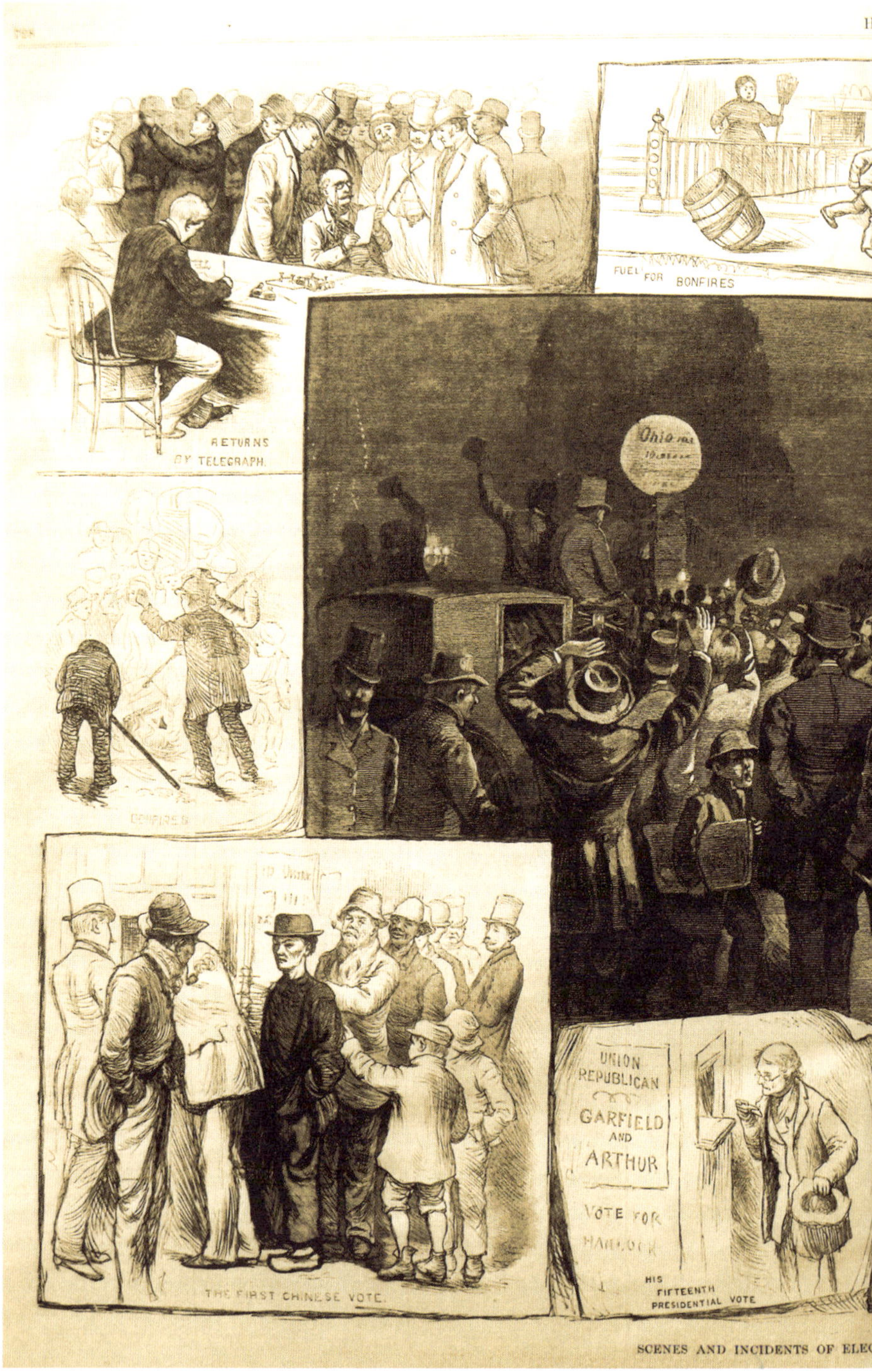

ILL. 4: A magic lantern used for presenting election results (*Harper's Weekly*, November 24, 1866. 744). The event had taken place around midnight, Nov. 6-7, 1866. The Magic Lantern Castle Museum, San Antonio, Texas.

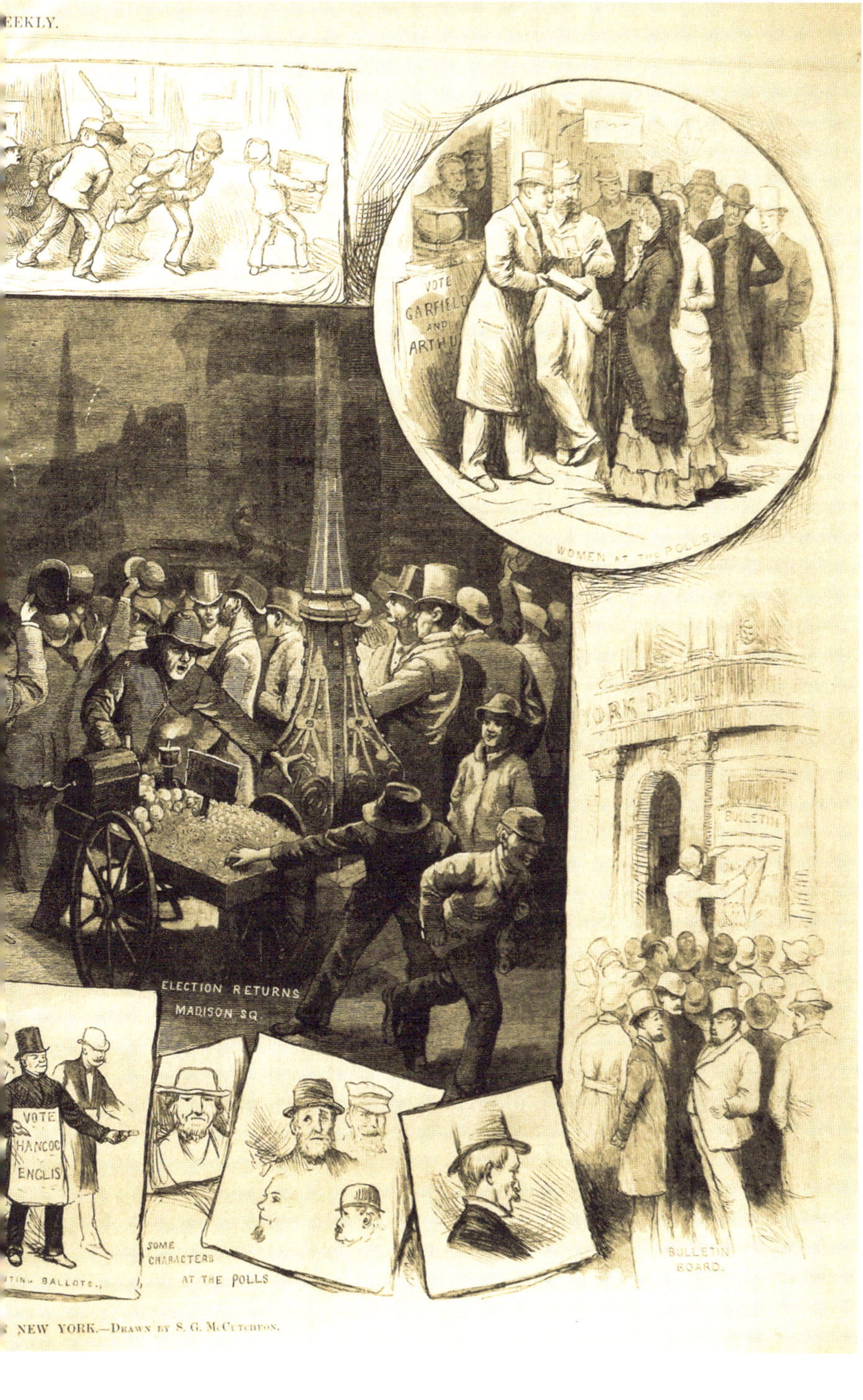
EEKLY.
VOTE
GARFIELD
AND
ARTHUR
WOMEN AT THE POLLS
ELECTION RETURNS
MADISON SQ.
BULLETIN
VOTE
HANCOC
ENGLIS
SOME
CHARACTERS
AT THE POLLS
BULLETIN
BOARD.
NEW YORK.—Drawn by S. G. McCutcheon.

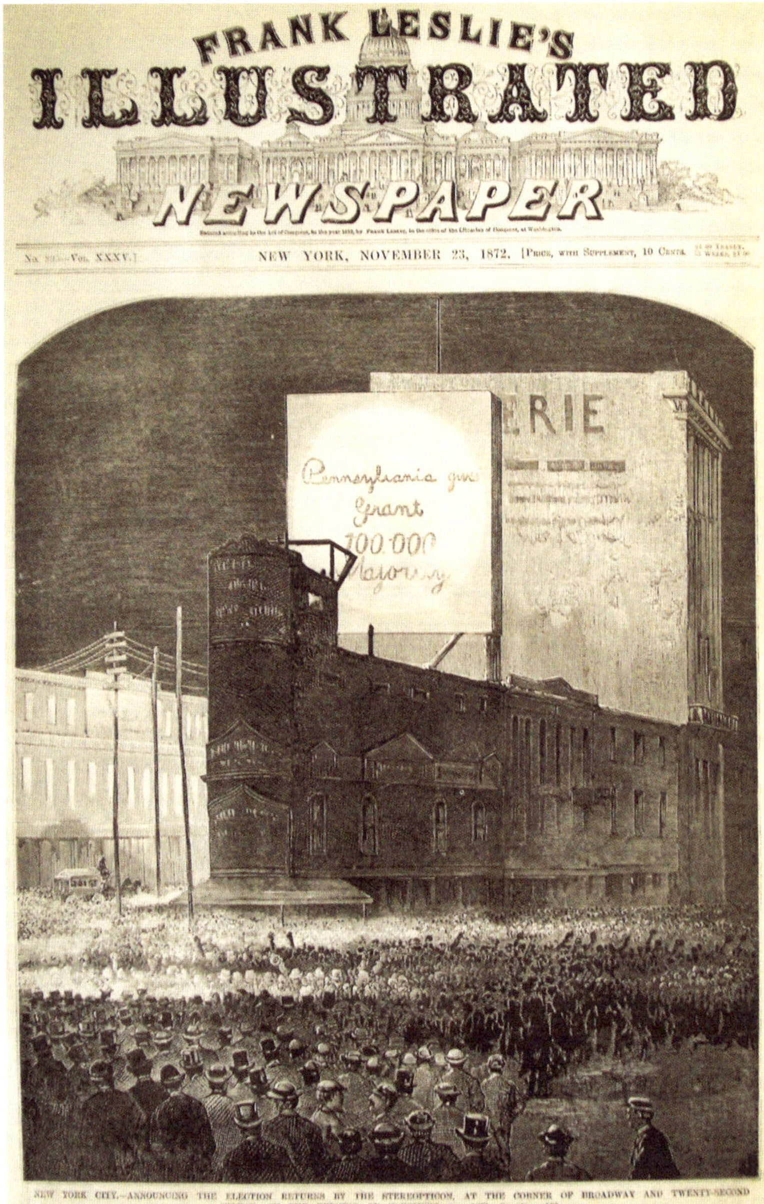

ILL. 5: Magic lantern presentation of election results, *Frank Leslie's Illustrated Newspaper*, Nov. 23, 1872 (cover). The Magic Lantern Castle Museum, San Antonio, Texas.

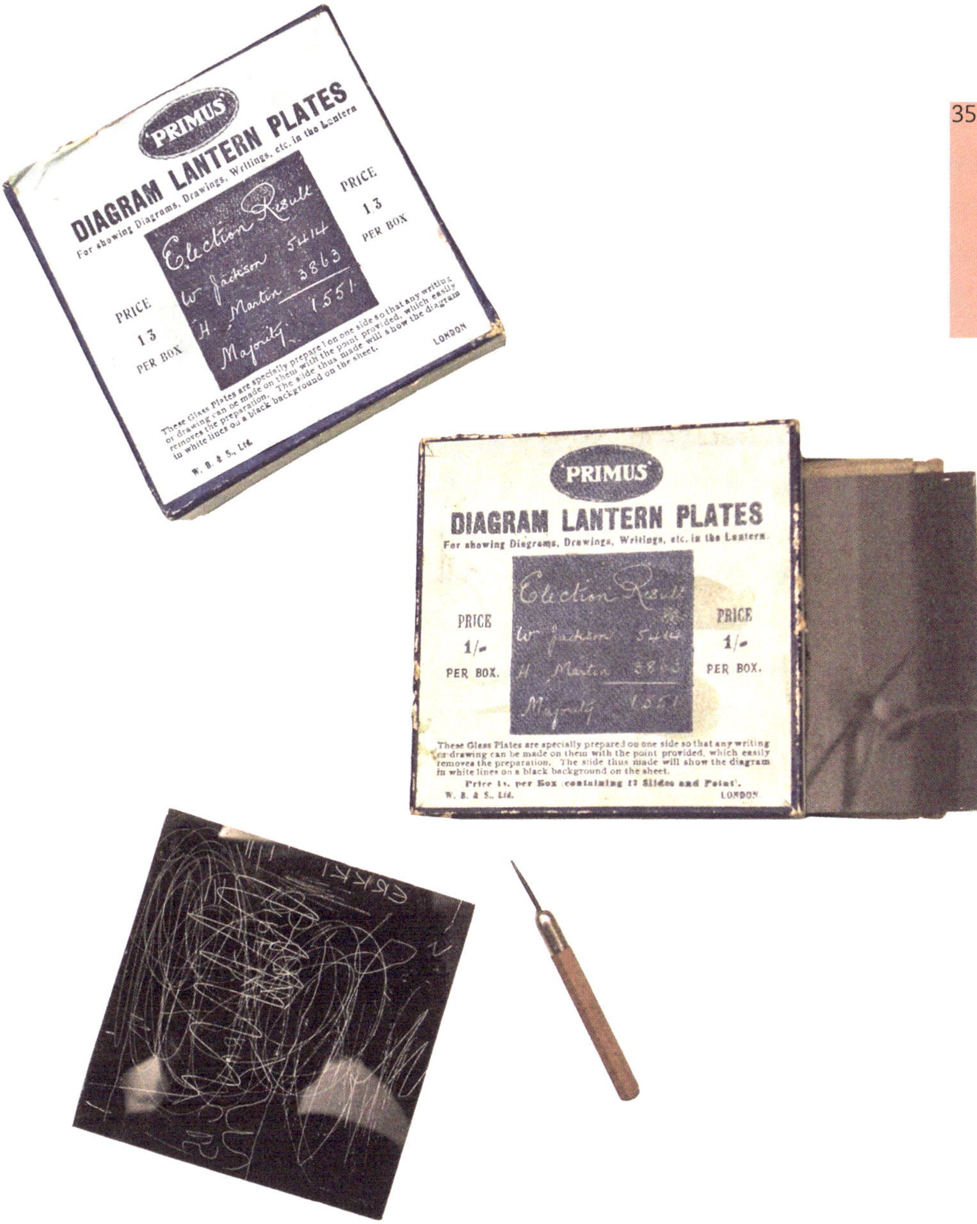

ILL. 6: "Primus Diagram Lantern Plates," blank magic lantern slides used to announce election results. W. Butcher & Son, London, early 20th century, author's collection.

The world-as-attraction on Robida's " Immense Glass Plates"

A constant interplay existed between the emergent public media displays and their discursive shadows as Albert Robida's *Le Vingtième Siècle*, an illustrated narrative about the Parisian society of the next century, demonstrates. What makes *Le Vingtième Siècle* particularly interesting, and separates it from many other futuristic fantasies of the time, is the prominent role Robida has given to media and communications. The central aspect of Robida's fantasy is the 'téléphonoscope,' an imaginary audiovisual extension of the telephone that permeates the society. The téléphonoscope is a veritable panacea, serving any imaginable communication need: "the suppression of absence, surveillance made easy, the theatre brought to your home" (73, author's trans.). It functions, anachronistically speaking, both as a broadcasting terminal and as a videophone. By peering into its 'glass plate' (*plaque de cristal*), the users can enjoy both live and recorded performances from the opera and witness the latest news. They can also communicate with each other and meet remotely face-to-face.

Particularly interesting is the *Epoque*, the audiovisual newspaper of the future, which is available for home subscribers via the téléphonoscope as four daily editions plus a breaking news service.[20] But the *Époque* can also be experienced outside the newspaper's headquarters in Paris on two "immense glass plates, twenty-five meters in diameter." (Robida 199). They stand on tall and high scaffoldings and can be seen from the boulevard below, the windows of the neighbouring houses and the balconies surrounding the newspaper building. The one on the left side of the building is dedicated to advertising; a 'calligraphist' draws ads on paper, and an 'ingenious electrical apparatus' reproduces them on the glass plate in 'gigantic characters.' The one on the right transmits news from around the world, transmitting the Chinese civil war of 1951 and other dramatic events of the moment to the thrilled Parisians in real-time. When the reporters roaming the world point their 'small pocket-telephonoscopes' to a scene, enlarged images immediately appear on the large plate in Paris, accompanied by sounds from the scene.

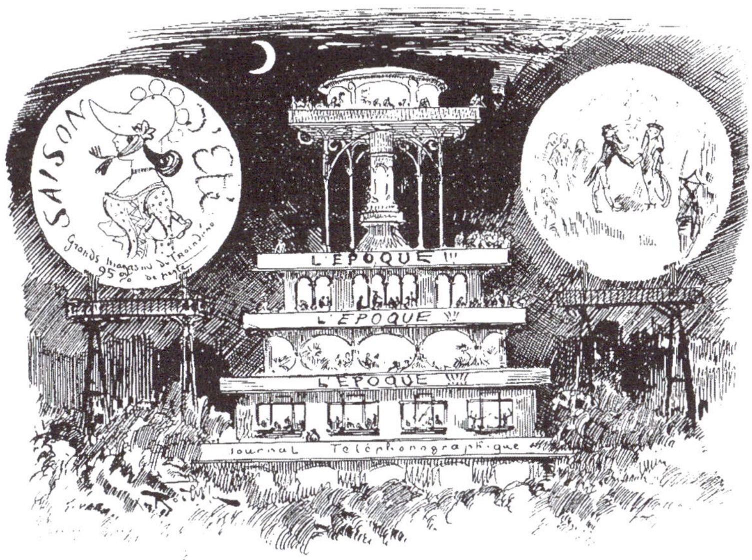

ILL. 7: *L'Époque*, Alberta Robida's imaginary 'telephonographic' newspaper, from *Le Vingtième siècle* (1883).

Although Robida does not say it explicitly, home subscriptions were probably meant as the *Époque*'s major source of income. The gigantic public displays that thrilled the residents strolling on the boulevards were above all a publicity gimmick rather than an interest-free public service. At the time when *Le Vingtième Siècle* was published, the corporate appropriation of public space was well on its way, as the ruthless strategies used by the Yellow journalism were soon to prove. Particularly in the United States, the fiercely competing newspaper corporations were not content with just reporting world events; they did their best to trigger such events themselves and used any strategies to gain attention and promote sales. In addition to sensational headlines in large print, their repertory of effects included exaggerated illustrations, made-up news stories and colour supplements with early comic strips (including the Yellow Kid that gave Yellow journalism its name).

During the Spanish-American war of 1898, not only the newspaper publishers but also the early film exhibitors got involved in similar activities, searching for a quick profit by exploiting the pub-

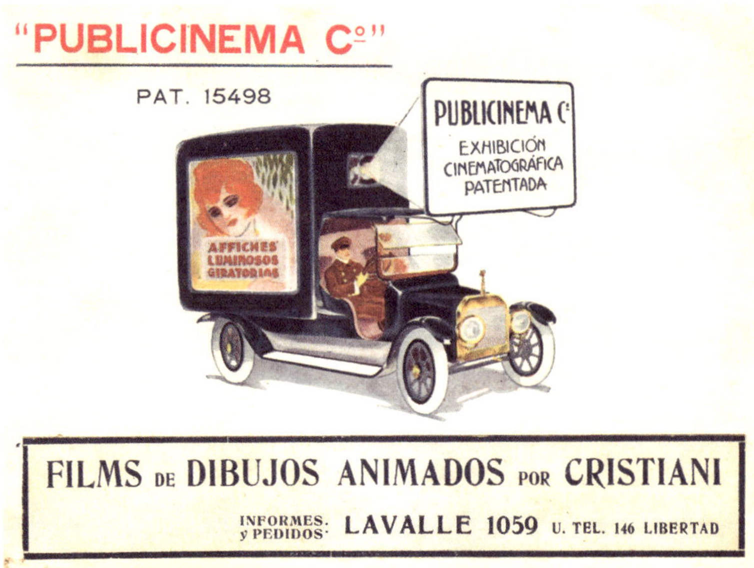

ILL. 8: **Mobile advertising projection by Publicinema Co, postcard, Spain, 1920s. (Author's collection).**

lic's thirst for real-life attractions. Sensational events were brought to the screen as close to real-time as the filmic medium allowed. When authentic film footage was not available, the sensational events were simply re-enacted with actors and special effects (Musser 146). Film posters joined the repertory of classic attraction devices, persuading bystanders to pay the fee and enter the hall where films were shown. The culture of attractions thus became entangled, not just in economic competition for the eye but in the politics of the artificial and the simulation of the real as well.

Coda: Los Angeles 2009

In a few short months, the media landscape of Los Angeles has undergone a major transformation. With astonishing speed, the traditional billboards flanking the freeways and surrounding busy intersections are being 'modernised' into dynamic, super bright LED billboards. Hundreds of them have already been converted and more are in the process of being transformed. Unlike what the outdoor advertisers told the credulous or nonchalant city authorities, the LED billboards are essentially a new medium. Whereas a traditional

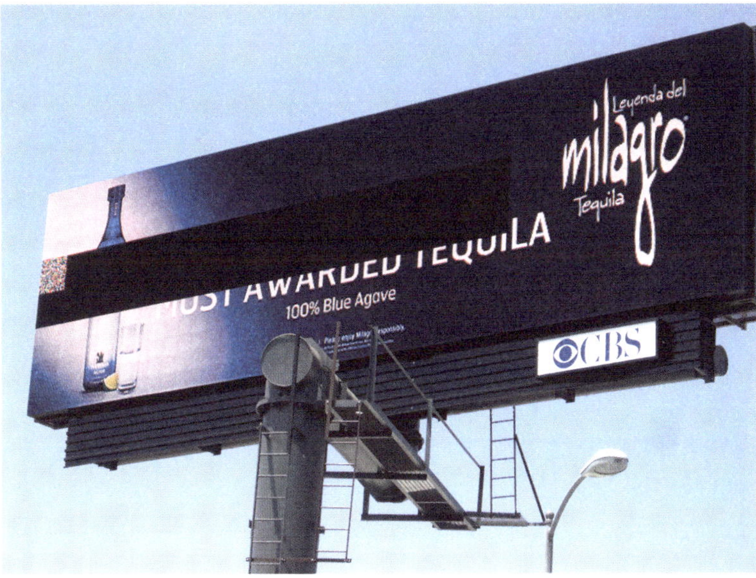

ILL. 9: **Crashed LED Billboard, Los Angeles, 2009, photograph by the author.**

billboard displayed just one printed advertisement at a time, the new ones extend the principle of 'heavy rotation' – familiar from commercial radio and music television – to the public urban environment. Ads flicker past the eyes in a rapid succession. Drivers waiting for the traffic-lights to change are exposed to a commanding new visual spectacle that does everything it can to catch their eyes.

The huge matrixes of thousands of tiny back-lit LEDs glow with a power that makes the messages visible in bright sunlight, not to say anything about the night. Those who are unfortunate enough to live under their glow have begun to experience 'false sunrises,' and have lost the privilege of enjoying the darkness of the night altogether. A social movement is rising, demanding public regulation or even the removal of the new glowing monsters. Whether it will have any impact in a thoroughly commercial environment dominated by corrupt politics and a general capitulation in front of the interests of corporate media and crony capitalism remains to be seen.[21]

I have chosen to conclude by jumping ahead in time to assure the reader that the developments described in this article have more than just academic or antiquarian interest. As we have seen, the emergence of public outdoor media did not take place automatically along a well-trodden path. Neither the roles the urban screens play nor the forms they take have ever been self-evident. Rather, they have been caused by economic, political and social developments accompanied by highly divergent discursive commentaries, cultural debates, practices of looking and social struggles. Media archaeological excavations of the factors, attitudes and forces involved in turning public outdoor media into artificial interest-ridden environments enveloping our lives can provide us with weapons to defend ourselves against discursive fabrications and corporate excesses – like the ones taking place in Los Angeles at the time of writing.

Notes

1. Malcolm Barnard has noted that in advertising 'information' and 'persuasion' can never be clearly separated from each other. I agree.
2. This aspect of Benjamin's work has been analysed well by Norbert Bolz and Willem van Reijen (71-2).
3. Signs of change include the series of Urban Screens conferences, and publications such as *First Monday's* Special Issue #4: Urban Screens: Discovering the potential of outdoor screens for urban society, http://www.uic.edu/htbin/cgiwrap/bin/ojs/index.php/fm/issue/view/217.
4. Polemically, Colomina argued that Le Corbusier's work undermined, rather than supported, the dichotomy between high art and mass culture.
5. This happened probably in the 1870s, although the *Oxford English Dictionary* mentions a British example from 1851: "The bill-boards of the Park [...] still continued to style the Park 'The Theatre'." This does not seem to be directly related to the later American usage.
6. Repr. in Gudis (186).
7. Dir. Ray Enright. Young lovers, interpreted by Ruby Keeler and Dick Powell, are travelling in a street car. He falls asleep and sees a dream featuring his girlfriend and other females in a fantastic stylised dance spectacle that takes place in an adscape turned into a dreamscape.
8. Author's translation.
9. Wolfgang Schivelbusch sees their origin in medieval bonfires. Already in the 17th century they were developed into an 'artform' with strict rules and own aesthetics executed by fireworks masters. See Schivelbusch (137-39).
10. Later, the French used them during the colonial wars in Africa to scare away the enemy, thus proving the ideological and military benefits of a 'blinding' technology (ibid. 57).
11. Emphasis added.
12. In *The Shocking History of Advertising* Turner records a commercial magic lantern projection on the Trafalgar Square in London on Trafalgar Day, 1894. Ads for "pills, blacking, and watches" were projected on the side of Nelson's Column and the pillars of the National Gallery. In *The Times*, a reader "suggested 'jamming' the advertisements by a more powerful beam" (126-27).
13. Trade card, undated (c. 1860s), author's collection.

14. Undated broadside (c. 1880s) in the author's collection. The exhibition in question was at the corner of Broad and Middle streets (city unknown) at 8 o'clock. The broadside mentions earlier presentations in Charleston (South Carolina), Augusta, (Georgia), and Hinesville (Georgia). Babbitt's soap works was based in New York City.

15. P. 744. The event had taken place around midnight, Nov. 6-7, 1866.

16. For example, *Frank Leslie's Illustrated Newspaper*, Nov. 23, 1872 (cover); Oct. 25, 1884 (cover); Nov. 17, 1888. 223-4; Nov.15, 1890. 262; *Harper's Weekly*, Nov. 17, 1888. 877; *Collier's Magazine*, Vol. XXXIV, No. 4 (Oct. 22, 1904), cover. I have found these from the archives of the Magic Lantern Castle Museum, San Antonio, Texas (thanks to Jack Judson).

17. This is confirmed by T. H. McAllister's catalogue: "LANTERN ADVERTISMENTS for temporary use – Election Returns, etc. – can be easily made by writing or painting them on glass, with India Ink or with the 'opaque' used by Photographers" (35). Two boxes of such slides, with a needle-pointed stylus, have been preserved in the author's collection. They are titled "Primus Diagram Lantern Plates For Showing Diagrams, Drawings, Writings, etc. in the Lantern" and produced by Butcher & Son, Ltd, London. Cover illustration shows a picture of a slide with election results.

18. "A Great Democratic Editor in the Greatest Democratic City Sheds Light on a Dark Subject", *Judge*, Sept. 25, 1909. Although the cartoon is hand-drawn, Pulitzer's magic lantern can be identified as a common cheap model sold by Sears-Roebuck around that time. The cartoonist may have used their mail-order catalogue as model.

19. Publ. Feb. 1, 1805 by Rudolph Ackermann, London (author's collection).

20. Twice a week, however, the newspaper publishes a richly illustrated paper edition, the *Époque Illustrée*, meant for readers in provinces or foreign countries. The illustrations are snapshots from the newsfeeds provided by the téléphonoscope.

21. See Cathcart.

Works cited:

Barnard, Malcolm. "Advertising: the Rhetorical Imperative." *Visual Culture*. Ed. Chris Jencks. London and New York: Routledge, 1995. 26-41, ref. 35. Print.

Bolz, Norbert, and Willem van Reijen. *Walter Benjamin*. Trans. Laimdota Mazzarins. New Jersey: Humanities Press, 1996. Print.

Cathcart, Rebecca. "Billboards Brighten Los Angeles Night, to the Anger of Many." *The New York Times*, Nov .6, 2008. A19. Print.

Colomina, Beatriz. *Privacy and Publicity: Modern Architecture as Mass Media*. Cambridge, Mass.: MIT Press, 1994. Print.

Crary, Jonathan. "Géricault, the Panorama, and Sites of Reality in the Early Nineteenth Century." *Grey Room*, 09 (Fall 2002): 5-25. Print.

"Election Day in New York." *The Century Magazine*, vol. LIII, no. 1 (Nov. 1896): 12. Print.

Elliott, Blanche B. *A History of English Advertising*. London: Business Publications Limited in association with B.T. Batsford Limited, 1962. Print.

First Monday's Special Issue #4: Urban Screens: Discovering the Potential of Outdoor Screens for Urban Society. Web. 20 Aug. 2010. <http://www.uic.edu/htbin/cgiwrap/bin/ojs/index.php/fm/issue/view/217>.

Gudis, Catherine. *Buyways. Billboards, Automobiles, and the American Landscape*. New York and London: Routledge, 2004. Print.

Gunning, Tom. "An Aesthetic of Astonishment: Early Cinema and the (in)Credulous Spectator." *Viewing Positions*. Ed. Linda Williams. New Brunswick: Rutgers University Press, 1995. Print.

– "The Cinema of Attraction: Early Film, Its Spectator and the Avant-Garde." *Wide Angle*, vol. 8, nos. 3-4 (Fall 1986). 63-70. Print.

Huhtamo, Erkki. "The Pleasures of the Peephole: An Archaeological Exploration of Peep Media." *Book of Imaginary Media: Excavating the Dream of the Ultimate Communication Medium*. Ed. Eric Kluitenberg, Rotterdam: NAi Publishers, 2006. 74-155. Print.

Jones, Francis Arthur. "The Most Wonderful Electric Sign in the World." *The Strand Magazine*. undated clipping. Quoted in Nye 52. Print.

Larwood, Jacob, [Hermann Schesoichaven] and John Camden Hotten. *The History of Signboards From the Earliest Times to the Present Day*. 1866. Eighth Edition. London: Chatto & Windus, 1875. Print.

Le Corbusier. "Fresque." *L'Ésprit nouveau*, 19. Quoted in Colomina. Print.

Marvin, Carolyn. *When Old Technologies Were New. Thinking About Electric Communication in the Late Nineteenth Century*. New York and Oxford: Oxford University Press, 1988. Print.

McAllister, T.H. *Catalogue of Stereopticons, Dissolving Apparatus, Magic Lanterns, Moving Picture Machines and Accessories*. New York: T.H. McAllister: April 1904. 35. Author's collection. Print.

Musser, Charles. *Before the Nickelodeon: Edwin S. Poretr and the Edison Manufacturing Company*. Berkeley, Los Angeles, and Oxford: The University of California Press, 1991. Print.

Nye, David E. *Electrifying America. Social Meanings of a New Technology*. 1990. Cambridge, Mass.: MIT Press, 1992. Print.

Plimpton, George. *Fireworks*. Garden City, New York: Doubleday & Company, 1984. Print-

R.A.S. "The Hudson Seen by Search Light." *New York Evangelist*, Sept. 16, 1897. 9. Print.

Robida, Albert. *Le Vingtième Siècle*. Génève and Paris: Editions Slatkine, 1981, facsimile of the original 1883 Paris edition. Print.

Robinson, David. *The Lantern Image: Iconography of the Magic Lantern 1420-1880, Supplement No.1*. Kirkby Malzeard, Ripon, North Yorkshire: The Magic Lantern Society, 1997. 4-5 (Fig. 122B). Print.

Rossell, Deac. *Laterna Magica – Magic Lantern*, Band 1 / Vol.1. German trans. Marita Kuhn. Stuttgart: Fuesslin Verlag, 2008. Print.

Rowlandson, Thomas. *Experiments at Dover or Master Charleys Magic Lanthorn*. Engraving, publ. July 21, 1806, London. Author's collection. Print.

Sampson, Henry. *A History of Advertising from the Earliest Times*. London: Chatto & Windus, 1875. Print.

Schievelbusch, Wolfgang. *Disenchanted Night*. 1983. Trans. Angela Davies. Berkeley & Los Angeles: University of California Press, 1995. Print.

Schuwer, Phippe. *Geschichte der Werbung*. Vebey: Editions Rencontre, n.d. Print.

Turner, E[arnest] S. *The Shocking History of Advertising*. New York: Ballantine Books, 1953. Print.

Venturi Robert, Denise Scott Brown, and Steven Izenour. 1972. *Learning from Las Vegas*. Cambridge, Mass.: MIT Press, 1993. Print.

Verne, Jules. *Paris au XXe Siècle*. 1863. Paris: Hachette, 1994. Print.

Weir, W. "Advertisements." *London*. Ed. Charles Knight. (London: Henry G. Bohn, 1851), vol. V. 33. Print.

Woodruff, Clinton Rogers. "The Crusade Against Billboards." *The American Review of Reviews*. Ed. Albert Shaw. New York: The Review of Reviews Company., vol. 36 (July-December 1907). 345-7. Print.

The Haptic Interface
On Signal Transmissions and Events

BY BODIL MARIE STAVNING THOMSEN

The appreciation that media, far from being neutral message carriers, actually transform ideas as well as relations has been broadly agreed to since Marshall McLuhan, Joshua Meyrowitz and John Tomlinson's accentuation of the capacity of electronic media to produce new kinds of 'proximity', 'intimacy' or technologically-based reinventions of face-to-face communication. While in literary cultures the viewer has become specialised in decoding written and printed texts in a linear fashion (looking for cause and effect, as well as key terms bringing the pattern of narration to the foreground), in the electronic culture, the perceiving experience of the eyes, the ears, and the skin to grasp expressive qualities and changes has been foregrounded. The liveness of electronic media connects everybody within a performative and mediatised culture (Auslander).[1] In contemporary culture, virtual spaces are as real as physical spaces to everyone over the age of two.

In this article, I will discuss how we might understand various forms of almost tactile (or 'haptic;' cf. definition later) imagery presented before our eyes in various forms of electronic as well as digital transmissions of so-called real-time recordings. I propose to study these very clear depictions of 'the signal noise' of the medium and its relation to software art in connection with video art of the 1960s. This perspective is chosen partly because the first video artists were very aware of the close relation between cybernetic systems and video art, which we have more or less forgotten, partly because this non-transparent image-type constantly makes us aware that the interface screen is more than a representation. Its dynamic, ever-changing material (the software and the electronic and digital signal), is just as visible and must therefore be taken into consideration when examining new media. So when I use the word 'signal' in the following it relates to software data or the electronic signal (or both), and it is my ambition to show how we might be able to reflect these as 'haptic imagery' that has been explored in video art as well as in software art since the 1960s.

In his manifesto, *Cybernated Art*, video artist Nam June Paik accentuates the signal as the foundation of so-called 'pure relations':

> Cybernetics, the science of pure relations, or relationship itself, has its origin in karma. Marshall McLuhan's famous phrase 'Media is message' was formulated by Norbert Wiener in 1948 as 'the signal, where the message is sent, plays [an] equally important role as the signal, where [the] message is not sent' (227).

An archaeological way of looking at media will in other words be attributed to the way the shift from sign (and object) to signal (and software) has affected the images that are displayed on the new types of interface screens that we employ today. The signal is not just that which gives form to various objects. The signal is not just that by which 'fictions' are created. The software carries information, and this information is part of the image that in this context (and in keeping with Les Levine's definition, cited below) might be called hardware. The significance of software is more or less left unspoken in today's art criticism, and texts seldom have the keen insight of Levine's, which was a part of his *Systems Burn-off X Residual Software* (1969) presented at the exhibition *Software – Information Technology: Its Meaning for Art* at the Jewish Museum in New York in 1970:

> Software is the programming material which any system uses, i.e. in a computer it would be the flow charts or subroutines for the computer program. In effect software in 'real' terms is the mental intelligence required for any experience. It can also be described as the knowledge required for the performance of any task or transmission of communication. They say: 'It's going to be raining tomorrow' is software. All activities which have no connection with objects or material mass are the result of software. Images themselves are hardware. Information about these images is software. All software carries its own residuals. The residual may take the form of news, paint, television, tapes or other so-called 'media'. In many cases an object is of much less value than the software concerning

> the object. The object is the end of a system. The software is an open continuing system (255).

So according to Levine we are dealing with 'software residuals' in our contemporary culture of performativity, where art has taken the form of events. They carry their own transmission report within, and it is this report that I will be referring to as *haptic*, as the visibility of the signal, which is just as important as what the image is portraying. Jay David Bolter and Richard Grusin distinguish in their book *Remediation* between *immediacy* meaning the creation of the illusion of depth as well as the erasure of media as artistic production, and *hypermediacy* meaning reflecting media and a high level of awareness in framing it within the aesthetic. I would like to add to this distinction that Levine's definition of art as one of software's 'residuals' must lead to art that can be described as a kind of hyper-(im)mediacy, wherein the signal transmission is the 'real' aspect of a highly media-reflective practice. I will address this type of contemporary art work as corresponding to the art world of the 1960s, when it became evident for the first time that the transmission of an event was just as real as a 'first-hand experience', as explained by Levine:

> The experience of seeing something first hand is no longer of value in a software controlled society, as anything seen through the media carries just as much energy as first hand experience. We do not question whether the things that happen on radio or television have actually occurred. The fact that we can confront them mentally through electronics is sufficient for us to know that they exist [...] In the same way, most of the art that is produced today ends up as information about art (255).

This also means that all kinds of electronic media capable of transmitting real-time could be new material for art production. It also means that real-time or so-called direct transmissions of events on TV have increased, since the widespread use of the internet. In the contemporary art scene, performativity and mixtures between media and so-called 'fiction' and 'reality' are only a few outcomes of Levine's insight: That the signal events of electronic data "carry just as much energy as first hand experience" and in this sense "exist" and "happen". The challenge to art historians is that the mental

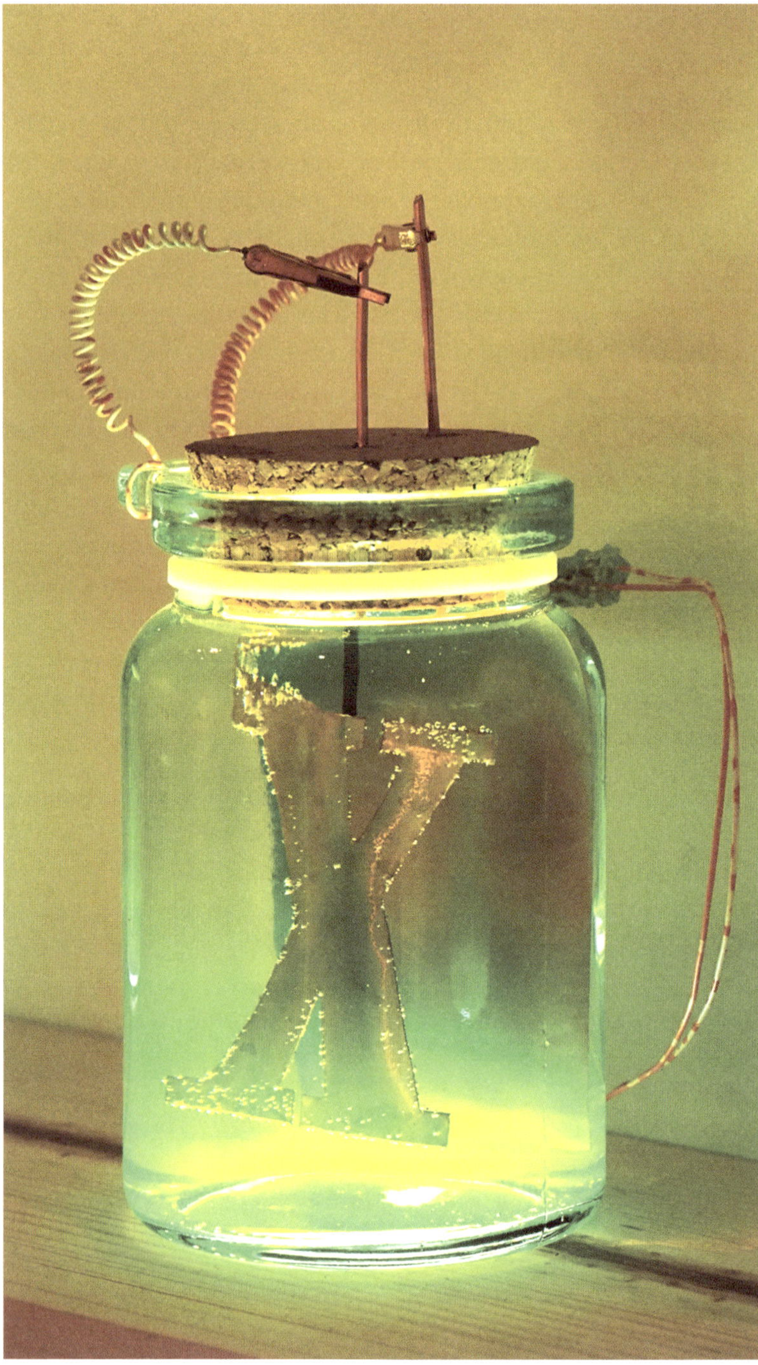

ILL. 1: Paul DeMarinis': *Messenger* (1998).

decoding of an electronic signal or software can be just as real, touching or affective as an encounter with a work of art situated in real physical space (cf. Gade and Jerslev). The "liveness of decoding" stems from the fact "[t]hat software is an open continuing system" and that the actual decoding is 'live' at the same time as you sense time as something that might be sensed directly, without its expression in spaces, movements and bodies. The video artists of the 1960s and 70s surely saw it that way. Paik stated in an interview from 1979, that "the fundamental concept in television is time" meaning that "in television, there is no space or image either, but only electronic lines" (Deleuze, *Cinema 2* 331), . This shift from sign to signal, or from seeing the image as the object of study to seeing it as the "end of a system", as Levine does, was in culture in general – and certainly in media studies in the 1970s – neglected. In line with Walter Benjamin's argument (from 1936) on the loss of aura in art works, when distance to the audience is not maintained since electronic images minimised the reproduction time, telecommunicative media like the telegraph and the telephone have not until recently been the subject of works of art (see Paul DeMarinis' *The Messenger* (1998) and Mark Hansen and Ben Rubin's *Listening Post* (2002-05)). And even then, it is striking how old, almost religious ideas of immediacy seem to

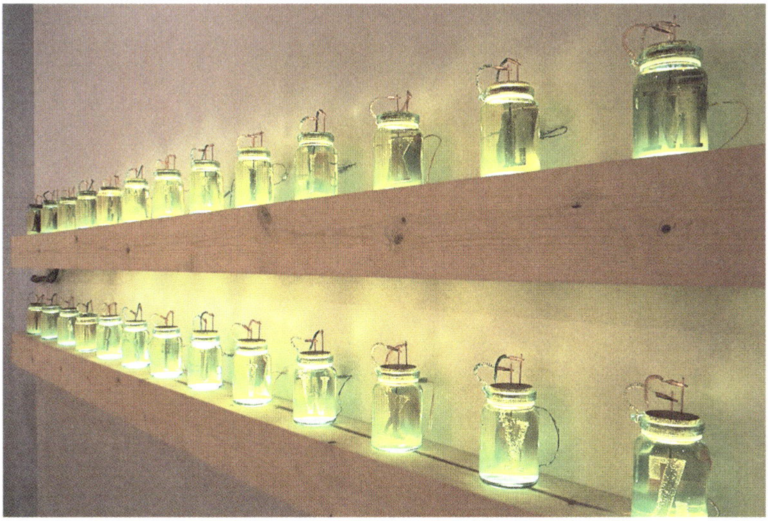

ILL. 2: Paul DeMarinis': *Messenger* (1998).

cling to those highly media-reflective works, as expressed in the text accompanying the exhibition of *Listening Post* (June 2006-May 2007) on the web site of The San Jose Museum of Art:

> For centuries, the soaring buttresses, vaulted ceilings, and luminous stained glass of cathedrals, along with hymns and chants, have transmitted that which is beyond expression. Using algorithms, software, and data mining, Listening Post generates a similar experience around what sometimes seems beyond comprehension. Hansen and Rubin's art facilitates a human-level connection to the immeasurable scale, vast content, and nano-immediacy of our communications universe (Pilo).

It is my aim to address the new "signaletic material" (Deleuze, *Cinema* 2)[2] of contemporary art as something that is neither "beyond expression" nor mere "information", in line with another aspect in Benjamin's "The Work of Art in the Age of Mechanical Reproduction," namely his use of the term 'tactile.'[3] Benjamin writes on 'tactility' in order to relate the automatic image of the camera and the montage of film to modern life in the new metropolises of Europe, aligning the filmmaker's operation to the procedures of the surgeon. Whereas the magician, like the painter, "maintains a natural distance from reality, the cameraman [like the surgeon] penetrates deeply into its web" (Benjamin). Deleuze does something similar when writing about the electronic image and its 'cuts' on the screen, functioning as an opaque site between brain and city:

> And the vertical of the screen now [in electronic media] has only a conventional meaning when it ceases to make us see a world in movement, when it tends to become an opaque surface which receives, in order to disorder, and on which characters, objects and words are inscribed as 'data'. [...] But when the frame or the screen functions as instrument panel, printing or computing table, the image is constantly being cut into another image, being printed through a visible mesh, sliding over other images in an 'incessant stream of messages', and the shot itself is less like an eye than an overloaded brain endlessly absorbing information: it is the brain-information, brain-city couple which replaces that of eye-Nature (*Cinema* 2 266-7).

Although Deleuze does not make much use of the term 'haptic' in his books about film, it is very important in his book on Francis Bacon, *The Logic of Sensation*, as well as in his and Félix Guattaris' description of nomadic or smooth space in *A Thousand Plateaus*. In order to describe how the electronic and the cybernetic signal, the cathode and the anode, are visible in the image transmission of the contemporary screen of real-time, I will introduce the Deleuzian use of the term 'haptic' in this field. In doing so, it is important not to forget the opaqueness of the electronic real-time screen, as Lev Manovich clearly describes it:

> In older, photographic technologies, all parts of an image are exposed simultaneously, whereas now the image is produced through sequential scanning – circular in the case of radar, horizontal in the case of television. Therefore, the different parts of the image correspond to the different moments in time. In this respect, a radar image is more similar to an audio record, since consecutive moments in time become circular tracks on a surface. What this means is that the image, in a traditional sense, no longer exists! And it is only by habit that we still refer to what we see on the real-time screen as 'images'. It is only because the scanning is fast enough and because, sometimes, the referent remains static, that we see what looks like a static image. Yet, such an image is no longer the norm, but the exception of a more general, new kind of representation for which we do not yet have a term (99-100).

In the case of the radar, what Manovich describes as "circular tracks on a surface" are what I am trying to describe as 'the signaletic' or 'haptic' noise of the real-time transmission, and the inclusion of the opaqueness of the screen and its user is what I refer to as 'the haptic interface'. In other words, I propose the term 'haptic' to cover the scanning noise and the 'images' of the real-time screen. This embodiment of time within the signal, which is visible as noise in all kinds of real-time screens (electronic and digital), should not be confused with the embodiment of space, which is the case in connection to haptic technology, where the individual body is very much seen as an entity, strengthened by new media. Every work of art or design that takes Deleuze's use of the term 'haptic' into serious consideration is bound to reflect its own material, for only on the surface of the screen is the medium made visible as lines, dots, modulating shadows etc. It is thus important to stress that the artists I mention in this article all tend to explore 'the haptic interface' as hyper-(im)mediacy rather than as 'immediacy' and 'embodiment of space.'

The exploration of the haptic signal in video art of the 60s

Let me first introduce the term 'haptic' in relation to the term 'optic'. My use of the word 'haptic' originates from Austrian art historian Alois Riegl. In his book, *Die Spätromische Kunstindustrie*, he uses the Greek word 'haphe' (meaning to grab, to touch) in order to make explicit the capacity of visual perception to experience a kind of 'touch' when looking at patterns, carvings and details in woven materials, like some ornaments and carpets. Riegl analysed this feeling of 'touching with the eyes' in relation to the term 'haptic'. The optic capacity is active whenever the visual decoding is more oriented towards lines and perspective in depth. The haptic quality will normally be found in surfaces inspected at close range. Riegl related the haptic capacity to short-sightedness, and the optic capacity to long-sightedness. In *A Thousand Plateaus* by Deleuze and Guattari, describing the nomadic qualities in rhizomatic structures and deterritorialisation, haptic perception is often mentioned. Haptic or smooth space is described as a possible response to variations and changes in physical spaces as well as artistic ones, when lines are active *between* dots and points, but do not create conjunctions nor connect one point to another. Instead, a haptic line has no beginning and no end, and its law is variation. It has expression, but no form, and it creates repetition and rhythm without symmetry.

An example of how a haptic perception would actually decompose or decode a classical painting is shown in *Zerseher*, Joachim Sauter's 1992 design proposal for museums in order to involve the audience in various interactions. This is an early example of how the impression of a haptic real-time experience can be animated by an intermediary computer calculation. The relation between the decoded, haptic animation of an optically organised painting and its reconstruction, when the onlooker moves on, nevertheless gives a clear demonstration of the software's signaletic operation and its relations to the user and the image portrayed. This design demonstrates, what Søren Bro Pold has defined as the main characteristics of the interface of the computer when understood (according to Frieder Nake) as an "instrumental medium" (Nake):

> The purpose of the interface is to represent the data, the dataflow, and data structures of the computer to the human senses, while simultaneously setting up a frame for human input and interaction and translating this input back into the machine. Interfaces have many different manifestations and the interface is generally a dynamic form, a dynamic representation of the changing states of the data or software and of the user's interaction. Consequently, the interface is not a static, material object. Still it is materialized, visualized, and has the effect of a (dynamic) representational form (Pold 2).

The relation between optic and haptic imagery is in other words integrated in the way we perceive the interface: as a dynamic relation between the visual representation on the screen and the software data of the electronic signal. And since "[t]he software is an open continuing system" (Levine) that cannot be "fully grasped [...] as a [material] form" (Pold 18) like the canvas of a painting or the paper of the writing its haptic manifestations (the visible, opaque pixels of the screen) become an important part of the interface. The haptic 'software noise' obstructs the ideal of transparency so often associated with the computer as functionality as it is often understood in engineering traditions and in the field of Human-Computer Interaction (HCI). This relation between haptic and optic associated to information technology saw one of its first artistic manifestations on film as early as 1968 in Stanley Kubrick's *2001: A Space Odyssey.* The strange interlude of haptic space (the shake-pattern on the astronaut's face-helmet-screen) and optic perspectives in galactic space (the 'Stargate Corridor' displayed on the space ship's window screen) was made possible by a construction, the so-called 'Slit-scan machine', built by special-effects supervisor Douglas Trumbull. His and Kubrick's collaboration in marrying basic cinematic techniques to computer and video sciences inspired, according to Gene Youngblood, a lot of artists working with the new video media of the 60s and 70s (Youngblood 156). In *Expanded Cinema*, Youngblood's remarkable collection of interviews with film and video artists anticipating the digital interfaces of today Kubrick's *A Space Odyssey* is mentioned numerous times.

In those days, when a lot of energy was fuelled by drugs, live experimental music and spaceships to the moon, it is no wonder that people used words like 'karma,' 'cosmic' or 'psychedelic' to describe their ambitions. Jordan Belson, for example, produced audio-visual light shows, kinetic live visuals with electronic music, and audio experiments with sound artist Henry Jacobs that anticipated Belson's later work with digital images (for example *Demon Seed* 1977). The three brothers, John, Michael and Mark, sons of James Whitney, created different kinds of cybernetic art, wherein pattern and experience were combined (*Lapis* 1963-66). Michael Whitney's *Binary Bit Patterns* (1969) shows mathematical patterns "permuting into other shapes, and an ornate, almost baroque, visual style softens any mathematical dryness" (Youngblood 236). The Whitney brothers' own vision for the future is to create:

> [a] kind of "kinetic wallpaper", which could be rear-projected onto the translucent walls of a room at close range in ultra-high resolution using large format film and special lenses. One would live in a home whose very walls were alive with silent kinetic activity (Youngblood 236).

Youngblood's book can be seen as an archive of artistic experiments with the haptic possibilities of combining media in the smooth surface of the electronic screen. John Stehura, who made *Cybernetic* 5.3 in four years (completed in 1969), "combined computer graphics with organic live-action photography" (Youngblood 239), and Stehura states in an interview that his "explorations in computer language led [him] back to conventional animation, back to the paintbrush – but a computerized paintbrush" (Youngblood 239). In order to create *Cybernetic* 5.3, he developed a meta-language (called 'Model Eight'): "a control system to control control systems" (Youngblood 244). In Stehura's description of the meta-language of Model Eight, a kind of meta-cybernetic machine, we find certain analogies to the haptic qualities mentioned by Deleuze and Guattari. Stehura states:

> It consists of a set of operators to work on one-, two-, or three-dimensional patterns: sensory patterns, music, drawings, motion, and so on. It's not a computer language which is operated one point at a time, but rather functions non-sequentially on large blocks of data (Youngblood 244).

The real-time experience was also highly praised in the 1960s and the 70s. Peter Kamnitzer's *City-Scape* (1968) was an attempt to create a real-time experimental site, where a simulated environment let you try different solutions to various problems. But the idea of real-time experiences had its arenas partly in the popular light shows and happenings, partly in the new video art. The light shows and happenings comprised elements from painting, film, electronic music events, the rock scene, jazz, performance art, underground beat poetry readings and scientific experiments, in order to create immersive visual and sound experiences. The integration of the physical bodily experience of space was certainly a basic concern in those experiments and happenings, but artists were also engaged in the real-time experience of the signal. Anyone who has seen D.A. Pennebaker's documentation of Jimi Hendrix's feed-back performance standing opposite the amplifier, followed by Hendrix burning his electric guitar at the Monterey Pop Festival in California, can testify to the effects of creating real-time electronic sound signals. This mixture of sound produced by Hendrix's hand and the feed-back noise from the amplifier squealing is a perfect example of a haptic interface.

The electronic feed-back signal meant new possibilities for the music scene as well as for the video art scene. If you do the same thing as Hendrix did with his guitar with a video-camera, placing it too close to its monitor, it squeals visually. This noise or 'feed-back' can create effects of echo, reverberation, and mirrored images folding into one image with no cuts between them. Video artist Robert Arn explains: "the system is itself a source of almost infinitely varying patterns, merely echoing the shape of the screen and the texture of the scan raster" (Arn 187).

The experience of 'live signals' is even imbedded in the 'salt-and-pepper pattern' of the raw video-tape referred to as 'white noise'.

The power of the naked signal is repeated in every decoding of electronic images, as the magnetic signals have to "be relived" in order to be seen, as Barbara Buckner explains in her unpublished manuscript from 1978: "Light and Darkness in the Electronic Landscape: Some Aspects of the Video Image":

> The process of video image scanning and recording is the process of converting reflected light as seen by a camera eye and coding this light energy as intelligence in the form of a sequence of voltages over time and decoding that arrangement into radiated and transmitted light in the monitor (Buckner 1978).

This technological procedure inspired Buckner and other artists from the 1970s to use the term 'immediacy' to describe the forces of the 'video-tape,' the preferred name for the video recorder at that time. Buckner also notes another aspect of video-tape, namely the possibility of mixing and inserting, in order to create a "multi-layered multi-colored new image composite".

This obviously leads directly to contemporary computer-simulation and modulation. In an interview, Brice Howard[4] expresses his visions of the electronic signal in video and television in a way that combines the haptic interface I have tried to explore, involving a thin space at the surface of the monitor, as well as the actual, experienced *now* of the real-time interface that we increasingly experience today. He says:

> The cubic space with which you are dealing in this newer mode of television is of a different order entirely [different from a stage designer's conception of space]. The only space which is valid is the space on the surface of that monitor. [...] I'm saying that it isn't in the studio, it's in the monitor. [...] [T]elevision is an electronic surface whose very motion is affecting the motion that you're putting into it. And what is really the richest part of television, less its technology, less its cubist nature, less its incredible colorations and shapes and motions and excitements – it's *now*, it's capturing the damned *actual* with all of its aberrations (Youngblood 285).

The fabrication of the sense of *now* within the machine/man connection was more or less what fascinated most video artists of the time. Video artist Eric Siegel created variations of geometric patterns in his so-called 'video-synthesis,' manipulating the intensity with which the electronic signals were scanned in the monitor. Paik manipulated the video-signal by external forces, such as magnets.

In this context, I want to turn to a closer examination of two works of art that seem to reflect *both* the man/machine interaction as a real event *and* the closed circuit system of the interface, namely Levine's *Contact: A Cybernetic Sculpture* (1969), and *Interface* (1972), by Peter Campus. *Contact: A Cybernetic Sculpture* consists of:

> eighteen monitors and eight cameras mounted in a sleek eight-foot stainless steel console, nine monitors and four cameras on each side beneath plastic bubble shields. [...] the cameras produce close-ups, mid-range and wide-angle views as images shift from screen to screen every five seconds. Each monitor screen is covered with a colored acrylic gel so that a given image may be seen in nine different colors as it swirls through the closed-circuit system (Youngblood 340).

In this work, Levine is trying to "synthesize man with his technology" presenting "people as software" (op. cit.) and, in keeping with his statement, cited at the beginning of this article, he prefers software to hardware when dealing with the televised image or signal. Within this scope it is possible to combine the feed-back or interface circuit of the electronic signal and its viewer with the event, as will be defined at the end of this article. Levine explains:

> Contact is made not only between you and your image, but how you feel about your image, and how you feel about that image in relationship to the things around you. The circuit is open. [...] television is constantly re-wiping itself and printing over all the time, so that depending on what information is available at any given moment the image will be different. So there's really no image. No definite image. [...] television has this quality: it always somehow looks the same, but it's always doing something different (Youngblood 340f).

The constant re-wiping of the signal creates a sense of immediacy or of – as I have chosen to term it – 'a signaletic event' that replaces the artistic image within this new machine/man connection, as diagnosed by Peter Weibel in his article "The Apparatus World – a World unto Itself".

With this in mind, let us look at Campus's *Interface*. This work is an installation with a big sheet of transparent glass behind which a video camera is placed. In front of the glass a projector transmits the camera signal in a closed circuit system. When a person stands in front of the glass, his/her image is both mirrored and projected in real-time on the glass. What he/she sees is a double image of him/herself that can even interact, if placed opposite each other. The mirror representation and the projected representation of the person can relate spatially through the mirror by way of the actual presence of the art gallery guest, although they cannot physically touch. This description of the interface space – both creating a sense of immediacy and hypermediacy – is both elegant and very precise. It can actually explain how contemporary haptic interfaces on TV, film and computers are created by combining an actual sense of phenomenological space with the decoding of 'live' signals transmitted in a closed circuit system. This work of art makes us sense the virtual meeting between two kinds of representation. The paradox is that the glass functions both as a physical hindrance to an actual meeting and as the real possibility for a human/machine interaction to take place in that same surface. The presence of the person in the installation is fundamental for creating new interfaces within the closed circuit of the two machines.

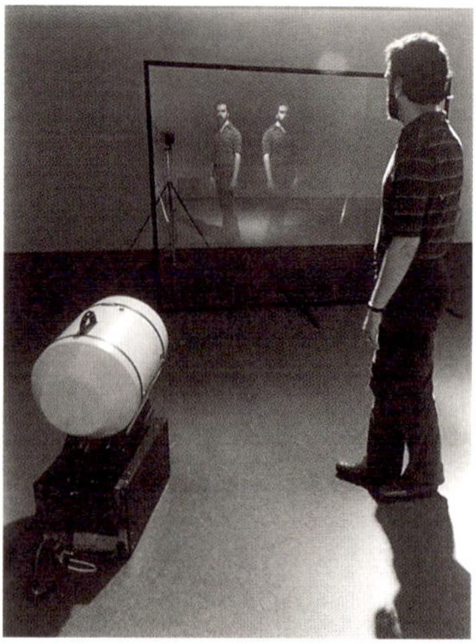

ILL. 3: Peter Campus: *Interface* (1972).

The 'signaletic event' in art, television, and digital media

Finally, I want to mention that the ability of new media since the 1960s to create those kinds of 'signaletic' events, in which the 'live' decoding of the electronic signals is essential for the sense of real-time experience and haptic involvement, should be understood in a broader philosophical context as defined by Deleuze and Alain Badiou. Although different in perspective, they both refer to the event as something which you cannot conceive in referring to the factual occurrences happening in physical time and space. In order to explain why the French Revolution or May 1968 became events that changed the existing world, you have to search for philosophic explanations. An event creates a new conception of truth but a political as well as an aesthetic event is, furthermore, something that cannot be of a certain nature. There needs to be uncertainty as to whether or not something has taken place. Infinity and ambiguity inspire doubt – and thought. An event can only be an event and thus mark some kind of truth if it is believed to be a rupture of life forces. It is my belief that new media artists from the 1960s up until today have been able to integrate the live-effect of the electronic signal so that the aesthetic events of modernism, described by Badiou and Deleuze, could actually be overridden by a new kind of post-modern event, where the machine/human interface, combining virtual and actual, could create new kinds of haptic interfaces.

A remarkable Danish example of this is Lars von Trier's television series *The Kingdom* (1994 and 1997) as well as his movie *Antichrist* (2009), in which the visibility of the electronic noise of television's magnetic decoding (i.e. salt-and-pepper patterns) as well as the pixels of digital media indeed permeates the screen. *The Kingdom* marked a post-modern approach to television and electronic media in general that can also be seen in works of software artists like Mark Napier or Lynn Hershmann. Napier's comment, in 2007, regarding his animations of the Empire State Building as information-based, and as organic and malleable human flesh, is convenient here:

> Increasingly we live and navigate in a world composed of energy: electrical, magnetic and light. [...] Digital media infuse our lives as never before. In this media environment, power

> is no longer associated with physical objects, but with the persistence of ideas in the collective consciousness of the media (*Mark Napier debuts new software art at bitforms gallery in New York*).

This is a great concluding remark, since it relates the haptic electronic interfaces of our daily routines to the skin of our senses, without necessarily needing so-called haptic devices like gloves or glasses to dive into virtual 3-D worlds.

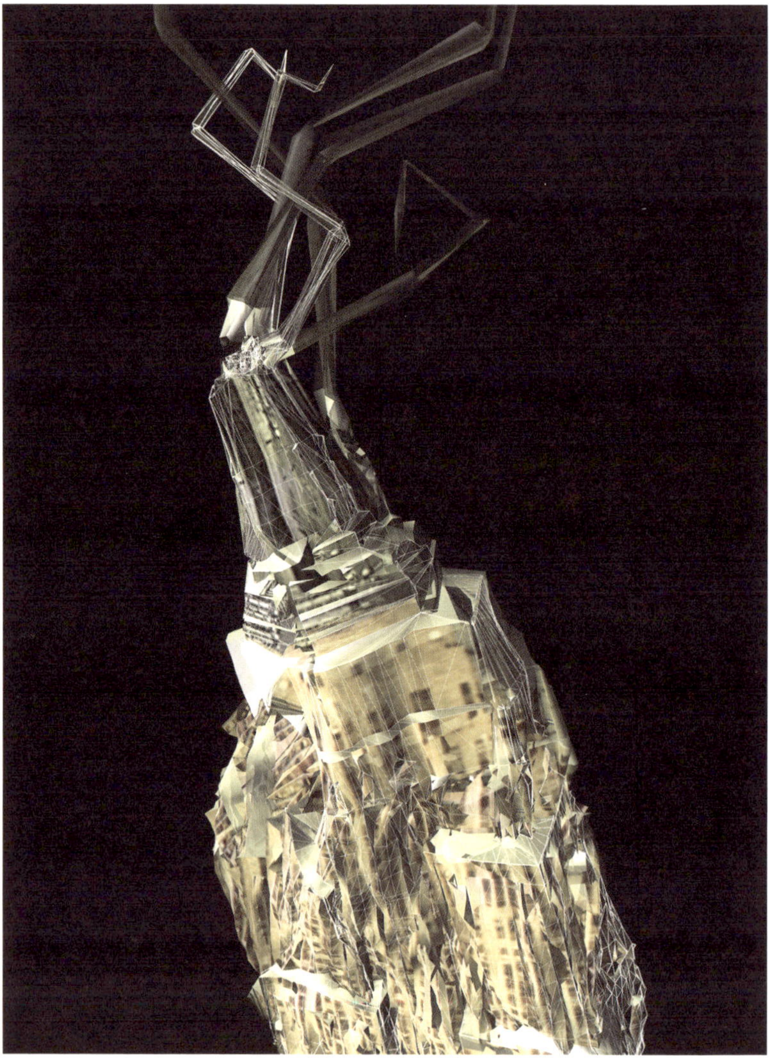

ILL. 4: Mark Napier: *Smoke* (2007).

Notes

1. Since the late 1980s, the term 'performativity' has become a key concept within interdisciplinary studies of modern western cultures. The speech act theory of J. L. Austin *How to do Things with Words* has since influenced cultural anthropology, theatre studies, social sciences and gender studies. The study of how cultural interactions and identity formation have to be performed within the rituals and patterns of everyday practices focuses on the dynamic processes that generate cultural meaning. In this context of performativity, art as well as media can be seen as events contributing to cultural processes.
2. Deleuze uses this term in *Cinema 2* when he wants to stress (in opposition to Christian Metz) that the components of the movement-image of film "is neither a language system nor a language" but "a plastic mass, an a-signifying material" that "includes all kinds of modulation features: sensory (visual and sound), kinetic, intensive, affective, rhythmic, tonal, and even verbal (oral and written)" (29). As Deleuze does for the film media, I am aiming at describing the 'signaletic material' of electronic media that 'grounds' the message or the narration, but that is not 'given' as message or narration.
3. Walter Benjamin uses the term 'tactile' according to Alois Riegl's use in the first edition of *Spätrömische Kunstindustrie* (Wien 1901). In the subsequent edition in 1902 Riegl substitutes 'tactile' with 'haptic' in order to underline the eye's role as a sense organ.
4. Howard was the director of the National Center for Experiments in Television (NCET) at KQED in San Francisco and inventor of the term 'videospace', in 1971 (cf. Gibson's *Cyberspace*).

Works cited

Arn, Robert. "The Form and Sense of Video." *Eigenwelt der Apparate-Welt. Pioneers of Electronic Art*. 1973. Ed. David Dunn. Linz: Ars Electronica, Vasulkas, 1992. Print.

Auslander, Philip. *Liveness. Performance in a Mediatized Culture*. London and New York: Routledge, 1999. Print.

Austin, J. L. *How to do Things with Words*. 1955. Oxford: Oxford University Press, 1978. Print.

Badiou, Alain. *Being and Event*. 1988. Transl. Liver Feltham. London, New York: Continuum Intl. Pub. Group, 2006. Print.

Benjamin, Walter. "The Work of Art in the Age of Mechanical Reproduction." *Media and Cultural Studies*. 1936. Eds. Meenakshi Gigi Durham and Douglas Kellner. London: Blackwell Publishing, 2006. Print.

Bolter, Jay David, and Richard Grusin. *Remediation. Understanding New Media*. Massachusetts and London, England: MIT Press. Cambridge, 1999. Print.

Bitforms Gallery. *Mark Napier debuts new software art at bitforms gallery in New York*. Press release. Web. 12 Aug. 2010. <http://potatoland.com/april2007/press_release_bitforms_april_2007.html>

Buckner, Barbara. *Light and Darkness in the Electronic Landscape: Some Aspects of the Video Image*. Unpublished manuscript presented at the Collective for Living Cinema, Feb. 1978. Web. 31 Aug. 2010. <http://www.experimentaltvcenter.org/history/tools/ttext.php3?id=6&page=1>

Deleuze, Gilles. *A Thousand Plateaus*. 1980. Minneapolis: University of Minnesota Press, 1987. Print.

– *Francis Bacon: The Logic of Sensation*. 1981. Minneapolis: University of Minnesota Press, 2002. Print.

– *Cinema 2: The Time-Image*. 1985. Minneapolis: The Athlone Press, 1989. Print.

Gade, Rune, and Anne Jerslev *Performative Realism*. Copenhagen: Museum Tusculanum Press, 2005. Print.

Kaprow, Allan. "'Happenings' in the New York Scene." *The New Media Reader*. Eds. Noah Wardrip-Fruin and Nick Montfort. Cambridge, Massachusetts and London, England: MIT Press, [1961] 2003. 84-88. Print.

Levine, Les, Theodor H. Nelson and Nicholas Negroponte. "From Software – Information Technology: Its Meaning for Art." 1969. *The New Media Reader*. Eds. Noah Wardrip-Fruin and Nick Montfort. Cambridge, Massachusetts and London, England: MIT Press, 2003. 249-257. Print.

Manovich, Lev. *The Language of New Media*. Cambridge, Massachusetts and London, England: MIT Press, 2001. Print.

McLuhan, Marshall. *Understanding Media: The Extensions of Man*. New York: McGraw Hill, 1964. Print.

Meyrowitz, Joshua. *No sense of Place. The Impact of Electronic Media on Social Behavior.* Oxford: Oxford University Press, 1985. Print.

Nake, Frieder. "Kalkulierte & kalkulierende Zeichen. Der Computer als instrumentales Medium." *Vom Sinn multipler Welt. Medien und Kunst*. Eds. Volker Demuth und Robin Wagner. Würzburg: Könighausen & Neumann, 2000. Print.

Paik, Nam June. "Cybernated Art." *The New Media Reader*. 1966. Eds. Noah Wardrip-Fruin and Nick Montfort. MIT Press. Cambridge, Massachusetts and London, England. 2003. 229. Print.

Pilo, Michela. *Listening Post*. San Jose Museum of Art. Web. 12 Aug. 2010. <http://2006.01sj.org/content/view/756/128/>.

Pold, Søren. "Interface Realisms: The Interface as Aesthetic Form." *Postmodern Culture*. 15.2 (2005). Web. 12 Aug. 2010. <http://muse.jhu.edu/journals/pmc/v015/15.2pold.html>.

Riegl, Alois. *Spätrömische Kunstindustrie*. 1901/02. Berlin: Gebr. Mann Verlag, 2000. Print.

Tomlinson, John. *Globalization and Culture*. Cambridge: Polity Press, 1999. Print

Weibel, Peter. "The Apparatus World – a World unto Itself." *Eigenwelt der Apparatewelt. Pioniere der elektronischen Kunst*. Ed. David Dunn. Linz: Ars Electronica, Vasulkas, 1992. 15-9. Print.

Youngblood, Gene. *Expanded Cinema*. Toronto and Vancouver: Clarke, Irwin & Company Limited, 1970. Print.

THROUGH: Sensation and Perception

LONE KOEFOED HANSEN
The Interface at the Skin

SØREN BRO POLD
Interface Perception:
The Cybernetic Mentality and
Its Critics: Ubermorgen.com

The Interface at the Skin

BY LONE KOEFOED HANSEN

> If success in communication was once the art of reaching across the intervening bodies to touch another's spirit, in the age of electronic media it has become the art of reaching across the intervening spirits to touch another's body. Not the ghost in the machine, but the body in the medium is the central dilemma of modern communications (Peters 224-5).

At 14:55 on 21st December 2007 my two mobile phones beeped at the same time. I immediately rushed to read the messages that had caused the beeping. I was certain that both of them were from my friend in Singapore, who was due to give birth to a son that day. To make sure I got the news immediately, I knew she would MMS both of my phones, and the double beeping worked like a personal ring-tone, only mediated through several devices. It felt like a poke, and it even had the same effect: I jumped up from the chair in excitement reaching for one of the phones. On the display the message popped up and there he was, one hour old, squinting his eyes towards the lens of my friend's mobile phone camera and looking slightly annoyed with the sudden change in climate. It was nothing like being there in person, but it was the closest I could get, and Earth actually did seem to shrink quite a bit as the display in my hand evidenced the existence of a very new human being who had come into this world just one hour ago, 6,500 miles away.

110 years prior to this incident, my grandmother was born. She spent most of her life working hard on my grandparents' small farm, lived to be almost 100 years old, and I'm not sure she ever heard about the mobile phone even though it did exist in 1997 when she died. Her life almost embodies the rapid development of technology, but even though the history of (digital) technology could probably be told from the viewpoint of her life that is not the reason why I mention her. I mention her because she once told me this little story about an experience she had when she was in her forties: It was spring, maybe summer, and she was working alone in the field.

She had been bending over for a while in order to work on something on the ground when all of a sudden, and for no apparent reason, the hairs on her arms rose. At the same time – or at least it felt like it was at the same time – she just knew that her mother was no longer alive. She explained to me how she got up slowly because her back was stiff from working, walked home, made herself a cup of coffee and prepared herself for the news, which – as she expected – arrived not long after she got home from the field. It appears that she got the feeling of the death as it actually happened, a couple of kilometres away.

Whether my beloved grandmother was psychic, had a vivid imagination, or maybe actually had an invisible connection to other people, is not the main concern in this context. What is interesting, however, is the similarity between the two stories; a poke or a touch that – although of an immaterial nature – immediately makes the receiver realise what is going on. The stories obviously span major emotional issues like life and death, past and present, but on a less dramatic level they are also tales of personal and emotional communication happening through some kind of medium – be it a modern technological one (as a sort of telepresence) or an inexplicable communication happening through 'the ether' (as a sort of telepathy or mind-reading).

The notion of 'telepresence' is not new within new media art and interface aesthetics. Coined by cognitive scientist and mathematician Marvin Minsky, the term has been widely addressed by artists (e.g. Eduardo Kac or Paul Sermon) as well as researchers and theorists – e.g. Jonathan Steuer (who primarily relates it to virtual reality), and Kac (who writes that art creating a telepresence experience highlights that "immediate perceptual encounters are expanded by a heightened awareness of what is absent, remote" (182)). Thus, telepresence is not a matter of disappearing into or immersing oneself in another world entirely, but instead a matter of sensing two worlds simultaneously with one world affecting the other. Similar definitions are put forward by Lev Manovich (167) and briefly by Gordon Calleja (84).

Telepresence could be understood as a techno-scientific term for (or a technological adaptation of) the primarily spiritual and psychological term telepathy, where one person is capable of sensing another person without having actual visual or physical contact.

The term telepathy is highly contested ground, and one of the major figures in telepathy research at present, Rupert Sheldrake, is looked upon with high regard as well as with contempt and hostility depending on the scientific paradigm people subscribe to.[1] Regardless of whether 'true' telepathy exists or not, technology research and development that might lead to a situation where something similar to telepathy is possible is currently in vogue. As Anthony Townsend, director of technology development at the Institute for the Future, writes:

> Yet today, the interest in telepathy is not in verifying its existence, or understanding its physiological or supernatural mechanisms, but rather in replicating its functionality through engineering (46).

It is the nature of, and the conceptual background for, this interest in 'telepathic functionality' that I will investigate in this article, although the engineers and designers themselves probably have not contemplated the resemblances between their designs and the telepathy topos.

The *Skin Probe Project* contrived by Philips Design in 2006 is an example of a design project that instantiates 'telepathic functionality' through connecting bodies and minds by using the skin. The project is comprised of two experimental dress prototypes: Biofeedback sensors in the two dresses read and emulate the body by measuring its data on the skin (e.g. pulse and amount of sweat) in order to subsequently display the results on the fabric. In this way, a Skin Probe dress becomes a 'second skin' that explicitly aims to be an interface to the body's 'raw' flesh and implicitly aims to be an interface to the wearer's mind.

By using the notion of telepathy as an analytical starting point for understanding the concepts at stake in this project, I will demonstrate how the dresses re-enact a resilient communication paradigm where it is (in theory) possible for communication to be effortless and without misunderstandings. Consequently, I will discuss how the Skin Probe dresses gained attention both on blogs and in traditional news media, because they tapped into an old dream about being intimately connected to others – brain-to-brain or body-to-body – and that this dream, or topos,[2] is to be found in many other (also very early) communication technologies. The dresses are somehow a fusion of my mobile phone and my grandmother's psychic sensibility, as they express an ability to sense intimate feelings and communicate them digitally.

Accordingly, the goal of this article is to argue that the viral marketing of the dresses relies on a reinterpretation of what Imar de Vries (using the mobile phone as an example) calls "ideal communication," even though Philips Design may not have consciously remediated the historical precedents. The dresses are one example of how current technologies and their interfaces seem to be built in the light of recurring dreams, and that even when communication channels and media change, the agenda for communication does not necessarily change at the same time.

The dream of ideal communication

The well-known communication model (1948) by mathematicians and information technologists Claude Shannon and Warren Weaver describes communication as transmission; an idea is transferred from sender to receiver in a process where the idea is transferred into language by the sender and then again transferred into an idea in the receiver's head. During this process, the idea is affected by noise in at least three places: when the idea is transformed into language in the sender's head; when the actual exchange of words between the sender and receiver takes place; and when language is transformed into idea in the receiver's head. This model has mothered a long range of transmission communication models all focusing primarily on the noise aspect.

Where Shannon and Weaver saw language as the channel through which messages are transmitted, many theories about media communication use the transmission model to describe how different media add different kinds of noise to the messages transmitted, and to describe how (and why) some media are better than others at getting messages through. Some talk about bandwidth – the amount of realistic impacts available to the senses: the more bandwidth, the better the communication possibilities. Depending on the medium (i.e. the coding of the message) there is a greater or lesser chance that what you think you communicate is also what other people think you say.

As most readers probably know, the transmission models of communication have a nice, clean way of looking at communication through media, but this model is also contested ground. It is highly questionable if the foundation of the argument (that there is a noise-free message in the first place) holds water and, as media theorist Joshua Meyrowitz points out, this view on the relationship between communication and the medium is quite reductive: When any medium is understood as a channel (a "conveyor belt" (7)) through which a message travels from sender to receiver, communication is reduced to being a question of transmitting information, and a medium is reduced to being a noise-adding device. The point made by Meyrowitz is that there are inherent problems with any channel as it always adds noise to the message while the message 'travels through' it, which is why it is equally important (and maybe even more rewarding) to study the structural and environmental properties and implications of media.

Since the transmission model of communication – the channel metaphor – is the metaphor on which the artefacts presented later in this paper are based, I will be taking this as my starting point. Interestingly, the more nuanced ways of understanding communication (through media) are rarely noticeable in commercially conceived projects – maybe because the dream of the existence of a message core is alluring, as it promises that we humans actually know exactly what we want and what we wish for. And if we actually know what we want, it makes perfect sense to understand communication as something that can be transmitted to someone else, and it makes perfect sense to hope for a medium that will enable a noise-free transfer of our needs, thoughts and wishes to other people.

Accordingly, the transmission models of communication implicitly operate with a belief in immediacy: that it is possible for a medium to make 'clean communication' happen. By addressing the issues of noise and bandwidth it is implied that there is such a thing as noise-free communication, even if it is only theoretical: a 'true' message devoid from noise, a core content that is transferable (at least in theory). This also means that there is a possibility of a medium whose channel does not add noise; which, by inference, means that the immediacy of communication, and thus the immediacy of the medium, is important. I will return to this argument shortly, but first we need to understand the dismal side to this way of understanding communication.

Bridging communication chasms

In his book *Speaking into the air*, John Durham Peters defines communication as an inherently contradictory term since it is always both a bridge and a chasm: The bridge makes contact possible, but it never actually removes the distance between the brinks. According to Peters, this contradiction drives a never resolved urge for finding a way to communicate 'ideally' – that is with the least possible gap between the brinks (and preferably no gap at all). Or, as de Vries describes it when he voices reservations about the subjectivity embedded in the word 'ideal':

> [T]he concept of 'ideal' is of course problematic, in the sense that its interpretation is an exceedingly personal matter [...] 'ideal communication' will be referred to [...] as perpetual contact, the fulfilment of 'sharing one's mind with another'; in other words, as ubiquitous and pure communication without misunderstanding (1).

Simultaneously, Peters argues that almost all debate about communication can be seen in the light of how technology impacts people's understanding of how communication takes place. Technology makes new kinds of connections (or bridges) possible, but has also been inserted into the discourse on – and thus the understanding of – communication as a phenomenon:

> 'Communication' is a registry of modern longings. The term evokes a utopia where nothing is misunderstood, hearts are open, and expression is uninhibited [...] How did it become possible to say that a man and a woman 'are tuned to different frequencies'? (de Vries 2)

Not only has technology opened up a long line of possible communication channels, but these channels have in return greatly influenced our way of thinking about communications technology. In other words, technology is a big part of the communication discourse. To paraphrase Lev Manovich's term 'interface culture', which highlights the fact that the interface is also a cultural phenomenon, technology is not only a communication tool but also a cultural and discursive agent of, or frame for, communication. "We connected really well", a friend of mine recently commented when she had been on a date, thus implying that they had had a good rapport. There is something inherently mechanical in this metaphor; in my inner eye I saw women establishing connections with wires at an old-fashioned phone central.

According to Peters, communication paradigms surfaced as an important area of research with the rise of telecommunication technologies and electricity as they made (especially verbal) communication possible, independent of place. Suddenly communication literally took place 'in the air':

> Thanks to electricity, communication could now take place regardless of impediments such as distance or embodiment. The term conjured up a long tradition of dreams about angelic messengers and communication between separated lovers [...] (5).

As Peters argues, the very thought of direct connections between people – brain-to-brain or heart-to-heart communication – was not new, it just resurfaced due to the sudden appearance of a technology that seemed to make direct communication possible, or at least within reach. Or, to put it in a less techno-deterministic way, finally someone invented a technology that seemed to make the much desired smooth communication possible. Technologies like the telegraph and electricity were seen as obvious metaphors for bridging the aforementioned gap between what you think you communicate and what other people think you say. The idea was that if you could transmit sound without wires, why should you not be able to transmit thoughts the same way? Thus, it suddenly became plausible that thoughts also existed 'in the air' even though no-one had been able to prove it yet. Maybe, some people thought, the technology that would prove the existence of (and facilitate listening to) thoughts *outside* the head and not only inside the head had simply not yet been invented? Even in this perspective, however, there were still problems to overcome, but they seemed easier as they appeared to be of a technological and not an interpersonal kind. As long as problems could be solved by inventing a suitable technology, all hope was not yet dead:

> Interpersonal relations gradually became redescribed in the technical terms of transmission at a distance – making contact, tuning in or out, being on the same wave-length, getting good or bad vibes, or "Earth to Herbert, come in please!" Communication in this sense makes problems of relationships into problems of proper tuning or noise reduction (Peters 5).

> Thought was not a sign expressed by a body but, as one psychical enthusiast put it, "a dynamic force or an X-form of energy." The problem of 'communication,' in this view, was one not of love or justice, but of proper tuning or channeling (Peters 104).

In other words: Good communication became a matter of possessing a good 'tuner' both literally (with a physical antenna and good hardware) and figuratively (with good social skills). Technology used to be able to help us with the literal part of tuning only, whereas social tuning was an individual matter that, when taken to the extreme, involved some kind of psychic capability – as in the phenomenon of telepathy or mind-reading. Even today, technology is often still understood as something that can provide considerable help, both when it comes to technical solutions to communication and when it comes to providing a strengthening of social skills in communication. Thus, the dream of flawless or ideal communication is nourished by, and reliant on, advances in technology. Conversely, the opposite power relation is also significant, as advances in technology are highly influenced by the recurring dream of communication without noise or flaws. This idea of noise-less or direct and immediate communication had an important peak in the late 19th century when the dream of immediate and instantaneous communication received a boost, resulting in the coinage of the term telepathy.

Telepathy

The concept of mindreading or thought transference can imply anything from the common ability to understand other people's behavioural pattern and hence to a certain extent their feelings (cf. Nichols and Stich) to the mystic realm, where mindreading is the ability to read exact thoughts in other people's minds. As I mentioned in the beginning of this article, telepathy is a slightly broader term as it denotes that someone is able to sense someone or something else without spatial constraints, and this 'something' need not be actual thoughts.

Telepathy was coined in the late 19th century as electricity and radio waves were invented and became widespread.[3] The theory of thought transference was not unknown, but with the advent of electricity it suddenly became clear that the transfer of thoughts and feelings between people might also be an invisible but actual physical phenomenon and not witchcraft. Nowadays, telepathy or thought transference is not accepted in the mainstream, and that may also have been the case back then. However, as professor in comparative literature Roger Luckhurst points out, it was a time when many different scientific genres worked with the notion of the brain being able to do more than people could grasp (78). Pamela Thurschwell lists Freud as another example (albeit Freud is now seen as being in a different category) of how investigations into the brain's ability to communicate on a subliminal level took place, thus changing people's ideas of the connections between brain and body. The body was gradually becoming understood as a container of information, and the self was understood as layers of supra- and superliminal consciousness; Freud's version of the subliminal consciousness being one way of understanding the invisible acts of the brain, mind-reading being another:

> According to F.W.H. Myers (1843-1901), automatic writing, table-rapping, hallucinations, clairvoyance and dreams [were] all attempts by the subliminal self to deliver information to the supraliminal self [...] the human subject, in its combination of psychic and bodily automatisms and symptoms, is a relay station for information [...] both [Myers and Freud] participate in a version of a late nineteenth-century hermeneutic project in which the subject is understood both as a text to be read and a space through which information flows (Thurschwell 18-9).

Basically, Thurschwell argues, a large number of researchers were investigating the invisible properties of the world (including several aspects concerned with the connections between brain and body) from so many points of view that it seemed almost a matter of repression to suggest that not everything had invisible properties and layers.

Not only was the brain's way of functioning up for debate, it was also debated because more established and reputable kinds of research (e.g. medical and natural science) were working from an assumption that everything had invisible properties, which technology was just about to prove the existence of. In the late 19th century, research into invisible properties was an 'inter-phenomenon' – everyone was researching the potential invisible properties of everything, and this happened across all research categories (Luckhurst 79). Louis Pasteur's germ theory, for instance, was verified in the 1890's. We now know that the theory about 'invisible' germs holds true, and that germs actually cause a lot of trouble even though we are unable to sense them, but in the late 19th century the transmission of invisible germs seemed just as (im)plausible as the invisible transmission of thoughts (Luckhurst 78).

Thus, in the late 19th century, people were gradually becoming aware of the invisible properties of several phenomena, and the leap from sounds consisting of waves (which can be verified by tuning forks) to brain activity also resulting in 'waves' in the brain did not seem that big.[4] The logic was that if brainwaves were actually waves, it should be possible to measure them just like sound can be measured with the help of tuning forks. Following this, the next logical step would be to not only measure them but figure out how to transmit them in the same way that sound waves can be transmitted. As a consequence of this thought, and despite some people attacking the concept of thought transference and calling it dubious, the Society of Psychical Research set up a laboratory in London in order to conduct more rigorous research into the phenomenon of transmitting brainwaves. According to Thurschwell, this is where 'thought transference' was coined as *telepathy* which, Thurschwell further argues, was not at all a new idea – it was just a new way of investigating it:

> Genealogically linked to the older concept of sympathy and the newer word empathy, telepathy is also related to love – the desire for complete sympathetic union with the mind of another (14)

The desire for complete sympathetic union with another person's mind is also addressed in the book *When old technologies were new* by Carolyn Marvin, where the connections between early communications technology and the dream of 'ideal communication' are laid out:

> Recurring anecdotes about electrically enhanced private conversations were often organized around the telephone, but the most fantastic projections concerned the prospect of eliminating all barriers, even wires, to the distant loved one. This communications topos was worked in endless variations, traced to antiquity, elaborated in a hundred hypothetical futures. The power of new electrical technologies to effect effortless intimacy between friends was perhaps the commonest of all prophetic themes about communication (154).

In her book, Marvin mentions a plethora of examples of how late 19th century technologies were influenced by – and gave rise to – dreams of uncomplicated and immediate interpersonal communication. One of her examples is an idea for a future technology where two people, through mutual transplantation of a small piece of skin from each other's arms, would be able to communicate through the alien skin now being part of one's own body (154). A very poetic vision indeed, albeit maybe slightly impractical should one either have many friends or happen to lose the friendship of the original owner of the skin.

Slightly more practical is the contemporary mobile phone, which also relies on the desire to always be able to engage in some kind of communication, be it a text message, a phone call or a third possibility. Nokia's corporate slogan almost says it all: "Nokia – Connecting People". As de Vries also points out, the underlying ideology is still that new technology (e.g. the mobile phone) will help us reach and understand each other quicker and better than before (10). In reality, we often experience gaps in mobile phone communication, but it is undeniable that the technological development is focused on providing access to a number of instant and 'true' communication possibilities – the latest being video calls and MMS as more 'realistic' versions of voice calls and text messages, respectively. On a more conceptual level, and regardless of the communications technology involved, when people dream of uncomplicated communication, they dream of communication where transmission noise is as good as eliminated and where a connection is always possible. In other words, they regard flawless and ideal communication as something that is both immediate/instant and immediate/direct.

Immediateness

As addressed by Jay David Bolter and Richard Grusin, the paradigm of immediacy has always been important for new media (or technology as such), and it continues to be a major selling point:

> Transparent media [...] desire to get past the limits of representation and to achieve the real. They are not striving for the real in any metaphysical sense. Instead, the real is defined in terms of the viewer's experience; it is that which would evoke an immediate (and therefore authentic) emotional response. Transparent digital applications seek to get to the real by bravely denying the fact of mediation (53).

Thus, the concept of transparent immediacy relies on a(n implicit) belief in a core content – there is something 'more real' behind the reality of the representation as it is only a re-presentation and not a presentation. In Bolter and Grusin's book, *Remediation: understanding new media*, dealing with the way in which each new medium builds on, comments on and incorporates earlier media, immediacy is defined as one of two central and equally important aspects of remediation; the other aspect being hypermediacy. In transmission communication terms, immediacy can be said to be the dream of noise-free communication, whereas hypermediacy is focused on the nature of the noise-adding channel. In representational terms, one could say that transparent immediacy is representation camouflaged as presentation – it is supposed to be *as if* the represented phenomenon is in front of us. Conversely, hypermediacy is presentation only, as it is concerned with the presentational aspects of the medium; about *how* the medium represents. The quest for immediacy has driven many commercial products as well as research projects in interface design and in the human-computer interaction (HCI) community, where the aim has been to provide absolute certainty about the nature of the core content (e.g. the possibilities in a computer application):

> What producers of new media artifacts are selling are experiences of immediacy. They engage in an ongoing struggle to define or redefine immediacy or authenticity of experience in a way that particularly enhances their own products. Often the immediacy of the product is expressed as transparency: you can see through the product to the ostensible reality behind it (Bolter and Gromala 69-70).

The dream driving the search for immediacy is that we will be able to forget all about intermediary layers (interfaces or noise-adding layers) and be brought to 'know for a fact' instead. Thus, this belief in the possibility of erasing the perception of the medium itself in order to reach the "immediate (and hence authentic) emotional response" is the primary reason why designers and developers of, for and in any medium more often than not strive for transparent immediacy (Bolter and Grusin 53).

Still, this endemic quest for authentic communication is, as Peters, Luckhurst, Thurschwell, Marvin and also Bolter and Grusin argue, not unique to digital technology. Computers in all forms are just the newest examples of how new technologies are not just novel but also part of recurring topoi.

Another important meaning of the term 'immediate' is concerned with instantaneity, which – as I mentioned above – is another important topos for digital communication (including mobile phones): Ideal communication is not only precise, it is also instantaneous. As with the telegraph and Morse code, the landline phone and voice, the mobile phone and its ability to reach everyone anywhere with either voice or text also promotes novel possibilities for instantaneous communication. In all of these cases, however, the 'core desire' is less about accurate content and more about the here-and-now. As a technology, the telegraph prioritised speed over argumentative accuracy, and curator Matt Locke refers to the text message as also being more concerned with time than content when he refers to how "Japanese children send blank text messages to each other as a way of saying a quick 'hello'" (Locke). Locke also argues that the mobile phone is able to create temporary intimate zones that happen as a consequence of the mobile phone's ability to connect people anywhere, unlike the landline phone that is always situated 'permanently' in the same zone.

So two meanings of the word *immediate* are at play when it comes to the relationship between technology and the dream of ideal communication, which is what most technologies seem to have been trying to accomplish since electricity came into general use: immediate as in instant, and immediate as in close, near and direct. It appears that both are part of Nokia's corporate slogan "Nokia – Connecting People," and the mobile phone is generally understood (and advertised) as being capable of immediately making people feel less distanced from each other. I received a photo of my friend's newborn son lying in a bed on the opposite side of the Earth, so the mobile phone does actually sometimes make the world seem smaller. Sometimes bridges are actually instantly built over physical distances when the mobile connects the people at both ends, be it via voice, text or pictures.

What the mobile phone is not good at, however, is building bridges over the communication chasms present in face-to-face communication. No technology has yet been able to reduce the transmissional noise coined by Shannon and Weaver even though it has been a prevalent topos at least since electricity became common. The development of the mobile phone has focused on the difficulties of remote communication, and all mobile phone companies have tried to find a technical solution to the obvious communicative breakdowns that occur when people are not able to see, feel and sense each other because this would be a 'killer application'. The pursuit of this solution can be analysed by using telepathy and mind-reading as metaphors, since communication is as much about sensing other people's reactions and feelings as it is about hearing what they say.

Much of this sensing takes place through facial expressions[5] and body language, but even though being in the same space is better than being apart when it comes to what we can call emotional or telepathic sensing, we are still not in a perfect world when it comes to ideal communication. One of the reasons is that some people are good at presenting a 'stiff upper lip' or a 'stone face', and another of the reasons is that some people are bad at reading others. This problem is the main foundation for technology developers when they design with the 'telepathy topos' in mind.

Skin Probes

As previously mentioned, Design Probes is a research initiative undertaken by Philips Design in order to "track trends and developments that may ultimately evolve into mainstream issues that have a significant impact on business" (Philips, "Design Probe Program: Skin"; Philips, "What are Design Probes?"). The *Skin Probes* project[6] is a way to investigate possible modalities of future social interaction by using wearable computing; in this case dresses with embedded biometric sensors and LEDs:

> The dresses show emotive technology and how the body and the near environment can use pattern and color change to interact and predict the emotional state (Philips "Design Probe Program: Skin").

Skin Probes comprises two dresses that are supposed to "express the emotions and personality of the wearer" (ibid.). By engaging in the Design Probe research initiative, with *Skin Probes* being one of several prototypes, Philips wish to investigate (hence the word 'probe') the future market of mainstream technology. These dresses make an interesting project because it is implicitly assumed that (digital) technologies have the ability to mediate human signals and human perception in a way in which the sign-system is bypassed.

The *Bubelle* dress (Ill. 1) expresses a blush. It contains two types of biometric sensors: a heart rate sensor and a galvanic skin response sensor. *Bubelle* is meant to monitor your anxiety level by calculating the sensors' measurements and letting the software decide if you should actually be blushing right now. The idea – based on scientific studies on bodily reactions to different kinds of emotions – is that if your heart rate is suddenly high and you sweat a little bit there is a high probability that you, along with most people, would be blushing. Consequently, the dress blushes for you by lighting up the LEDs contained in the fabric of the dress, if the measured data complies with the data regarding when people normally blush.

The *Frisson* dress (Ill. 2), or rather bodysuit, is gooseflesh remediated through LEDs as the bodysuit's visual appearance changes according to the wearer's state of excitement. The dress has long and

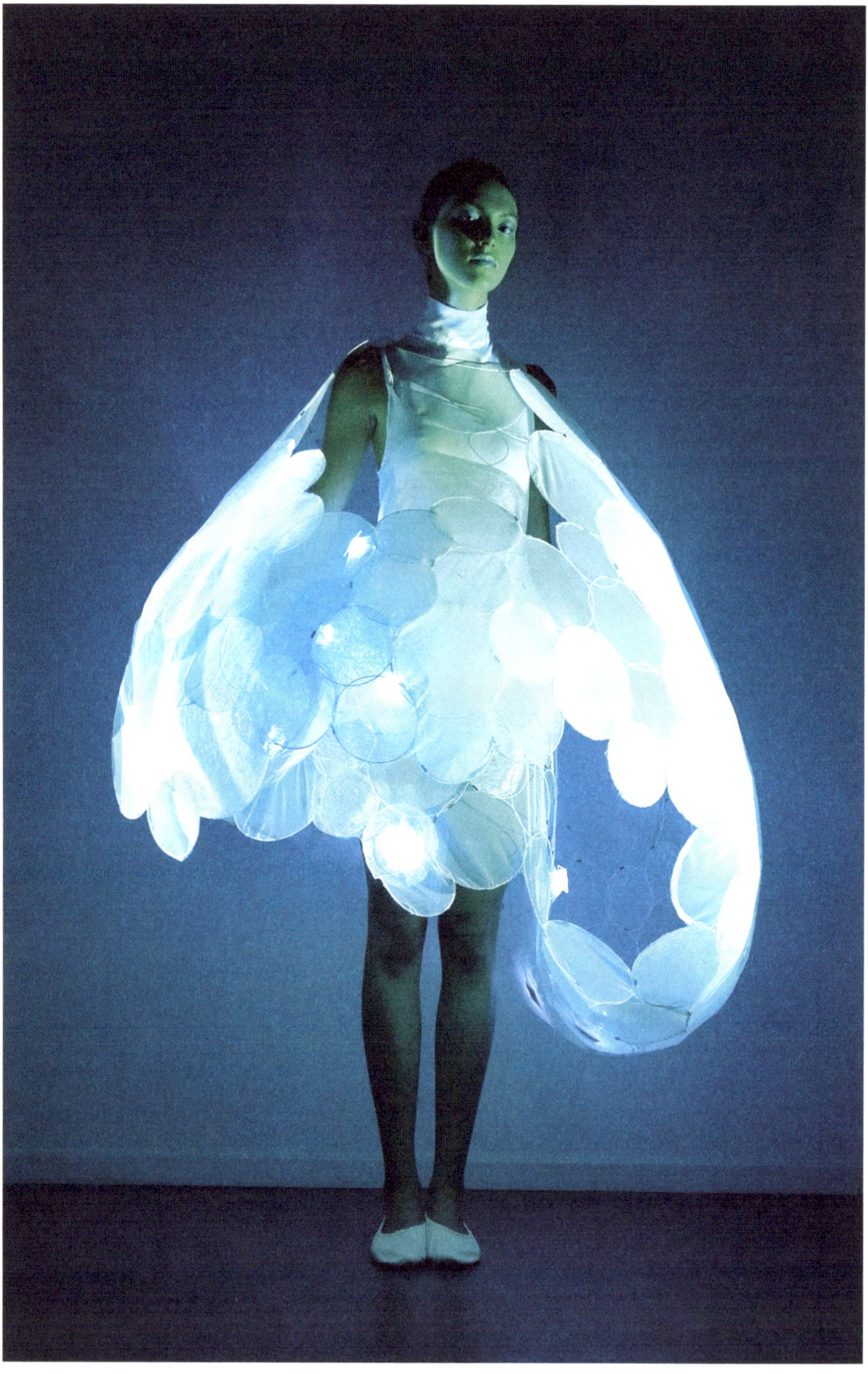

ILL. 1: The Philips Skin Probe *Bubelle*, promotional photo.

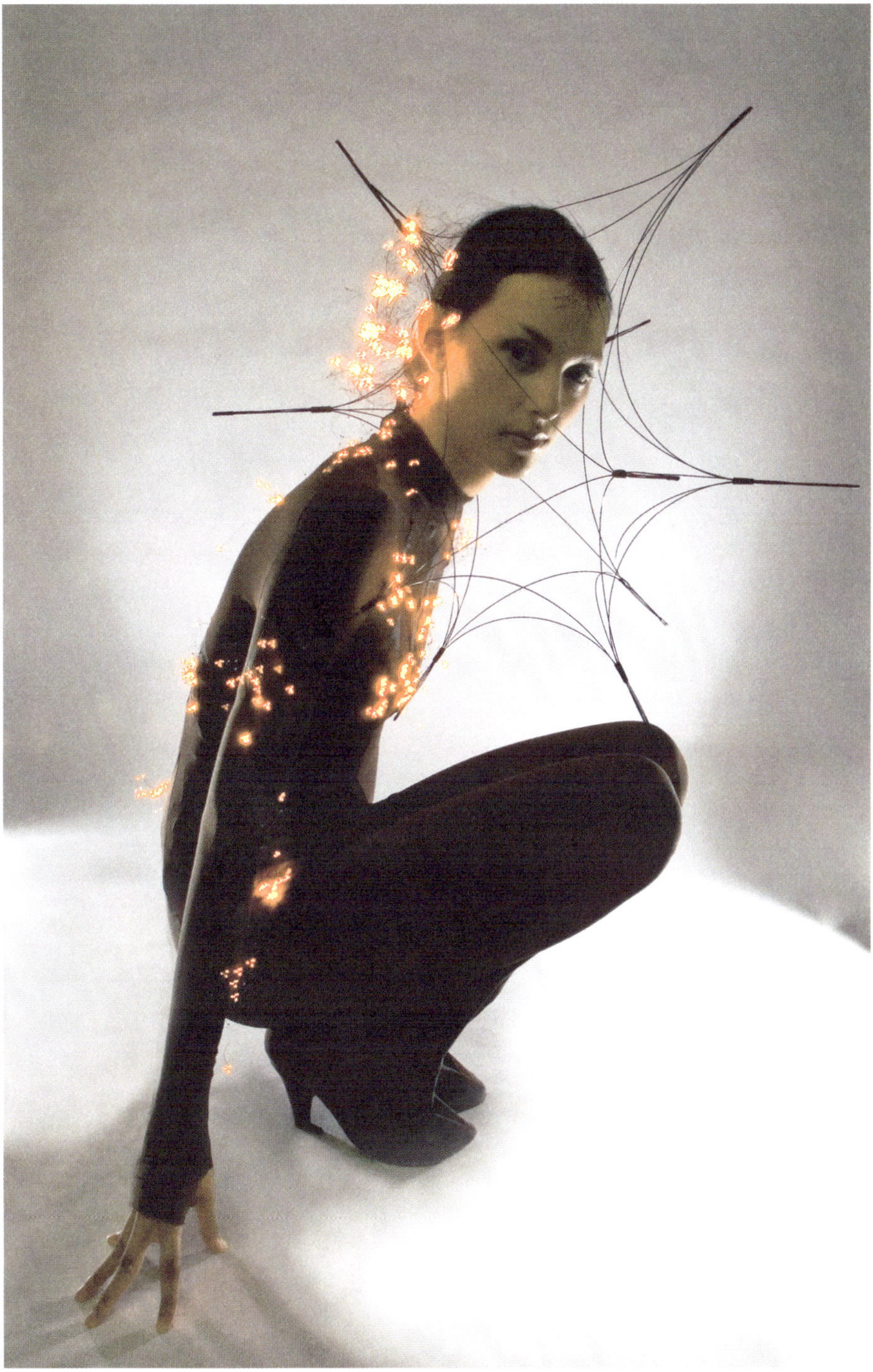

ILL. 2: The Philips Skin Probe *Frisson*, promotional photo.

very light copper tentacles that are modelled after the antennae of an insect. The ends of the tentacles light up when brushed or blown on, and by performing calculations on the sensors' data, the dress thus emulates the way skin 'rises to the occasion' and becomes goose pimpled. It is implied that the moving of the tentacles is likely to be a result of the sensation of another body being close to yours and that this sensation would have caused excitement.

As pointed out by Philips Design, the idea behind *Skin Probes* is to construct technologies that express the emotions and personality of the wearer. The project is technical (as Philips is basically a company of engineers making hardware), but it is of course based on how the group envisions the potential use of the technology. As Philips Design further writes in the press material about *Skin Probe*:

> The SKIN probe project is part of the program [of Design Probes] and challenges the notion that our lives are automatically better because they are more digital. It looks at more 'analog' phenomena like emotional sensing, exploring technologies that are 'sensitive' rather than 'intelligent'. Two outfits have been developed as part of SKIN to identify a new way of communicating with those around us by using garments as proxies to convey deep feelings that are difficult to express in words.

The concept of (or the idea behind) these *Skin Probes* is that they make visible some of those aspects we have a hard time sensing consciously even when being very close to other people and, as such, the dresses 'enhance' social communication. In the current 'analogue' world, we may be able to vaguely sense that something is going on in or with our communication partner, but since we do not have certain knowledge, it can be tricky to both begin and sustain a fruitful conversation. Accordingly, the aim of the dresses is twofold: to make social interaction more immediate, and to convert potential interactions into highly probable ones. The general idea being that by knowing more about each other – by getting certain knowledge – we will be able to use this knowledge to communicate better and more often. So, allegedly, Philips has set up ways for social interaction to become easier, better, more meaningful and more exciting with the help of algorithms and digital technologies.

Philips' rhetoric is a study worth its own essay, as the company uses a terminology that implies quite a few things about the benefits and detriments of the current interface culture. However, a brief touching on some of the more interesting implications of the above quote is relevant here as the quote implies a split between mind and body – or between the controlled and 'cold' thoughts of the brain and the immediate and 'warm' state of the body. The split occurs in often used dichotomies like 'emotional sensing' vs. 'technologies'; 'sensitive' vs. 'intelligent'; 'deep feelings' vs. 'words' and, finally, in 'digital' vs. 'analogue'. Like the woman Kraka from the Nordic Sagas,[7] *Skin Probes* miraculously seems to bypass all of these dichotomies by introducing the garment as an interface and thus mending the split between the intelligent mind and the sensitive body. Here, the garment of the dresses is part technology, part organic matter, and whilst it covers the body it also exposes it. With Bolter and Grusin one could say that *Skin Probes* remediates the skin. The dresses are part digital and part analogue, and despite the algorithmic brain of the embedded computer, this computer is almost a part of the body of the wearer through the biometric sensors.

So it seems as if Philips Design has ended up equating the wearer's body to a computer in which the flow between input and output is a matter of cause and effect. The body has been appropriated and relabelled so that it becomes a container of information receiving input and sending output via the interface of the skin. In this way, an attempt is made to remediate the skin into an interface or a medium as immediate as it gets. Thus, while the dresses are permeated by hypermediacy (they display technology as fashion), they also embody the dream of ultimate communication transparency as the hybridity between the analogue and the digital enables certain knowledge of the 'deep feelings' of the wearer.

I will return to this supposedly transparent communication after a quick detour into a brief investigation of why a project like this is also important to Philips.

Performing Philips

These dresses do not only seek to establish connections between the body, the dresses and the surroundings – they also have a very performative side to them. As is the case with fashion and clothes in general, this performative side includes aspects like the expression of self, the performance of oneself and the making of a fashion statement (cf. visual culture theorist Malcolm Barnard). But while the *Skin Probe* dresses obviously carry the same overall performance connotations that fashion and clothing do, they are first and foremost a spectacular performance of the Philips brand.

The spectacular nature of the project lies in the fact that it catches the eye. Evidently, one of the main purposes of the whole Design Probes research initiative is to create showcases that establish Philips as a trendy, cutting edge company and as a cool brand. The many spectacular projects of the Design Probe program – *Skin Probes* and its sister projects – are probably seeking to attract buyers as well as innovative and creative employees.

With respect to the spectacular performance of Philips, the project proved to be efficient even though only Philips knows if it was also effective: the dresses were widely blogged and were also mentioned in traditional media.[8] So, viewed as a viral brand-marketing campaign, the project was definitely a success. It did very well in striking the right note of Internet spectacle, so it is safe to say that the performance of the Philips brand was successful.

The project is spectacular in several other ways as well, and one of them is its visual appearance. Beautiful, stunning and slightly odd dresses photographed advantageously, featuring a slim female model and focusing on the specific features of the dresses (the LEDs and the pointy appearance of *Frisson*). The form factor of the dresses alone would possibly have made the headlines, since it leans on the appearance of the parade dresses of haute couture in the fashion industry. On top of the spectacular form of the dresses, they are visually striking due to the embedded lights, which may have been the primary reason why the pictures travelled the blogs. LEDs are considered cool and are always a hit – something containing LEDs seems to be worth taking pictures of, as the response to the various projects from Grafitti Research Lab (amongst them *Throwies*[9]) indicates. As technology, LEDs 'belong' to the computer and to the Internet era as they look good in print but are particularly stunning on the backlit screen of the computer.

Furthermore, it is hard to imagine the dresses getting worldwide online coverage in early 2006 if they had been emitting anything other than light. Take sound as an example: Sounds are a lot more difficult to present online, especially if the viewer/listener has to be able to make a connection between the data source and its auditory representation. Sound is temporal, so video would have been needed; video would have meant larger files, and since really fast broadband was not as widespread in 2005 (when I have to assume the project was conceived) as it is now, and since YouTube was launched in 2005 and hence not yet ubiquitously present on the web, a video presentation of Skin Probes would have been presented in a very poor video and sound quality.[10] Furthermore, auditory output would have prevented most conventional, printed media from presenting the dresses. Similar arguments are even more valid for any other non-visual output type (vibrations, smell, pressure etc).

The point of all this is to underline that the *Skin Probe* project was of course made for a specific purpose with a specific medium (or transmission channel) in mind. The research initiative is not just about future technologies, even though this ties in nicely with the many earlier attempts at, and dreams of, connecting two minds that I presented previously. The project is also about creating breaking news. I will briefly conclude on this aspect of performing Philips towards the end of this article.

Performing communication

Leaving aside their striking visuality, the *Skin Probe* dresses are spectacular because they visualise communicative signals that most humans almost desperately wish they were able to perceive consciously. The primary spectacular aspect of the dresses thus lies in their functional properties, where physical signals are remediated and where the remediation promises that there are 'deep feelings' to be 'conveyed'. This psychological bias makes the dresses the newest example of an artefact or a service that promises to make communication, and thus understanding of other people, less complicated. Expressed polemically, these dresses are gadgets designed to satisfy the geeky gadgeteer who falls for easily understandable eye-candy and who is lacking so much social competence, and maybe even social intelligence, that s/he is only able to understand other people when they can be translated into algorithms. It is, however, not as easy to dismiss *Skin Probe* as yet another useless gadget as one might think because the project is also a performance of the concept of communication.

My argument is thus that *Skin Probes* in general and *Bubelle* in particular are a new occurrence of the telepathy topos embedded in many other communication technologies throughout time. The *Bubelle* dress reacts to internal stimuli as the sensors are turned towards the body, towards the skin, promising some kind of closeness to the mind by being close to the skin. *Bubelle's* touching of the skin promises a touch of the mind, acting as a translating membrane between inner self and outer appearance. The wearer of *Bubelle* may be in her own bubble (bubelle) both figuratively, because she has a mental shell surrounding her (cf. Locke), and literally, through the name and form of the dress; but she is not isolated as her surroundings are actually able to access her 'true' feelings on the outside of this bubble. In the dominating paradigm of *Bubelle*, physical reactions are taken literally and are, in this case, furthermore assigned predominance.

Even though the dresses are spectacular in their appearance, the most spectacular aspect of the dresses – especially *Bubelle* – is that they apparently do what 'we' have been dreaming of for ages. They seem to make visible what our bodies and hence our minds 'actually' feel, and they appear to aim at finally closing the communication chasm described by both Peters and de Vries:

> All media we have seen so far have one thing in common: they were initially perceived as trying to bridge space and time to such an extent that people would be able to communicate without obstacles and without misunderstanding. Fear of miscommunication and restoration of the natural balance of our extended sense-organs is what drives us to improve existing media (de Vries 13).

As de Vries argues, most media have been conceived owing to the fear of miscommunication. The same argument is relevant when technology moves into clothing and other artefacts because these artefacts also seem to fall into the transparency trap: they are close to the body, a closeness that the project effortlessly translates into also being close to the mind and thus the 'true self' of the person. Where the goal so far in many media has most often been to obtain interface transparency (cf. Bolter and Grusin; Bolter and Gromala), *Skin Probes* also addresses another kind of transparency: the telepathic transparency where we know what goes on inside another person. Following this, the dresses are visually striking examples of a dominant development strand focusing on envisioning technology as something that ultimately has no interface as the project subscribes to the paradigm of ultimate transparency – hypermediacy is not the conceptual goal here, even though the dresses in themselves do nothing but point at their own mediacy. Conceptually and rhetorically, *Skin Probes* subscribe to the paradigm of the perfect and invisible servant responding to our needs even before we are aware of them ourselves.[11] Furthermore, by regarding the skin as a membrane for the mind, *Bubelle* becomes the interface to emotions, feelings and other traditional mind-reading topics by reading signals from the skin. The body underneath can, apparently, never lie.

In this respect, the dresses are mind-reading machines that monitor the body to reveal the mind; the design builds on the archetype of the lie detector although the dresses appear to be much more sophisticated because they promise more nuances than just true or false. However, as is the case with lie detectors, there is still a chance that the interface 'lies' because all it does is read data, even though this data stems from a living body. Based on the popular assumption that the brain controls the body's functions, and (more importantly) based on the equally popular assumption that while the brain does control the body's moves, much of this control happens on a subconscious level, *Bubelle* addresses the skin as a way of getting to facts and 'pure data' from the 'inner self' of the wearer.

So even though the body does often react in certain ways according to emotions, *Bubelle* (like a lie detector) still only reads data. This data is then processed through digital algorithms written with the same cultural bias as our individual interpretation of the algorithms' results. It is thus possible to argue that noise is added in two places even though the dresses appear to comprise noise-free communication. First of all, noise is added because the programmer and the designer's cultural backdrop is a culture in which we believe in the primacy of the body's signals when it comes to finding the 'truth'. Secondly, noise is added because the interpreter is embedded in the same discourse – but unfortunately two similar noise patterns do not cancel each other out.

Signs of data and discourses

All *Bubelle* reads is signals: it reads the body's actions and physical energies, but these actions need not be reactions to specific or certain feelings; energies are not purely denotative signs that signify a specific and unmediated source. Rather, as signs they are always subject to a culturally specific interpretation. Literally, the body becomes a data source – a site playing host to a diversity of 'true' or 'false' feelings that we are now allegedly able to distinguish between because of this new technology.

Furthermore, at this point in time, the dream of flawless communication appears to have reached another level as digital technologies now allow for information processing on the body of communicators. By introducing sensors which are able to read the body's signals, these signals are highlighted as signs and not only physical processes. The *Skin Probes* project takes the symbolic understanding of blushing literally and converts the symbol so that it becomes reality. It is assumed that if a specific combination of data can be read from the wearer's body, this automatically means that the person is experiencing a specific emotion. Affect becomes effect.

To put it in semiotic terms, the *Skin Probe* dresses have an iconic expression but they 'pretend' that the indexical and the symbolic are identical; that the symbolic has been engulfed by the index. The interface is normally thought of as a semiotic relation between sign and data, as something mediating otherwise incomprehensible digital data. In *Skin Probes*, however, the interface seems to have transformed from a semiotic relation between data and expression into a direct translation, where the expression seeks to be pure and uncamouflaged data. The body is seen as a container of information just waiting to be tuned into, in order for the world of interpersonal communication to become 'a better place.' Luckily, Philips communicates, the company's designers and engineers have come to the rescue as they have found a way to extend the skin, thus finally enabling us to penetrate the skin and get access to the raw and unmediated flesh. Ironically, this sign-system bypass takes place in a dress that apparently gives access to the 'real' and unmediated communication of the body, although the staging is highly dependent on the fact that the dresses are visually stunning. Thereby the dresses become signs in themselves; well-executed marketing artefacts that signify Philips as a highly innovative and remarkable company.

So while *Skin Probes* dresses are not very successful readers and displayers of the dress wearer's mind, they are certainly very successful readers and displayers of latent technological hopes and desires and, not least, of the Philips brand. Or, to use the Townsend-inspired phrase 'telepathic functionality', the dresses fail in being functional with regard to telepathy, but they succeed in being functional signs of a resilient techno-discourse.

Concluding remarks

As is probably apparent by now, I find this mind-reading aspect, as re-proposed by *Skin Probes*, interesting but also limited. It is limited because it renders the more complicated feelings and desires invisible at best, obsolete at worst. What was interesting about both the principle of telepathy in the late 19th century and my two anecdotes at the beginning of this essay (especially the most recent one with the MMS) was not the receiver's ability to feel exactly what the sender felt or thought. The most interesting part of both telepathy in its broader definition (non-verbal communication of sensations and feelings but not actual thoughts) and my anecdotes was how these messages signified (deep) emotions and how they enabled a non-verbal emotional connection between two people. In the case of the MMS, it was not so much a matter of me feeling exactly what my friend felt as she gave birth to her baby boy. It was a matter of her conveying a feeling which also evoked a feeling in me, even though it was not at all the same feeling. I was happy and proud of her son, but in a completely different way than she was.

Communication technologies working close to the skin are able to connect bodies – to transfer signals appearing on one body to another body's skin, thus creating a sensation on another person. But unlike what the *Skin Probes* project strives to do, these connections do not need to aim to make people aware of each other's thoughts or feelings in order to be interesting. They do not need to try to pass through the skin in order to get to the core of the person (literally and figuratively). Instead, they (like other interfaces and communication technologies) could aim to allow for interpretations. Allowing people to interpret the connections, their signals and their signs, so that the interface does not try to penetrate the skin but instead aims to keep the interface *at* the skin, where the sign-system will not be bypassed but will become embodied instead.

Notes

1. Rupert Sheldrake has conducted various experiments on the subject of telepathy on both humans and animals ranging from investigating how many people are able to determine when they are being looked at, to investigating how dogs seem to be able to sense when their owner returns home almost 10 minutes before it happens. Further, his idea of 'morphic resonance' describes how new behaviour patterns of e.g. laboratory rats can surface elsewhere at the same time in other rats, thus implying that there is some kind of 'ether' that connects all living beings. See Sheldrake's own website for further references and abstracts of his books, papers and talks on the subject.
2. Topos is a term commonly used by media archaeologist Erkki Huhtamo, and it denotes the concept of a theme resurfacing through time, making the current resurfacing a single instance of a general theme. Huhtamo has analysed this concept several times, thus aiming at a deeper historical understanding of concepts like interactivity ("From Cybernation to Interaction") and arcade gaming ("Slots of Fun, Slots of Trouble: An Archaeology of Arcade Gaming"). See also Huhtamo's article in this volume.
3. The context of the many innovations in that era is that Thomas Edison invented the light bulb in 1879 and built the first power plant on Manhattan in 1882 (one of the first large-scale power plants in the world). The power plants made experiments with, and theory about, electromagnetic waves possible. The possibility of transmitting predetermined sounds through the air via radio waves was demonstrated by the German physicist Heinrich Hertz in 1886.
4. In this day and age we believe brain activity to be a result of a combination of chemical processes and very small electric impulses, and there is a tendency to believe that all brain activity can be not only measured but also explained with the help of neuro scans etc. We do not know yet if this theory will be dismissed at a later point in history, but the belief is a sign of the dominating scientific paradigm of our time nonetheless.
5. Which is also the reason why emoticons in written, digital communication (IM, SMS, email) are widely used.
6. Philips' naming of the project is not consistent in the available material. It is sometimes referred to as "SKIN: Dresses", sometimes as "SKIN probes" and sometimes with the alternative spelling of "Skin Probes". I have chosen the latter name.
7. The legend of Kraka's marriage from the Nordic Sagas (770-842) is about how Kraka had to solve a difficult riddle in order to meet the man she would later marry. Part of the riddle was to meet him neither clothed nor naked. She solved the impossible dichotomy by covering herself in her long hair fastened by a fishing net, thus bypassing the understanding of both hair and clothes.
8. Furthermore, the project won the "Red Dot" Award for '"best of the best'" design concept 2007 (Philips, "Philips Design SKIN probe receives prestigious "best of the best" in red dot award").

9. *Throwies* is an interesting case since it was the first open source graffiti project coming out of eyebeam's Graffiti Research Lab and it instantly made GRL famous in the blogosphere. *Throwies* is a simple project: a throwie is an LED taped to a battery and a magnet. The battery fuels the LED and the magnet enables it to stick to metallic surfaces. Thus, if you make thousands of throwies, you can 'tag' any metallic surface with lights and consequently transform any metallic surface into a light installation. *Throwies* have since conquered the world, as there have been public performances in almost every large western city. Even I have thrown a throwie.

10. A video was later posted on YouTube, where the official *Skin Probe* video from Philips Design has had 63,835 views to date, which is not much considering the sender. In comparison, the sister Probe project Electronic Tattoo has been viewed 705,297 times – almost 12 times more than the dresses. The reason could be that the Electronic Tattoo Probe project itself (and thus also its presentation) is clearly designed for video: it features a very sensual and erotic video where movements are key as a naked woman's caressing of a naked man causes his skin to 'grow' a tattoo. (Philips, YouTube channel).

11. For a discussion of the relation between new technologies and the invisible servant, see Lynne Hamill's account.

Works cited

Barnard, Malcolm. *Fashion as Communication*. 1996. 2nd ed. London: Routledge, 2002. Print.

Bolter, J. David and Diane Gromala. *Windows and Mirrors. Interaction Design, Digital Art, and the Myth of Transparency*. Leonardo. Cambridge, Mass.: MIT Press, 2003. Print.

Bolter, J. David and Richard Grusin. *Remediation: Understanding New Media*. 1999. Cambridge, Mass.: MIT Press, 2000. Print.

Calleja, Gordon. "Digital Games as Designed Experience: Reframing the Concept of Immersion." PhD dissertation, IT-University Copenhagen, 2007. Web. 2nd Nov. 2009. <http://www.gordoncalleja.com/GordonCalleja_Digital_Games_as_Designed_Experience.pdf>.

de Vries, Imar. "Mobile Telephony: Realising the Dream of Ideal Communication?" *Mobile World: Past, Present and Future*. Eds. Lynne Hamill and Amparo Lasen. Computer supported cooperative work. New York; London: Springer, 2005. 11-28. Print.

Hamill, Lynne. "Controlling Smart Devices in the Home." *The Information Society* 22.4 (2006): 241-49. Print.

Huhtamo, Erkki. "From Cybernation to Interaction: A Contribution to an Archaeology of Interactivity." *The digital dialectic*. Ed. Peter Lunenfeld. Cambridge, Mass: MIT Press, 1999: 96-110. Print.

– "Slots of Fun, Slots of Trouble: An Archaeology of Arcade Gaming." *Handbook of Computer Game Studies*. Eds. Joost Raessens and Jeffrey Goldstein. Cambridge, MA: MIT Press, 2005. 3-21. Print.

Kac, Eduardo. "Dialogical Telepresence Art and Net Ecology." *The Robot in the Garden: Telerobotics and Telepistemology in the Age of the Internet*. Ed. Ken Goldberg. Cambridge, Mass.: MIT Press, 2000. 180-96. Print.

Locke, Matt. "Wireless Culture Performs in the Temporary Intimate Zone." *Horizono*, 4 (2002). Web. 1st Nov. 2009. <http://www.horizonzero.ca/textsite/touch.php?is=4&file=7&tlang=0>.

– "Light Touches – Text Messaging, Intimacy and Photography." *Receiver*. 4 (2004). Web. 2nd Nov. 2009. < http://www.vodafone.com/flash/receiver/09/articles/pdf/09_04.pdf>

Luckhurst, Roger. *The Invention of Telepathy, 1870-1901*. Oxford: Oxford University Press, 2002. Print.

Manovich, Lev. *The Language of New Media*. Cambridge, Mass.: MIT Press, 2001. Print.

Marvin, Carolyn. *When Old Technologies Were New: Thinking About Communications in the Late Nineteenth Century*. New York: Oxford University Press, 1990. Print.

Meyrowitz, Joshua. "Analyzing Media – Metaphors as Methodologies." *New England Conference on Teaching Students to Think*. University of Massachusetts, Amherst, 1980. Print.

Minsky, Marvin. "Telepresence." *Omni* June 1980: 45-51. Print.

Nichols, Shaun and Stephen P. Stich. *Mindreading: An Integrated Account of Pretence, Self-Awareness, and Understanding Other Minds*. Oxford Cognitive Science Series. Oxford, New York: Clarendon; Oxford University Press, 2003. Print.

Peters, John Durham. *Speaking Into the Air: A History of the Idea of Communication*. Chicago, Ill.; London: University of Chicago Press, 1999. Print.

Philips. *Design Probe Program: Skin*. 2006. Web. 17 Aug. 2007. <http://www.design.philips.com/about/design/portfolio/researchprojects/article-14935.page>.

– "Philips Design SKIN Probe Receives Prestigious 'Best of the Best' in Red Dot Award: Design Concept 2007". 2007. Web. 2nd Nov 2009. <http://www.design.philips.com/about/design/portfolio/research-projects/article-14935.page>.

– YouTube Channel. Web. 2nd Nov 2009. <http://www.youtube.com/user/PhilipsDesign>.

– *What are Design Probes?* 2009. Web. 2nd Nov. <http://www.design.philips.com/probes/whataredesignprobes/index.page>.

Shannon, Claude Elwood and Warren Weaver. *The Mathematical Theory of Communication*. Urbana: University of Illinois Press, 1949. Print.

Sheldrake, Rupert. Home page. Web. 2nd Nov 2009. <http://www.sheldrake.org/homepage.html>.

Steuer, Jonathan. "Defining Virtual Reality: Dimensions Determining Telepresence." *Communication in the Age of Virtual Reality*. Eds. Frank Biocca and Mark R. Levy. Hillsdale, N.J.: L. Erlbaum Associates, 1995. 33-56. Print.

Thurschwell, Pamela. *Literature, Technology and Magical Thinking, 1880-1920*. Cambridge Studies in Nineteenth-Century Literature and Culture, 32. Cambridge: Cambridge University Press, 2001. Print.

Townsend, Anthony. "Thinking in Telepathic Cities." *Towards a Philosophy of Telecommunications Convergence*. Ed. Kristof Nyiri, 2008. 41-51. Print.

Interface Perception

The Cybernetic Mentality and Its Critics: Ubermorgen.com

BY SØREN BRO POLD

> During long periods of history, the mode of human sense perception changes with humanity's entire mode of existence. The manner in which human sense perception is organized, the medium in which it is accomplished, is determined not only by nature but by historical circumstances as well (Benjamin 222).

Walter Benjamin suggested in the 1930s that the mode of human perception changes historically. Human perception is not only governed by nature, biology and its slow evolution, but our perception acts, is organised and accomplished through media that are also governed by historical circumstances. For example, we do not only see the world with our eyes; our seeing is also accomplished and takes effect in a way that is governed by semiotic and material media, which are historical constructions in our reality.[1] We may still see with the physiological eyes of the hunter and gatherer, but what we perceive has changed a great deal when we watch reproduced images or film or read a text. And if we want to understand the social, historical and cultural role of perception, we have to examine how media and representations challenge and change our way of perceiving and simultaneously incorporate certain modes of perception in their own technological and material form.

A current significant example of this is the cybernetic interface. This kind of interface is constructed through a remediation of older representational forms such as images, film, texts and sounds, complete with their various traditions, genres and media characteristics, like linear perspective, film editing grammar, the conventions and designs of the pages, sound design and musical styles (Bolter and Grusin; Manovich). But the contemporary interface also incorporates cybernetic feedback and interaction. It allows the user to interact with its representations, and it registers the user and his/her interactions through input devices, sensors and tracking. In this sense the interface simultaneously builds on media history and aesthetic traditions of how to represent things in ways that are distinguishable and meaningful to human perception, and it constructs its own perceptional feedback loop.

In this article, I will argue that it is important to follow this interface perception in order to understand our current social, political and cultural reality. But when we look at an interface, we only see half of it, since the machinic, cybernetic part is largely hidden from our senses, though it still has effect. In order to take a closer look at these effects and discuss interface perception, I will look to some contemporary net art projects by Ubermorgen.com. Ubermorgen.com consists of lizvlx and Hans Bernhard, who started his artistic work with the net art group Etoy in the 1990's. Ubermorgen.com has received numerous awards and distinctions, e.g. at ARCO (Madrid), Transmediale and Ars Electronica, has exhibited around the world and received a great deal of media attention, some of this undercover as part of media activism such as [V]ote-Auction. I divide Ubermorgen.com's projects into outward-reaching activist projects and more inward-oriented psychological and epistemological projects. Of the former, I shall focus on Google Will Eat Itself (2005-09), which is the first project of the EKMRZ (ecommerce) trilogy, and my example of the latter is the *Psych|OS* cycle (2002-09).

While writing this article, *Ubermorgen.com – Media Hacking vs. Conceptual Art* has been published with an overview of Ubermorgen.com's work until date and with short essays by a number of writers (e.g. Inke Arns, Florian Cramer and Jacob Lillemose also present in this volume). Florian Cramer puts Ubermorgen.com into an art historical perspective of net art and the avant-garde and shares my description of the double character of the work: "It is simultaneously reflexive and actionist, introverted and extroverted, it is melancholy put into action, hyperactive melancholy, acted out a high personal risk in it, running battles with lawyers, the courts and personal burn-out" (Cramer in Ludovico 187). Both these two strands of Ubermorgen.com's work are, however, united in exploring the contemporary networked interface, and I find both the differences and the similarity illuminating in my attempt to understand interface perception.

First, however, I will elaborate on mediated and cybernetic perception. My argument will primarily address seeing, but a seeing that is thoroughly synaesthetic and thus connected to the other senses, e.g. in the way that seeing is related to a perceptional, cultural and mental experience in Ubermorgen's projects. Towards the end of the article, my exploration of the interface mentality leads me to psychotropic drugs, bipolar disorder and ADD following Ubermorgen.com in a discussion of how art reflects cultural changes in perception.

Media culture, perception and the interface

Walter Benjamin pointed out how a distracted and tactile perception developed as a response to the challenges of modern life – sometimes as a defence against the speed and intrusive nature of modern visuality, sometimes as a therapeutic or overwhelming shock in order to shock the senses into perceiving again, which is necessary in order to avoid unconsciously adopting the manipulations of the media in propaganda, spin etc. Several historians of visuality have pointed out that a new sort of mediated perception was gradually trained in the course of the 19th century (Crary *Techniques of the Observer*...): a construction of a new mobile, virtual gaze (Friedberg), and a disjunction of the near space from the distant far space such as it is experienced while travelling in a train, or in a panorama (Schivelbusch). Several of these studies were explicitly written as media archaeological prehistories to discover the effects of digital media in relation to perception.

What is found in embryo in the 19th century was developed in the 20th century and further amplified by the ubiquitous screens of our century. The disjunction of near and far space and the mobile gaze are still important sensory characteristics when driving a car in *Grand Theft Auto* or shooting your enemy in *Counter Strike*, but the interface also contains a cybernetic feedback-loop between recipient and interface. Interfaces contain an action-reaction pattern, which, through sensors, input devices, tracking, data-mining and surveillance, registers the recipient and incorporates his/her responses and reactions – it is this mechanism that is sometimes marketed as 'interactivity'. Cybernetic feedback was invented by the father of cybernetics, Norbert Wiener, as a way to control machines by measuring their actual performance in real-time and feeding the results back in a continual loop. The functioning of feedback is, according to Wiener, "to control the mechanical tendency towards disorganization; in other words, to produce a temporary and local reversal of the normal direction of entropy" (*The Human Use of Human Beings* 25). Wiener moves on to consider cybernetics as a general vision for organising – if not controlling – a modern liberal humanism.[2]

This cybernetic interaction takes place on many levels since, as Florian Cramer points out elsewhere in this book, interfaces exist on many levels between hardware, software and humans. Interfaces exist from the intra- and inter-machinic as procedure calls and commands in the code and between layers of code, between machines and in networks, to human-computer-interaction and human-computer-human-interaction, e.g. on the Internet. In addition, interface logics spread as cybernetic processes in culture at large, say in economic exchanges, strategic communication and poll-based democracy. Things are packaged in measurable units which feed back on themselves in cybernetic loops – a key characteristic of our contemporary interface culture.

This cybernetic interface culture can be expressed as a cybernetic interface-cultural feedback loop in five phases, moving outwards from the internal systems through representation, interaction, reception and to culture:

1. **System**: In the internal systemic processes of the machine, for example the procedural calls and self-references – the way the systems run and are maintained – and how these system processes are also a model of human perception.[3]
2. **Semiotics**: In the sequence or selection of output signs (e.g. images, sounds, text and signs for interaction) that is presented at the interface, where the selection process is further regulated by the cybernetic circuit between the interface and its contexts and users.
3. **Interaction**: In the way the interaction is communicated and modelled in the interface, e.g. as input devices, and represented by buttons, menus, metaphors, staged perspectives etc. Here

we have the staging of the use-situation and the user – which, to a large extent, is what interface design is about.

4. **Reception**: As the recipient's horizon of expectation and interpretation; we increasingly expect that we can interact with representational, aesthetic artefacts (e.g. as we can interact with the fictional space in a computer game, with music in remix culture, or with knowledge in Wikipedia).[4]
5. **Culture**: As an interface culture, a culture that increasingly adopts itself to and repeats this cybernetic interface-cultural feedback loop – often blindly and unknowingly.

The transmission between the phases – from the system to culture and back again (as human culture in itself becomes increasingly ready for digitisation and systematisation, and as systems simultaneously become more adept at handling culture) – is in itself cybernetic as feedback loops that translate one phase into the next.[5] Consequently, each phase presupposes and contains the others, and the system is reinforced by the continuing dynamic development, in fact in itself a loop.

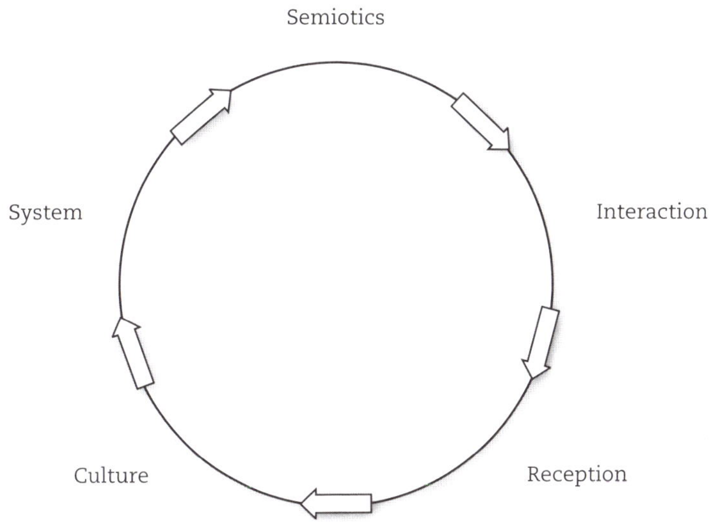

ILL. 1: The interface-cultural feedback loop.

The interface itself is actually a sense organ – it integrates still crude but far-reaching sense apparatuses, which are sometimes embedded in networks and procedural calls between layers of code and at other times are modelled or mapped on the human senses (hearing, touch and sight). Furthermore, it is multi-medial and cross/syn-aesthetic in a specific way: It treats all data as a sort of generalised, statistical text, with no access to the ontology or semantics of the data, such as the image character or the meaning of the text, but only to its behaviour and relations.[6] One can argue that the interface measures the senso-motoric body of the recipient through input devices and reads his/her semiotic activity through analysis of clicks, choices and input; a process which is often utopically advertised as a more or less direct coupling on the consciousness allowing the machine the ability to establish a direct connection between mind and machine. In this way, it can give the recipient what he/she wants even before he/she has formulated the wish, and as such it can be the perfect butler, partner or surveillance apparatus.

However, as we all know, it does not work seamless nor without errors or mismatches. Unfortunately, or perhaps fortunately, computers only observe our semiotics statistically, with no real access to the semantics and ontology. This statistical scanning can be quite effective, but there is still space for artistic exploration in the misunderstandings and mismatches, which can help our culture to develop a critical understanding of this defining cultural technology. We need art to teach us the effects of the interfaces, which run, partly hidden, cybernetically, under the surface of our culture. I will continue by looking at two art projects that act in the cybernetic feedback loop in order to demonstrate how art critically explores the cybernetics of the interface.

Ubermorgen's interface activism

The interface connects machine, representation, reception and culture, as we have seen in the interface-cultural loop explained in the model above, but we are only slowly seeing and learning the consequences of this, even though they are already pervasive. On one hand, the interface is a functional tool with which one can perform various tasks and automations. On the other hand, it is a representational medium used for cultural production and experience. Exactly this chimerical character of the computer, which Frieder Nake characterises as an "instrumental medium", which is simultaneously a machine and a representational medium, is distinctive for the interface and its cultural potential. It renders the signs and representations functional, as when one moves and double-clicks icons in order to start processes and carry out transactions and simultaneously enters the functional machine into the domain of semiotics and thus reception, interpretation and culture. In fact, the system both measures and interprets; while the viewer him/herself simultaneously is fed into the system, tries to beat its cybernetic system by partly becoming one him/herself, and reflects on the cybernetic process and its cultural implications.[7] In this way, the cybernetic interaction and feedback connects the representational and the functional, and even though these connections are not seamless, the chimerical character of the interface pervades both the machine and the medium and influences the culture around it.

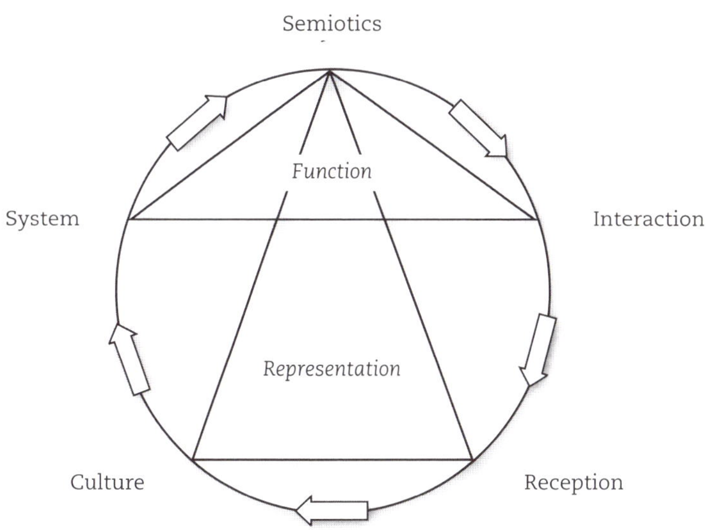

ILL. 2: The interface-cultural feedback loop with triangles of function and representation.

As stated in the introduction, Ubermorgen.com has worked with the interface in ways that both reach outwards to culture through net actvism and in others they are more concerned with sense perception, recognition and the cybernetic mentality. Often their work provokes reactions from media, audiences, and the companies and institutions that become involved. Especially pieces such as Etoy's Hijack, Ubermorgen.com's [V]ote Auction, Amazon Noir and Google Will Eat Itself are good examples that try to extort the cybernetic discourse economy of the net culture and turn it back against itself – a kind of cybernetic criticism of a cybernetic culture. However, simultaneously some of Ubermorgen.com's works are directed towards the psychological, perceptional or epistemological, especially the works around the *Psych|OS* project, where Ubermorgen.com and Hans Bernhard project a somewhat autobiographical, vulnerable subject into focus.

While these two strands of Ubermorgen.com's work at first glance seem very different, they are in fact related as the two sides of the interface – the functional and the representational. Some projects reach outwards in order to examine a cybernetic culture; others look inwards to examine how this culture influences and stresses the subject and perception. As such they also critically explore the effects of the cybernetic interface-cultural loop I presented in the above: What happens when machines and humans become more closely interrelated in culture?

GWEI – disrupting the feedback

Google Will Eat Itself is an example of how Ubermorgen's activist projects are turning the cybernetic feedback mechanism back against itself, thereby adding noise to the system and disturbing its order. As the artists (Ubermorgen's Hans Bernhard and lizvlx, Alessandro Ludovico and Paolo Cirio) themselves argue, Google has established a market monopoly by becoming the 'giant middleman.' In cybernetic terms Google accomplishes the feedback mechanism, mapping the content of the internet and giving it back to people through packaged services such as the company's search engine, gmail, blog and video services (Blogger, YouTube, Google-video). Furthermore, Google controls advertising on the net through adwords. As such, Google has

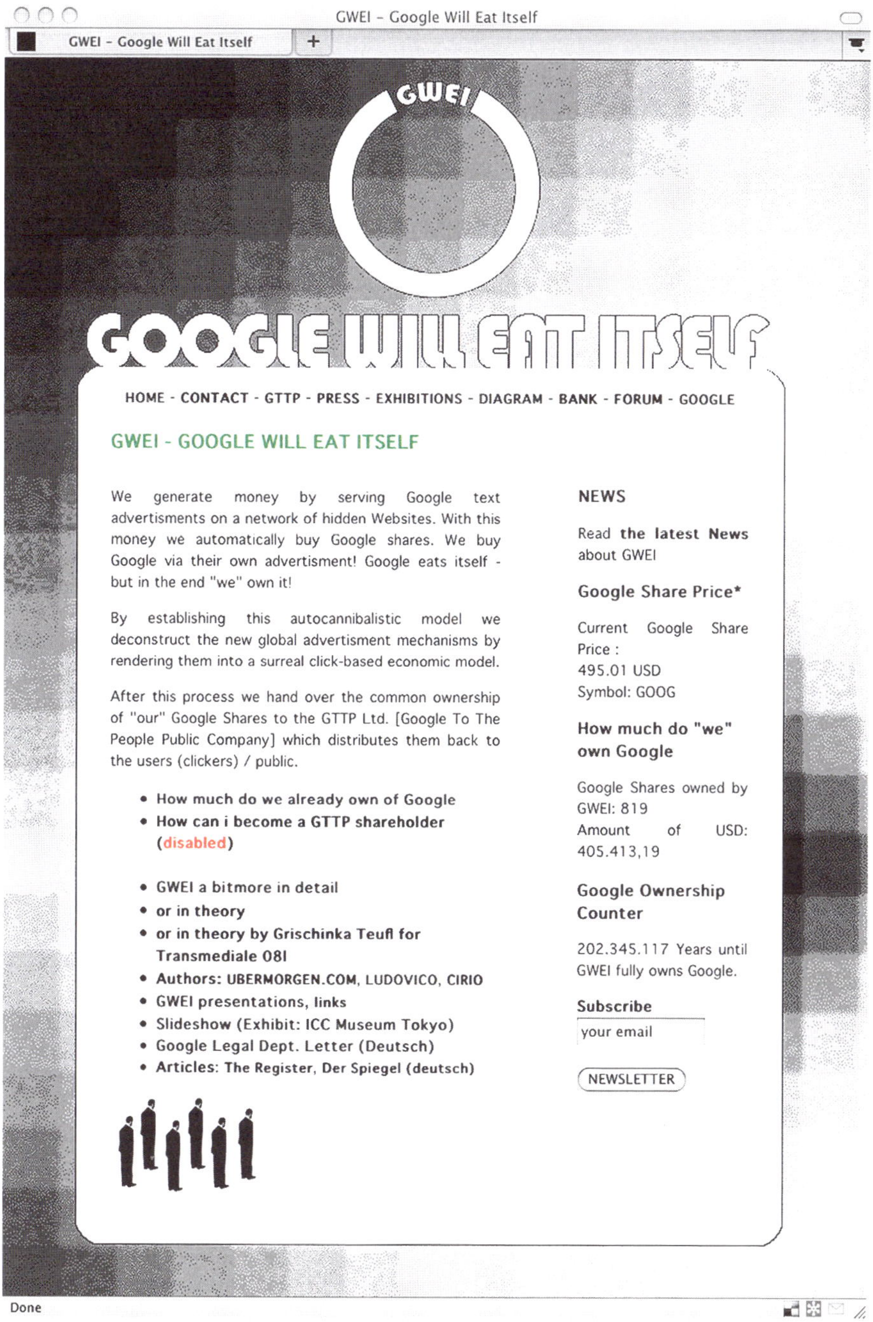

ILL. 3: Ubermorgen.com: *Google Will Eat Itself*, (gwei.org).

become the dominant accomplisher of the net, its market and the access to it, thereby giving the company enormous powers and knowledge that alone make it worth keeping an eye on this 'funny dictator.'

The way the project critically examines this cybernetic feedback middleman is by "hacking the Google self.referentialism," in praxis by launching a humoristic parasite (Bernhard et al.). This is done by creating a hidden website with adwords and generating fake clicks on the ads. This creates revenue from Google, which is fed back into Google via buying Google shares thus gradually (in 202 million years!) Google will eat itself and be redistributed to the people through GTTP, Ltd. (Google To The People). Even though this project probably cannot harm Google seriously, the company has felt threatened to the extent that it has sent cease-and-desist letters and for a period banned the website from the search engine. Ironically, this made things worse for Google, as a search for *GWEI* consequently only displayed websites about the ban – the censorship has currently ended.

The project strikes at Google in three interrelated ways: Firstly, by disrupting and misleading the advertisement chain through fake websites and fake clicks, resulting in no real display of the advertisements to human eyes and thus no real generation of human traffic. Secondly, by critically demonstrating the power of Google, and by forcing Google to take countermeasures such as censorship.[8] Furthermore, the project not only hacks Google's advertisement chain, but also Google's own worth by buying shares with the revenue from the fake, and jokingly threatening to take over Google and redistribute it to the people. As Hans Bernhard puts it, it is hard to evaluate the value of Google shares because the Google share is highly volatile (Mancuso). Google's market value is itself a cybernetic system that one can interact with through the shares, parallel to the ways in which the Etoy artist group interacted with the shares of the eToys online children's toy store in the Toywar project; however the 'new' cybernetic economy of the Internet has apparently become more stable than before the dot-com crisis.[9]

In this way, the project fundamentally attacks Google's role as the 'giant middleman' or the accomplisher of the feedback that sets up the Internet as a market, and it does so by disrupting and misleading the feedback, by spending the revenue from the misled feed-

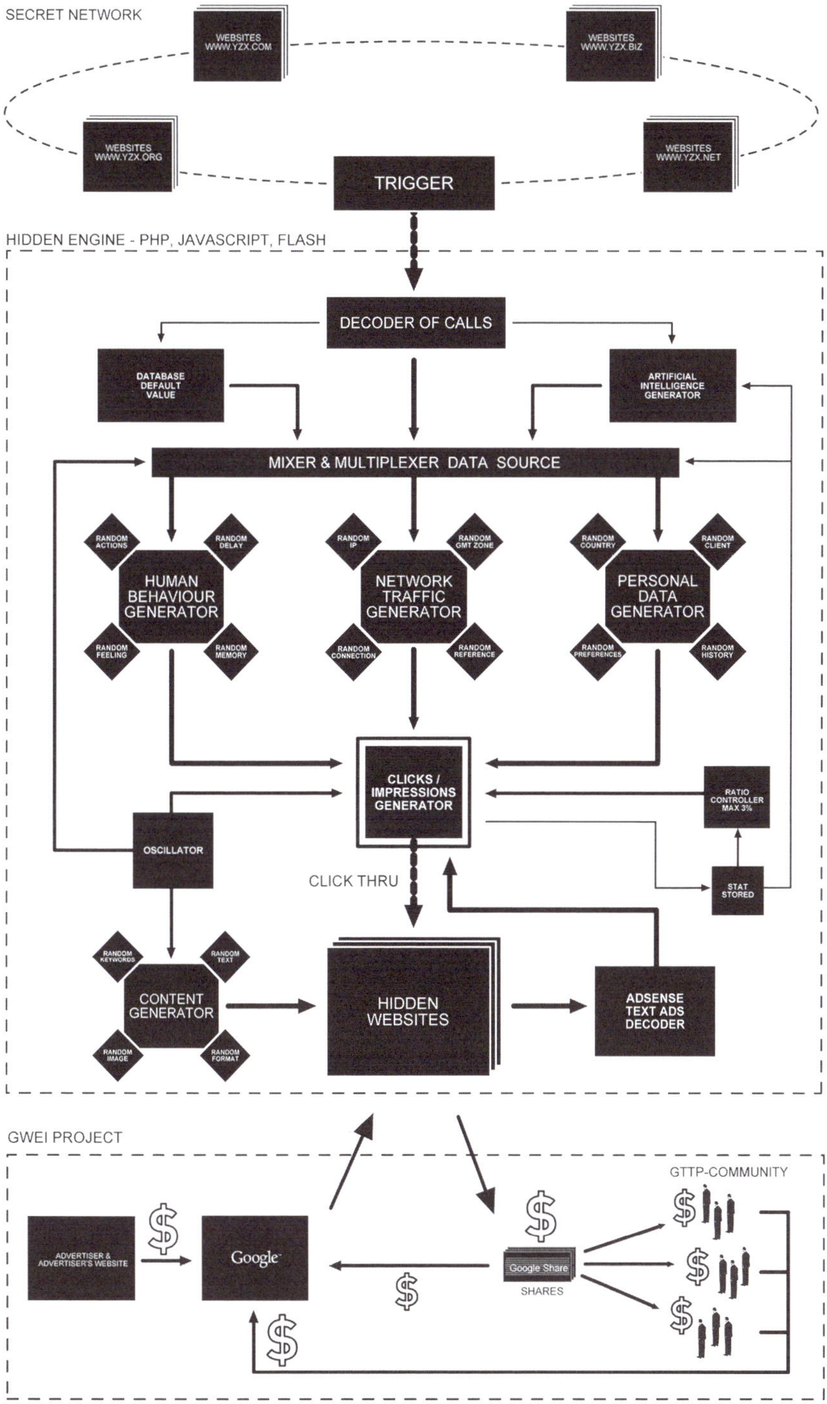

ILL. 4: Ubermorgen.com: *Google Will Eat Itself* diagram showing the system.

back to make Google eat itself and, in doing all this, critically revealing Google's power.

Psych|OS - Cybernetic noir

There are other projects that focus on the activism-oriented dimension, such as the *(F)original* project and its generators, *Amazon Noir*, which attacked the Amazon website through the "Search inside the Book" feature, stealing and redistributing copyrighted books (cf. Dieter), and *[V]ote Auction*, with its slogan of "bringing capitalism and democracy closer together" by making a web-based auction house for votes. But there are also other kinds of projects that are more inwardly oriented towards psychological, mental dimensions: thematising the conditions for perception, recognition and psychology – most are collected under the fitting *Psych|OS* headline. As the following quote implies, these projects are initiated out of a personal disease, though it is not the autobiographical dimension that interests me here, but the relations between media, perception, identity and drugs. Even though the project is autobiographical, there is also an explicit artistic distancing from the merely personal in the presentation and the references to the fictional Blairwitch Project:

> In October 1994 three student filmmakers disappeared in the woods near Burkittsville, Maryland while shooting a documentary. A year later their footage was found... http://blairwitch.com: *The Blairwitch Project*.
>
> In March 2002, Ubermorgen's Hans Bernhard experienced a manic outbreak [bipolar affective disorder] in Capetown, South-Africa. He was airlifted to Austria – General Hospital Vienna. Two and a half years later, Ubermorgen found video footage of his stay at the Mental hospital - Station 4B, Department of Psychiatry. They decided to release the material unedited, only with minimal contextual information to go along with:
>
> "We are the children of the 1980s. We are the first internet-pop-generation. We grew up with radical Michael Milken [The King of Junk Bonds] and mythical Michael Jackson [The King of Junk Pop]. Hans Bernhard is loaded with 10 years of internet & tech [digital cocaine], mass media hacking, underground

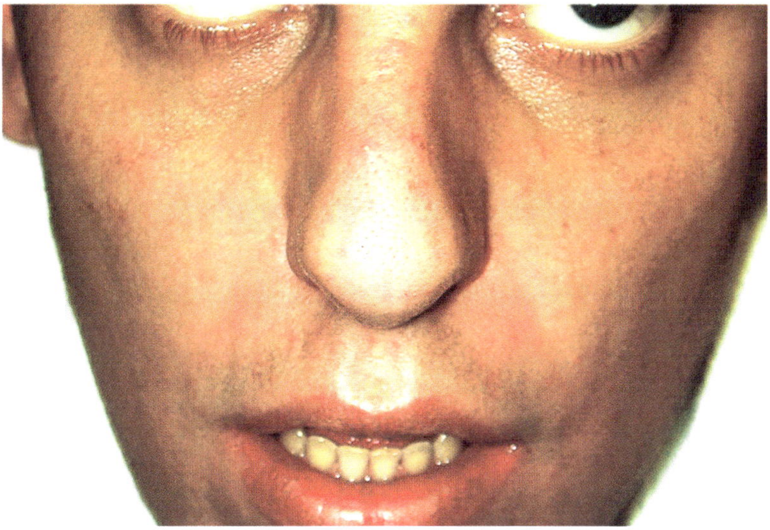

ILL. 5: **Ubermorgen.com: *Psych*|OS Cycle – Hans Bernhard Self-portrait.**

> techno, hardcore [illegal] drugs, rock&roll lifestyle and net.art jet set [etoy]. His neuronal networks and brain structures are similar to the global synthetic network he helped build up and maintained subversive activity within. And now they are 'infected' by a manic-depression [WHO ICD-10, F31.1.], both Hans Bernhard and The 'Network' are infected by this structural disorder. (...)" (Ubermorgen).

This text is kept in Bernhard/Ubermorgen's typically explicit, slogan-like rhetoric, and though many nuances are omitted, it is worthwhile to follow the project as a solemn reflection on the interrelations between our perception, psyche and the media. This is emphasised by how the project was exhibited in Dortmund at Hartware Medien-KunstVerein, according to the description on the website:

> The Installation is a common projection, a sensitive membrane [the screen] which serves as a thin skin which is penetrated by light and onto which a unique reality is projected. This membrane moves if you touch it or it curls if you blow: the image twists. The membrane represents the human and the network – it is hypersensitive.[10]

The installation showed Bernhard's own video footage from the mental hospital. The interface in the installation is a thin, fragile membrane in both concrete and metaphorical ways that one can physically interact with in the installation, and this interface represents both the human mentality and the network, which is disrupted by drugs, technology and mania. Ubermorgen further argues that our collective media mentality is becoming manic, abusing technology and drugs:

> Waves of mania and depression are running through the technical, social and economic structures. Contemporary high-tech societies deal with hardcore brains using bio-chemical 'agents' to control the internal information flow, we call them psychotropic drugs (Ubermorgen).

The medical diary, Hansbernhardblog, has entries on Hans Bernhard's drug and food consumption every day since 2005, where he lists the drugs he is prescribed; often drugs that act primarily upon the central nervous system where it alters brain function, resulting in changes in perception, mood, consciousness and behaviour. Furthermore, the *Psych|OS* project contains the *Psych|OS* generator, which through a question and answer process generates a prescription mocking a diagnosis and rendering it into a cybernetic machine.

The cybernetic interface culture is articulated in the *Psych|OS* project through its darker sides, producing a cybernetic mentality complete with cybernetic diseases, diagnosis, treatments and cures. Ubermorgen.com demonstrates this with a personal blog, which, instead of being a medium of individual expression, portrays the subject through lists of the medical and nutritive inputs, indexed and linked to pharmaceutical information. Furthermore, diagnosis and prescriptions are left to a cybernetic machine, the *Psych|OS* Generator, and the subject of the *Psych|OS* project, the drugged and hospitalized Hans Bernhard, is left passive, with no personal memory, identity or free will. This also distinguishes the 'Hans Bernhard' of the *Psych|OS* project from the real Hans Bernhard – the project is presented in a cool and unsentimental tone, remarkably cleansed of any romantic attempts at glorifying the mental disease.

ILL. 6: **Ubermorgen.com: *Psych|OS* Cycle (video stills).**

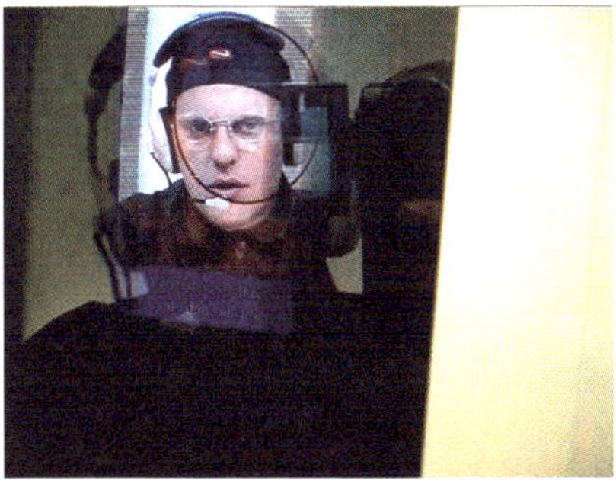

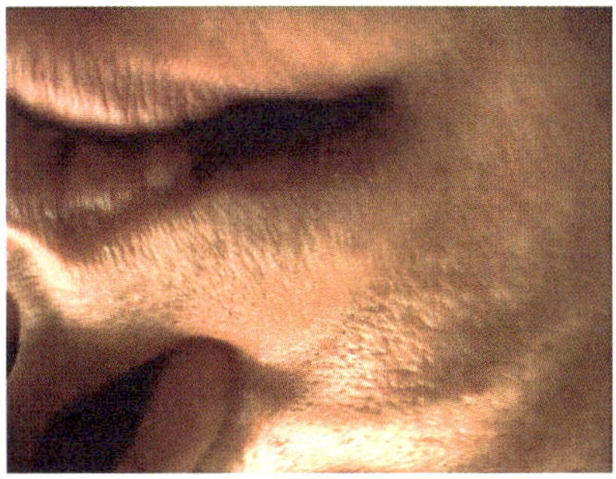

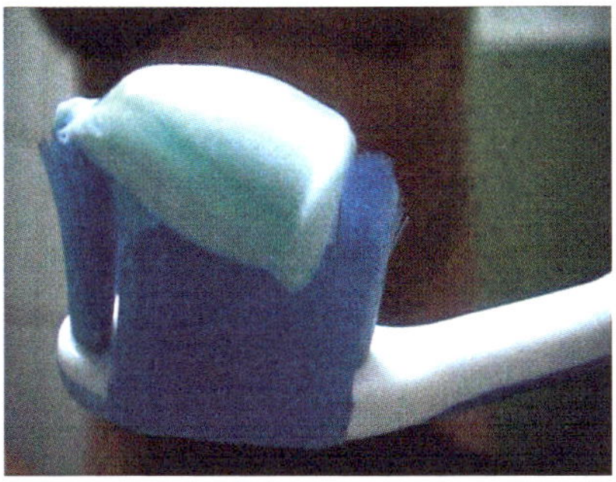

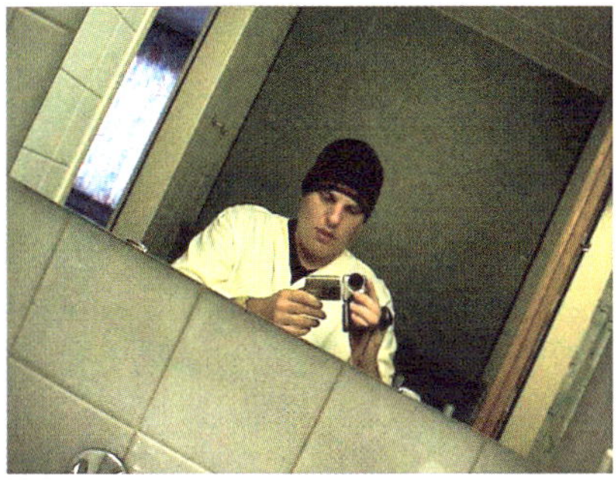

BERNHARD M 23 07 1971
Luzius
A PS102
PSY/Station 4B
Pat.Zl: 901-20311/02/0204

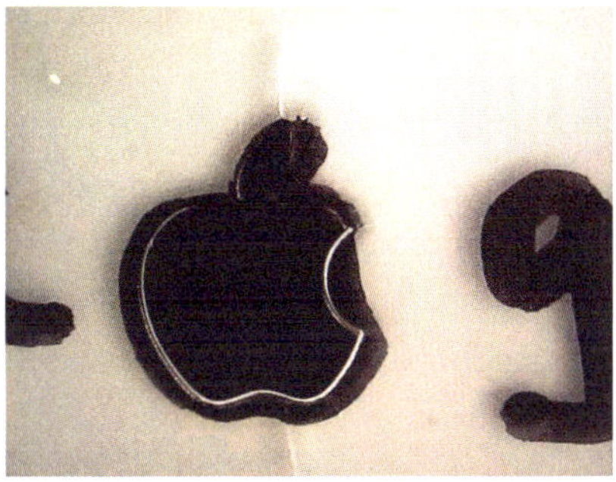

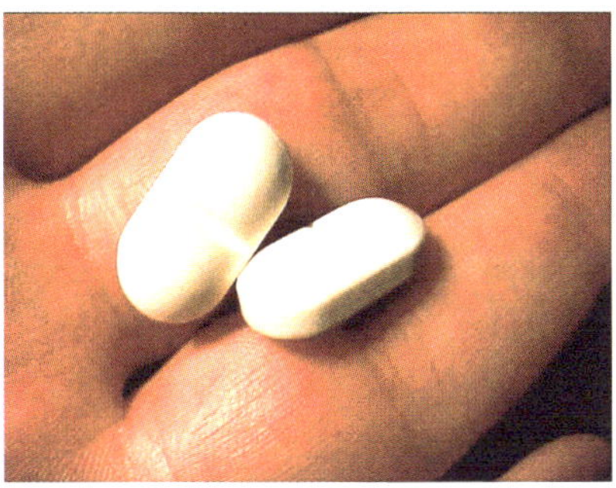

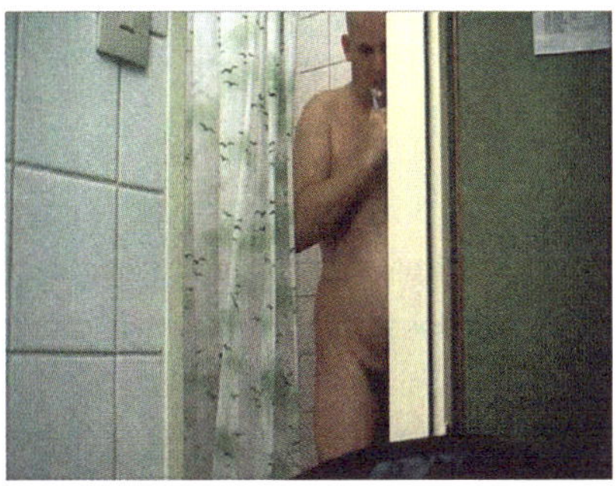

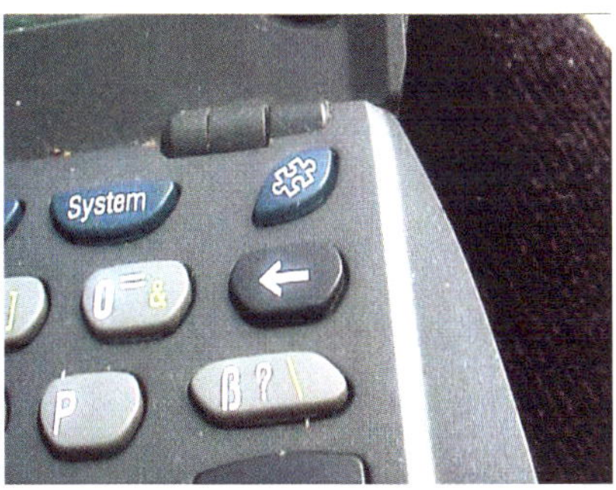
System

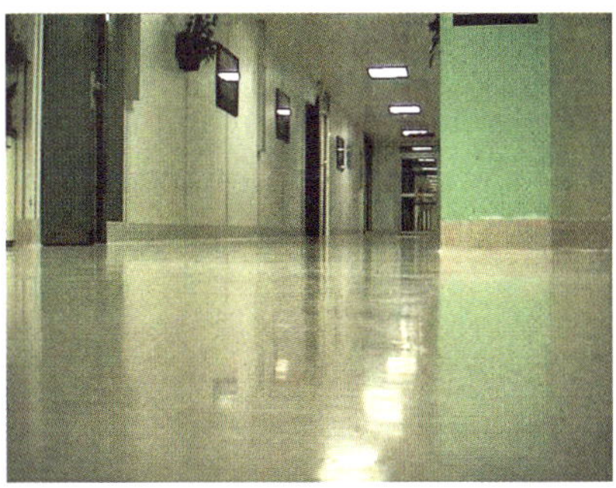

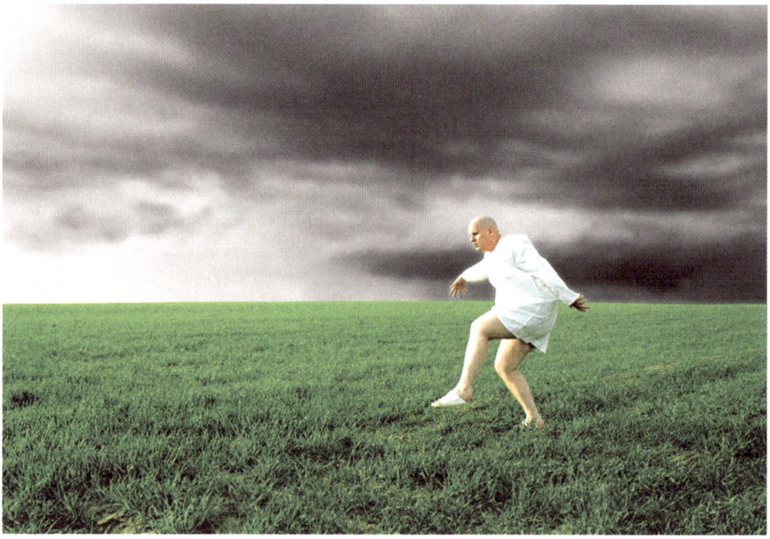

ILL. 7: Ubermorgen.com: *Psych|OS Cycle – Hans 2.*

The conditions for criticism

Does this noir-cybernetics work as criticism? Can we learn any analytic or methodological tools from it? Well, as GWEI's Paolo Cirio says, it is difficult to criticise the cybernetic system from a distanced standpoint and with clear rational paroles:

> The only way to avoid this process is to do strange things and to behave highly unusual. The more noise you inject into their data base, the more difficult it is for them to understand who you are. To be free means to be unpredictable (Mancuso).

This might even be too romantic! The cybernetic processes of Google and others do not need to "understand who you are"; they only need to be able to map you and your behaviour and relate you to the cybernetic system through feedback. Furthermore, unpredictable behaviour is a basic substance of information, according to information theory.[11] However, there is a possible lesson at another level, if we look at the artistic strategies of the projects – how they perform a *noir* cybernetics: Disrupting the feedback, attacking the mechanism and feeding the system with itself might be a viable strategy, since it will render the system potentially unstable, and consequently lead to some kind of recognition of the workings of the system. Likewise the system, or the people struggling to maintain it, will try to reject the noise and malfunctioning, as was the case with Google's banning of *GWEI* from its search engine. As Norbert Wiener points out in discussing intention tremor and Parkinson tremor, excessive feedback potentially leads to a breakdown of the system's ability to reverse entropy and thus order chaos. He hopes to be able to use cybernetics to cure this disease (*The Human Use of Human Beings* 163 ff.).

Consequently, the conclusion must be that cybernetic criticism must be cybernetic in its form in order to enter into the system, but also an outspoken meta-reflection of the machine in order to avoid merely confirming the order of the system and becoming a speechless part of it, as just another wheel in the machine, or a banner ad on the front page of the cybernetic spectacle. This way *GWEI* manages to both enter into the system, use it to gain maximum effect, and disrupt it in ways that forces it to defend itself, whereas *Psych|OS* portrays the crisis of the cybernetic interface mentality.

Interface mentality

Are cybernetic interfaces a cure for our diseases, a necessary updating of our sense perception, or does cybernetic information technology make us sick? It is difficult to judge whether it makes sense in medical terms to speak of parallels between Bernhard's bipolar disorder/manic depression, the Internet network and his activities in it, and the related psychotropic drugs. It is, of course, complicated in both medical and cultural terms to compare such phenomena and distinguish between cause and effect, related to the discussions about whether video games and multitasking lead to ADHD (Attention Deficit Hyperactivity Disorder) or ADD that can be found flourishing on the Internet. But if we for a moment skip the more strict scientific descriptions of cause and effect and look at perceptual alterations and how they are experienced in art and culture, such as suggested in the Benjamin quotation in the opening of this article, we might recognise experiences of even our everyday life with software.

If we look at how our software and operation systems perform, invading our concentration through millions of more or less helpful suggestions, disturbances and multitasking options, there seem to be parallels, and I guess we all feel a bit attention-deficient after a stressful day at the office, trying to achieve some concentration in the midst of emails, telephones and the all-invading software upgrades with their annoying prompts to re-start your computer.[12]

When the software and hardware upgrades are insufficient to cope with modern reality, we are constantly urged to reinvent, develop and renew ourselves through adaptability, and there is a thriving industry ready to help us by 'upgrading,' 'reprogramming' or 'overclocking' our brain and 'hacking our performance' through smart guidelines and smart drugs.[13] We might draw a parallel to the industrial society of the 19th century where new diseases, cures and drugs were created and many artists were exposed. For example, hysteria and neurasthenia with cures such as magnetic therapy were much in vogue and many artists such as Charles Baudelaire and Edgar Allen Poe used hashish and opium (Lyhne). Our current networked information society also has its characteristic diseases and cures that affect sensitive information workers, including artists and intellectuals, such as stress, ADHD, anxiety disorders and functional disorders.

In *Suspensions of Perception,* Jonathan Crary points to how attention has become increasingly essential through modernity in both work and cultural activity, and that we live through a topical "immense social crisis of subjective dis-integration", which is "metaphorically diagnosed" as a "deficiency of 'attention'" (1). To Crary, concentrated attentiveness signifies a strict control of perception that excludes large parts of the sensed – e.g. when navigating in traffic or concentrating on writing and reading this article. In a comment on the diagnosis and medical literature of ADD, Crary writes:

> The diagnosis of ADD in adults is increasingly linked to feelings of underachievement, in such a way that any sort of economic shortcoming or social insecurity is now understandable in terms of failure to apply oneself attentively to the ideologically determined standards of performance and 'achievement'. In a culture that is so relentlessly founded on a short attention span, on the logic of the nonsequitur, on perceptual overload, on the generalized ethic of 'getting ahead,' and on the celebration of aggressiveness, it is nonsensical to pathologize these forms of behaviour or look for the causes of this imaginary disorder in neurochemistry, brain anatomy, and general predisposition" (36).

Clearly, Crary does not see ADD as a disease but as a sign of a social crisis. He even explicitly links this to screens and interfaces as "methods for the management of attention that use partitioning and sedentarization, rendering bodies controllable and useful simultaneously, even as they simulate the illusion of choices and 'interactivity'" (75). Whereas the subject in romanticism was interiorised, this is now reversed in a cybernetic interface:

> The inwardness of what Hegel called romanticism is not so much exceeded here as it is paradoxically turned inside out, into a condition of externalization: attention as a depthless interface simulates and displaces what once might have been autonomous states of self-reflection or a *sens intime* (79).

ADHD, stress, anxiety disorders, functional disorders and bipolar disorder are definitely separate phenomena that should not be equated too quickly, and if one suffers from any of these it does not help to know that it might be a sign of a social crisis. Also, I do not aim to make an argument that is valid within psychology or medical sciences. The aim here is to discuss art and how it reflects cultural changes in perception.

Perceiving interface perception

The interface works in two ways, translating the machine to us and us to the machine. It renders the computer sensible, and it is the sense-organs of the computer, whereby it becomes a part of human culture. This double sensory process entails a contemporary relationship between interface and perception: Perception becomes mediated and cybernetic. However, as the interface-cultural loop in the above pointed out, this relationship is not purely techno-biological, but draws on complex cultural processes, where culture, human-beings, organisations, societies, increasingly incorporate cybernetic behaviour. This is further implemented through becoming accustomed to interfaces (on the web, on the job, in computer games, in social software and Web 2.0), but also through management guidelines, understanding of self-development from popular self-help psychology, from education, and finally from drugs and medication. Consequently, we do not see a direct coupling between human perception and the machine, but a cultural process that artists can interact with, and that can be critically analysed and reflected.

It is potentially misleading to make excessively harsh comparisons and connections, which will easily lead us to a one-sided understanding of technology and hinder our capacity to engage critically with it on several levels. Still, I believe we see a central effect of digitisation here; that artefacts and representations become data injected in a cybernetic interface-cultural loop, and that we begin to see and understand the world in this way too.

I hope to have demonstrated through analysis of two digital art projects that systems, semiotics, culture and perception are related in a cybernetic interface-cultural loop, which can also be a perspective on larger societal and political issues such as new public management or the topical dramatic increase in the consummation of Fontex and other antidepressant drugs. This interface-cultural loop is difficult to acknowledge because we are part of it and, like a website that knows our preferences or a VR-simulation, it wraps itself around our sense-perception and subjectivity. But as these projects have demonstrated, even though the effects are massive, it does not work seamlessly, but through semiotics, representation and culture. Through artistic exploration it can be experienced.

It is tempting to conclude by asking whether this development is fundamentally evil, alienating, damaging – or thrilling, dynamic and perhaps even democratic? Perhaps it is an unavoidable development of our visual culture, sense perception and market economy? Developing our sense perception and culture accordingly, in keeping with the time, is definitely necessary in order to not just be immersed in the cybernetic spectacle. We need to develop, experience, understand and culturally integrate cybernetic perspectives and interface perception in order to experience the changing conditions that the interface sets up for perception, experience and culture.

THANKS to Hans Bernhard for letting me reproduce images, the anonymous reviewer for useful suggestions, and Stacey Cozart Madsen for corrections on the language.

Notes

1. Cf. also Wartofsky, who argues that "the forms or modes of perception, its structures themselves, are historically variant; that this variation is related to *historical* changes in the forms or modes of human action (or *praxis*)." Perception is for Wartofsky "a highly evolved and specific mode of human action or praxis" which is "mediated by *representation*". Furthermore, Wartofsky writes that "it is by the variation in modes of representation that perception itself comes to be related to historical changes in other forms of human practice, and in particular, to social and technological practice." (189).
2. Wiener develops the idea of cybernetic as a way of organising society in *The Human Use of Human Beings* but withdraws somewhat in his later speech "Men, Machines, and the World About" where he argues for understanding the machines and warns against worshipping it (72). N. Katherine Hayles explores this apparent change and in order to explain it she describes how the cybernetic feedback loop in fact undercuts Wiener's liberal humanism, how he "looks into the mirror of the cyborg, but then withdraws" and tries unsuccessfully to restrict cybernetics from societal issues. (Hayles 108). However, as discussed below, cybernetics continued to play an important social role as a way to control and manage.
3. This description of machines and humans itself clearly draws on (second order) cybernetics in how it sees the human and other entities (systems) as self-contained systems with internal cybernetic feedback-loops (cf. e.g. Hayles' description of the second order cybernetics of von Foerster, Maturana and Varela and Luhmann).
4. As my oldest son said some years ago, when he was about five, well accustomed to children's games, and saw on the web a plain photograph of a house that we had rented for our summer holiday: "Click on it so we can get inside!" – This episode (although it should not be over-interpreted) does give some evidence that perception and recipient expectations are changing towards the expectation of dynamic and interactive representations. In education, too, there is evidence that children brought up on computer games expect to continue this kind of explorative reception in their learning.

   Valery Grancher's web paintings also illustrate this. They absurdly comment on how we begin to see images as interfaces by reversing the process and turning an interface into a painting. (http://www.nomemory.org/webpaint/data/text.htm (21/12/2007)).
5. N. Katherine Hayles describes how cybernetics is fundamentally without borders between humans and machines and between phases and disciplines: "Border crossings accomplished through analogy include the separation between flesh and world (sense perception), the transition between one discipline and another (for example moving from the physiology of living organisms to the electrical engineering of a cybernetic machine), and the transformation of embodied experience, noisy with error, into the clean abstractions of mathematical pattern" (Hayles 98).
6. This is what Hayles sees as a shift from content to pattern, which she also traces in structuralism's and de Saussure's concept of language as a system: "Thus, perception, mathematics, and information all concentrate on pattern rather than content. As data move across various kinds of interfaces, analogical relationships are the links that allow pattern to be preserved from one modality to another. Analogy is thus constituted as a universal exchange system that allows data to move across boundaries. It is the *lingua franca* of a world (re)constructed through relation rather than grasped in essence" (Hayles 98).

7. The process of playing a computer game has been described in this way by e.g. Friedman as an aestheticisation of our cybernetic connection to technology. An art installation that directly explores cybernetic sensation through an eye-tracking mechanism that measures what the viewer looks at and generates new sets of images from a media art database based on this measurement is *Eye-Vision-Bot* (Scherffig; Pold "The Critical Interface").
8. In this way it is parallel to Christophe Bruno's Adwords project, which worked by disrupting the semantics (cf. Pold "Literature from Page to Interface...").
9. The Etoy Toywar project took place around the turn of the millennium and documentation can still be found at http://toywar.etoy.com/, in Pold "Litteratur I Nettet..." and Wishart and Bochsler.
10. The quotation continues: "The sound is played quietly via speakers and very fat via earphones. The room is bright with daylight so the mood of the viewer is influenced by the weather outside. There is no difference to a room in a mental hospital" (Ubermorgen).
11. N. Katherine Hayles describes how information theory with Shannon and Weaver views the unpredictable: "Heuristically, Shannon's choice was explained by saying that the more unexpected (or random) a message is, the more information it conveys" (Hayles 102). This also holds true culturally, e.g. if one thinks of marketing or perhaps the art market, that the game is driven by differentiation in order to attract attention. So the romantic rebel becomes the new market leader, which does not necessarily mean total defeat, but definitely that it is not possible to stay outside of the system.
12. As Lev Manovich has pointed out, the logic of software and its underlying databases are primarily paradigmatic, promoting alternatives and substitutions instead of syntagmatic cause-and-effect relations and a temporal or narrative way of ordering the world. When this becomes excessive as information overload, it counteracts distinctive, qualitative ordering and the creation of cohesion (Manovich 212 ff.).
13. Cf. book titles such as *Mind Performance Hacks (TM) – Tips & Tools for Overclocking Your Brain* (Ron Hale-Evans, O'Reilly, 2006), *Upgrade Your Brain: Boost Your Memory, Think More Clearly, and Discover Your Inner Einstein* (John Middleton, Perigee Books 2007) or the concept of Neuro-Linguistic Programming.

Works cited

Benjamin, Walter. *Illuminations*. Transl. Harry Zohn. Reprint ed. New York: Schocken Books, 1985. Print.

Bernhard, Hans, et al. "Hack the Google Self.Referentialism." *Google Will Eat Itself*, 2005. Web. 12 Aug. 2010. <http://gwei.org/pages/texts/theory.html>.

Bolter, Jay David, and Richard Grusin. *Remediation : Understanding New Media*. Cambridge, Mass.: MIT Press, 1999. Print.

Crary, Jonathan. *Suspensions of Perception: Attention, Spectacle, and Modern Culture*. Cambridge, Mass.; London: MIT Press, 1999. Print.

---. *Techniques of the Observer on Vision and Modernity in the Nineteenth Century*. October Books. Cambridge, Mass.: MIT Press, 1990. Print.

Dieter, Michael. "Amazon Noir: Piracy, Distribution, Control." *M/C Journal* 10.5 (2007). Web. 12 Aug. 2010. <http://journal.media-culture.org.au/0710/07-dieter.php>.

Friedberg, Anne. *Window Shopping: Cinema and the Postmodern*. Berkeley; Oxford: University of California Press, 1993. Print.

Friedman, Ted. "Civilization and Its Discontents: Simulation, Subjectivity, and Space." *Discovering Discs: Transforming Space and Genre on Cd-Rom*. Ed. Greg Smith. New York University Press. 132-150. Print.

Hayles, N. Katherine. *How We Became Posthuman Virtual Bodies in Cybernetics, Literature, and Informatics*. Chicago: University of Chicago Press, 1999. Print.

Ludovico, Alessandro, ed. *Ubermorgen.Com – Media Hacking Vs. Conceptual Art*. Basel: Christoph Merian Verlag, 2009. Print.

Lyhne, Vagn. *Savnets Vellyst Charles Baudelaire I Det 19. Århunderede*. Århus: Klim, 1990. Print.

Mancuso, Marco. "Gwei, against the Nice Dictator." *Digimag* 11, Feb. 2006. Web. 12. Aug. 2010. <http://www.digicult.it/digimag/article.asp?id=506>

Manovich, Lev. *The Language of New Media*. Cambridge, Mass: MIT Press, 2001. Print.

Nake, Frieder. "Der Computer Als Automat, Werkzeug Und Medium Und Unser Verhältnis Zu Ihm". *Menschenbild Und Computer. Selbstverständnis Und Selbstbehauptung Des Menschen Im Zeitalter Der Rechner*. Ed. H. Buddemeier vol. Medienkritische Reihe 3. Bremen: Universität Bremen, 2000. Print.

Pold, Søren. "Litteratur I Nettet: En Litterær Retssag - Eller Hvordan Litteraturen Vandt Legetøjskrigen." *D-Day På Kasernen 7 Foredrag Fra Konferencen "Æstetik Og Digitalisering: Tradition Eller Revolution?"* Eds. Lars Kiel Bertelsen and Søren Pold. Aarhus: De Æstetiske fag, Multimedieuddannelsen, 2001. 9-17. Print.

– *The Critical Interface*. Proceedings of the 4th decennial conference on Critical computing: between sense and sensibility, ACM Press. 2005. 109-112. Print.

– "Literature from Page to Interface: The Treatments of Text in Christophe Bruno's Iterature." *Electronic Book Review*, Feb. 2007. Web. 12. Aug. 2010. <http://www.electronicbookreview.com/thread/electropoetics/textualized>.

Scherffig, Lasse. *It's in Your Eyes -- Gaze Based Image Retrieval in Context*. Ed. Hans H. Diebner. Karlsruhe: ZKM | Institute for Basic Research, 2005. Print.

Schivelbusch, Wolfgang. *Geschichte Der Eisenbahnreise Zur Industrialisierung Von Raum Und Zeit Im 19. Jahrhundert*. Geschichte Fischer; 1680. Ungekürzte Ausg. ed. Frankfurt am Main: Fischer Taschenbuch Verlag, 1989. Print.

Ubermorgen. Psych|OS. Video/Installation/Web. 12. Aug. 2010. <http://www.hansbernhard.com/X/pages/video/index_long.html>.

Wartofsky, Marx W. *Models: Representation and the Scientific Understanding*. Dordrecht: Springer, 1979. Print.

Wiener, Norbert. *The Human Use of Human Beings: Cybernetics and Society*. 2nd ed. New York: Da Capo Press, 1988. Print.

– "Men, Machines, and the World About." *The New Media Reader*. Eds. Wardrip-Fruin, Noah, and Nick Montfort. Cambridge, Mass.: MIT Press, 2003. 67-72. Print.

Wishart, Adam, and Regula Bochsler. *Leaving Reality Behind: The Battle for the Soul of the Internet*. London: Fourth Estate, 2002. Print.

BEHIND: Representation and Computation

What Is Interface Aesthetics, or What Could It Be (Not)?

BY FLORIAN CRAMER

'Interface aesthetics' is a textbook example of a term which seems easy to grasp, but which turns into a can of worms when taken literally and examined more thoroughly. Its two constituent nouns, interface and aesthetics, are subject to whole libraries of philosophical, technological and artistic debate.[1] Should interface be most generally defined as "a surface forming a common boundary of two bodies, spaces, phases," as in Webster's Ninth Collegiate Dictionary, thus including chemical, biological and sociological notions of interface and interfacing? Or should the term, in a media studies context, more narrowly refer to computer interfaces? Does aesthetics refer to judgments of perception, as first defined by Alexander Baumgarten in the 18th century and still maintained by Jean-François Lyotard (in *Lessons on the Analytic of the Sublime*)? Do we mean aesthetics as the philosophy of art, from Hegel to Adorno, even in the context of interface research? Or should the latter use a combination of both, as in the contemporary aesthetic theory of Jacques Rancière (in *Aesthetics and Its Discontents*)? Or does aesthetics, in a computer interface context, boil down to the colloquial notion of the 'look-and-feel' of software and hardware controls?

Historical-critical studies of the evolution of look-and-feel from the Xerox Star to the contemporary iterations of Windows, Mac and various Linux/Unix graphical user interfaces, or that of web browser software from Mosaic to Firefox and web pages from HTML 1.0 to XHTML+CSS[2], would be useful and are overdue, especially if they could reflect the relation of computer interfaces to their contemporary audiovisual cultures: How, for example, did web and browser design, pop cultural flyer aesthetics, and the information design of TV news stations interfere in the 1990s? What is the link between the early use of vintage user interface and game aesthetics in Internet art, 8-bit music and the contemporary renaissance of analogue media? However, none of these examples could represent the whole of 'interface aesthetics' without oversimplifying both the notion of aesthetics and that of computer interface. As Wendy Chun points out,

> Analyses of digital media that concentrate on the *appearance* of user interfaces or on high-level software miss what is fundamentally different about so-called computer-mediated communications: the fact that they are arguably human-mediated communications (249).

In computing, interfaces could be technically defined as anything acting as a common boundary or link between machine components – whether on software or hardware level – or between human operators and the human-designed machines. Still, it would be rather problematic to include common social links between humans as 'interfaces', since that would either imply a cybernetic-behaviourist explanation of human behaviour through machine functions, or exhaust itself in superficially sexy, yet vague and ultimately unsatisfying analogies of social and machine connecting devices. There is the risk of inflating 'interface' into yet another humanities hype word such as 'text', 'performativity' and (last but not least) 'media' in the past.[3]

What could, however, be gained from comparing computer and social interfaces would be insight into epistemological limitations of computer interfaces stemming from the fact that computers are deterministic, purely syntactical and thus cognitively very limited machines (Searle). This could open up critical perspectives on the superimposition of formalisms onto society and culture. Still, the word 'interface' itself may be too technologically laden to save such social interface research from technodeterminism. The term is, in the end, as problematic as other 1990s cyber metaphors such as 'virtual reality' or 'the operating system art' (Wulffen).

If computer interfaces link machine components to each other and to human operators, then a systematics of computer interfaces would include:

1. *hardware-to-hardware interfaces* (CPU sockets, buses like PCI and USB, modems and network cards)
2. *hardware-to-software interfaces* (modern CPU instruction sets that no longer correspond to the physical hardware design)
3. *hardware controllers for software functions* (such as joysticks or remote controls for software players)
4. *software-to-hardware interfaces* (classically: operating system kernels and hardware drivers)
5. *software-to-software interfaces* (plug-in interfaces, file formats, protocols, most generally: application programming interfaces [APIs])
6. *human-to-hardware interfaces* (keyboards, mice, screen and audio feedback, all controller and feedback devices)
7. *human-to-software interfaces* (user interfaces).
8. With the exception of audiovisual displays and medical devices, advanced computer *hardware-to-human interfaces* are mostly science fiction, while it would be plausible to think, for example, of computer-generated bank and insurance statements and reminders as software-to-human interfaces.

Out of these eight possible interfacings, media studies have historically privileged one, the human-to-software user interface, using it often enough as a synonym of the term 'interface'. The trend was set with Brenda Laurel's – terminologically still precise – anthology *The Art of Human-Computer Interface Design*. Lev Manovich's essay "The Interface as a New Aesthetic Category" from 2000 uses both terms (interface and human-computer interface – in the sense of human-software interface) interchangeably. Interface, in that definition, becomes a synonym of a perceptive 'medium', much like optical devices in Renaissance philosophy,[4] only that the former is specific to computing technology.[5] Interface aesthetics then is simply how humans – respectively computer users – perceive the world via the organisational and sensory structures programmed into the device.[6] The question, however, is whether such a model of the "Interface as a New Aesthetic Category" is not about phenomenology rather than aesthetics, since by itself it is concerned neither with judgment of taste nor with art. For Manovich, a primary function of computer interface art is to challenge the "idea of content pre-existing the interface", thus suggesting different subject-medium-object relationships that ultimately prove the power of the medium. While Manovich is careful not to reduce human-computer interface to GUIs and look-and-feel, but includes data organisational structures like hierarchical file systems and hypertext in his consideration, the interface aesthetics he proposes could be criticised not only for its exclusive (yet typical) focus on human-computer interfacing, but also for using interface as a factual synonym of media and aesthetics as a synonym of phenomenology.

Humanities media studies have simultaneously restrained and inflated the notion of interface, comparable to the 'restrained rhetoric' that the structuralist Gerard Genette observed in modern philology since Giambattista Vico: the notion of rhetoric was gradually reduced to the figures of speech (tropes) of the elocutio, and ultimately to the single – yet vastly expanded – trope of the metaphor (160).[7] Interface, in its general sense of a common boundary, could conversely be considered the cybernetic sibling of metaphor, the Greek word for 'transfer'.

Another issue is the restraint within the very concept of the 'user interface,' with its inscribed difference from a 'programming interface' or API,[8] and hence implied separation of 'users' from 'programmers' based on different access privileges to machine functions granted by the respective interface. While the API is, as pointed out above, supposed to work purely as a software-to-software interface, for example as the communication channel via which a media player program interfaces with a song database, its juxtaposition to a user interface is ultimately arbitrary. In 8-bit BASIC computers like the Apple II, Commodore 64 or Sinclair ZX, on the Unix command line, in MIT's Lisp machines and even in Alan Kay's Smalltalk-based graphical user interface developed at Xerox PARC, the user interface was also a programming interface and vice versa. The contemporary computer art form of 'Live Coding', such as in Adrian Ward's and Alex McLean's Perl-based musical performances and in jodi's ZX Spectrum video *All Wrongs Reversed* ©1984, demonstrates how APIs can be employed as user interfaces. As a matter of fact, every act of computer hacking – in the 'black hat' sense of breaking a system open – boils down to a tactical misuse of an API as a user interface. A good example is John Draper's legendary use of a Cape'n'Crunch toy whistle to deactivate AT&T's tariff time switch: the touch tone frequencies of the dial were designed as the telephone user interface, and the whistle's 2600 Hz frequency as a programming interface was withheld from ordinary customers but turned into a user interface with the help of the technology provided in the cereal package.

Aesthetics, in a simple sense of perceptive transparency or opacity – aided by such aesthetic factors as pleasing rendering of visible, audible and touchable controls versus the sublime obscurity of a hidden programming interface – is a common mode of choice of drawing the line between the two levels of access in interface design. On the other hand, human-computer interfaces are often designed to lack convenience as a software-software or hardware-hardware interface. Good examples are graphical PC software that requires programmed mouse movements for scripted automation, or the need for a mechanical device to switch on a personal computer remotely. According to the ideals of both computational elegance and hackability, however, the threshold between human-computer and computer-computer interfaces should be smooth if not altogether absent, thus doing away with the dichotomy of programmer and user, designer and consumer.

Such design considerations imply that notions of aesthetic pleasantness also exist in all types of so-called computer-to-computer interfaces: software-to-software, hardware-to-software, software-to-hardware, hardware-to-hardware. Programmers' discussions on mailing lists and Internet forums are ripe with debates over whether an API or a hardware design is 'ugly' or 'beautiful',[9] thus reiterating both classical 18th century categories of aesthetic judgment and, on a larger historical horizon, Pythagorean and Platonist ideas of the transcendence of beauty in mathematics, arts (music) and cosmology. Donald Knuth's *Art of Computer Programming* and Steven Levy's hacker credo that "you can create art and beauty on a computer" refer to this latter pre-modern notion of art as beauty, but neither to 18th century aesthetics with its notion of art as comprising beauty, the sublime and ugliness alike, nor to aesthetics as historical philosophy of art after Hegel (Knuth; Levy).

In the extreme yet not untypical case, the computer engineering notion of art as beauty simply boils down to the internal elegance of a logical design, algorithm or equation, which at best corresponds to the beauty of its visualisation, such as in fractal geometry. It is a concept of aesthetics that could not be farther away from contemporary aesthetics like Rancière's, or Nicolas Bourriaud's influential contemporary art manifesto *Relational Aesthetics*, regardless of the latter's borrowing of software engineering terminology. The kind of computer art that has adopted it, such as the Artificial Life works mentioned in Manovich's essay, is also the one that has fully removed itself from contemporary art discourses outside a science and technology lab-based media art system. These gaps in the notions of aesthetics play a key role in the overall widening gap between the two cultures of science and humanities, engineering and contemporary art.

Ever since BBS underground cultures of the 1980s[10] and net.art of the 1990s, 'hacks' and intentional crudeness of software and hardware design have been embraced as an alternative computer aesthetic.[11] By themselves, they perfectly conform to classical philosophical notions of the sublime as the antipode of beauty. Edmund Burke's 18th century *Investigation into the Origin of our Ideas of the Sublime and Beautiful* lists pleasure and pain, terror, obscurity and suddenness among its effects and attributes (Section VII). In hacker/cracker aesthetics, they turn into pleasure and pain of hardware and software interfaces, terror of the desktop, obscurity of the API, and suddenness of operating system crashes. This fits traditional and contemporary aesthetics, including Lyotard's equation of the aesthetic sublime and a postmodern experience of "incommensurability of reality" (in *The Postmodern Condition*). It is an aesthetic, however, that constitutes itself as the symmetrical opposite of neo-Pythagorean beauty ideals that have governed computer science from Knuth to fractal geometry, the 'art and beauty' of the white-hat hacker culture described by Steven Levy, and the human/computer interface designs of mainstream, high-tech media lab arts. In the end, such dialectics helped to stabilise and reinforce 'media art' as a separate art system based, with few exceptions,[12] on pre-modernist aesthetic parameters.

The contemporary (visual) art system is, unlike electronic art, music or film, no longer defined by a medium or occupation with media, but first of all by its own system.[13]

In order to succeed, contemporary art relies on informed, up-to-date systemic references to the art context, its languages and institutional frame.[14] Ever since abstract painting and Duchamp's Ready-Mades rid visual art of both pictorial representation and specific media, but left framing and context, this has been the exclusion mechanism of a modernist and contemporary art aesthetics that only appears to be permissive and all-inclusive with regard to work and practices that count as art. As it has become crucial for artists to produce the 'right' contextual reference, art is no longer defined by the autonomy of its products – whether solid objects or ephemeral practices – but by doing the right thing in the right place at the right time within the art context.[15]

Contemporary art has become systemically incompatible with technological aesthetics because it has no interest in any relations, interfacings and mediation whose art references are either lacking or not up-to-date. Expressed positively, technological and media aesthetics may have spotlighted critical blind spots of an allegedly 'post-media' contemporary art system,[16] and, clashing with Kant's opposites of knowledge and judgments of taste respectively logic and aesthetics, gained punk hack appeal. This is what net and software art demonstrated roughly between the mid-1990s to the mid-2000s. But what remains when this impulse has worn out? Even a comprehensive interface aesthetics reflecting interface as user interface *and* API, hardware *and* software, beauty *and* debasement misses the mark of any critical contemporary aesthetics unless it deliberately stretches the notion of 'interface' to a metaphor of the social and the art system. Or, in the many worst cases that have already happened, it boils down to the glorification of new technology as the better contemporary art, be it in iPhone lifestyle, Web 2.0 hype or media theoretical glorification of sorting algorithms and CPU instruction sets.[17] Yet none of this is as provocative as Marinetti's glorification of a race car as more beautiful than the Nike of Samothrake; an aesthetic judgment that has become the common street sense of any car geek anyway and, if applied to computers and the Internet, boils down to the stock neoliberal ideology of the 'creative industries' superseding the autonomous arts.[18]

Aside from mere aesthetic preference, serious philosophical and political issues are involved. Ever since Martin Heidegger in "The

Question Concerning Technology" applied fundamental ontology to technology, to the effect that technology became an a priori of the human condition instead of a human product, there is a technological sublime in media theories from McLuhan to Kittler. As second nature, technology may arbitrarily take the place of Kant's natural beauty or the mathematical and dynamic sublime. This means that we are no longer overwhelmed by mountain ranges or thunderstorms, but, for example, by the pervasiveness of computing. If, with Lyotard, a sublime experience of computing has its share in the experience of incommensurability, it obscures the fact that the reality of computing is based on constructed designs and policies that can be changed.

Modern aesthetic theories are likewise difficult to apply to computing and its interfaces. Kant's notion of the dynamic and mathematical sublime may lend itself to cinema or virtual reality gaming, but hardly to any contemporary audiovisual or tactile computer user interface, and even less so to more abstract computer-computer interfaces.

However, the whole mapping of aesthetics and interface remains a speculative stretch given Kant's juxtaposition of aesthetics and logic.[19] His notion of beauty as "pleasure without interest"[20] does not lend itself to technical thinking that recognises beauty in perfect functionality. In a more contemporary discourse, computer culture and engineering may fit, to some degree, Rancière's "ethical regime of art" (in *The Politics of Aesthetics* 20), where artists are craftspeople and their products are judged by truthfulness of representation – as opposed to the later "representative regime," where art gains its autonomy, but is still defined by its making and a modernist "esthetic regime" of simultaneous autonomy and engagement with everyday life (21). While these regimes, or periods, can be usefully mapped onto the development of computational visual arts within the 20th century, from early depictive computer graphics via representational neo-Renaissance audiovisual installation art in the manner of Bill Viola and Jeffrey Shaw (Grau) to social-contextual and interventionist Internet art since the 1990s, they can hardly be applied to the design of the technology itself. Rancière's notion of aesthetics is simply too narrowly bound to literature and visual arts. Not even lending itself to the history of music and sonic arts, it could be mapped onto applied arts and technical designs at best via crude analogy.

Interface design thus marks a blind spot of modern aesthetic theories just as much as, for example, food. Cooking is perhaps the most basic cultural practice that integrally involves aesthetics in the original 18th century sense of judgments of taste, yet exists outside the definition of fine and even applied arts.[21] Wherever cooking was brought into modern and contemporary arts – from Marinetti's futurist cuisine, Daniel Spoerri's *Eat Art* of the 1960s and Gordon Matta-Clark's artist restaurant *Food* in the early 1970s to Gordon W.'s cooking performances since the 1980s and Rirkrit Tiravanija's cooking installations and interventions since the 1990s (Bourriaud 25, 30) – it was less about food as an aesthetic phenomenon (akin to visuals or sound) than about food as a social means, both in its contextual friction with the art system and communal refunctioning of art spaces. Bourriaud's own definition of 'relational aesthetics' as a "theory consisting in judging artworks on the basis of the inter-human relations which they represent, produce or prompt" fails to reflect this latter, crucial aspect without which 'relational art' would just be a fancy neologism for sociocultural art (112).[22]

If food is thus a medium – both in the Fine Art sense of an artistic material and in the communication studies sense of an information transmitter – allowing an audience to relate differently to itself and the art system, is it not then also an interface in the general dictionary sense of "a surface forming a common boundary of two bodies, spaces, phases"? And is not relational aesthetics, with its nominal indebtedness to the computer term of the relational database,[23] describing an art, and aesthetics, of interfacing? Next to the dangers of cybernetic superimpositions of machine models onto society, or vice versa, anthropomorphising the machine, the notion of a 'social interface' is simply too broad to be useful. What, in culture, is not a 'social interface'? Ultimately, 'social interface' boils down to a synonym of 'communication medium', with only a minor semantic shift from community to society and from mediation to interconnection. Naturally, this does not mean that there is no social dimension in human-computer and computer-computer interfaces. Quite the contrary: the social dimension lies precisely in those dumb, unsexy and typically non-aesthetic – not immediately visible or tangible – formalisms of hardware and software and their interference with human life, from day trading algorithms to insurance risk algorithms, bank account balancing software, to the behavioural modelling in Web-based social networking software.

There are, in other words, no human-human 'social interfaces' to be modelled on human-computer or computer-computer interfacing without reductionism. With its subtitle *From Judgment to Calculation* (i.e., if one borrows from Kant: from critical (aesthetic) reasoning to formal processing) Joseph Weizenbaum's 1976 book *Computer Power and Human Reason* tackles exactly this issue and obsoletes further arguments here. The opposite, however, is just as true: Every human-computer and computer-computer interface also acts as a 'social interface' in the sense of the (by definition: formally constrained) computational operations it lends to (as an enabling technology) and superimposes on (as a controlling device) human practices (Fuller; Chun). Yet the terms 'interfacing' and 'interface' become meaninglessly broad when thus referring, in cybernetic terminology, to any kind of feedback and feedback device.

Even when founded on narrower, colloquial notions of both interface and aesthetics, interface aesthetics may have its place as a critical approach within both media studies and computer science; namely when it is considered as a paradigm rather than a certain perspective, when it insists on the *aisthesis*, perceptibility, of all computer feedback. If an API can be as ugly as a GUI, then it is also a user interface, with the aesthetic perspective shedding light on the politics of interface denominations. It still means that 'interface aesthetics' will remain a quite restrained subset of aesthetics and never suffice for a critical perspective on electronic arts. To embrace aesthetics and subjectivity as tools for the critical analysis of technology may, conversely, help to avoid reductive cybernetic equations. Aesthetic judgment remains, after all, the least computable form of analysis and decision, for purely technical reasons.[24]

Notes

1. For an encyclopedic historical overview on aesthetic theory, see Pochat. At the time of writing, I am not aware of any comprehensive research of the meanings, applications and history of 'interface'. A taxonomy was attempted in the article "Interface" that I co-authored with Matthew Fuller for the volume *Software Studies* (Cramer and Fuller 143).
2. Some useful practical research work has been done on various GUI history web sites for which the Wikipedia article *History of the graphical user interface* (http://en.wikipedia.org/wiki/History_of_the_graphical_user_interface) delivers up-to-date pointers, and in Olia Lialina's research on the "Vernacular Web" (http://art.teleportacia.org/observation/vernacular).
3. As pointed out by Søren Pold in correspondence with the author.
4. As, for example, in Athanasius Kircher's *Ars Magna Lucis et Umbrae*, 1646, and Jan Amos Comenius' *Labyrinth of the World and Paradise of the Heart*, 1631.
5. "The interface shapes how the computer user conceives the computer itself. It also determines how users think of any media object accessed via a computer" (Manovich).
6. Or, in Manovich's words: "In short, far from being a transparent window into the data inside a computer, the interface brings with it strong messages of its own." This is a variation of the classical media theoretical paradigm, from Innis to Kittler, that the medium determines (or is) the message.
7. The similarity to contemporary media studies is all the more striking since the restraint of interface to graphical human-to-software-user interfaces has led research to focus on the visual metaphors implemented in those interfaces, such as in Laurel, ibid.
8. API = application programming interface.
9. An example: As of November 2009, the source code comments of the current Linux operating system kernel (version 2.6.30) contain 382 mentions of the word 'ugly' compared with 14 mentions of 'beauty' or 'beautiful'.
10. As documented on the site http://www.textfiles.com.
11. Alexei Shulgin's *Fuck-U-Fuck Me*, http://www.mediaartnet.org/works/fuck-u-fuck-me, with its designed obscenity of the hardware-to-user interface, is a good example.
12. Such as: interventionist and activist media art, and Internet art that strongly related to the language and system of 20th century and contemporary art.
13. As reflected, for instance, in the song *Art is a luxury* by the Rotterdam-based music group Coolhaven: "Art is a luxury / starving people don't paint / maybe they scream a lot / art is a luxury / but as far as expression is concerned / that's very meagre / art is a luxury / throw the poop shot on the canvas / colorful society can't put them in a square / when you talk to me / you talk to yourself / art is a luxury / because it only talks to itself".
14. The curator Marius Babias accordingly defined art as a 'para science' building "upon the history of art and styles, on preceding developments" to which "everyone wanting to do art has to relate"; translated from a German interview in the Berlin paper Zitty, July 30, 2008, http://www.zitty.de/kultur-kunst/16840/.
15. Rirkrit Tiravanija, whose 1990s cooking performances are quite second-hand in comparison to Matta-Clark in 1970s and subcultural artists like Gordon W. Zealot in the 1980s, comes to the same conclusion in an interview with Ben Lewis for the BBC Documentary *Art Safari: Relational Art*, 8 July 2004, http://www.ubu.com/film/relational.html.
16. See, for example, the contemporary art web site http://www.postmedia.net.
17. This tone was set by Friedrich Kittler's techno-deterministic media theory of the 1990s and became the theme of such events as the "Takeover" edition of the Ars Electronica Festival in 2001.

18. If experimental digital art is merely content with the aesthetic debasement or subversion of computer interface subversions, it runs the risk of ending up as the court jester of those industries.
19. "That which is purely subjective in the representation of an object, i.e., what constitutes its reference to the subject, not to the object, is its aesthetic quality. On the other hand, that which in such a representation serves, or is available, for the determination of the object (for or purpose of knowledge), is its logical validity" (Kant, *Critique of Judgment* 23).
20. "Interesseloses Wohlgefallen" (Kant, *Kritik der Urteilskraft*).
21. 'Food design' most commonly refers to the visual styling of food rather than its preparation and taste.
22. Compared to Bourriaud, Adorno's posthumously published *Aesthetic Theory* is surprisingly fresh in its refusal to bless either practices or objects, respectively autonomy or sociality of art: "The dual nature of artworks as autonomous structures and social phenomena results in oscillating criteria: Autonomous works provoke the verdict of social indifference and ultimately of being criminally reactionary; conversely, works that make socially univocal discursive judgments thereby negate art as well as themselves."
23. Coined by the IBM research Edgar Codd in 1970 according to Wikipedia, http://en.wikipedia.org/w/index.php?title=Relational_database&oldid=326505871.
24. Unless one is still a hardcore believer in artificial intelligence.

Works cited:

Adorno, Theodor W. *Ästhetische Theorie*. Frankfurt a.M.: Suhrkamp, 1970. Print.

– *Aesthetic Theory*. London: Continuum 2005 (1970). Print.

Baumgarten, Alexander Gottlieb. *Aesthetica*. 1750-1758. Print.

Bourriaud, Nicolas. *Relational Aesthetics*. 1998. Paris: les presses du réel, 2002. Print.

Burke, Edmund. *A Philosophical Investigation into the Origin of our Ideas of the Sublime and Beautiful*. 1757. Oxford University Press, 1990, Section VII. Print.

Chun, Wendy Hui Kyong. *Control and Freedom*. Cambridge, Mass.: The MIT Press, 2006. Print.

Codd, Edgar. *A Relational Model of Data for Large Shared Data Banks*. Communications of the ACM, 13.6 (1970). 377-87. Print.

Comenius, Jan Amos. *Labyrinth of the World and Paradise of the Heart*. 1631. Print.

Cramer, Florian, and Matthew Fuller. "Interface." *Software Studies*. Ed. Matthew Fuller. Cambridge: The MIT Press, 2008. 143-9. Print.

Fuller, Matthew. *Behind the Blip, Essays on the Culture of Software*. Brooklyn: Autonomedia, 2003. Print.

Genette, Gerard. "La rhetorique restreinte." *Communications* 16 (1970). 158-71. Print.

Grau, Oliver. *Virtual Art*. Cambridge, Mass: MIT Press, 2003. Print.

Hegel, G.W.F. *Aesthetics*. 1831. Lectures on Fine Art. Oxford: Clarendon, 1975. Print.

Heidegger, Martin. "The Question Concerning Technology." 1953. *Basic Writings*. San Francisco: HarperCollins, 1977. Print.

Kant, Immanuel. *Critique of Judgment*, Oxford: Oxford University Press, 2007. Print.

– *Kritik der Urteilskraft*. 1790. Berlin: Akademie-Verlag, 2008. Print.

Kircher, Athanasius. *Ars Magna Lucis et Umbrae*. 1646. Print.

Knuth, Donald E. *The Art of Computer Programming*. Reading, Mass.: Addison-Wesley, 1973-1998. Print.

Laurel, Brenda, ed. *The Art of Human-Computer Interface Design*. Reading, Massachusetts: Addison-Wesley, 1990. Print.

Levy, Steven. *Hackers*. 1984. Champaign, IL: Project Gutenberg, 1986. Web. 31 Aug. 2010. <www.gutenberg.org/etext/729>.

Lyotard, Jean-François. *Lessons on the Analytic of the Sublime*. Stanford: Stanford University Press, 1994. Print.

– *The Postmodern Condition*. Minneapolis: University of Minnesota Press, 1984. Print.

Manovich, Lev. "The Interface as a New Aesthetic Category." *Through the Looking Glass*. Ed. Patrick Lichty. Cleveland: Beachwood Center for the Arts, 2000. Web. 31 Aug. 2010. <http://www.voyd.com/ttlg/textual/manovichtext.htm>.

Marinetti, Filippo Tommaso. "Manifesto della cucina futurista", *Gazzetta del Popolo*, Torino, 28 August 1930. Print. Web. 31. Aug. 2010. <http://www.railibro.rai.it/articoli.asp?id=484>

Pochat, Götz. *Geschichte der Ästhetik und Kunsttheorie*. Cologne: DuMont, 1996. Print.

Rancière, Jacques. *Aesthetics and Its Discontents*. Cambridge: Polity, 2009. Print.

– *The Politics of Aesthetics*. London: Continuum, 2004. Print.

Searle, John C. "Minds, brains, and programs." *The Behavioural and Brain Sciences*. 3 (1980): 417-424. Print.

Shulgin, Alexei. *Fuck-U-Fuck Me*. Web. 31 Aug. 2010. <http://www.mediaartnet.org/works/fuck-u-fuck-me>.

Weizenbaum, Joseph. *Computer Power and Human Reason*. San Francisco: W.H. Freeman, 1976. Print.

Wulffen, Thomas. "Betriebssystem Kunst." *Kunstforum International* 125 (1994). Print.

The Computation of Space

BY DRAGANA ANTIC AND MATTHEW FULLER

0. Preface

For the purposes of this discussion, we would like to stress two points: Firstly, that an interface is understood here in the sense of being any process or structure that brings computational events into correlation with what is outside them, including other computations. Secondly, that interfaces can also be figured as the relations and structures introduced between entities and processes by computational processes which may enfold or link them (Cramer and Fuller). We propose to think through the question of computation and interface in these terms with specific reference to the production of space.

With the increasing abundance, though not necessary visibility, of embedded and ubiquitous computing, the billions of processors used outside of what we can call the now classic 'face to screen' interfaces, interface also means those devices involved in interpellating computation into multiple kinds of relation with processes as diverse as car automation systems, weather monitoring, traffic control, intruder alarms, food production, building information systems, wireless networks and mobile phones. Such devices act as interpretation and actuation triggers of location, movement, information flow, pattern recognition, temperature, optometry and so on.

In such contexts computation often occurs between multiple processors. These, 'Central Processing Units' which are, along with screens and keyboards, one of the privileged 'sites' of computing, are decentred in a way in which a process on one computer acts on or with a process in another, each only carrying part of the interaction. This is the condition of network computing, one in which questions of access to energy and the topology of landscape and weather also couple with questions of routing and calculation (Perkins). But the network between computers is only part of the situation. In addition, the multiplication of kinds of computation in space, through sensors and actuators, monitoring systems and the like means that the actions of those entities, events and processes that they handle are also involved in computational processes. Such a situation replicates, in a certain way, the prehistory of electronic computers "when computers were human" (Grier), because calculations pass through people and are arrayed around them in books of tables, writing desks, slide rules, annotations, methods systems of education and other forms of interface to the space and conditions of computation. The additional factor being that in such cases of distributed computation, the computers may also consist of weather patterns, chemical growths, sensors on tennis courts, the behaviours of markets and the movements of targets.

Recent theories of distributed cognition, such as those of Andy Clark (1997) and Ed Hutchins (1996), or in situated cognition as in the work of Lucy Suchmann (1987) which show how objects and processes in the environment act as prompts and armatures of thought, as well as the discussion of memory and embedded thought in much media theory (Innis), come at this problem from another direction, establishing the possibility of understanding computation as something being constituted in a 'field' rather than being solely located in specific sites. Such a field can be understood in terms of its spatial needs and effects, but it can also prompt us to think about computation as a spatial activity or one that can be articulated, rendered in spatial terms. One of the means of coming to grips with such a spatial understanding of computation is through architecture, urban planning and other kinds of spatial practice.

Architecture's relation to number and calculation is extensive and multiform, covering the history of the discipline and particularly its relation to engineering from the point when:

> In the fifteenth century we are at a period when numbers are beginning to be attached to (these) geometrical figures, in order to establish a link between abstract mathematical speculation and the figures, without being restricted to empirical ratios of displacement (Gille).

We do not propose to trace this relationship here but to suggest it as a possible means for entering into and experiencing the contemporary conditions of computation as a spatial and cultural domain. The following text proposes a short reading of the place of computation and of software in contemporary architectural practice and then of folding this process inside-out, configuring spatial ordering as a computational process by means of simple algorithmic experiment.

As such, what we hope to do with this text is to bring computation and spatial design and experience into a more open set of relations, in which its tractability and tensions tangle with perception, thought and the handling and capacities of multiple kinds of materials including the symbolic. In doing so, we also aim to generate reflection on the nature of interface when, in something of an extension of distributed computing, it becomes something increasingly co-extensive with what it handles.

1

'Technological progress' has generated many new materials and incorporated computation into many levels of their fabrication. This has established the possibility to create a new diversity of spatial forms and to identify experimental methods of construction that weave the foundational abstraction of computation into their fabric. Once the joints are in place, however, or the welds are made, the process of creation stops. We have yet to experience a space that is fully computational. This text aims to suggest a small means of doing so.

The architect Bernard Cache has described the Constructivist project as something that is not finished but is present as an abundant resource, of the imagination and of the synthesis of spatial formations coupled with social dynamics and multiplicative powers of abstraction. Aside from its typological visual characteristics, what constructivism allows for is this coupling of the abstract and the social, turning them both into concrete material that can be experimented with in the here and now but also allowing the fullness of the dimensions that they exist upon to become palpable, thinkable and, more importantly, to be worked in.

Despite having the capacity to think things through from the level of the multiple interactions of many parts by virtue of their 'non-standard' interaction, much contemporary work on materials in architecture amputates its potential by staying solely within the domain of what it characterises as material. This is the continuing folly of engineers or of architects who consider themselves as only special high-expertise servants or savants whose role is clearly demarcated. Instead, we propose that form-finding goes on at many scales, including the social.[1] Cache's image of Constructivism allows not for some codified vocabulary of forms but for a sense of working with plasticity and constraints, affordances at any level of reality that may be to hand or that may yet be invented.

2

The current intensification of the mathematisation of space and spatial processes no longer allows us the option of failing to understand concrete space in terms of the abstractions that are woven into it. In order to understand the city, one has to understand it at multiple scales, not simply at those of the local and the global but as something that emerges out of interacting waves of force and materials operating at scales involving the following:

- The informational normalisation of space, such as traffic control, security or logistics systems
- The weaving of informational space into the fabric of the city, layering it in with typologies of form characteristic of earlier eras, the mediaeval or modern city
- The increasing production of forms of matter ready to correspond to its informational modelling, what Kas Oosterhuis (2006) calls file to factory production but also at the 'lower' scale of nanotechnological fabrication and the 'higher' one of pre-emptive actuations of whole futures via computer simulations
- The increasing incorporation of previously 'expert' knowledge of computing into popular cultures
- The development of algorithmic culture as a compositional force in areas such as music
- The development of architectural software based upon the interaction of parameters rather than (ideal) forms
- The increasing generation of organisational forms, especially in institutions, that are designed to meet the needs of informational schema, such as quality audits, before other considerations

Within this context, we propose an experiment that may help tease out some further possibilities in thinking through the production of space at a relatively high level of abstraction and also as something immediately made and experienced. But alongside the way in which informationalisation has mutated and layered urban space, it is also useful to first think about how it has developed a particular sub-set of practices within – architecture.

In terms of recognising software as a new material within architecture, a number of directions of its usage within different architectural practices are readily identifiable:

Case 1: Software as 'a tool', the most general and widespread use of software. Architects use AutoCAD, 3D Max, Maya, Rhino and Adobe Photoshop instead of a pen. They use software for faster drawing and quicker production of their design. In projects such as *Maxilla* by Stealth Unlimited,[2] which parametrically generates large-scale urban layouts, additional software is developed to work inside AutoCAD and a spreadsheet program. In such cases, software becomes less of a tool and more of a machine.

Case 2: Software as 'a material' for sculpturing buildings. Some architects, such as Lars Spuybroek[3] and Greg Lynn,[4] use software as a means for sculpting the space they are working on. They do not use software solely as a tool for production but more as a means for creating shapes and forms that are not possible to produce or present on a sheet of paper. Here, software is used more intuitively in the process of creation.

Case 3: Software participating in the design process. This practice questions the position of the architect as an ultimate designer. Cache took part in the creation of the software Top-Solid that, among other features, has the facility to work with an implementation of parametric design. This suite of applications was originally made for the "drafting, design and manufacture of products,"[5] but architects took on the exploration of the possibilities of its implementation in their practice. Parametric design is determined by the constraints on the structure to be made. These are fed into the software and a correspondingly narrow or broad spectrum of possible results can be derived and tweaked. The composition or structure produced by the architect in this way is a numerically determined geometry. A great advantage is that the architectural design produced in this way can be immediately manufactured in the factory or workshop because all the elements of the construction have their precise specifications.

Case 4: Software as an 'interactive media' or augmentation of space with software. Architects and designers, such as Attila Kovacs,[6] Mark Goulthrope (of the atelier dECOi),[7] Daan Roosegaarde[8] and others, use these in direct application to architectural elements in space, such as façade walls. In this way, they intend to create a playful and receptive architecture. Here, software and hardware are additions to the space and not its essential elements.

When making an architectural design for a building, an architect develops a programmatic model of how a building should be used. He or she creates a sort of 'programming table' for the planned life of the inhabitants inside the building. Even the most farsighted architects of Modernism, excited by every new machine that appeared: cars, grain processors, aeroplanes, machines used in factories, did not see beyond the functionality of the machines and the aesthetics that followed this functionality. They did not imagine the possibility of a machine as an abstraction – the algorithmic logic by which a certain machine works in order to make such a logic applicable to their architectural concepts. Instead, they saw a building 'as a machine' in a purely functional sense: a house that works as perfectly as a machine. What, however, would a constructivism of the abstract machine imply?

3

Whilst computation offers the mechanism of fixing, of logical or social identity and the schematic formatting of realities, it also manifests the possibility of synthesis and of the generation and development of mathematico-material drives in which permutation becomes the compositional principle. In his text "A. and Pangeometry"

(1925), El Lizzitsky states that the realm of irrational numbers allows that "We now enter a realm that cannot be directly registered by the senses, that cannot be demonstrated, that follows from a purely logical construction and therefore represents an elementary crystallisation of human thought." It is the vastly productive alienness of mathematics from ordinary experience of the world that provides the power released when its scalar level is brought into composition with others.

A question one might ask regarding the principle of identity to be found in the logical preposition 'A is A' is about the conditions in which it is uttered. If it is a computation specifying, say, the uncorrupted transition of an email from one point to another, that is one thing: a guarantee of an adequate transmission. If it is a statement made by an entity placed in a position to determine one or the other or both of the instances of A in a case where A is, from the perspective of another scale, equal to more than A, or something other than A alone, one is left with neither certainty nor accuracy. Such a statement might also equate to a violation.

Asking such questions means that logical structures, even those as simple as 'this equals that,' need to be understood in terms of the grammars they also weave between entities in the world. It is not possible to adequately describe an entity such as a city in logical terms without substantial loss, nor by a mathematical description that would not itself be larger than the city. Nevertheless, the violence of logical reason, the way it opens itself to ridicule, but also its power, is in part generated by its capacity to map relations between entities. But this is often a process in which the act of mapping is itself excluded.

Perhaps it is possible to think this through with reference to minimalist sculpture and thus onto space. If we are to take a square of magnesium or of slate, as in the work of Carl Andre, and identify each of the entities as corresponding to the logical statement A, each additional statement of A corresponds to each A in the sculpture. However, what Andre's work allows us to understand and literally feel, especially in the case of the magnesium, in terms of a heat differential between the viewers' feet and the metal, is that each enunciation of A takes place in a way that is displaced in time and space from other elements but also in arrangement with them.[9] Each square of slate or magnesium has minor differences in quality, which might be derived from manufacturing and shipping processes, from their handling whilst entering the category of 'art,' or from the long timescale of the material's geological gestation. Each square, like a time slice of cells in a cellular automata, is placed in varying relation to the other entities in the composition. Thus there is a grammar of differentiation inherent to the repetition of what is ostensibly a 'same.' This minor differentiation alters the meaning of 'A' without, however, necessarily altering it at the scalar level of logic or of the statement which describes the work at the level of matter-of-fact linguistic articulation. That they are brought together by a description of sameness at a certain scale also produces the capacity for the sensing of their differentiation. Finding the means to articulate the traction or compositional force that logical statements have on other scales of reality allows us to understand them also as materially productive.

4

A formalisation of the field of computation was achieved in 1936 by Alan Turing. His concept was very simple. He imagined a machine that would be capable of carrying out any achievable calculation by means of an algorithmic process. The genius of his idea consists in its position as a meta-algorithmic statement. It produces an algorithm by means of which, as far as it is currently known, all other algorithms or 'effective procedures' for the purposes of computation may be written.

The standard model of a Turing Machine consists of an infinite tape divided into cells of equal dimensions, positioned one next to the other.[10] Before the machine starts working, the cells are blank. When the machine starts working, each cell may be filled with a symbol from some finite alphabet. This alphabet contains a special symbol to identify a blank cell. The Turing Machine also contains a scanner or a head that scans the cells reading what is written in the cell, carrying out any instructions given in the 'programming table,' recording the results of instructions and writing another symbol according to the 'programming table' set up. Instructions might include functions such as copying a string of symbols, deleting a symbol, moving the head a specified number of positions in one direction, writing a specified symbol in the current cell carrying out a concatenation or addition. Each computer language differentiates itself by making certain kinds of such activities, including far more complex ones, more or less built in and accessible by more or less condensed rather than convoluted commands. What is crucial about the Turing Machine is that anything that can be fully formally described within the terms of this abstract machine.

Whilst it forms the crucial logical substrate of all current computers, the Turing Machine is, by and large, an imaginary machine. That is to say, it is rare for anyone to actually set out to make it manifest both at the level of concept and as material practice, with pencil, paper, and the human computer originally imaged by Turing. Whilst much of what is revealed by such an exercise is a) the mundanity of computation carried out as a task (Grier), and b) the normally imperceptible speed with which electronic computers carry out such work, it is possible, and perhaps fun as an exercise, to set it out. Equally, it is possible to construct a basic set of symbols corresponding not only to actions within the Turing Machine but also to the manipulation of spatial elements 'outside' of it. It would also be possible to feed the results of the actions carried on at the level of work with materials back into the Turing Machine as the results of computations, or to carry out part of the computation in the handling and behaviours of the materials.

5

What we would like to propose is a logical continuation of the list of four tendencies in architecture listed as 'cases' above. But instead of augmentation, as a move in architectural-computational evolution, we suggest a merging of the logic of the machine, in this case that of Turing, and the logic of the architectural space with all of its connotations, social, cultural, formal, mathematical etc. What we suggest is a creation of a space that will function in algorithmic manner. We suggest three ways in which this might happen:

1. Creating an algorithm that will deal with a specific number of basic forms (i.e. as a simple sub-set of all numerically determinable shapes, the Platonic solids: sphere, cube and cone; or using another set such as fogs, slimes and blobs) which

will when executed create a form and, depending on the algorithm(s) used, might even create a different form with the same elements on every execution.

2. The accent is on shape; creating an algorithm that will deal with only one element (i.e. sticks or tiles). A result of the algorithm is a structure composed by specific mathematical rules.
3. The accent is on structure; creating an algorithm that when executed establishes a specific kind of state of a space and when the machine/space passes certain steps:
   a. A space may go through different states within itself – metamorphosis of the space.
   b. A space may provoke or elicit different states within observers – metamorphosis of the inhabitants and constructors of the space.

3.a. The metamorphosis of the space would imply that a space changes its numerically describable characteristics, such as size, volume, colour, shape, sound, texture etc. There is a possibility of having a database of different materials this space can use. The states of this space are changed with the input of the inhabitant but related to a previously programmed algorithm. A more illustrative example could be in having parametric design software running real-time, not only inside the computer but in a working space. The software might run a space so that an inhabitant could change all the elements of a space and programme the shape, colour, size, texture, he or she wants to live in until it is time for another experiment. This might be like living inside a sintering machine[11] or a space equipped with swarms of 'always-on' Computer Numerical Control (CNC) drills.[12] Equally, one can imagine using a magnetic fluid that can reciprocate in creating shapes with programmable forces or, over a larger area, banks of particles interacting with positional sound waves. This would be an ever-changing, perhaps interestingly nightmarish, space.

3.b. The metamorphosis of the inhabitant of the space would be concerned with the experience one has whilst inside it. One might argue that the modernist grid itself proposes a universal machine corresponding, when reduced to one dimension, to an infinite stretch of cells. Are we not simply proposing a greater degree of formalisation? To inhabit and co-construct such a space would be a significant way of both coupling and uncoupling sensual and cognitive experience in a vivid interplay generated by the momentary degree of emphasis in working with the space. We imagine that the spatial entities and processes thrown up by such procedures would allow people to more fully experience the logical and computational scales in which they exist. As an extension of this argument, and in resonance with the continuing potential of constructivism by opening up a mechanism for the generation of spatial entities, such a project might tend to induce access to a conceptual feel for the relations of dimensionality whose multiplying interlocking scales compose life.

6

In an exercise we have produced for the Calculation Space project at Transmedia[13] we will use a mechanism of the Turing Machine to compose and shape an architectural space. The goal is to write a 'programming table' composed out of a set of algorithms that when executed will create a shape. Instead of using an electronic computer we return to human computers, calculation by project participants, alongside pencils and paper, simple construction materials. The structure for this exercise is:

- Decide whether to operate via a predefined matrix to which materials are aligned or alternately by using the form-finding capacities of the materials. (Turing's 'infinite tape' may be translated into an infinite 3D matrix since architectural space in computer terms has often been defined with x, y and z axes.)[14] If using a matrix, define and create it.
- Identify the material (i.e. wooden rods, balloons, paper strips, string etc).
- Create an algorithm for shaping an individual material element. For instance by trimming or filling with water, sand or air. These elements will make a composition when processed through further algorithms – 'what' is composed.

- Create an algorithm for positioning created elements – 'where' they are composed, whether in the matrix or in relationship to other elements.
- Create an algorithm for composition of created elements – 'how' they are composed.
- Create an algorithmic routine for the observation and adjustment of the shaping, positioning and composition of elements.

This is only one in a line of experiments possible to produce in relation to this field, staging new encounters between abstract machines and the experiential and social working of space. A number of questions naturally arise from such work, including discussion of the generation of adequate notation and scripting symbols and how far the Turing Machine as logical substrate or pretext remains adequate when different compositional forces, such as other data structures or even imagination, take over.

Notes

1. For a useful set of arguments, see Hensel and Mendes.
2. As the Rotterdam-based studio Stealth Unlimited note about their custom software, "The input comes from layouts of urban areas in an AutoCAD drawing and parameters saved in a Microsoft Excel spreadsheet. *Maxilla* generates the streets, envelopes and buildings from scratch." See http://www.stealth.ultd.net/stealth/05_maxilla.html.
3. See, Nox Architecture, http://www.noxarch.com/.
4. See, Greg Lynn Form, http://www.glform.com/.
5. http://www.topsolid.com/products/plm/.
6. See Attila Kovacs (1969-1970) "Electronic-cybernetic sculpture and wall."
7. In work such as the *Aegis Hyposurface*. 2004.
8. See Studio Roosegaarde, http://www.studioroosegaarde.net/.
9. i.e. Carl Andre, 144 Magnesium Square, 1969, Tate 10. In some models of the Turing Machine the 'scanner' moves and the tape is motionless. Others contain multiple tapes, although ultimately these distinctions are inessential.
11. A sintering machine is often used in rapid prototyping. Plastic granules are melted, layer upon layer, using computer-controlled lasers, in order to build up three-dimensional entities.
12. Computer Numerical Control is one means of directly manufacturing from file. Such drills, often with several heads working in different dimensions, carve directly into blocks of material.
13. Calculation Space, 2007, Transmedia, Postgraduate Program in Arts + Media + Design at Hogeschool Sint-Lukas, Brussels, http://www.transmedia.be/.
14. For a reading of a computational alternative to Cartesian co-ordinates see Mackenzie.

Works cited

Cache, Bernard. *Earth Moves, the Furnishing of Territories*. Trans. Anne Boyman. Ed. Michael Speaks. Cambridge: MIT Press, 1995. Print.

Clark, Andy. *Being There, Putting Brain, Body and World Together Again*. Cambridge: MIT Press, 1997. Print.

– *Natural Born Cyborgs, Minds, Technologies and the Future of Human Intelligence*. Oxford: Oxford University Press, 2003. Print.

Cramer, Florian, and Matthew Fuller. "Interface." *Software Studies, a Lexicon*. Ed. Matthew Fuller. Cambridge: MIT Press, 2008. Print.

Grier, David Alan. *When Computers Were Human*. Princeton: Princeton University Press, 2005. Print.

Gille, Bertrand. *The Renaissance Engineers*. London: Lund Humphries, 1966. Print.

Grier, David A., *When Computers Were Human*. Princeton: Princeton University Press, Princeton, 2005. Print.

Hensel, Michael, and Achim Mendes. "Morpho-Ecologies, Towards and Inclusive Discourse on Heterogeneous Architectures." *Morpho-Ecologies*. Eds. Michael Hensel and Achim Mendes. London: Architecture Association, 2006. 16-59. Print.

Hutchins, Edwin. *Cognition in the Wild*. Cambridge: MIT Press, 1996. Print.

Innis, Harold. *The Bias of Communication*. Toronto: University of Toronto Press, 1951. Print.

Lizzitsky, El. "A. and Pangeometry." *Art in Theory 1900-2000, an Anthology of Changing Ideas*, (2nd. Ed.). Eds. Charles Harrison and Paul Wood. Oxford: Blackwell, 2003. 317-21. Print.

Mackenzie, Adrian. "Losing Time at the PlayStation: Real Time and the 'Whatever' Body." *Transductions, Bodies and Machines at Speed*. London: Continuum, 2002. 146-71. Print.

Oosterhuis, Kas. "A New Kind of Building." *Crossover, Architecture, Urbanism, Technology*. Eds. Arie Graafland and Leslie Jaye Kavanagh. Rotterdam: 010 Publishers, 2006. 240-69. Print.

Perkins, Charles E. *Ad Hoc Networking*. Boston: Addison Wesley, 2001. Print.

Suchman, Lucy A. *Plans and Situated Actions, the Problem of Human Machine Communication*. Cambridge: Cambridge University Press, 1987. Print.

Turing, Alan. "On Computable Numbers, with an Application to the Entscheidungsproblem." 1936. Ed. Jack B. Copeland. *The Essential Turing*. Oxford: Clarendon Press, 2004. 58-90. Print.

GEOFF COX
Means-End of Software

MORTEN BREINBJERG
Poesis of Human-Computer Interaction: Music, Materiality and Live Coding

CHRISTIAN ULRIK ANDERSEN
Writerly Gaming: Political Gaming

DOWN: Software and Code

Means-End of Software

BY GEOFF COX

Means to end

It has become common to replace a critical engagement of the graphical interface with what lies behind it: source code. Indeed, conventional interfaces tend to hide the workings of the computer and the complexity of its processes. In "There is no Software", Friedrich Kittler claims: "We simply do not know what our writing does" (quoted in Druckery 332), referring to the ways that graphical interfaces largely dispense with the need for writing and hide the *machine* from its users. To Kittler, this is activated on the level of hardware, wherein "so-called protection software has been implemented in order to prevent 'untrusted programs' or 'untrusted users' from any access to the operating system's kernel and input/output channels."[1] In such cases, the *means* are somewhat neglected for instrumental *ends* intent on implementing a certain degree of alienation from the production process. Part of the issue here lies in better expressing the processes that are running on a computer, and not least the relation between the writing, compiling and running of code, in order for the programmer and user to position themselves as an active part of the process.

There is nothing particularly unusual in this perspective. It draws upon a critical (and dialectical materialist) tradition to challenge the usual relations of production to reveal unevenness and lines of exploitation, based on a lack of transparency of process. In software production, the efforts of the programmer are often relatively hidden and remain subordinate to that of the end-product. As with the work of the programmer, the source code that lies behind software also remains relatively hidden and consequently difficult to consider as an integral part of the work of software, and indeed to consider as an interface in itself. In response, it is tempting to emphasise process rather than the product – not the object of software but the *means* of software. Indeed, software – often rather loosely described – is more than just the program and the activities of programming, it also includes a large amount of other material required for the program to run – and only when taken together can this be strictly referred to as software.

There are numerous examples of software art (not the artwork resulting from software but software *as* artwork) that have drawn attention to aspects and combinations of these activities. Aesthetic practices related to software have also drawn attention to the interface and interactions of coding, the code object and its execution – separately and together – stressing the means over ends. But clearly the relation is more complex than even the tendency (in critical work) to privilege means over ends. The aim of this paper is to go beyond this, using the example of live-coding, and explore (somewhat speculatively) the *means without end of software*.

Perhaps the relations are better articulated as dialectical. Walter Benjamin considered the relation between aesthetics and politics as such in order to stress that: "all efforts to render politics aesthetic culminate in one thing: war" (234). The suggestion of this essay is that a further engagement with the distinction between means and ends of software is similarly political (if not dialectical). One might think of the current intellectual property wars that characterise the production of software and culture in general – often referred to as 'softwar'. Again, citing Benjamin, on the one hand: "Only war makes it possible to mobilize all of today's technical resources while maintaining the property system" (234); and yet on the other, technology also demonstrates the potential to disrupt established property relations. This is indeed exemplified in the struggles over intellectual property and the 'dead end' of proprietary software.

For the most part, software compiles code into an executable version that 'locks-down' the source to protect proprietary interests, including intellectual and artistic capital. That the source code might be considered an integral part of the artwork, or even the artwork itself, remains outside the imagination or will of the software/art market, obsessed for the most part with conservative property rights. The trick of the software capitalist is to hide the content (or labour) under a deceptive form (the user interface), rather than to reveal the contradictions of value and hence divisions of labour involved in production.

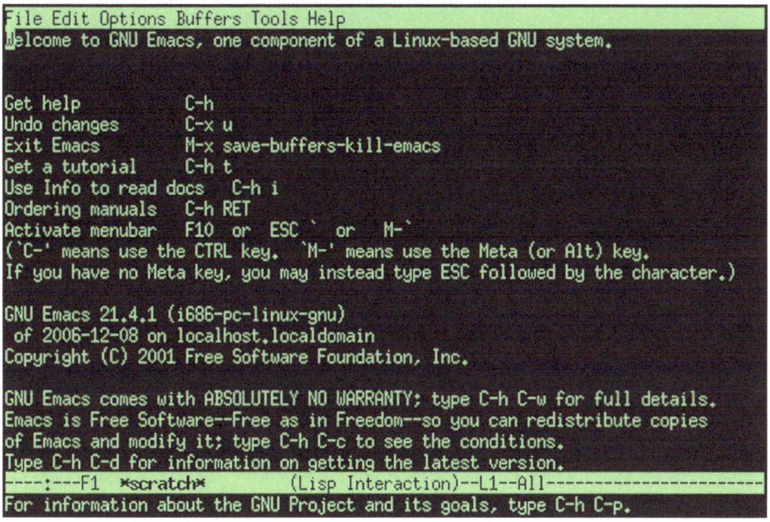

ILL. I: Launching GNU Emacs.[2]

The assumption I am making is that software performs a kind of work ('codework' if you prefer), and that social relations are expressed not simply between people but between people and machines (including technologies, institutions, and architectures). If software works, it can also be seen to express a kind of agency through its interactions with people (often referred to as 'machinic agency'). Source code promises action whether executed or not. This is somewhat verified in the ways that all kinds of work have become more like software, in the ways it is performed through collaborative and communicative networks (what the autonomists refer to as 'immaterial labour'). Consequently, the control of communications, and the machinic labour related to communications technologies, has become a key site of antagonism.

In software production, the contradictions that arise from free and open source principles are bound up with the way society by both encouraging and limiting software development: on the one hand by employing technical possibilities that facilitate free and easy information sharing, and on the other by exploiting commercial benefits through free labour and proprietary licensing. Cast in terms of means and ends, what is required to engage politics is to focus on the performative/communicative means itself and to make sure this remains in the public realm. The Italian philosopher Paolo Virno explains in *A Grammar of the Multitude*:

> If the publicness of the intellect does not yield to the realm of the public sphere, of a political space in which the many can tend to common affairs, then it produces terrifying effects (40).

With some of these ideas in mind, the essay explores the abstract relation between means and ends of software by making reference to interlinking ideas expressed in Hannah Arendt's essay "Labor, Work, Action," Virno's "Labor, Action, Intellect," and Giorgio Agamben's short collection of essays *Means Without End*. All make reference to Aristotle's claim, in his *Nichomachean Ethics*, that action is an end in itself: "For while making has an end other than itself, action cannot; for good action itself is its end" (quoted in Virno 52). For Agamben, the disruption of the false distinction between means-end presents the possibility of *means without end*. If there has been a tendency to think of software as a means to an end, how might we begin to conceive of it as a means without end? This is the means-end of this paper, so to speak.[3]

Means as end

The means, or the performative aspect, is what lies hidden behind the surface of software. This issue is made evident in Inke Arns's "Read_Me, Run_Me, Execute_Me" essay, suggesting that the performative dimension lies repressed in relation to code (her subtitle is "Software Art and its Discontents", which in itself makes a reference to Freud's "Civilisation and its Discontents"). Perhaps programming might offer therapeutic assistance in putting the programmer in touch with his/her, and indeed culture's, sublimated desires – that which is repressed under capitalism (to paraphrase Félix Guattari). That freedom of speech relates to relatively un-repressed free and open source software, is maybe one of the analogies that leads Arns to discuss software's performative dimension through its relation to speech-act theory. She is paraphrasing John Langshaw Austin's *How To Do Things With Words* to express "that language does not only have a descriptive, referential or constative function, but also possesses a performative dimension" (185).

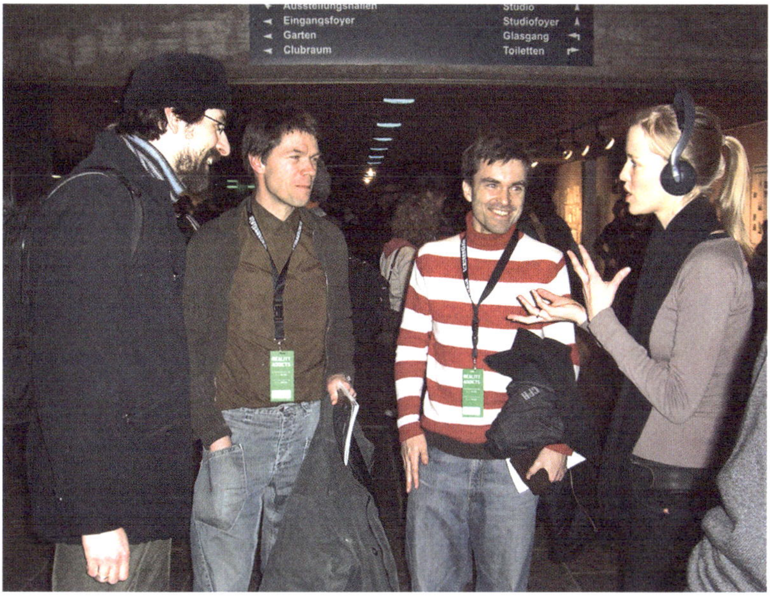

ILL. 2: **Christophe Bruno, *Human Browser* (2005).**

Speech is like program code in that it says something and does something (Arns 186).[4] Indeed, words determine actions and events, and there is something fundamentally performative in this. Also paraphrasing Austin, Virno says: "In the assertion 'I speak,' I *do* something by *saying* these words; moreover, I declare what it is that I do while I do it" (90). Virno's interest in speech emanates from how work is increasingly bound to speaking and the use of communications technologies (Christophe Bruno's *Human Browser* is a good example of a human-machine interface in this connection, see Ill. 2).[5] A software program is particularly articulate in this sense, as it both says something and acts upon the instruction in an efficient way. It is this sense of action that software art might exploit, by challenging the expectations of the normative action.

The emphasis on action in itself makes an important distinction from work or labour. This is what Hannah Arendt identifies in her essay "Labor, Work, Action" (from a lecture of 1964) to emphasise how labour (poiesis) and action (praxis) tend to be under-acknowledged in relation to work. Human labour is embedded in work only in as much as it is required to generate an income. Even in Marx's writings, Arendt maintains, labour is tied too firmly to work at the expense of action. The end product is as a result of a production process entirely separate from its possible uses – what Arendt calls "determined by the category of means and end" (175). Work is different from mere labour in which production and consumption are part of the same process like life itself (as both production and consumption are labour activities).[6] Emancipation of work from the workers is mainly possible when the worker is not merely a *tool-maker* but a labourer wherein the tools become part of the labouring process in itself (a machine in other words). Arendt's example is the deployment of labour-saving gadgets in the kitchen, gadgets in tune with the body or replicating the body's movements and rhythms (175). This would suggest that although software may perform work in itself, it cannot be considered labour unless tied to the labour and body of the programmer.

The important issue here is how software undermines established distinctions, in a similar way to how the work of art does not fit what Arendt describes as the *means-end* chain by not being useful and thereby resisting commodification (177). Although the assumption might be made that software is generally more useful than a mere work of art, the work of software art is more uncertain in this connection. In fact, much of software art is trying to break out of the commercial imperative to be useful to the market but also offers the potential to be useful outside of market forces.

For Arendt, human action (or praxis) lies in this realm of uncertainty as something that cannot be fully known but that is crucially bound up with the principle of freedom. Action is the ability to begin something new and as such the highest human achievement. Following Aristotle, Arendt's point is that action simply cannot be avoided. This is the case in her distinction between contemplation and action (what she refers to as *vita contemplativa* and *vita activa*), from which she concludes that an active life cannot be avoided (167). She explains that rather than think that all action ends in contemplation or that all contemplation necessarily leads to action, it is not possible to go through life without acting in it, whereas contemplation is optional.

Making reference to Arendt's essay forty years later, Virno confirms that the once unquestionable separation of labour (or poiesis), action (or praxis) and intellect has since dissolved. Whereas Arendt argued that politics imitates labour, he thinks the opposite, where labour imitates politics, or indeed that poiesis has taken on the appearance of praxis (50-1). That labour takes on the form of political action or, more to the point, has depoliticised action, exemplifies what Virno refers to as the current "crisis of politics, the sense of scorn surrounding political praxis today, the disrepute into which action has fallen" (51). He thinks that the purpose of any activity is increasingly found in the activity itself. Like Arendt, Virno further explains the point by making reference to Aristotle (also quoted earlier): "For while making has an end other than itself, action cannot; for good action [understood as ethical conduct and as political action, Virno adds] itself is its end" (52). Good action is required to break the means-end chain.

Drawing upon Arendt's observation that the performing arts have a strong affinity to politics, Virno explores action through the idea of *virtuosity* by looking at the special attributes of the performing artist. A performance is characterised by its lack of an end product, or at least a product that is indistinguishable from the performance itself. Virno further links virtuosity to speech as a phenomenon that has purpose in itself, that does not produce an end product independent of the act of speech and that operates in a publicly organised space. In saying this, he is affirming that labour itself is performative as it is bound to speaking and the use of communications technologies (or in this context is software-like, perhaps). He continues: "It is enough to say, for now, that contemporary production becomes 'virtuosic' (and thus political) precisely because it includes within itself linguistic experience as such" (56).[7]

Virno asks: "What is the *score* which the virtuosos-workers perform? What is the script of their linguistic-communicative *performances?*" (63). The answer is bound to the concept of 'general intellect' as the "know-how on which social productivity relies", as an "attribute of living labour" (64-5).[8] Know-how refers to the ways in which workers learn skills but also to the rules of social behaviour by which labour-power is reproduced and abused. The script, score and source code for this is not determined and does not have an end product in sight. In this way, the script, score, or source code can be considered uncertain, indeterminate and thereby full of radical potential. If potential is largely commodified under capitalism, then logic demands that positive potential must remain without end product, remain in the public realm (free and open) and remain performative – without end.[9]

Means

A performance operates in real-time and has its own sense of purpose or fulfilment, in parallel to the way that a computer program undermines the distinction between its function as a score and its performance (something Florian Cramer has previously referred to) (18-24).[10] In such a case, the score is *not* detached from the performance – or the program code from its potential action (even if only executed on a metaphoric level). It would appear that many of the attributes associated with virtuosity that Virno outlines could be applied to programmers who are required to demonstrate their technical and cultural agility in a social context. In the area of livecoding, programmers make music in keeping with the expressive qualities of live performance, by coding in real-time (using the command line interface, for example):

> Live coding is where computer programming becomes performance art; improvising a performance using a programming language. This is made possible by the dynamic programming languages at the heart of all live coding environments. Sections of code are interpreted and added to a running program, so that a musician may enact thematic changes without a break in the sound. Thus the usual design-implement-test development cycle is discarded in favour of immediate actions and reactions more suited to creative exploration.[11]

There is a certain transparency of process, and performances present the source code for public display. TOPLAP (Temporary Organisation for the Promotion of Live Algorithm Programming) has established some working principles in this respect, and (quoting from their manifesto) explain:

> Code should be seen as well as heard [...] Performance involves continu[a] of interaction, covering perhaps the scope of controls with respect to the parameter space of the artwork, or gestural content, particularly directness of expressive detail.[12]

In live-coding performances, the intention is to open up what would otherwise seem to be determinate processes of how music is generated. Any resulting sense of improvisation relies on a predictive understanding of complex processes and an awareness of the transformative potential of code. In this sense, it breaks out of the means-end chain of following instructions without interpretation (and as live music, some of the post-production issues associated with recording, distribution and the market). The intervention of the programmer allows for a less deterministic approach and openness to other transformative possibilities, such as the possible and often unpredictable actions that result when a program runs, including the return of errors.

In the case of live coding performances, human-machine agency is foregrounded. The program performs the music with the programmer, both relaying instructions and acting upon them in a more uncertain way. In "Real DJs Code Live", Alex McLean explains:

> By describing a musical idea in code, we're describing it at a higher level than if we're entering notes into a sequencer [...] I've tried sequencers and found it a slow, difficult, maddening way of doing music. There's an atmosphere of musicians being subservient to software. It really limits the kind of music that can be made. [...] Live coding places the human right back in the creative process so you can't really call it "computer-generated" any more (quoted in Andrews).

Any sense of agency assigned to code relies on the relation of "code's existence as both expression and process" (Mackenzie 141). Arguably, live-coding goes further as the act of coding becomes a prototype for its further action; what Adrian Mackenzie calls "an entity that the code-index is held to represent" for software in general (his example is 'extreme programming'). In this way, coding work – writing, compiling, and running code – comes to represent software as a whole. Code becomes privileged in a way that is simultaneously a simplification of the process and at the same time a challenge to the normative relations of software production and its further usage. Mackenzie clarifies the point:

> Making code and coding into a prototype for software production seems very recursive, but in terms of the contestations of agency associated with software, the primacy of coding can be seen as asserting the identity of programmers as the originators of software (141).

Software remains unfinished in socio-technical terms, and without end. To Mackenzie, the 'performativity of code' challenges the commercial imperative of software development and also the social relations associated with this. Like the work it does, the coding performance disrupts the false distinction between "coding as form and code as force" (178).

The performativity of the code object is characterised in this way by Mackenzie, making reference to the Linux operating system. The Linux kernel has a particularly unstable relation to commodified software and hardware as the most pervasive example of free/open source software development (taking the file and process of the Unix-like operating system) and through the enforcement of its GNU General Public License.[13]

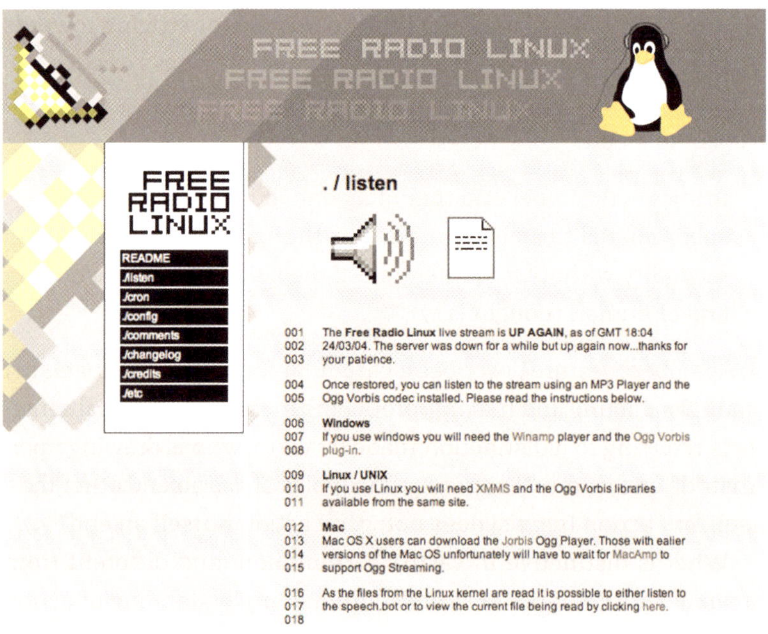

ILL. 3: *Free Radio Linux* by r a d i o q u a l i a (2001).

Free and open source software development is enacted through an ongoing collective and collaborative labouring process. As a socio-technical description of performance, Mackenzie describes Linux as a performative speech act that produces an uncertain relation between the code object (the Linux kernel) and the code subject (the programmers), and thus challenges its property relations and corporate relations of production (13). To Mackenzie, Radioqualia's *Free Radio Linux* is a performance in this sense: The source code of the Linux kernel (the core component of the GNU/Linux operating system) was webcast over the Internet, using a speech synthesizer to convert the 4,141,432 lines of code into talk radio. Thus Linux can be seen to demonstrate collective social action, or as a positive implementation of general intellect in Virno's terms. It disrupts the false distinction between means and ends.

Means without ends

In "Notes on Politics," Agamben explores the consequences of the disruption of means and ends. With reference to what he calls "being-generic" (or the common), he asserts that the expression of politics is reliant on the "free use of the common and as sphere of pure means" (118). He refers to the mistake of striving towards "finality without means" or a higher end (of happiness or equality) as much as the mistake of imagining process or mediality only with respect to an end:

> Politics is the sphere neither of an end in itself nor of means subordinated to an end; rather, it is the sphere of a pure mediality without end intended as the field of human action and of human thought (117).

To Agamben, gesture describes a particular form of action that is set apart from acting and making/producing in the conventional sense. He is referring to a distinction made by Varro, who is drawing upon Aristotle once more: "For production [poiesis] has an end other than itself, but action [praxis] does not; good action is itself an end" (57).

What is distinctive in Varro's formulation (and different from previous interpretations) is the additional understanding of action associated with gesture that is neither a means to an end (production), nor an end without means (praxis). The claim is that gesture disrupts the false distinction between means-ends and occupies mediality itself:

> *The gesture is the exhibition of a mediality: it is the process of making a means visible as such.* It allows the emergence of the being-in-a-medium of human beings and thus it opens the ethical dimension for them (58).

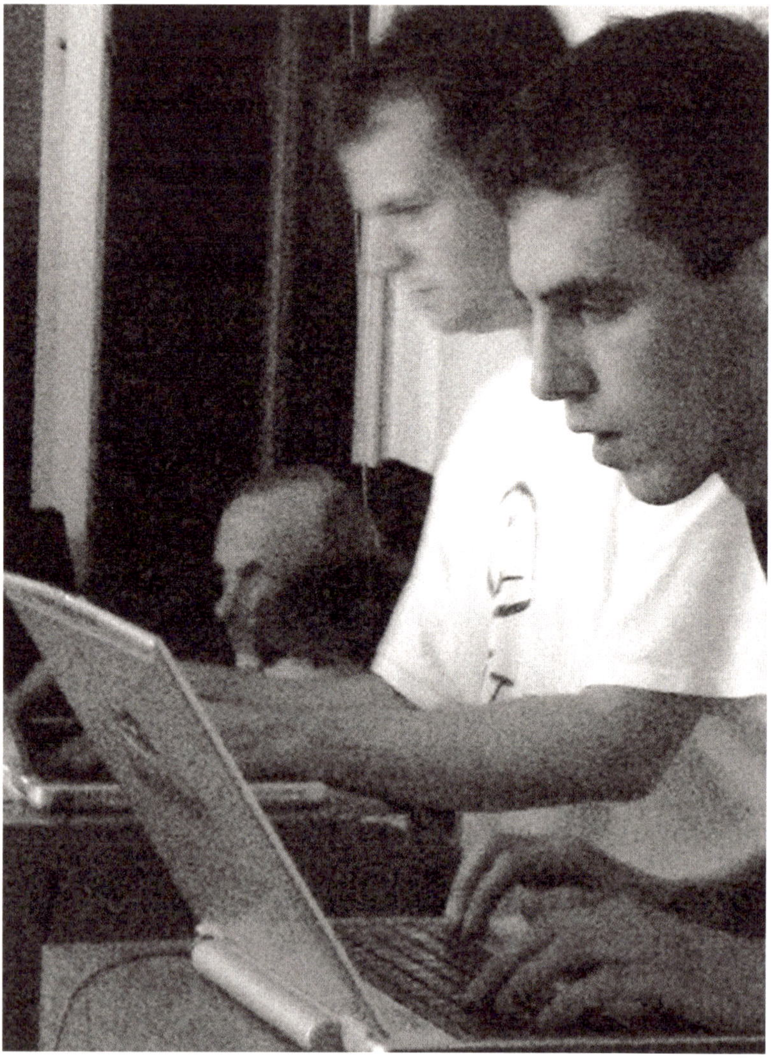

ILL.4: slub, live coding performance.

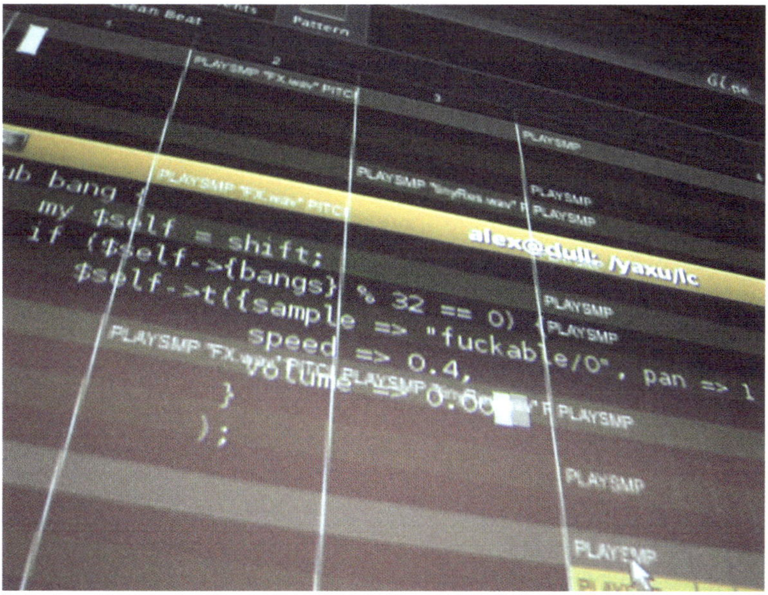

ILL. 5: **slub, projected screen during performance.**

Gesture also evokes a live coding performance – making means apparent and embodied and describes a mediality that breaks down the distinction between the means and ends, in as much as the score is not detached from its performance. On a formal level, live coding demonstrates a tendency towards a disruption of the false distinction between the means-end of software and the possibility of imagining software process or mediality without end. Sadly, what appears repressed in live coding is the ethical dimension. Yet, there is an emerging discourse around live coding, not least developed at the *LOSSLivecode2007* festival and subsequent events (incidentally, L.O.S.S. stands for Linux Open Source Sound Project, established to encourage and promote music created with open source software and the Linux operating system). The call for the festival read as follows:

> 'Live Coding' is the creation of software while it is being executed; the software in turn generating music or video. Thanks to dynamic programming languages, the live coder is able to

> modify and extend their program without restarts, their music and/or visuals growing with the code that describes it. This way of working allows instant results for every sourcecode edit. Programming becomes a fast, creative process – expressive enough that a whole audio/visual performance may be created *as software* [my emphasis].[14]

Software in this inclusive sense expresses dynamic interactions at the level of language itself – as good action – and the event of language is political in as much as it relates to the free use of pure means. This lies in the realm of language in terms of the act of speaking (evoking free software as in free speech, not free beer): "the act itself of speaking" (Agamben 115).

Similarly, live coding expresses its means at the level of embodied communication or speech – as prototypical software – with code and coding challenging normative socio-technical relations, expressing a form of agency and asserting the value of human intervention. Rather than software cast as a means to an end (its functional application), or an end without means (closed-off, locked down by commercial imperatives), this practice comes close to what Agamben describes as the "sphere of a pure and endless mediality" (59). In terms of the aesthetics of the interface, the suggestion is to conceive of occupying the interface (or, as others have suggested, of thinking about interfacing as an active state). The essay advocates the development of software practices that disrupt the false distinction between function and further use in this way: that do not make the mistake of striving towards ends without means or the mistake of imagining means only with respect to an end. Instead, the argument is for the possibility of software without ends.

End

Notes

1. Kittler is referring to his own previous work, "Protected Mode" (33-44). In "There is No Software," Kittler sees these tendencies (of the graphical user interface) as a rejection of the principles of the Turing machine in identifying hardware as an algorithm for computation. To Kittler, this is a commercial imperative occluding his belief that software does not exist as a machine-independent faculty. This simplification makes recent work in software art that does not require a computer all the more important, if not radical.
2. GNU Emacs is an extensible, customisable text editor — here launched from the interface of the UNIX terminal. See <http://www.gnu.org/software/emacs/>.
3. This chapter is a further elaboration of my earlier essay "Software Actions", in Joasia Krysa (ed.). *Curating Immateriality*. New York: Autonomedia 2006. 69-79.
4. The performative aspect of speech is evidently social and context-bound, broadly differentiated in linguistic studies as the distinction between syntactic and semantic realms – emphasising the performance (or 'parole') that is generated from the rules ('langue'). Software art is concerned with both, but arguably places emphasis on the performative aspect according to recent commentaries.
5. In Bruno's *Human Browser*, a human actor, using wireless headphones, hears a text-to-speech audio that comes directly from the Internet in real-time, and simply speaks the words.
6. Broadly describing the same activity, the distinction between work and labour is hard to fathom: Arendt quotes Locke: "the labor of our body and the work of our hands" (170). Arendt points out that most European languages make similar distinctions: 'arbeiten' and 'werken' in German; 'laborare' and 'fabricari' in Latin; 'ponein' and 'ergazesthai' in Greek. It seems that the human body is given over to labour, the reproductive process, the biological and the link to the human organism (even the pains of birth are associated, of course). Thus labouring is tied closely to the cycles of life itself, and consumption in a general sense, indeed it "corresponds to the condition of life itself" (172).
7. For more on virtuosity, see Virno's "Virtuosity and Revolution: The Political Theory of Exodus."
8. The source of the concept 'general intellect' is a section in Marx's *Grundrisse* called "Fragment on Machines" written in 1857-8, in which he describes that at a certain point in capitalist development, real wealth will be measured not on labour time in production but on technological expertise and organisation. The autonomists, like Virno, use the term to describe the ways that technical expertise and socialised labour work together. This demonstrates both positive and negative tendencies, both releasing and limiting possibilities for future transformation.
9. That action might operate without end evokes Theodor Adorno's comments in his essay "On the Fetish Character in Music and the Regression of Listening," but here the emphasis is different again. To Adorno, the score is partly a purer form, more closely associated with production that affirms use value, rather than the exchange value of the performance itself. In the former, the listener is encouraged to become a producer by executing the score, and in the latter, a consumer of the commodity form of music. In this sense, use-value is privileged over exchange-value.
10. Although program code is like other so-called 'natural' languages, there are crucial differences in that words of natural languages do not generally do what they say. On the other hand, artificial languages generally do – they tend towards a means to an end – with execution determined by the code. Here, I am referring to software that disrupts this distinction at the level of the interface.

11. See <http://www.elec.qmul.ac.uk/researchopenday/>.

An alternative definition is given on Wikipedia:

"Live coding (sometimes known as interactive programming, on-the-fly programming, just in time programming) is the name given to the process of writing software in realtime as part of a performance. Historically, this technique has been around since computers were used to produce early computer art, but recently it has been explored as a more rigorous alternative to laptop DJs who, live coders often feel, lack the charisma and pizzazz of musicians performing live." <http://en.wikipedia.org/wiki/Live_coding>.

To give more detail to its history:

"Live Coding began during the 1980s, primarily with FORTH and Lisp. In recent years new live coding environments and languages such as Chuck, Fluxus, Impromptu and SuperCollider 3 have appeared, with enthusiastic communities growing around them. Live Coding performances have also used PureData, Scheme, Perl, Haskell, Ruby, Python..."

<http://livecode.access-space.org/>.

12. See <http://toplap.org/index.php/ManifestoDraft>.

TOPLAP was formed in 2004 to support open dialog between live coders. On the web site <http://toplap.org/>, the acronym is defined more playfully: (Temporary|Transnational|Terrestrial|Transdimensional) Organisation for the (Promotion|Proliferation|Permanence|Purity) of Live (Algorithm|Audio|Art|Artistic) Programming.

13. See <http://en.wikipedia.org/wiki/Linux_kernel>.

14. *LOSSLivecode2007* festival, held in Sheffield UK, 20-22 July 2007, in association with Access Space, TOPLAP and lurk <http://livecode.access-space.org/>.

Works cited

Adorno, Theodor. "On the Fetish Character in Music and the Regression of Listening." *The Culture Industry: Selected Essays on Mass Culture*. Ed. J.M. Bernstein. London: Routledge, 1991. 26-52. Print.

Andrews, Robert. "Real DJs Code Live." *Wired*, 07 March 2006. Web. 12 Aug. 2010. <http://www.wired.com/science/discoveries/news/2006/07/71248>.

Arendt, Hannah. "Labor, Work, Action" (from a Lecture 1964). *The Portable Hannah Arendt*. New York: Penguin, 2000. 167-181. Print.

Aristotle's *Nichomachean Ethics*, VI, 1140 b q.

Arns, Inke. "Read_Me, Run_Me, Execute_Me: Software and its Discontents, or: it's The Performativity of Code, Stupid." *Read_Me: Software Art & Cultures*. (Edition 2004). Eds. Olga Goriunova and Alexei Shulgin. Aarhus: Digital Aesthetics Research Centre, University of Aarhus, 2004. 176-193. Print.

Austin, John Langshaw. *How to Do Things with Words*. Cambridge: Harvard University Press, 1962. Print.

Benjamin, Walter. *The Work of Art in the Age of Mechanical Reproduction*. [1936]. Trans. Harry Zohn. *Illuminations*. London: Pimlico, 1999. Print.

Cramer, Florian. "Concepts, Notations, Software Art." *Software Art: Thoughts, Read_me festival 1.2*, catalogue. Eds. Olga Goriunova and Alexei Shulgin. Moscow: Rosizo, State Centre for Museums and Exhibitions, 2002. 18-24. Print.

Giorgio Agamben. *Means Without End: Notes on Politics*. Trans. Vincenzo Binetti and Cesare Casarino [1992]. Minneapolis: University of Minnesota Press, 2000. Print.

Kittler, Friedrich. "There is no Software," *CTheory* (1995). Web. 12 Aug. 2010. <http://www.ctheory.net/text_file.asp?pick=74> (also in Timothy Druckery (ed.). *Electronic Culture*. New York: Aperture, 1996. Print).

– "Protected Mode." *Computer, Macht und Gegenwehr. InformatikerInnen für eine andere Informatik*. Eds. Ute Bernhardt and Ingo Ruhmann. Bonn, 1991. 34-44. Print.

Mackenzie, Adrian. *Cutting Code: Software and Sociality*. New York: Peter Lang, 2006. Print.

Virno, Paulo. *A Grammar of the Multitude: For an Analysis of Contemporary Forms of Life*. Trans. Isabella Bertoletti, James Cascaito and Andrea Casson. New York: Semiotext(e), 2004. 40. Print.

– "Virtuosity and Revolution: The Political Theory of Exodus." Trans. Ed Emery. *Radical Thought in Italy*. Eds. Paolo Virno and Michael Hardt. Minneapolis: University of Minnesota Press, 1996. 188-209. Print.

Poesis of Human-Computer Interaction
Music, Materiality and Live Coding

BY MORTEN BREINBJERG

In this article, I will discuss contemporary approaches to music composition and performance rooted in a poesis of human-computer interaction. This will be a poesis belonging neither to humans nor nature alone, which the classical understanding of poesis as either 'techne' or 'physis' implies. Instead, it is founded on human beings interacting with computers and utilising the ability of computers to carry out tasks of their own in accordance with a specified 'logic of decision' written in a program.

Central to my discussion is the idea of software as artistic material and programming as an artistic act, and how this changes the practices of music composition and performance.

The focus of this discussion of the poesis of human-computer interaction is not on intelligent machines, the potential of artificial intelligence, or the use of computers to edit recorded music as often seen in popular music software packages. It is rather to investigate an approach to music composition and performance that explores the interactive and algorithmic nature of modern computers, and at the same time reflect on how this changes the way in which music is being composed and performed, i.e. conceptualised, prescribed and executed.

I will start by looking at two examples. The first is ixi software, a new approach to screen-based instrument design; and the second is live coding, a new performance-based art form. Although ixi software is a project of development and live coding an art form, both of them emphasise the materiality of software and human-computer interaction as a complex and mediated process. So while they *prima facie* seem very different in their approach to music composition, they distinguish themselves from other contemporary approaches that use the computer as a music automaton, a simulator (e.g. fractal music) or a remediated interface (Bolter and Grusin).

ixi software

ixi Connector is "a screen-based interface for musical performance on computers" (Magnusson 162) that can be downloaded from www.ixi-audio.net. It uses generative algorithms in the form of first-order Markov chains[1] to decide how *actors* move around in a network of *connectors*. As can be seen in Ill. 1, the network looks almost like a plumbing system of interconnected pipelines. Networks of greater or lesser complexity can be designed by patching together connectors of different shapes and with different numbers of outlets. Up to eight actors can simultaneously move around inside the network, and probability charts decide which route they will take. For each actor a sound volume and a tempo (the time lag between moving from one connector to another) can be set. When actors enter a connector either a sound sample is played or a midi note is sent to an external synthesizer. Beside the shape and the probability chart, properties of the individual connector encompass sound, sound pitch, sound volume, and midi note and midi volume. In the words of its designer, the ixi Connector is, like other ixi interfaces, a pattern-generating machine (Magnusson 165).

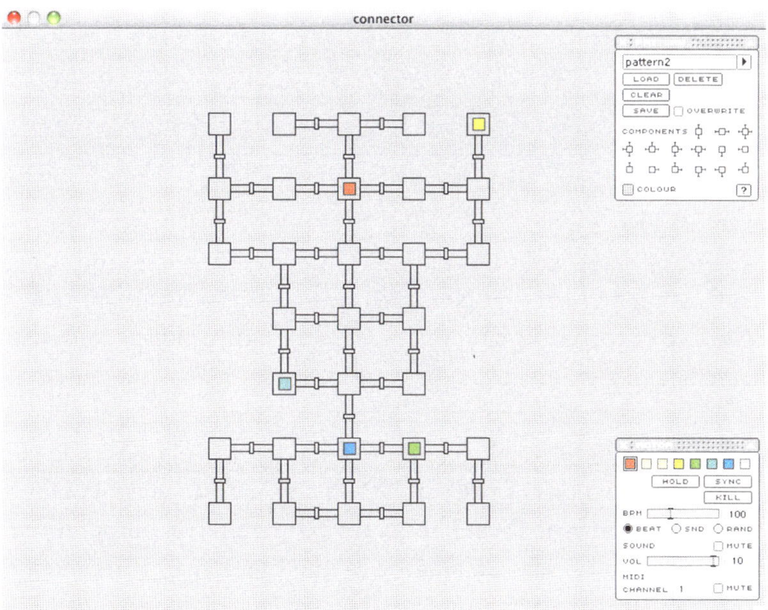

ILL. 1: The interface of ixi Connector.

Connector is being developed as part of an experimental research project called the *ixi software project*, led by Thor Magnusson and Enrike Hurtado Mendieta. The project develops prototypes for screen-based musical instruments, and started in 2000 as a critical response to the interface and interaction design of commercial music software. Unlike ixi, commercial music software is primarily designed to edit recorded music, which is then synchronised, juxtaposed and layered on separate tracks, and organised sequentially on a time line. The interfaces of commercial software are typically well known from the use of earlier music media technologies like multi-track tape recorders, effect units and mixers and standard music notation, and in general they simulate the workflow and technologies of analogue studio production. These older media technologies are now represented, or rather remediated, in the software's graphical user interface.

In ixi Connector, as in all of the prototypes of ixi software, we are faced with a reification of musical ideas that are different from commercial music software. In ixi Connector there are no time lines, no tracks and no linear sequencing. Instead, music composition is conceptualised as consecutive choices among different possibilities and as a result of interactions among different elements in a system. In addition, traditional elements of graphical user interfaces like buttons, knobs and sliders are avoided, although floating palettes and drop-down menus are used.

The aim of the ixi software project is to avoid remediation of traditional musical tools and thereby the ways in which music is conceptualised in those technologies. That is why the project inscribes itself in an avant-garde tradition of music, seeing new technology as a way of subverting, or at least getting around, the historical understanding of music, as well as the constraining practices of music composition and production present in commercial music software.

Live coding

Live coding is a rather new performance-based art form in which sound/music or visual expressions are programmed during performance. As stated by the software artist and musician Adrian Ward: "Live coding is the activity of writing (parts of) a program while it runs" (Ward et al. 243). Staged, and with their laptop screens project-

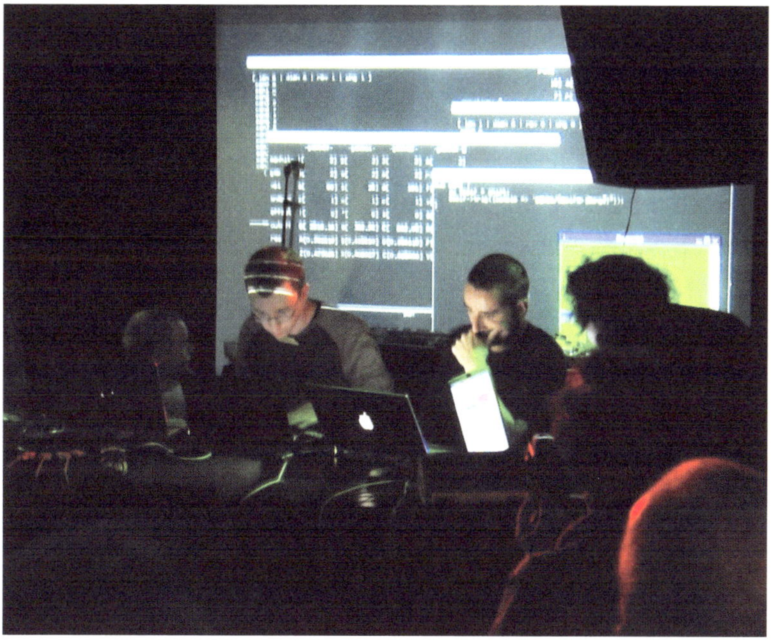

ILL. 2: **Live coding performance, ReadMe 2004.**

ed so that the audience can see the program being written, live coders perform their music while formulating and describing algorithms, typically in a textual, interpreted programming language as can be seen in Ill. 2.

In addition, as can be seen in Figure 2, transparency is an important aspect of live coding performances. The action of the performer, what he/she writes and manipulates, as well as the machine program and the interaction between the two, must be visible. As a result, the "code should be seen as well as heard" so that the intention of the coder can be followed and the processes carried out by the machine understood (Ward et al. 247).

Taking advantage of computers as algorithmic machines using often dedicated programming languages for music composition, live coders avoid the remediated interface of commercial music software. Instead, they seek access to the machine in a way that is more in line with its nature. Controlling the flow of data, defining criteria for selection and iteration at run-time, they use the full potential of the machine (Collins 322). As hinted at by composer and computer music researcher Nick Collins, the use of programming languages results in a greater freedom of expression since the constraints and ideological understandings of music contained in the rigid metaphors of commercial music software can be transcended. Instead, a programming language allows musicians to take advantage of the algorithmic nature of the computer and – most important of all – its programmability.

Although significant differences between the use of ixi software and programming languages exist, ixi designers and live coders express commonalities in their view on software and in their approach to music performance and composition. Both react against the rigid metaphors of commercial music software interfaces and the way in which they normally allow computers to be interacted with.

Their ideal of software interaction is rooted in qualities specific for computers, i.e. algorithmic calculations, randomness, generativity and programmability, among other things. These are qualities that permit music to be composed and generated in real time by rules written in the code of the software; rules that allow music to emerge and unfold differently, depending on the way in which the parameters are set and interpreted, both by the user operating the software and the software program itself. Unlike in commercial music software, it is no longer the ability to edit music that is being explored but rather the ability to create music in a mediated context of writing, reading and executing algorithmic procedures. This aspect, alongside a genuine interest in the nature of the software itself, defines the central part of the aesthetic endeavour taking place.

In addition, they share a view on software as more than a tool. Both ixi software and software for live coding may be regarded by analogy to musical instruments, but they can never be understood instrumentally, that is as simple means to obtain musical goals. As stated by Adrian Ward et al., live coding "deeply connects algorithmic causality with perceived outcome and by deconstructing the idea of the temporal dichotomy of tool and product it allows code to be brought into play as an artistic process" (244). As such, code is more than just a tool for making software work and music play; code itself becomes an object of interest and a part of the materiality that is being explored. Hence coding becomes an expressive act.

Likewise, Thor Magnusson (165), referring to the concepts of Michel Beaudouin-Lafon, explains that ixi software cannot be categorised as simply an interaction instrument because it is already a musical instrument in its own right.[2] In Magnusson's understanding, music results from a mutual semiosis of software and user. As such, the user becomes just another actor of a semiotic system that already includes the ixi instrument. Thereby, the software and the user engage in an act of communication that challenges the normal hierarchy of human and technology and regards the tool concept of technology as inadequate.

Both live coding and ixi software invite us to consider the conditions in which music is composed and performed by exploring and staging another relation of human-computer interaction. A relation that builds upon the basic characteristics of the machine (the computer as a machine), primarily its speed of execution, generative and programmable nature, and which regards these features as fundamental for the making of art/music. In doing so, live coding can be said to "acknowledge the conditions of its own making – its poesis" (Cox 161).

Poesis

The ancient Greeks made a distinction between two kinds of poesis, i.e. two kinds of ways in which things come into being. The first, labelled *techne*, refers to that which is made by humans; the second, labelled *physis*, refers to that which is made by nature. In "The Question Concerning Technology" from 1953, Martin Heidegger discusses this distinction in relation to modern technology and explains that *physis* is a kind of becoming of something out of itself as opposed to *techne*, which is a becoming of things by someone else, for instance an artist or a craftsman.

In the realm of *techne*, the human hand actively creates things with the help of technology. Technology can therefore be seen as a means to an end, leading to an understanding of technology that Heidegger refers to as instrumental (5). As an instrument, technology is used in the process of bringing forth or rather, as Heidegger puts it, in the process of revealing. In the context of modern technology, Heidegger claims that it cannot be understood simply as instrumental since modern technology orders humans to bring forth and reveal in a certain way, which includes regarding nature as a standing reserve, i.e. as something controllable that can be transformed and regulated.

What concerns Heidegger is that although it is correct that technology in some sense is instrumental (a means to an end) and also causal, this does not define its nature. What characterises its nature or what is true about (modern) technology is that it challenges or requests us as humans to reveal nature as a standing reserve. Hence we are no longer the masters of technology, since technology forms the basis of our conception of nature: a conception that is deeply rooted in virtues of modern science, e.g. formalisation, rationalisation and efficiency. As a consequence, the clear distinction between humans as subject and technology as object, which is inherent in an understanding of technology as tools, has to be abandoned, including the idea of our control over technology. Technology is not something we can deselect, it is something we live through and as such it becomes a condition of life. Consequently, the essence of technology is not something technical – a technological artefact – it is a way of living, perceiving and acknowledging. So to understand the essence of modern technology we must, according to Heidegger, recognise how technology orders the way in which we bring forth and reveal, and he himself points to art as the place where the truth of technology can be revealed (35).[3]

Tools and machines

Regarding classical categories of technology, tools are easily understood within an instrumental understanding of technology since a tool is considered to be an artefact that is under full control and used for producing and/or converting materials. As a tool, technology holds no value in itself. Its value relates only to the goal and the activity that it serves and fulfils. The operator is the driving force behind the tool and as such he or she is in command, although of course it can be said that the inherent functionality and design of the tool frame the possibility of actions. Nonetheless, humans are supposed to be superior and can, as masters, pick or choose.

But other categories of technology, like automata and media, challenge the tool metaphor as well as the instrumental understanding of technology. An automaton is considered to be an artefact "that can perform some reasonably complicated process that ends in a desired state (e.g. having produced a certain product) without human interference, although humans may need to provide its material, set its controls, and start it" (Andersen 184). A medium (the radio, the newspaper, the television etc.) is considered to be an artefact used for communication. As such, it can be understood both as a communication channel and a communication environment – but also as a language of its own (Meyrowitz).

According to the American philosopher Lewis Mumford, "the difference between tools and machines lies primarily in the degree of automatism they have reached" (10). The tool is less independent in the sense that it works in accordance with the motive and the skill of its operator. Therefore, automation invokes the aspect of autonomy since a machine can perform actions independent of human interference and without demanding a continuous input of human energy. As a consequence of the autonomy of the machine, a gulf between humans and technology opens up. Now humans are no longer the necessary executing force, and this changes their relation to technology. They no longer need to have knowledge of the way in which the machine is performing, or knowledge of how to create and perform the work of the machine. Their competences need only cover the ability to configure, monitor and adjust the machine, and to evaluate and interpret the quality of its output in accordance with certain more or less specified criteria: for instance, personal taste or more formalised criteria such as rules of good voice leading when talking about music.

Discussing the culture of simulation, media researcher Norbert Bolz argues that the role of the artist has changed from realising ideas to exploring and choosing from what the generative method (the machine) produces (177). Following Bolz's argument, the workflow of human-machine interaction would be one in which the machine is configured, its parameters set and adjusted during its performance, and the output (music, images, texts) evaluated alongside its production. If it is not satisfactory, the machine is reconfigured and/or its parameters retuned. As such, the result of the creative process that Bolz describes originates in a human-machine symbiosis.

Human-computer interaction: searching for the truth of the machine

In "The Apparatus World – a World Unto Itself," the artist and curator Peter Weibel discusses automation in relation to art and subsequently the way in which automation in the form of machine-supported art, from the photo camera to the computer, "uncovers the fiction that art is a human place, a place for human creativity, unique individuality" (18). To stage his argument, Weibel refers to the British inventor Fox Talbot's remarks on the photo camera in a letter from 1839, quoting Talbot for saying "that by means of this device [the photo camera] it is no longer the artist who makes the picture but it is the picture that makes itself. The artist does not have to do more than set up the device in front of the object, the picture of which he wants" (17).

Although Talbot explicitly recognises that the picture is no longer a (sole) result of the artistic subject, Weibel condemns him for taking into consideration the "ideological resistance to the exclusion of the subject" when naming his book on photography *The Pencil of Nature* and not *The Pencil of Machine*, as Weibel believes it should have been titled. Refusing to acknowledge the creativity of the autonomous machine, the "sovereignty of the bourgeois subject remained untouched", Weibel claims (8).

Underlying Weibel's critique of Talbot is the question of whether art can be externalised. According to Weibel, the photo camera, as an autonomous producer of images, abolishes the definition of the author as the "one and only god of creation" (17). Following the technological development from the photo camera to the modern computer, Weibel describes how the image becomes automatically generated, transmitted, set in motion, manipulated and finally also calculated by machines. As a consequence, machines create autonomous worlds of sounds and images. At the beginning of the 20th century, art (painting) turned its back on representation and focused on the autonomy of its own materiality (its intrinsic laws and qualities). Likewise, the machine-generated and machine-calculated picture of today adheres only to its own logic, referencing to a semiotic relation (or a semiotic aesthetics as Weibel calls it) of medium, sign and virtuality. The image no longer represents a world or truth beyond itself, instead it produces its own.

Following Weibel in his critique of Talbot, the temptation to understand machine-based art in relation to the creative power of nature (physis), as the title of Talbot's book suggests, should be avoided. Otherwise it leaves the role of the creative subject unchallenged and prevents the nature of machine-based and (I would like to add) human-machine-based art from being discussed and understood. According to Weibel, the machine is already autonomously producing pictures, images, sounds etc. pointing to the fact that the subject (the author) is no longer a sole foundation for the creation of art. It is therefore necessary that we recognise the creative potential of the autonomous machine in order to understand the kind of art it can produce and particularly what the implications are for the way in which art is normally produced (*techne*), as well as the way in which we, through art, comprehend and understand the 'Apparatus World' around us. If we fail to acknowledge the importance of the machine, and if we (like Talbot) regard it in the light of nature, then its meaning remains unrecognised because we willingly accept nature as fundamentally inscrutable.

Perhaps even worse, the consequence of Talbot's act is that nature and the power of its creativity is understood within a technological context. This leads to taking a picture that we believe is of nature, whereas in fact it is a picture of what nature looks like when we look at it through the optics of technology. Referring to Heidegger, we could say that it is a picture of nature ordered by technology and therefore conceptualised in its image.

Live coding and ixi software explicitly admit the importance of the machine and ask for its essence in the context of composing and performing music. In doing so, and following the call of Heidegger and Weibel, they distinguish themselves from other computer-based music practices that utilise the computer as either a music automaton (generative music), a simulator (e.g. fractal music), or a remediated interface. In the last case the computer is used as though music today is still produced on the premises of the analogue music studio.

Ironically, regarding the practice of computer music composition, we find that *physis* continues to be an inspiration for many composers and musicians dealing with simulation and generative algorithms based on mathematical descriptions of natural phenomena. In their approach, music, like a flower, arises from within itself in accordance with enclosed rules of becoming, and as such it 'makes itself'. Using statistical distribution functions, fractal geometry, cellular automata, game theory etc., their interest in processes of creation outside the human reconnect art and nature in a way that somehow could be regarded as a search for 'the pencil of nature'. This is indicated by, for example, Brian Eno's metaphorical understanding of generative music: "Ordinary music is like engineering, where everything is built according to a plan, and it is the same every time you play it. Generative music is more like gardening; you plant a seed, and it grows different every time you plant" (Shachtman).

Commenting on Eno's comparison of generative music with the sowing of seeds, Adrian Ward et al. underline that in live coding the idea is not to produce music automatons (music machines) from which an endless stream of music can flow independently of human interaction. Instead they "advocate the humanization of generative music, where code isn't left alone to meander through its self-describing soundscape, but is hacked together, chopped up and moulded to make live music" (246). In live coding it is recognised that music unfolds in a process of human-machine interaction, on the terms of the machine, i.e. formalisation and algorithmic descriptions, and by choosing from, configuring, monitoring, re-writing and adjusting the machine.

Distributed agency

In the writings of Adrian Ward and Thor Magnusson it is underlined that music arises in a complex relation of coder/performer and software. Both of them are 'actors' in a larger system of interacting elements. In a recent article, media artist and researcher Julian Rohrhuber explains equally that interactive programming is not so much a question of control (the programmer's/subject's control over the software/tool/object) but rather a question of a 'distributed agency', meaning that the realisation of a satisfying musical output is not the "result of a random coincidence, but of the way in which program-text, synthesis process, sound and perception interact" (Rohrhuber 455). As interacting elements, the computer and the computer user enter a cybernetic loop of input/output, control, regulation and mutual communication, becoming involved in a continuous process of acting out in which the user communicates on behalf of his knowledge and experience, and the computer on behalf of its data and its program, which as a model portrays a certain 'world' with its own rules (Rohrhuber). The point is that in the context of live coding every aspect (user knowledge and experience, computer program and data) is dynamic and interacting.

Discussing digital poetry in comparison with printed text, N. Katherine Hayles argues that the poem is not only a distributed phenomenon consisting of data files, algorithmic structures, executable software and hardware, but also an interactive artefact that is significantly modified and determinated in a readerly and writerly process. Referencing Loss Pequeño Glazier and John Cayley, Hayles claims that programming is writing and that writing is exactly "a concrete act of making", and not a process in which the text, as a preconceptualised idea, is dressed in language (184). To write is to engage with the formal qualities of language that are the materiality of the medium, "whether or not it serves other ends", in a digital context that includes algorithmic declarations, procedures, protocols, software/hardware interactions, input/output configurations etc. (183).

Returning to live coding, we can see that we are dealing with a literary approach to music composition that reflects the literacy of computer programming and thereby its processual nature, i.e. the eventness of the act. While we could say that digital media in general move art into the domain of time, as when Hayles speaks of the digital text as an event more than an object, we have to remember that music per se is a time-based art form which also (due to music notation) has a long history of literacy. However, this literary tradition was broken by the appearance of analogue recording technology in the 20th century, which reified sound and made it an object of phenomenological investigations. As such, sound was no longer just a phenomenon in time but also a phenomenon in space, which could be stored as a media object in a sound library and retrieved for analysis, manipulation and composition. Sound recording and playback led to new approaches to music composition, as in the practice of Pierre Schaeffer, which originated from listening to sound objects and not writing them.

The music culture of today has long been dominated by operations of selection and compositing, or rather of cut, copy and paste taking on the legacy from Schaeffer. It is in this context that live coding introduces a 'literary turn' which uncovers the symbolic and literate nature of digital technology. Instead of working with remediated time processes of sound recording and sequencer-based music, live coding engages in a distributed process of performative writing, which rather owes its legacy to algorithmic composition and generative music.

However, in live coding the literary process is accelerated in time since algorithmic writing (the actual programming, i.e. the writing of music) now takes place in a live setting, which unfolds as a discourse between the programmer and the software model. Designating live coding as "just in time programming" (Rohrhuber), and/or "on the fly programming" (Wang), different live coders reflect the time-accelerated process of programming and the changes it brings about. For instance, Rohrhuber et al. point to the fact that in live coding the programmer is caught in two time structures: the time of the program and the time of the process in which the program is being modified. The time of the program is given by the rules that always operate based on previous states, i.e. the program operates based on its own history. At the same time the program is changed in a dynamic process of reading (the programmer listening to the results of the program) and writing (the programmer modifying the unfolding program to embrace new directions of his initial idea). Consequently, a basic disagreement is stated "between the programmer's time and the time of the program – each trying to reach their own aims, before they are ready again to take each other into account" (Rohrhuber 456).

What the texts referenced above point out as conditions of live coding, and in a broader context conditions of digital literacy, are processes of human-machine interaction from which music or literary texts unfold. Forming a distributed system of interacting elements, the readerly and writerly exchange between the human and the machine takes place in clashing and accelerated structures of time, in which the text and its history (the conditions of its current state) are constantly negotiated and changed. To quote Hayles again, the digital text (music, literature, images) is "less an object than an event, [and] emerges as a dance between artificial and human intelligence, machine and natural languages, as these evolve together through time" (187).

The concept of emergence is significant since it underlines that the text is something that is always in the process of becoming. Since the conditions of its own state are constantly being changed and rewritten, the text is not something that is revealed due to a preconceptualised idea or something that can be predicted beforehand. It takes its form from the unfolding negotiations of the interacting elements. Hence we recognise a poesis which is neither *techne* (humans revealing and fabricating objects by using tools) nor *physis* (the self-organising code of nature from whence that which does not exist comes into being). Instead, it is a poesis founded on a distributed system in which humans interact and communicate with machines, utilising their ability to carry out tasks of their own in accordance with a specified 'logic of decision' written in a program.

Conclusion

To conclude, I believe that although an important aspect of live coding and ixi software is the attempt to penetrate the remediated interfaces of commercial software in order to address the true nature of the machine, a more profound aspect is how live coding and ixi software, by engaging with the materiality of the software and the literacy of programming, openly address and reflect the conditions of the music made and performed. Accepting that the software and the human are both elements in a distributed system, live coding and ixi software acknowledge what Talbot did not and avoid a naïve understanding of software as either remediated tools or autonomous machines from which a second nature springs. Live coding and ixi software thus help us to recognise what is true about technology, and to acknowledge the conditions of the music composed and performed – i.e. its poesis, a poesis that cannot be recognised as either physis or techne.

Notes

1. A first-order Markov chain (named after the Russian mathematician Andrey Markov) is a discrete random process in which e.g. the next state of a randomly changing system depends only on its current state.
2. In "Instrumental Interaction" Michel Beaudouin-Lafon distinguishes between domain objects, which are objects of interest, and interaction instruments, which are tools or artefacts by which we manipulate domain objects (Beaudouin-Lafon 448). What Magnusson argues is that ixi software is more than an artefact/tool to manipulate music. As a musical instrument it qualifies also as a domain object in its own right, or at least one could argue that the concepts of interaction instrument and domain objects are blurred when we speak of musical software instruments or creative software in general. See also Bertelsen, Breinbjerg & Pold.
3. Of course, we should bear in mind that Heidegger refers to art as such, and thus to art as another approach to the perception, recognition and conception of the relation between humans, technology and nature, and not to specific genres of art.

Works cited

Andersen, Peter Bøgh. "Acting Machines." *digital media revisited*. Eds. Gunnar Liestøl, Andrew Morrison and Terje Rasmussen. Cambridge, Mass., London, England: MIT Press, 2003. 183-213. Print.

Beaudouin-Lafon, Michel. *Instrumental Interaction: an Interaction Model for Designing Post-WIMP User Interfaces*. Proceedings of the SIGCHI conference on Human factors in computing systems. ACM, 2000: 446-53. Print.

Bertelsen, Olav, Morten Breinbjerg, and Søren Pold. *Instrumentness for Creativity: Mediation, Materiality & Metonymy*. C&C 2007: Proceedings of the 6th ACM SIGCHI Conference on Creativity and Cognition. ACM, 2007: 233-42. Print.

Bolter, J. David, and Richard Grusin. *Remediation: Understanding New Media*. Cambridge, Mass., London: MIT Press, 2002. Print.

Bolz, Norbert. "Basic Features of the Culture of Simulation." *Billeder fra det fjerne/Images from afar*. Eds. Anders Michelsen and Frederik Stjernfelt. Oslo: Akademisk Forlag, 1996. 173-177. Print.

Collins, Nick, Alex Mclean, Julian Rohrhuber, and Adrian Ward. "Live Coding in Laptop Performance." *Organized Sound* 8.3 (2003): 321-30. Print.

Cox, Geoff, Alex McLean, and Adrian Ward. "Coding Praxis: Reconsidering the Aesthetics of Code." *Read_Me Software Art & Culture*. Eds. Olga Goriunova, and Alexi Shulgin. Aarhus University Press, 2004. 161-74. Print.

Hayles, N. Katherine. "The Time of Digital Poetry: From Object to Event." *New Media Poetics*. Eds. Adalaide Morris, and Thomas Swiss. Cambridge, Mass., London, England: MIT Press, 2006. 181-209. Print.

Heidegger, Martin. "The Question Concerning Technology." *The Question Concerning Technology and Other Essays*. New York: Harper & Row Publishers, 1977. 3-35. Print.

Magnusson, Thor. *Screen-Based Musical Interfaces as Semiotic Machines*. Proceedings of the 6th International Conference on New Interfaces for Musical Expression. IRCAM, 2006: 162-7. Print.

Meyrowitz, Joshua. *No Sense of Place*. New York, Oxford: Oxford University Press, 1985. Print.

Mumford, Lewis. *Technics and Civilization*. San Diego, New York, London: Harcourt Brace & Company, 1934. Print.

Rohrhuber, Julian, Alberto de Campo, and Renate Wieser, *Algorithms Today: Notes on Language Design for Just In Time Programming*. Proceedings of the 2005 International Computer Music Conference, 2005: 455-8. Print.

Shachtman, Noah. "New Eno Music Gets 'Generative'." *Wired* 27 Oct. 2001. Web. 7 August 2009. <http://www.wired.com/culture/lifestyle/news/2001/10/47670>.

Wang, G., and Perry Cook. *On-the-fly Programming: Using Code as an Expressive Musical Instrument*. Proceedings of the 4th International Conference on New Interfaces for Musical Expression, 2004. 138-43. Print.

Ward, Adrian et al. "Live Algorithm Programming and a Temporary Organisation for its Promotion." *Read_Me Software Art & Culture*. Eds. Olga Goriunova, and Alexei Shulgin. Aarhus University Press, 2004. 243-61. Print.

Weibel, Peter. "The Apparatus World – a World unto Itself." *Eigenwelt der Apparatewelt. Pioniere der elektronischen Kunst*. Ed. David Dunn. Linz: Ars Electronica, Vasulkas, 1992. 15-9. Print.

Writerly Gaming: Political Gaming

BY CHRISTIAN ULRIK ANDERSEN

Computer games are aesthetic interfaces per se. Opposed to the functional dimension of a pragmatic software interface (as in the editing of text or images for example), a game interface highlights an experiential and aesthetic dimension of the interface. Having fun interacting with the game, enjoying the graphics and audio etc., is what drives the player to play (Andersen 159-63). The question of aesthetics in the computer game interface is frequently linked to the relationship between game, player and reality. This relationship can appear in various ways.

A game interface is a visual and auditive representation of various algorithmic processes within the computer, and what is particular to the game interface is that the representation of the computer very often looks and feels like the real world. The level of visual and auditive detail is usually extremely rich and sometimes even based on real events (ranging from Champions League football to World War 2). Often, aesthetic judgements of games are based on this reality effect in the game. This representational relationship is, however, not the only one to consider. The virtual worlds do not just 'look', 'sound' and 'feel' real – the relationship also depends on the player's interests and activities, on the ways the player uses the game and the ways of using that are staged in the game as an aesthetic experience.

Whilst playing, you disappear into the game's cybernetic world; you learn to master this world by jumping from one rooftop to another, driving a car or letting civilisations battle. Games are software created just for fun. In this case, the relation between game and reality is not only representational but also implies that the game is a consumer product. Computer games are 'consumer games' – market products made for entertainment, based on an aesthetic and experiential urge to entertain and be entertained.

Yet another relationship appears when you look at the skills the player obtains by playing games. Through the game, the player may train his or her social competences (e.g. bargaining), cognitive competences (e.g. reaction), or intellectual competences (e.g. language). Usually, the skills are obtained involuntarily, meaning that they appear as side effects of the real goal: entertainment. At times, designers succeed in turning the game into a didactic tool. This is usually referred to as 'serious gaming'. Games are used to train particular behaviour in the real world. Games teach pilots to fly, soldiers to fight, children to do maths, or – as advertisements – buyers to buy ('advergaming'). Computer games are 'user games'; professional tools for training and learning disguised as aesthetic experience.

We need to distinguish between various aesthetic strategies in computer games. The experience and aesthetics of computer games can be used to seduce the player by resembling reality or being real fun. They even provide a seductive way of acquiring pragmatic skills. Games may, however, establish yet another relationship between game, player and world. Some games explicitly work within a political sphere and address the player as a civil person – instead of a consumer or a professional user. The aesthetics of the computer games' interface is not only a question of resemblance to reality, having real fun or the entertaining acquirement of real skills, but also about supporting a democratic public sphere. It is about aesthetics as well as politics and action.

Computer games can be political in many ways. By definition, they involve a ludic and playful interaction with the computer that deconstructs the interactive world and points to the underlying cybernetic procedures of the computer. Players are always reminded of the underlying procedures of the game, exploring the properties of the software, finding out how things work (Andersen 183, 235). Playing is political in the sense that it always involves an awareness of the medium and its seductive strategies: The player *reads* the computer medium and not just the game world. Playing may, however, also be political in the sense that it reflects an act of production. In some games there is an aesthetic of production that can be highly political. Here, playing is something other than mere participation, playing is *writing*. This article will present a fundamental understanding of how ludic activities can be political by including the authorship of games, as well as analysing the way in which playing as writing can function as political actions in different contexts: on the Internet, in a software culture and in urban settings.

The background of political gaming: The Landlord's Game

In aesthetic research, often focusing on the experience of art, games can easily be dismissed as trivial, just for fun. Without doubt, having fun is constitutive for the playing of games. If it is not entertaining to submit to the rigid rules of games, players usually refrain from playing them. However, as argued by several game researchers, not just paintings, movies and novels but also games allow us to address political, social and cultural values in an aesthetic expression (Bogost; Frasca; Galloway). Games can speak to our assumptions and worldviews.

Using games in this way is in fact neither a new thing nor strictly related to computer games. Elizabeth J. Magie originally patented the board game *Monopoly* from 1934 as *The Landlord's Game* as long ago as 1904. Allegedly, Magie created the game to explain how 'the single tax theory' of Henry George enriched landlords and impoverished tenants. The original intention was to demonstrate the negative consequences of private monopolies on land (Berg and Judd).

The game of *Monopoly* clearly demonstrates the fun of being a landlord and having 'tenants'. Perhaps *The Landlord's Game* was too successful in its demonstration? Paradoxically, *Monopoly* turned what was (at the time) a serious political statement into entertainment and a huge commercial success. Could we imagine the abuse of minors by Catholic priests as a game? Would this trivialise a tragedy, or does it allow us to say something about abuse, oppression, the responsibilities of neighbours and authorities etc.? Despite the risk of indifference, attempts to address political or cultural values in games are in fact made (the game *Pedopriest* actually exists). Perhaps these political games, existing both on the Internet and elsewhere, deal with another kind of 'ludic' behaviour where having fun exceeds the trivial?

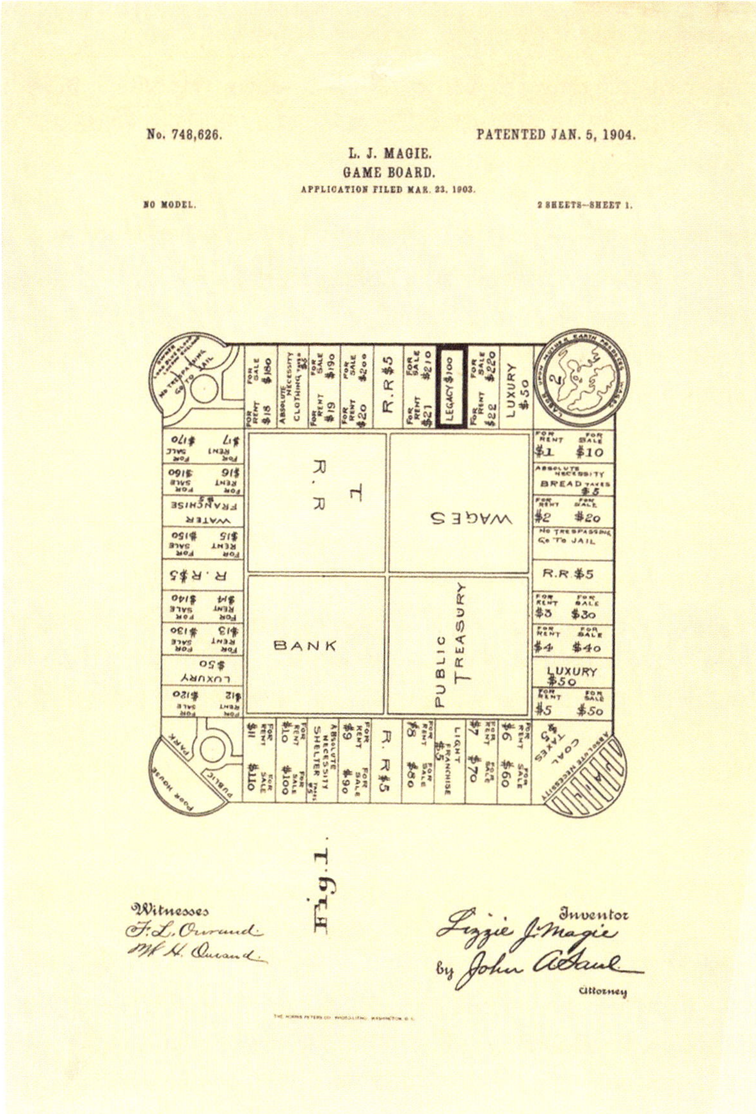

ILL. 1: Original patent drawing of Elizabeth J. Magie's *Landlord's Game*.

Games and politics: From 'writerly' to political

All games contain politics. Any representation or simulation reflects a particular perspective on the world. In a game, this worldview is revealed either in the presentation of the game world and what *has happened* (depiction of a world through a background story, a perspective, game characters, objects, etc.)[1] or in a demonstration of what potentially *could happen* (demonstration of a world through interaction with a dynamic system).[2]

However, decoding the rhetoric of a game through an analysis of agency, storytelling, navigation of space and system dynamics only partly covers the political statement of a game. Whether exclaimed orally, in writing or by moving images, a statement also inherits its political nature from the person speaking – the victims of abuse and oppression, the workers, the women, the children, an ethnic or religious group etc. The act of taking responsibility of authorship is crucial. What makes *The Landlord's Game* political is precisely the fact that the author was a Quaker woman who wished to address the inherently unfair dynamics of a taxation system built upon a particular worldview. The political articulation of a right to express oneself and taking responsibility of authorship is intrinsically related to a 'writerly' behaviour.

The notion 'writerly' derives from Roland Barthes' literary theory. To Barthes, writerly characterises a particular way of reading associated with the open texts of modern literature. In a 'readerly' text, reading is predetermined by the author and aimed at reconstructing the 'proper' meaning of the text. A writerly text addresses the reader as an active producer of meaning rather than a passive consumer (Barthes 10). A writerly text is open to interpretation, and the reader may actively re-write the text by restructuring its different layers (historical, symbolic, hermeneutical etc.).

A writerly aspect of digital texts was also highlighted in the heyday of hypertext and electronic literature in the nineties. In certain interpretations it is related to the hypertext structure itself, where the user is seen as the producer of the text (e.g. George P. Landow). However, as pointed out by game researcher Espen Aarseth, even though navigating a hypertext or configuring a game may constitute forms of interactivity, this is by no means equivalent to the user actively contributing to the meaning of the text (Aarseth 64). A writerly game implies that the text is open at a structural level. The player must be able not just to experience the effect of a predetermined meaning (a rule or a 'script') by means of navigation and configuration, but also to affect the meaning of the text by rewriting it and adding to its structure (rule-making, 'scripting' or what Aarseth labels 'textonic' behaviour). Applying the notion of a writerly text to a game must necessarily take a structural openness into account. Being writerly means contributing to the structure of the game, the behaviour, the rules and the events of a game.

Involving users in the creation of games is nothing new to the gaming community. Gamers are not just 'readers' playing games; they are often 'writers' actively participating in the construction of the games, exceeding the mere navigation and configuration of the game. Players contribute to games by creating objects in games that form the course of events in the game: for example characters in a massively multiplayer online role-playing game who can engage in conversations, form guilds and create player events. Players also often access the actual coded/scripted layers of the game to cheat, apply new rules, reconfigure the user interface ('macros'), create new worlds ('skins') etc. In other words, the possibilities of player involvement in the creation of games seem infinite.

A writerly behaviour is, as such, by no means controversial. It contains no political action. Even hacking, cheating and reconfiguration and other types of access to coded layers, which in most types of proprietary software (Windows, Word, Photoshop etc.) are restricted or even prohibited, are actually expected in computer games. Game software has always been relatively open with built-in options for scripting and configuring the game's engine. Player scripts and game reconfigurations must be seen as part of the developers' business model. Game developers often rely on the creativity of the players when developing future versions of their products. To understand how a player contribution or writerly behaviour can constitute a political act, one must consider how the player actually contributes to the game.

To understand a structural openness in the game and the act of writing as a political attribute, one has to understand it as a specific aesthetic and literary quality. The hacking of the game, the rewriting of the rules etc. must be of a particular kind, questioning and challenging prevailing meanings and control mechanisms. The French philosopher Jacques Rancière has pointed to such a political aspect of a writerly action.[3] To Rancière, the aesthetic, literary quality of writing lies not merely in the perfection of form and the beauty of language but in the ability of the writing to designate something common. It points to that which does not have ownership. A literary quality of writing points to a condition in language "in which relations of propriety and authority remain undefined" (Hallward 36). The literary thus applies to ways of writing "that circulate without a legitimating system defining the relations between the word's emitter and receiver," as Rancière puts it (Rancière, "Literature, Politics, Aesthetics: Approaches to Democratic Disagreement (Interview with Solange Guenoun and James H. Kavanagh)" 7 – qtd. in Hallward 36).

In the context of political computer games, one may say that these games circulate outside the regular games' preservation of a particular relation between game emission and game reception – explicitly the relation between market and consumer, producer and programmer, society and citizen. A literary and aesthetic quality of this kind of political, writerly gaming is thus that the games remain open, undetermined, and that this openness must offer the possibility of a performative action that destabilises an existing hierarchy of meanings, roles and experiences.

In the following, I will demonstrate how gaming can incorporate a writerly aspect as an aesthetic, literary, destabilising and political action. I will demonstrate how these games, despite a similarity in their incorporation of a writerly/literary aspect, involve different kinds of interests and relations between game, game-writer, player and world. The categories I suggest thus place themselves at very different locations in the cultural landscape – on the Internet in an activist environment ('game activism'), in the area of software art ('game modifications'), and in the urban space within the area of intervention art (New Digital Games Movement – with a reference to the *New Games Movement* of the seventies). They seek to de-normalise the relation between game and player, between programmer/programming and pragmatic function, and between society and citizen respectively.

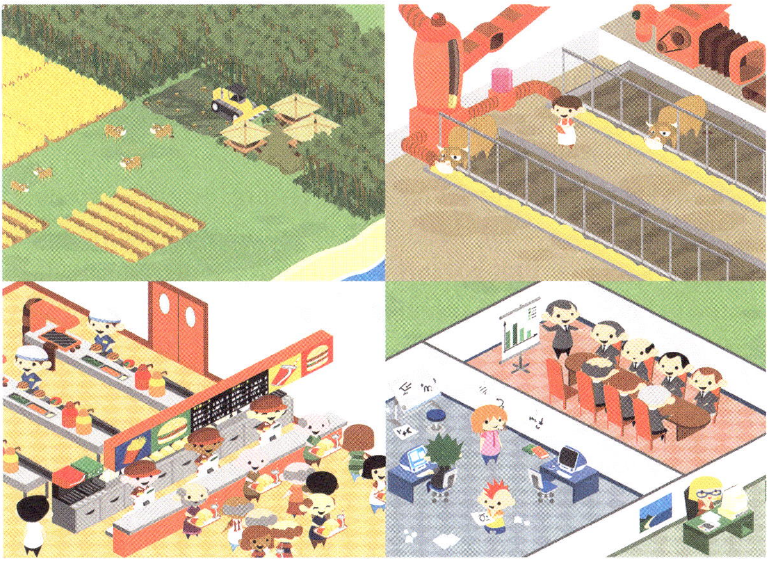

ILL. 2: In *The McDonald's Video Game* the player controls the production of fast-food (by permission from Paolo Pedercini).

Game activism: The McDonald's Video Game

A large quantity of political computer games are found on the Internet in an activist environment determined to revolt against the established attitudes of the prevailing system – a kind of net activism. Visiting these websites one will find games that challenge the meaning of the War on Terror, work, homosexuality etc. According to one of the genre's leading designers, Paolo Pedercini from Italian Molleindustria, a common presumption amongst political game designers is that games are able to reach an audience which is otherwise unreceptive to political discussions, and that games are well suited to stage and question a world perceived as a system. As game theorist Ted Friedman states, it is much easier to create Marx's *Das Kapital* as a game than as a movie (Dugan).

The real political (and aesthetic) dimension does not, however, lie in the ability to create an insight into particular, supposed mechanisms of society. Rather, it lies in the will to express an attitude through a game as a performative action – when the player him/herself starts emitting attitudes. Pedercini and Molleindustrias' own *McDonald's Video Game* is a good example.

McDonald's is a 'tycoon game'. Tycoon games are not games that can be won but are rather simulations of systems. Players construct buildings, zoos, roller coasters, railroads and so forth, and the object is essentially to construct and accumulate as much wealth as possible by auditing and maintaining the system. In *McDonald's*, you build and sell burgers. To maintain a satisfactory production of burgers it is necessary to cut rainforest, exhaust land, add industrial waste to cow fodder, bribe environmental organisations and nutritionists, and so forth. Consequently, the game is a rather explicit exclamation of the factors that govern the global fast food industry – a kind of enlightening of the player as to 'what things are really like'. At the same time, and much more importantly in understanding its political/aesthetic qualities, the game has a built-in critique of the computer game itself.

According to Pedercini, Will Wright, the designer behind the well-known game *SimCity*, claims that when designing games he does not consider their political dimensions. Everything is created to entertain the player. This is of course surprising because *SimCity* seems extremely overt in its political evaluation of the player's actions – you cannot nationalise all property, certain ways of doing things pay off and others do not etc. Pedercini calls the game industry "the dictatorship of entertainment" and argues that games are never entertainment alone. Games are always political because they deal with cultural and ideological issues. The object of the *McDonald's* game is thus not so much to entertain as it is to de-mystify "the political neutrality of the entertainment products ('it's only a game'), by making games whose main point is not to keep the player hours and hours in front of a screen" (Dugan).

As Pedercini suggests, the implication of the dictatorship of entertainment even reaches beyond emitting a dominant ideology disguised as entertainment. The entertainment of the user may be regarded as a dictatorship in itself. The player of a computer game needs to be active – but only within the magic circle of the game. After all, playing a computer game is a very mute activity. So, through entertainment software, the consumer is pacified and silenced – not as a player, but as a citizen. Pedercini breaks this silence by becoming writerly – that is, by becoming a producer and not just a consumer of a game. He creates a game that in its presentation of a game is almost a caricature of a game. By doing this, he escapes his destiny as a player subordinated to 'the dictatorship of entertainment'.

When playing *McDonald's*, what fascinates is not only the exposure of the fast-food industry, it is also the humour and the parody of a game. Through laughter, the player finds a community with the game and becomes involved in the process of being transformed into a producer, subverting the relationship between emitter and receiver, game and player, market and consumer.

In short, Pedercini plays with the computer game as a personal expression and this little game undermines what Rancière would call "the distribution of the sensible." The game opens for experiences that are not otherwise allowed. Through a game loaded with a personal perspective, the player deliberately manifests him/herself and demonstrates that he or she still has at least the possibility of imagining a destiny beyond "the dictatorship of entertainment".

Game mods: Max Payne Cheats Only

Another kind of writerly gaming is found within the field of software art. One could call them 'art games'. 'Game' is perhaps not the best term to use, because a large proportion of these 'art games' are modifications of games that in many cases are not even playable.

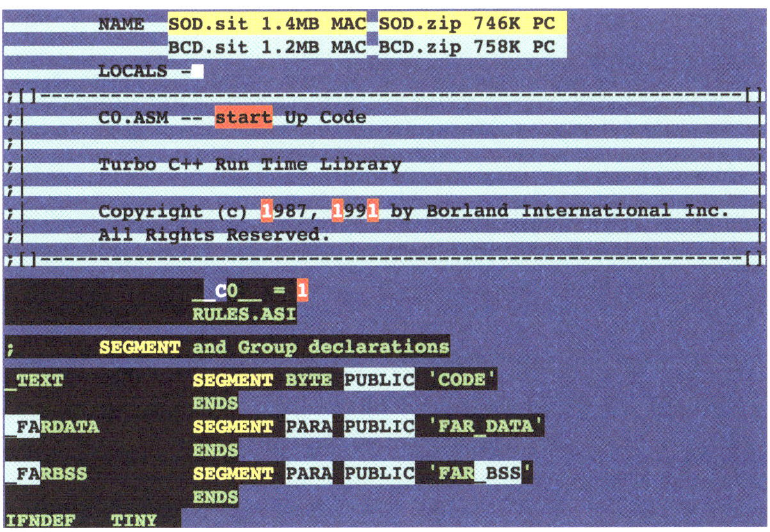

ILL. 3: The web page where the game *SOD* can be downloaded (by permission from Jodi).

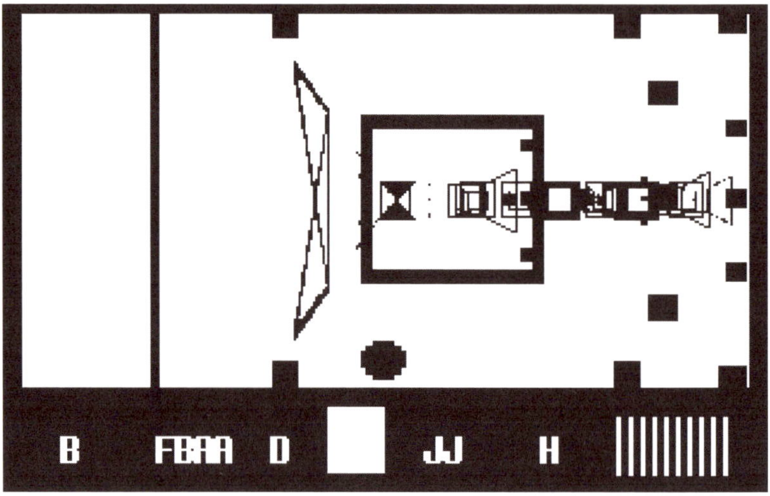

ILL. 4: The game *SOD*, a modification of the 3D shooter *Wolfenstein*, as a constructivist landscape (by permission from Jodi).

The genre is not new but has existed since the dawn of the 3D game engine. One of the first (and most famous) examples is Jodi's *SOD* – a modification of the 3D shooter *Wolfenstein*, replacing the otherwise realistic game with a constructivist landscape.

More recently (in 2006), Jodi has made another contribution to the genre in their work *Max Payne Cheats Only*. Here, they have turned the shooting game *Max Payne* into a surreal world where the characters are staged as grotesque sculptures twisted in absurd positions, with the soundtrack being turned into gabbling speech and other similar details.[4] As often in Jodi's games extracts of code appear on the screen and also the title of the work suggests that these glitches are a result of coded actions ('cheats').[5] The writing, the code of the game, seems to be of crucial importance. How are we to understand this?

One obvious option is to regard the appearance of a coded level as a rebellion against the game as a symptom of a non-writerly use of the computer. As such, the video game *Pong* (1972) is a symbol of a new era in computer interaction design. Whereas the user was previously someone who knew the language of the computer, the code,

Pong made it possible for anyone to interact with the computer through direct manipulation and images that (though simple) refer to a recognisable domain – the game of tennis.

Florian Cramer has described the invention of the graphical user interface as a media separation, a separation of text and images. The graphical user interface transforms the user from a producer of text/code to a reader of its images, and what was naturally united in the computer, the unity of data and process, becomes separated and alien (Cramer 100). One might even say that 'the user' as such is born the moment the media separation takes place. From having been the user's own machine, programmed and controlled by the user, the user is now staged as a recipient and spectator. As Florian Cramer suggests, one must seek to reintroduce a writerly form of computing – as a way of re-appropriating the computer (as in this article, also with a reference to Roland Barthes).

Reading Jodi's game modifications as a rebellion against the concealment of the code, the separation of image and text, they become a kind of avant-garde art. Modifying the game, dismantling the imagery and insisting on an otherwise hidden writerly aspect, they seek to do something to the interface similar to what Brecht did to the theatre: they reveal the otherwise concealed aesthetic aspect of the show, they reveal the illusion of the stage and the alienation of the user. However, this approach does not fully account for the writerly aspect of Jodi's game modifications. It seems, though, as if there is something else at stake as well in the game modification,

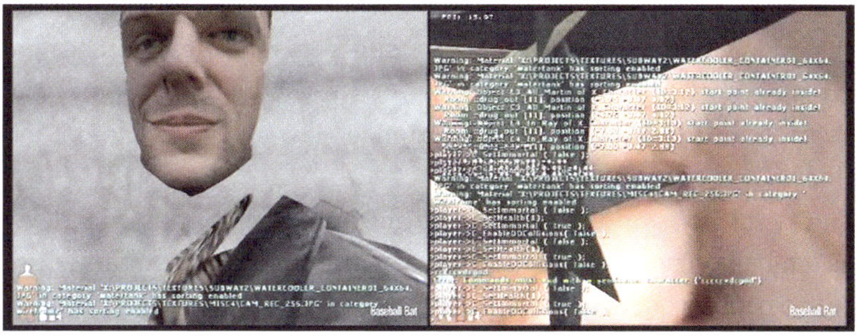

ILL. 5: *Max Payne Cheats Only*, a modified version of the popular game staged as a coded and surreal world (by permission from Jodi).

something other than just the re-appropriation of a coded, textual level.

Since the early days of computer gaming, players have made their own games. Many computer gamers now in their late thirties got their first computer (Commodore 64 or similar) in order to write games – or, at least, to copy the code from a game magazine. When the games became more complex, gamers modified existing games through access to the game engine. The game of *Counter-Strike*, for instance, was originally a player modification of the game *Half-life*. In other words, gamers have always been much more than mere users of graphical interfaces. They are not alien to the computer's attributes, and discussions about game behaviour are often intrinsically linked to a practice that involves a coded level behind the graphical user interface. Apart from the fact that one is a well-functioning, highly entertaining game and the other is not playable at all, *Counter-Strike* and *Max Payne Cheats Only* have similar characteristics in that they both highlight this coded/textual level of the game behind the apparent realism.

To understand the difference one must, I believe, focus on the performative aspect of writing the code. In the case of *Counter-Strike*, the player does not want to change his/her status as a player by re-writing the game. It is rather an act of game appraisal. Gaming culture is alive and loaded with creativity, but nothing in the act of modifying a game breaks with any norms – the behaviour is entirely expected.

The 'hacker's' game *Max Payne Cheats Only* is different. Software art is not a stage for gamers. Nor is it a stage for artists, in the classical sense. It is a stage for "people doing strange things with software" (as the title of the readme festival for software art a few years back indicates). In other words, one may interpret the software art culture as a scene for programmers who transform their otherwise functional, computer-scientific knowledge into a personal expression. In software art there are several examples of programmer artists who have had no relation to an art scene but who suddenly start to produce art. Some of them do not even see themselves as artists – just programmers.

It is a scene for people who do something which is unexpected. Instead of producing pragmatic software, the programmer starts using an artistic language. As the player in the activist game redistributes his/her universe of sense and experience by turning him/herself into a programmer and the game into his/her expression, the programmer redistributes his/her universe by turning him/herself into an artist who, by hacking a game, reveals the aesthetic of the computer as art. The noise, the flickering images, the surreal landscapes, the grotesque characters become the voice of the programmer who illegally interferes with a program and an existing system and aesthetics of production.

New Digital Games Movement: Who Wants To Be?

The third and last type of writerly gaming I would like to present has the physical world as its frame. In art terminology (which these games seem to induce), one would call them 'interventions'. Using games, they intervene in a social system. The aim of the intervention is to reveal or influence certain determining factors and thereby create growth for dynamics and change. I label this type of gaming 'New Digital Games Movement' – not because it represents an organised movement, but because it has several characteristics of the *New Games Movement* of the seventies.

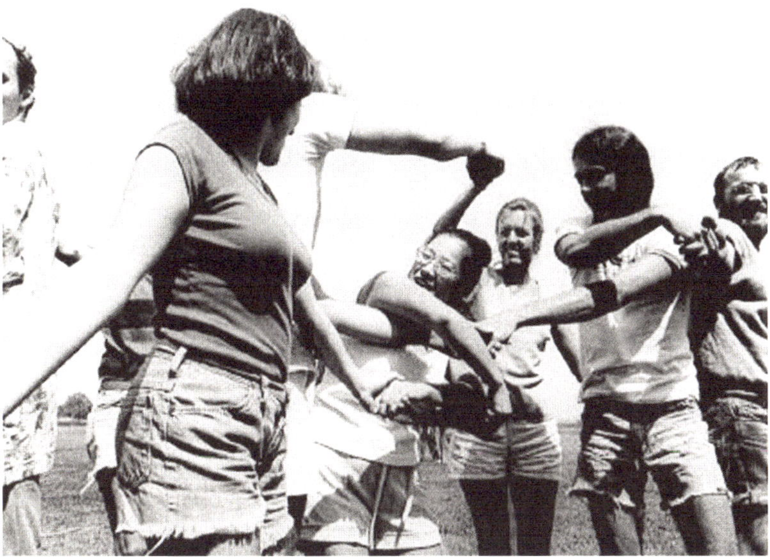

ILL. 6: The game of *Knots*, 1979 in Perkasie, PA at a local New Games festival (by permission from Lee Rush).

The *New Games Movement* is the source of numerous games that involve physical activity, and is primarily known today within pedagogical studies of movement and exercise. Originally, however, it was an offshoot of the peace movement – and it is this aspect that one must focus on to understand its political implications.

Stewart Brand, also the producer of *The Whole Earth Catalogue*, a catalogue aimed at providing means and tools "by which people could realize their own visions of living, shape their environment accordingly and share their adventure with others," saw the game as a powerful tool with which to realise new visions of living, and became the father of *The New Games Movement*. Brand regards the objective of a game as follows:

> You can't change a game by winning it, losing it or refereeing it or spectating it. You change a game by leaving it, going somewhere else, and starting a new game. If it works, it will in time alter or replace the old game (Fluegelman and Tembeck 137).

The game to be changed is the underlying system of Western combat that led to the Vietnam War: the strategic handling of 'the red enemy,' the replacement of body with power, and so forth. Changing the game's rules of war and combat cannot happen by just refereeing it differently or by acting differently – one must *leave* the game and create a new game, with new game rules that embody a different ideology. The new games are characterised by competition but also friendship, play, fun and a bodily sensitivity – the act of forgiveness is crucial to Brand (139). In this way, *The New Games Movement* was a movement aimed at constructing games that let people experience *other* game rules than the ones the prevailing system enforced.

It seems as if the digital intervention art scene has a similar interest in activating the potentials of gaming. One cannot define the scene as a movement as such today; what we see is more like a number of games that seem to evoke gaming – usually with digital aspects – as an artistic practice. Like the *New Games Movement* of the seventies, the new digital games movement regards playing games and having fun as something which is both a subjective experience and an experience of a larger collective with societal and political implications. In the *New Games Movement* these implications were tied to the peace movement and new visions of basic human correspondences. Today, in the new digital games movement, the implications are often, in addition, tied to new visions of the urban landscape – a landscape open not just to interpretation but also to re-writing.

In what way can an urban landscape be written? Though tangible and physical, the modern city may be regarded as a highly semiotic and coded landscape. This can be understood in several ways (Andersen and Pold). First of all, the modern city is a spectacular city (Pold; McQuire). Through architecture, sound, visual media and signs, the urban landscape guides its inhabitants and forms the experience of the city. As an example, the urban mall with its billboards and music coming from stores is a spectacle, seducing and adapting its inhabitants to a materialist, commercial culture. Secondly, the modern city has a non-visual, informational, coded, encrypted layer that is tied to control structures behind the surface of the city – often involving computer transactions. As documented by Bruno Latour and Emilie Hermant, the city (cafés, monuments, streets etc.) is constantly under surveillance, leading not only to a mediated view on the city (e.g. a map perspective on traffic) but also to a reconfiguration of the city (e.g. the guiding of traffic) (Latour, Hermant and Shannon).

Finally, many contemporary cities have computers embedded in various contexts – what is commonly referred to as ubiquitous computing. The city does not only consist of architecture, signs and information; very often computers and the processing of information are used to augment the spectacle of the city or its control mechanisms. The inhabitants of the city can use personal devices such as the iPhone to map personal whereabouts; the city is plastered with (password protected) wireless networks etc.

Despite the negative effects of not being able to access the scripts of the city (being seduced by architecture, logged off a wireless network, unable to get access to personal computers etc.) scripted layers make the city an obvious setting for playing and having fun. One can drift along in the mall, enjoy the benefits of an iPhone application enhancing the experience of a space and place etc. In the perspective of the city as the scene for a writerly game with political implications, however, the city is an open structure where inhabitants play the city in order to challenge its spectacle, networks and control mechanisms.

One example of both using the effect of the spectacle and challenging the hidden networks of an urban area is found in the English artist collective The People Speak. In 2006, they were asked to create a mural in Bow – an area in East London. Instead of just using their own creative talent to create a picturesque mural that would most likely be sprayed with graffiti, the group consciously challenged the social system they were entering. Any image – and any mural – embodies a way of seeing. To ensure a democratic approach to the mural, The People Speak wanted to identify the different stakeholders.

In the neighbourhood of the mural they found, for instance, a group of people whose houses faced the mural and who were wealthy and socially very different to others in the estate's community, which included two housing companies (one private, the other public), a number of street gangs, and a large group of 'mute' inhabitants, who usually preferred to keep a low profile. Instead of representing the otherwise dominant actors, they made an effort to be neutral. As an alien presence in the community, they tried to stage a social event in the form of a game show. The object of the game show was democratic – to let everybody speak whilst having fun in a compelling game. Under the title *Who Wants To Be?* (with a reference to the TV show *Who Wants To Be a Millionaire*) the game show was set up in the public space in front of the mural. By expressing visions and voting on ideas in the show, the contestants affected the creation of the mural – visualised live using a variety of technical equipment.

In the end, The People Speak did not succeed in maintaining their neutrality. The outcome of the game shows was, in the eyes of the housing companies, very provocative as they included gang slogans, for instance. The People Speak adjusted the content and thereby became representatives of the ruling power. The mural was never realised and, as such, they failed to carry out the task. In a different perspective, however, the intervention was a success. They made it possible for inhabitants who were not usually accepted as actors in the community to have their say. Even though their alternative system of authority was overruled in the end by the existing regu-

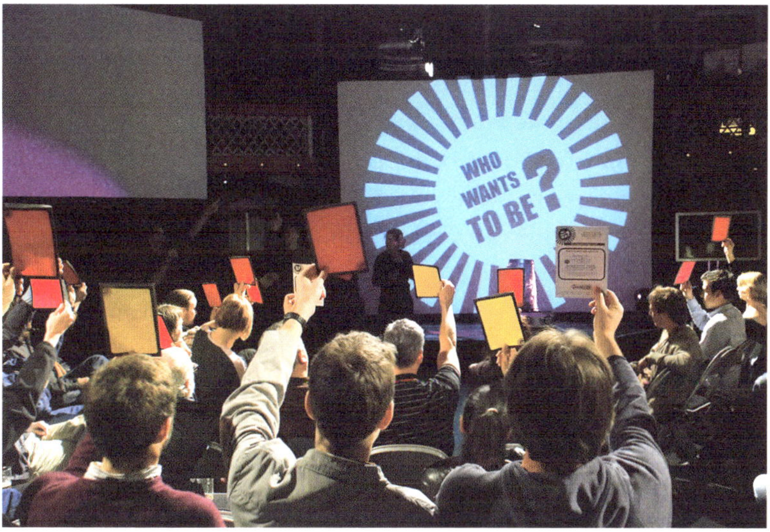

ILL. 7: **Giving people a voice through a decision game: *Who Wants to Be by* The People Speak (by permission from The People Speak).**

lations of power and control in the community, they at least envisioned a different 'game' based on different, democratic rules. The visualised mural and the game shows were the spectacular manifestations of this vision.

Consequently, the political and aesthetic quality of the project lies not in the aim of awakening a slumbering working class who ought to claim their material rights (cheaper rent for instance), but in challenging the existing system by giving the people their own spectacle and letting them play and speak – giving them a vote/voice.

Examples of contemporary ludic approaches to the city are numerous and plentiful in their expression. In many of them, the city merely works as a landscape providing the setting of the game (as in many alternative reality games and mobile games) – in a sense a parallel play universe in the city. In other games, however, the city is not turned into a game but its hidden scripts are instead something to be played with and challenged. Here, the game transgresses its own borderlines and reaches well into the political reality of the setting.

Noteworthy in this context is not only The People Speak but also the artist organisation Ludic Society. In their game *ToyGenosonic*, they address the use of RFID tags (Radio Frequency Identification) – used, for instance, to tag consumer goods in shops. Using a transformed Nintendo DS, players can navigate through the city by finding and scanning RFID tags, each generating a sound on the game console. The point of the game can be seen as a critique of how urban consumerism is dependent on informational surveillance and technical control mechanisms. A significant quality, however, is also the game's ability to engage people in play and let them experience how play performed in a physical and political reality can be the source of new visions of the city based on the players' own psychogeographic dérive. Drifting through the city with their modified game console, players may experience not only *that* ordinary consumer objects contain control mechanisms but also *how* this can be challenged by turning the control information into sound and a paradoxical space for play (Bazzichelli).

Writerly gaming: Playful redistribution of the sensible

What I label 'writerly gaming' – and what I have tried to demonstrate – are games that in their aesthetic qualities point to a literary, writerly aspect that subverts and destabilises a relationship between emitter and receiver, which is fixated by the dominant ideology. In the terms of Rancière one would say that a "distribution of the sensible" was at stake.

As Peter Hallward describes the philosophy of Rancière, his basic assumption is very simple: "Everybody thinks, everybody speaks" (Hallward 26). Everybody thinks but the prevailing ideology allocates people to different classes, not all of whom are authorised to speak. Rancière studies the mechanisms that "distribute the sensible" in its widest sense: what can be experienced, thought, sensed, felt etc. These mechanisms serve to differentiate acceptable practice from unacceptable practice. When everybody thinks and everybody speaks, it is an expression of a relentless struggle by some groups to avoid adjustment to the system and its distribution of classes and norms. The sensible experience is distributed by the dominant ideology, and the negotiation of the distribution seeks to cause turbulence.

One example of this can be found in Rancière's analysis of the 19th century working class. Surprisingly, he does not see the class struggle as a complaint about the distribution of goods. What's at stake is the social hierarchy's determination of life. The workers, who in a platonic worldview ought to work at day and sleep at night, redistribute the sensible by changing behaviour, challenging the norm, doing what is not authorised, making noise, adopting a different language, creating nocturnal poetry societies, making newspapers etc.

In their own way, the computer gamer, the programmer, the software artist, the Vietnam veteran and the inhabitants of Bow are condemned to convention, regulation, muteness – to sticking to their place. But what we see when gaming becomes writerly and the ludic becomes not a game but an approach to reality is "the possibility for anybody to appropriate for him or herself another ethos than the ethos suited to their condition" (Rancière, "From Politics to Aesthetics" 16) – a condition for dynamics and change.

The writerly aspect of the aforementioned games deals – in a similar way to the aesthetic revolution of the 19th century – not just with reclaiming material rights or the right to produce a game or code. It is characterised by the way it administers this writerly aspect. The writerly aspect of political games is aesthetic – it serves to enter into a dialogue with our world by de-stabilising, de-normalising and de-classifying a prevailing hierarchy of meanings, roles and power; and through play it initiates the participants in a vision of a different way of living, a different distribution of the sensible.

As seen in all the examples of writerly gaming, playfulness seems inherent to the act. Playing games is always about having fun. However, playfulness and other forms of ludic behaviour do not necessarily imply gay surrender to the rules and prescriptions of a game; the fun also involves cunning tricks, cheating and affecting the outcome. Writerly gaming is exactly about strategies (the ability to speak), cheating (the ability to assume unexpected roles) and affecting the outcome (challenging the existing hierarchies of meaning and control).

Notes

1. Hypothetically, when an archetypical WW2 first-person shooter contains a worldview it is partly because the player through the cut scenes and the game play experiences what it feels like to be an American solider trying to liberate Europe, getting shot at by evil-looking Nazis who possess lethal weapons.
2. *The Landlord's Game*, for example, is a demonstration of what happens when you monopolise land and make others pay rent.
3. Barthes' notion of writerly texts also bears political undertones. In the revolutionary spirit of the late sixties and early seventies, when the theory was put forward, a writerly text demands not just that the author should die but also that the reader should be born. Allowing the meaning of a text to remain plural and ambiguous liberates the reader from being a captive of the author's experience and addresses questions to the reader, promoting critical reflection and (writerly) action, which, one may claim in the light of history, also implies political reflection and action.
4. Videos can be found at http://maxpaynecheatsonly.jodi.org/.
5. All games have 'cheat codes', secret codes installed by the game programmers to change the mechanics of the game. These are used for playtesting or as 'easter eggs' for the players. More sophisticated 'cheats' include using special software to change the game mechanics.

Works cited

Aarseth, Espen. *Cybertext – Perspectives on Ergodic Literature*. Baltimore: Johns Hopkins University Press, 1997. Print.

Andersen, Christian Ulrik. *Det Æstetiske Interface – Computerspillet i en Interface-kultur og Interfacet i Computerspillet*. Aarhus: Digital Aesthetics Research Center, 2009. Print.

Andersen, Christian Ulrik, and Søren Pold. "The Scripted Spaces of Urban Ubiquitous Computing – the Experience, Poetics, and Politics of Public Scripted Space." (forthcoming).

Barthes, Roland. *S/Z*. Paris: Éditions du Seuil, 1970. Print.

Bazzichelli, Tatiana. "Toygenosonic." *Enter Action*. Århus: ARoS – Århus Kunstmuseum, 2009. 88-89. Print.

Berg, Kristian, and Graham Judd. *Early Monopoly*. 2004. Transcript. PBS, 28 June 2004.

Bogost, Ian. *Persuasive Games – the Expressive Power of Video Games*. Cambridge, Massachusetts: MIT Press, 2007. Print.

Cramer, Florian. "Exe.Cut[up]Able Statements: The Insistence of Code." *Ars Electronica: Code – the Language of Our Time*. Eds. Gerfried Stocker and Christine Schöpf. Ostfildern-Ruite: Hatje Cantz, 2003. 98-103. Print.

Dugan, Patrick. "Hot Off the Grill: La Molleindustria's Paolo Pedercini on the McDonald's Video Game" (Interview with Patrick Dugan)." *Gamasutra* (2006). Web. 6 Nov. 2009. <http://www.gamasutra.com/features/20060227/dugan_01.shtml>.

Fluegelman, Andrew, and Shoshana Tembeck. *The New Games Book*. A Headlands Press Book. California: Dolphin/Doubleday, 1976. Print.

Frasca, Gonzalo. "Video Games of the Oppressed: Critical Thinking, Education, Tolerance, and Other Trivial Issues." *First Person: New Media as Story, Performance, and Game*. Eds. Noah Wardrip-Fruin and Pat Harrigan. Cambridge, Massachusetts; London, England: MIT Press, 2004. Print.

Galloway, Alexander R. *Gaming*. Electronic Mediations. Minneapolis: University of Minnesota Press, 2006.

Hallward, Peter. "Jacques Rancière and the Subversion of Mastery." *Paragraph* 28 1 (2005): 26-45. Print.

Landow, George P. *Hypertext the Convergence of Contemporary Critical Theory and Technology*. Baltimore, Md: Johns Hopkins University Press, 1992. Print.

Latour, Bruno, Emilie Hermant, and Susanna Shannon. *Paris Ville Invisible*. Paris: La Découverte, 1998. Print.

McQuire, Scott. "The Politics of Public Space in the Media City." *First Monday* Special Issue #4 (2006). Web.10 Aug. 2009. <http://firstmonday.org/htbin/cgiwrap/bin/ojs/index.php/fm/article/view/1544/1459>.

Pold, Søren. *Ex Libris Medierealistisk Litteratur, Paris, Los Angeles & Cyberspace*. University of Southern Denmark Studies in Literature. Odense: Syddansk Universitetsforlag, 2004. Print.

Rancière, Jacques. "From Politics to Aesthetics." *Paragraph* 28.1 (2005): 13-25. Print.

– "Literature, Politics, Aesthetics: Approaches to Democratic Disagreement (Interview with Solange Guenoun and James H. Kavanagh)." *SubStance* 92 (2000): 3-24. Print.

HENRIK KAARE NIELSEN
The Net Interface and the Public Sphere

JACOB LILLEMOSE
Is There Really Only One Word For It? Software Vocabularies in the Expanded Field of Interface Aesthetics

INKE ARNS
Transparent World. Minoritarian Tactics in the Age of Transparency

OUT: Culture and Politics

The Net Interface and the Public Sphere

BY HENRIK KAARE NIELSEN

The Internet has since the mid-1990s established itself as an increasingly important space of social practice. In this process, the specific conditions that Internet communication constitutes for communicative interaction in general and political participation and opinion formation in particular might reasonably become the object of a correspondingly increasing, critical reflection. In a primarily theoretical discourse, this article will discuss central potentials and risks posed by the Internet in the perspective of the democratic public sphere. Initially, the concept of the public sphere will be critically qualified; then general features of the conditions of the public sphere in late modernity will be characterised and, finally, the specific properties and perspectives of the Internet and its interface will be discussed within this overall framing.

Conceptualising the public sphere

An obvious point of departure for a reflection on the concept of the public sphere is Jürgen Habermas' classic analysis of the rise and decline of the bourgeois public sphere in *Strukturwandel der Öffentlichkeit* from 1962. His thesis of decline, which characterised the public sphere of the highly developed bourgeois society as no less than 'refeudalised', has been severely criticised throughout the years – e.g. by the originator himself in the foreword of the new edition (from 1990) – and today should be regarded as merely of historical interest. But Habermas' conceptualisation of the basic idea of the bourgeois public sphere is still able to make a productive contribution to the discussion: namely the notion that mediation between contending private interests and overall governmental regulation should take the shape of communicative, reason-based interaction among citizens in a specific, differentiated sphere of practice.

Furthermore, in this differentiated sphere neither economic nor social status should be deciding factors, but only the better argument with a convincing reference to the common good. This basic idea is still of interest; partly in its capacity of a precise and differentiated reconstruction of the revolutionary bourgeoisie's conceptualisation of the good society which was destined to supersede absolutism; partly as the foundation of ideas on which the historical construction of the institutions of democracy actually took place, and which even today constitutes the legitimacy of modern democratic society.

This rational core of both the conceptualisation and institutionalisation of the notion of the public sphere is, in other words, still in a position to claim the status of reality as an immanent, normative guideline of social practice, even though its practical impact on the societal regulation of conflicts and distribution of resources may often seem marginal (Nielsen and Horn). However, Habermas does not limit his analysis to the historical reconstruction of a specific, class-bound self-conception and its hegemonic shaping of the principles of societal intercourse: He also refers to the public sphere and universal reasoning in a utopian-progressive sense as the necessary means to overcome the barriers to the realisation of a truly free, democratic society constituted by the systemic, reifying mechanisms of capitalism and bureaucracy. In this sense, the malaise of modern society is due to the fact that the principle of the public sphere has not in practice obtained the status in the regulation of societal intercourse to which it should be entitled in its capacity as the principle of democratic societalisation *par excellence* – and social emancipation thus refers to the correction of this malaise.

Since the early 1970s, Habermas' conception of the bourgeois public sphere as the adequate normative basis for general social emancipation in a highly developed modern society has been confronted with various types of criticism (Peters; *Social Text*; Calhoun). In this spectrum, Oskar Negt and Alexander Kluge's critical dialogue with Habermas' theory of the public sphere from 1972, *Öffentlichkeit und Erfahrung*, still positions itself as the most thorough and fruitful criticism, since it both acknowledges the central relevance of Habermas' project and, at the same time, develops an alternative point of departure for the concept of the public sphere, considerably expanding its theoretical field of vision.

As mentioned above, in Habermas' theory the concept of the public sphere refers to a specific, differentiated field of practice in which citizens interact dialogically under the auspices of universal, critical reason and – via the institutions of parliamentary democracy – discursively mediate between the privately organised spheres of society and overall state regulation. Negt and Kluge confront this notion with an expanded concept of the public sphere, which in principle includes all socially relevant forms of experience. Their concept of the public sphere, in other words, transcends modernity's separated fields of practice and integrates all types of collective formation of meaning.

The motivation for this expanded definition of the concept is that, according to Negt and Kluge, the conceptualisation of the public sphere by Habermas and the early bourgeoisie is characterised by strongly exclusive features, and is therefore not suited to serve as the general frame for reflecting all relevant social experience, which it claims to be. Their argument is not least that different backgrounds in terms of class, education etc. equip individuals quite unequally with respect to the competence to master abstract, universal reasoning. Furthermore, Habermas' focus on the public sphere as a differentiated field of practice neglects those types of concrete experience and socially relevant formation of meaning that originate in the private spheres of social life. This includes partly the experience of individuals from the process of socialisation in the family and the related formation of gender roles and general expectations regarding human intercourse etc.; partly the variety of work-related experiences comprising elements of heteronomy and social hierarchy in immediate cooperative relations, as well as the more anonymous mechanisms of compulsion and marginalisation of the market.

In addition, Negt and Kluge point to a specific, private type of experience of crucial importance to society, namely the subjective everyday life experience of all individuals, with unorganised, sensory-emotional impulses of resistance, compensating fantasies and daydreams of unspecific change, which emerge in the process of wrestling with an everyday life that in large part appears heteronomous. If these fragmented subjective resources of resistance are being processed and organised consciously and emancipatorily in a collective relation of practice, the emergence of what Negt and Kluge call the 'proletarian public sphere' is taking place. To be sure, we should not be disturbed by the reminiscences of the rhetoric of the early 1970s since, in spite of its obvious connotations, the term does not refer to a public sphere exclusively related to the working class. It represents a counter-concept to the bourgeois public sphere, based on *general* social experience and the multiplicity of concrete subjective resources marginalised by the concept of the bourgeois public sphere. The development of the proletarian public sphere is, in other words, propelled by these repressed subjective resources of resistance, and it can take the shape of processes of politicisation from below, the formation of subcultures, oppositional artistic movements etc.

If the diffuse impulses of resistance of everyday life are *not* being processed collectively and discursively in the shape of the proletarian public sphere, they remain private, unfocused dynamic forces that are activated not least in the individuals' imaginative exchange with the standardised models for wishful dreams offered by the industries of consciousness (commercial culture and media, advertising etc.). In this connection, Negt and Kluge suggest yet another concept, the 'public spheres of production', to characterise the type of collective formation of meaning and shaping of social spaces of practice represented by the industries of consciousness. Whereas both the bourgeois and the proletarian public sphere on their distinct premises are characterised by a critical, dialogical basic principle of exchange, the public spheres of production address the recipient in a monological, instrumentalising manner in order to channel his/her private fantasies and longings into a prosaic act of buying and consuming.

Late modern conditions of the public sphere

In the terminology of Negt and Kluge, the processing of collective experience in late modernity takes place on the basis of a relationship of increasing conflict between the bourgeois public sphere, the proletarian public sphere and the public spheres of production as principles for the formation of meaning and the institutionalisation of practice (Nielsen 2001). The bourgeois and the proletarian public spheres are both founded on the communicative societalising principle of civil society although they represent two different, conflicting variants of the principle, whereas the public spheres of production are founded on the expansive, money-mediated principle of societalisation of the market. In practice, social processes will often be characterised by a more or less pragmatic interplay between these different types of public spheres, but the basic relation of conflict and tension remains a reality, and the development of the variable power relations regarding their respective weight in the processing and organising of social experience is of crucial importance for the developmental conditions of democracy.

The intensification of the active, enlightened political participation of the population and thereby the strengthening of civil society's communicative mediation of social intercourse vis-à-vis the money-mediation of the market and the power-mediation of the state constitutes the precondition for the further development of democracy in the deliberative sense of the word (Habermas, *Faktizität und Geltung*; Cohen and Arato). However, it does not seem plausible that this process can be based solely on the Habermasian ideal of rational, universally arguing discourses. The process will have to comprise the reflection and integration of the multiplicity of subjective resources and sensory-emotional needs that constitute the dynamics of politicisation from below, but which, conversely, do not in themselves imply any overall, universal perspective. It is, in other words, necessary to conceptualise a productive, mutually enlightening and politicising interplay of elements of the universally reasoning, bourgeois public sphere and the subjective experience-processing proletarian public sphere.

Thus, in a perspective of democratic civil society, these two types of public spheres are interdependent: The bourgeois public sphere needs the proletarian public sphere as a driving force and as a diversifying, sensibilising counterpart in the realisation of the principles of universal normativity. The resources of the proletarian public sphere can only unfold democratically on the level of society as a whole if their dynamics and experience of conflict are being processed within the discursive framework of the common good[1] and in a qualifying dialogue with the aspiration for an overall ethical consensus of the bourgeois public sphere.

A few further distinctions might be clarifying in this context. If we define 'public space' as an overall concept for society's commonly accessible, physical or virtual fields of practice, characterised as they are by a variety of conflicting interests and formations of meaning, the term 'public sphere' could advantageously be understood as a question of the specific *mode* of processing experience. As we have seen, these modes (bourgeois, proletarian, productionist) constitute conflicting principles of interaction that are operational in the struggle for hegemony in public space. A 'public', on the other hand, signifies a collective of agents operating communicatively (in the mode of bourgeois or proletarian public sphere) in public space – ranging from the level of overall public debate over autonomous, single issue-orientated 'partial publics' to, in a general sense oppositionally defined, 'counter publics'.

In this conceptualisation, evidently, it makes no sense to speak of 'the public sphere' in terms of one, unambiguously demarcated space. The parliament-orientated public debate, operating in the mode of the bourgeois public sphere, coexists with – and engages in conflictual interplay with – a diverse multiplicity of partial publics and counter publics in the shape of social movements and subcultures processing and organising social experience and cultural needs in the mode of the proletarian public sphere.[2] Nonetheless, the parliament-orientated public debate maintains a special status in its capacity as the overall interpreter and organiser of the conflict experience of society, and thereby as the crucial forum for the ongoing creation of democratic political culture (Nielsen, *Demokrati i bevægelse*).

The processing of conflict experience, though, has hegemonic character in the sense that only those expressions of the proletarian public sphere that have contrived to establish themselves in an adequate position of power are able to leave their mark on the politico-cultural self-conception of society. But in spite of this tendency towards a selective processing of experience, the parliament-orientated public debate must – due to its overall mode of reflection in obligation to the discursive framework of the common good – be regarded as crucially important, also in respect to the autonomous partial publics' chances of contributing productively to the perspective of democracy in the civil society sense. At their point of departure, partial publics tend to orientate themselves toward special interests and needs connected to their own limited experiential horizon. Therefore experience-expanding learning processes in interaction with other partial publics, and not least with the universal mode of reflection of the parliament-orientated public sphere, are required in order to channel this dynamics of politicisation into a socio-politically qualified shape. In the following, the term 'democratic public sphere' refers to this perspective of the modes of bourgeois and proletarian public sphere interacting.

This draws attention to another central issue of the public sphere in late modernity. As pointed out above, the development of a democratic public sphere, capable of processing all relevant social experience, cannot be reduced to the universal form of reflection of the bourgeois public sphere. It must also comprise conflictual social action in which agents with different interests and points of view interact in common spaces of practice, have new experiences, challenge each other's dictums and in this process develop a consciousness of common concerns and mutual obligations in spite of the differences. Such spaces of practice, where informal encounters and processes of experience across partial publics take place, are increasingly scarce resources in late modern everyday life, and this fact constitutes a significant problem for the developmental perspectives of the democratic public sphere (Sennett).

Precisely in this type of communicative practice, in which individuals in a physico-spatial sense impose themselves on each other, agents may develop their own means of production to constructively comprehend and process conflicts in the immediate context of everyday life and on this basis also develop a capacity to understand and act in relation to overall societal conflicts. This type of experience thus implies crucial perspectives for a democratic civil society and for a public interaction that is able to combine the recognition of differences and the reflection of the universal principles of the common good.

The increasing absence of such mixed spaces of practice and experience in late modern everyday life is partly due to prominent features of urban development like the tendency towards separating groups of the population with different social and cultural backgrounds – and like the ongoing transformation of city spaces into zones of pure consumption at the expense of the physical and aesthetic facilitation of the activity of civil society. Instead of animating encounters between strangers and the reflection of common concerns across differences, public spaces in late modernity increasingly appear primarily as forums for the smooth, harmonising, consumerist appeals of the public spheres of production.

Furthermore, the development of the spaces of practice and experience of everyday life is intertwined with the dominant role achieved by the mass media in social and cultural life as a whole. The general conflict between the public spheres of production on the one hand and the bourgeois and proletarian public spheres on the other appears highly accentuated in late modernity due to globalisation's dramatic expansion and complication of the space of relations far beyond the horizon of everyday experience (Giddens). In this constellation, the mediation of experience by the mass media increasingly dominates the collective formation of meaning and, due to the genuinely incalculable nature of global relations, the media to a large extent tend to reduce complexity by aesthetic means: Complex conflicts are reduced to trivial narratives of good vs. evil, politicians are staged as medial consumer goods and offered as icons of personal identification rather than as representatives of political programmes etc. In addition, the mass media's progressively more marked status as competing market agents contributes to fragmenting public space, and their sensationalist profiling in the battle over market shares tends to marginalise the issues and agents of reflecting public debate. All in all, this strengthens the appeal of public space to the individual as a consumer at the expense of his/her incentive to engage in public reflection as a citizen.

In the perspective of civil society, this development of the late modern space of relations necessitates the mediation of knowledge that does not originate from the individuals' immediate everyday life experience. Under these conditions, forming an opinion and acting as a citizen on a competent level not only depends on communicative interaction in concrete spaces of practice and experience but also implies the ongoing acquisition of a large fund of knowledge on geographically remote conditions and non-lucid relations of exchange and interdependency between near and far. In the terminology of Negt and Kluge, this constellation requires an interplay between 'immediate experience' (understood as sensorily-based knowledge which the individual has acquired in direct, bodily and mental exchange with the world) and 'mediated experience' (knowledge acquired at second hand). Both types of experience are crucial preconditions for being able to orientate oneself in the modern space of relations, so the distinction between them is not aimed at granting immediate experience a monopoly on being 'real' but merely at pointing out a fundamental difference in respect to 'quality of reality' which implies perspectives for the conditions of possibility for democratic processes of empowerment.

As Dieter Hoffmann-Axthelm has argued, it is the basic principle of human formation of experience that we acquaint ourselves with the world through our senses and in analogy to the immediate, sensorily-based experience of our previous life history (Hoffmann-Axthelm; Nielsen, *Æstetik, kultur og politik*). Concurrently with the development and differentiation of this primary foundation of experience, the ability to practice an increasingly abstracting formation of analogy emerges and allows us to integrate mediated experience; but the sensorily-based patterns of immediate experience remain the turning point, also for the acquisition of mediated experience.

With respect to the potential of the late modern space of relations for developing a democratic public sphere with a productive interplay between the proletarian public sphere based on the formation of concrete, diverse experiences and the universal reflection of the bourgeois public sphere, the interesting question is thus whether the dominance of the media and mediated experience still allows the process of analogical acquisition sufficient scope to function and thus enable individuals to develop a competent identity as citizens. Or whether the sensorily-based potential and the ability to form experience-integrating analogies in reality are being exhausted under the present conditions, with a common lack of orientation and judgement as a consequence – which would leave the diffuse resources of resistance of everyday experience to the instrumentalising processing of the public spheres of production.

The potential of the Internet in terms of public sphere

The Internet with its specific medial characteristics is inscribed in this overall picture of the public space of late modernity. The virtual space of practice, to which the interface of the World Wide Web grants access, is correspondingly permeated by conflicts between the principles of the bourgeois, the proletarian and the productionist public spheres and the related, conflicting formations of experience and meaning. In respect to quality of experience, the Internet further represents an ambiguity: On the one hand it contributes by way of its mediality to the increasingly dominant status of mediated experience in society; on the other hand, by way of the interactive potential of the net interface, it must be regarded as an important part of the current condition of acquiring immediate experience.

In this connection, it is a central question for the potential of media use in relation to the public sphere, according to which the discursive principles of the concrete interface have been constructed: which possibilities of control and interaction it opens and closes, which implicit intentionality (commercial, artistic, political, technocratic or repressive in terms of surveillance) frames the interaction and formation of experience facilitated by the interface, and to which extent it makes a genuine, dialogical exchange possible. These features of the interface condition practices in the virtual field of action, but without determining them in a strict sense, in other words, the concrete use of the media, the process of 'interfacing' (Cramer), still implies scope for critical reflection and alternative, autonomous practice.

We are witnessing a continuous production of hot air around the issue of the Internet and its democratic potentials. For instance, Kevin Kelly, editor of *Wired Magazine,* has praised the net as one big "participatory democracy" where the global community of users are in total control of events; and *Time Magazine* regards the net as a "direct democracy" and has appointed "You", meaning every single Internet user, to "personality of the year." It is worth noting that in these descriptions *all* practice of individual agents on the net is per definition 'democratic', and it is therefore not surprising that the evaluation turns out so optimistically.

There are, however, a number of central issues that are left in the dark by these cheerful interpretations of the potentials of the net. For instance, it constitutes a crucial difference whether the individual in his/her practice on the net is acting in the role of critically reflecting, communicating citizen, as monologically acting market agent or as bureaucratically framed user of the services of the public sector. Only the first mentioned of these roles has democratic relevance, and even in this category not all net practice can be classified as democratic since anti-democratic elements are also active on the net and seek to spread their misinformation disguised as arguments.

Furthermore, the role of the citizen as such is under pressure on the Internet, which since 1993/94 has been the target of an immense process of colonisation by the forces of the market (Nielsen, *Konsument eller samfundsborger?*). The commercialisation of access to the net, the orientation of Internet regulations towards facilitating trade transactions, the increasing advertisement financing of all sorts of net activities, the massive and expansive presence of private companies etc. has to a large extent transformed Internet interaction into public spheres of production, where advanced communication technology is utilised in a targeted manner and beyond any critical dialogue in order to establish a direct link between the economic interests of business and the private desires and inclinations of the individual consumer. This practice is evidently generally considered legitimate, but it has absolutely nothing to do with democracy, if we thereby understand the reflective political organisation of the common concerns of society.

In the light of this process of commercialisation, Jodi Dean denies the Internet any relevance in the perspective of a democratic public sphere. According to Dean, critical civil society activity will also inevitably be absorbed by the dominant "communicative capitalism" on the net. This analysis seems, however, to be too deterministic, considering that the Internet still functions as a field of practice for a multiplicity of non-commercial agents, networks and institutions who use the net on their own terms. In spite of their discursive autonomy, these activities are nevertheless conditioned and restricted by the dominance of the market, in the sense that the market-defined competition in the virtual field of practice makes it considerably more difficult for autonomous civil society initiatives (whether they are political, social or artistic) to attract attention and establish themselves on the net. On the other hand, the phenomenon 'weblogs' proves that this restriction should not be exaggerated (Schmidt).

It will be a basic assumption in the following that if the Internet deserves particular attention in the perspective of a democratic public sphere, it must be on the basis of its own, unique medial properties and not just as an expanded and accelerated version of the traditional media. The expansion, the acceleration and immediate availability of gigantic amounts of information are, of course, in a quantitative sense, important new features of the Internet, but its qualitative innovation consists in its facilitation of decentralised two-way communication, i.e. its "many to many capability" (Rheingold). Apart from the interactive potential, the Internet also grants the individual an immediate opportunity to publish directly for a global public. So, in principle, the Internet constitutes a vast field of opportunity in the perspective of both the bourgeois and the proletarian public sphere.

However, the actual use of the net exploits the new medial possibilities of the interface only to a very limited degree. The Internet is to a large extent used as an ordinary mass media: Public authorities, political parties and agents of the market address their recipients via the net in the same one-way mode of communication that they have traditionally used in printed material and TV-spots, whereas dialogic exchange and debate is rarely offered (Nielsen 2007, *Konsument eller samfundsborger,* 115). Likewise, many users simply consult the net in order to read newspapers or check the news on TV stations' sites. Here, use of the net is further characterised by major social and educational differences: The younger, well-educated part of the population has competences to seek information independently and draws on a variety of sources, whereas the older and less educated typically turn to the sites of the large, commercial media, granting them a considerable position of power in respect to the hegemonic interpretation of the relations and conflicts of society (Klinenberg).

Apart from this, the Internet is first of all used for private e-mail correspondence, entertainment and the search for information, whereas politics plays a very marginal role in activity on the net as a whole. Furthermore, activity on the net is highly integrated into everyday practice: By far the main part of the communication takes place between family members, friends, colleagues and neighbours, and only a very marginal part involves participation in general discussions and exchanges with strangers on issues of common interest. According to the international surveys on Internet activity, its element of general, public interaction between citizens is, in other words, extremely limited. Or in other terms: Internet communication, which orientates itself towards the universal perspective of reflection of the bourgeois public sphere, remains so far of peripheral importance in comparison with the proportions of the public spheres of production and private communication on the net.

In this quantitative sense, it looks only slightly better for the elements of proletarian public sphere on the Internet since they also stand quite in the shadow of commercial and private net use. But in a qualitative respect the net represents a crucial new resource for the communication and processing of experience of autonomous civil society initiatives. A diverse multiplicity of social, cultural and artistic movements, subcultures etc. use the net for internal communication, public presentations, campaigning, organising demonstrations, putting pressure on politicians and media etc. In order to assess the potentials of the Internet in terms of democratic public sphere, however, it is crucial to be aware that these currents represent civil society practice which operates in both the physical and the virtual space of practice at the same time: Their activity originates in experiences and relations in 'real life' and in a common effort to bring about concrete changes, whereas virtual space is integrated as a supplementing frame for a common, inward formation of identity and as a public platform for outward communication.

In principle, the virtual space may in such contexts of practice contribute to compensating for the above-mentioned increasing scarcity of physical, urban spaces designed to facilitate the public, communicative interaction between citizens. In addition, virtual space offers the opportunity of creating communicative circuits and relations of practice that transcend the limits of physical space and thus open the perspective of a global civil society. Those movements and subcultures, using the Internet in this way in order to create critical, public reflection in an interplay with 'real life' practice in the shape of decentralised communicating forms of politics, are productively exploiting the uniquely new medial potentials of the Internet.

It is the strength of these forms of political participation that they, in contrast to the traditional hierarchical forms of party politics, offer the individual the opportunity of immediately and directly becoming a valid and active participant. Their weakness in the perspective of a democratic public sphere, on the other hand, is partly that they lack a democratically legitimising formal mandate, and partly that they will tend to fragment public, communicative interaction and marginalise the obligation of the agents in respect to reflecting society as a community of historical experience, including common politico-cultural values and standards of public interaction. Inwardly, these autonomous networks may function as highly productive publics based on the mode of the concrete, experience-processing proletarian public sphere, which develop both a strong, common identity and differentiating learning processes in relation to their respective topics. But outwardly this very combination of identity work and political commitment will often make them appear as monological partial publics with an exclusive focus on their own themes and interests.

As was pointed out earlier, this reflects a general limitation of the immediate horizon of experience of partial publics which it would be essential to overcome in an overall perspective of the democratic public sphere in late modernity. In other words, if the Internet is to be developed further as a space of practice of civil society and thus gain relevance in an overall perspective of a democratic public sphere, it implies that the partial publics transcend their particularistic self-presentation and create forums for common, transverse discussion. The perspective of this would be the emergence of a new political culture on the Internet which would integrate universalistic reflection and recognition of difference – and thus be able to operate within the discursive framework of the common good without invalidating the particular network identities.

So far, however, the partial publics have primarily appropriated the Internet as a medium for their individual needs, not as a medium for universal public reasoning. The explanation for this may certainly be that a need for overall public forums on the net has hitherto not manifested itself with sufficient urgency for the partial publics to foster the necessary initiatives. Needs emerging from practice will always be the decisive factors as to whether a medium is brought into play in relation to political issues. At the same time, each medium is characterised by distinct medial properties that facilitate and condition specific forms of realisation of the practice needs in question – and in this perspective the interface of the digital media carries features that in principle may contribute to weakening the developmental conditions of overall public forums on the Internet.

Until now, general experience indicates that 'pure' net communication, i.e. without interplay with 'real life' practice, does not provide optimal conditions for establishing democratic dialogue between citizens. Numerous analyses of political debates on the Internet show concurrently that a hyperactive minority typically conquers the scene and primarily utilises the public space of the net for monological proclamation of dictums (J. Jensen; Torpe; K. Jensen; Wilhelm; Rheingold). Corresponding tendencies occur in other, purely virtual forums: In spite of the medial potential of the weblog and the general image of blogging as a media of interactivity and dialogue, a closer view reveals the 'blogosphere' as dominated by the monological self-presentation of individuals and by the formation of groups that confirm unity inwardly but do not engage in outward dialogue (Lovink).

Similarly, the virtual communities that are unfolding in popular domains like *MySpace* serve the purpose of individual self-presentation, identity profiling and communication within a particular, private horizon rather than the facilitation of overall reflecting, democratic dialogue. Undoubtedly, these forums operating in the mode of 'public spheres of monological self-presentation' fulfil a need, but they represent a use of the Internet media which neither in the bourgeois nor the proletarian sense has anything to do with a democratic public sphere. Although the activity in the virtual communities of *MySpace* is defined by the users themselves, it is further framed by the public spheres of production since the portal is owned and run for profit purposes by the media tycoon Rupert Murdoch.

In other words, net communication that is not involved in an interplay with 'real life' relations appears to appeal to the individual as a self-centred consumer, i.e. to his/her private needs and special interests rather than to his/her capacity as a citizen orientated towards dialogue and the common good. The background for this tendency is complex but involves as a crucial element some characteristics of the interface of the World Wide Web and the virtual space of practice. As mentioned above, due to the medial possibility of interactivity, virtual space implies an element of formation of immediate experience, but at the same time it must be noted that this type of experience has a restricted quality. Whereas face-to-face interaction implies a broad-spectrum sensory relation in which the agents offer each other a complex response, adding a variety of nuances to the verbally-communicated content and thus throwing it into relief, the virtual encounter is characterised by a restricted, almost frictionless, sensory quality. As pointed out earlier in relation to the concepts of immediate and mediated experience formation, this distinction is not aiming at granting one type of interaction a monopoly on being 'real' but merely at distinguishing between different qualities of reality with different characteristics and potentials. Both face-to-face communication and virtual communication are absolutely necessary in the late modern space of relations, but due to their respective interactive sensory qualities they imply different degrees of involvement and mutual obligation between the agents.

In face-to-face interaction we offer our bodily integrity as a pledge to our commitment and credibility and at the same time demonstrate a degree of trust and recognition of the counterpart that we would not be able to communicate virtually – no matter what bandwidth the interface may reach (Böhme; Rheingold).[3] In addition, face-to-face communication is the form of experience in which we, in the perspective of our individual life histories, have developed our basic social competences and to which also, in later phases of life, essential dimensions of our judgement and ability to make qualified distinctions remain connected (Guggenberger). The fact that important political and economic negotiations and the settling of major agreements still necessarily imply face-to-face meetings – even though matters might technically very well be dealt with in virtual space – is a strong indication that this qualitative difference is actually operative in social practice. When complicated and important questions are at stake in economic and political relations (or in love relations, for that matter), and the highest possible degree of mutual trust is necessary, virtual communication is in other words insufficient – on such occasions the presence of the body and the sincerity of the face are required as guarantors.

A corresponding observation is made in the field of education via the Internet, where experience shows that the necessary mutual interest and trust between the interacting parties to the educational process on the net can only be established and maintained if virtual communication is supplemented by occasional meetings face-to-face (Lundvall). Furthermore, the participants of more informal virtual communities typically develop a need for also getting together in 'real life' every now and then since this quality of interaction is experienced as more binding and thus more consolidating for the community than the purely virtual relation (Rheingold; Heintz and Müller).

In other words, when purely virtual political debating forums seem to encourage agents to participate in a discourse of special interests rather than to commit themselves to reflecting the common good, an obvious explaining factor could be the restricted, almost frictionless, sensory quality of the interface and virtual communication which to a higher degree appeals to the expansive projection of one's own needs, wishes and dictums than to the complex reflection of both one's own and the counterpart's points of view in relation to the discursive framework of the common good. It is probably an even more central element of explanation that the agents of virtual communication neither in a physico-spatial, a bodily nor a social sense are dependent on one another: The communication is not associated with any common or mutual responsibility which might connect the agents in binding relations (Poster). Moreover, on this background, pure net communication will typically not encourage the development of a practical readiness among the participants to recognise each other's points of view and basic legitimacy to the extent that they are willing to seek agreement, make compromises and commit themselves to reflecting the common good – in other words: act as democratic citizens in public interaction.

Conclusion

As pointed out above, the Internet today represents an invaluable resource for partial publics and counter-publics operating in the mode of the proletarian public sphere and thereby for a reflecting, experience-processing, decentralised many-to-many communication which connects interaction in virtual space with relations and committed activity in 'real life'. In this sense, the Internet forms an important framing condition for a possible current development of an increased democratic participation in the shape of public civil society interaction. But as we have also seen, the partial publics so far exhibit considerable limitations in the perspective of an overall democratic public sphere due to their tendency to form closed circuits and to neglect the transversal dialogue within the discursive framework of the common good. In other words: On the Internet, the subjective, experience-processing communicative practice of the proletarian public sphere holds a relatively strong position, whereas the position of the universal reflection of the bourgeois public sphere so far remains weak.

If the communicative practice of the partial publics is to be able to contribute to a productive interplay between proletarian and bourgeois public spheres and thereby to the development of a participation-based, democratic civil society which is also competent in an overall, socio-political perspective, learning processes are necessary in which the diverse, autonomous communities of practice challenge each other dialogically and open their respective, particular horizons towards a universal public discourse. The Internet would still not be able to replace the classic mass media and parliamentary forums in respect to the overall processing and interpretation of the conflict experience of society, but the net might play an important role as the channel through which the partial publics combining 'real life' and net activity articulate themselves into the common public debate.

But these positive potentials of the Internet in a perspective of the democratic public sphere are at the same time flanked by a number of risks. As we have seen, the public spheres of production have established themselves in an extraordinarily strong position in the public space of the Internet and have shaped its dominant formations of meaning in the monological forms of private fantasies of consumption. In an interplay with the liberalist mainstream of political life, the agents of the public spheres of production thus – both in 'real life' and in the virtual space of practice – contribute actively to the positioning of special interests and immediate private preferences as the turning point of social practice, at the expense of the perspective of reflecting the common good.

The discursive hegemony of the public spheres of production further implies that the dominant formation of meaning concerning the Internet focuses on precisely those medial properties that aim at facilitating the user as a self-centred consumer who expects his/her own urges and needs to be satisfied immediately and without friction. The appeal of this promise of the net as an infrastructure for the realisation of private, monological wishful thinking is strong and so far tends to marginalise alternative formations of meaning with regard to the net as a possible forum for engaged dialogical exchange between citizens.

Finally, we should consider the risks to a democratic public sphere that emanate from the increasing, comprehensive governmental surveillance activity on the Internet and from the action-conditioning forms of control that are always implied in the very construction of the interface. It would in this respect be crucial for the developmental possibilities of a democratic public sphere that these forms of control be based on the communicative, critically reflecting principles of civil society and not on the formal principles of the market or the state. The potentials of the Internet in respect to a democratic public sphere are, in other words, closely connected to the question of the development of social and political relations of power – in the virtual space of practice as well as in 'real life'.

Notes

1. 'The discursive framework of the common good' conceptualises the common good not as a fixed entity but as an arena for a continuous, argumentative struggle about what, in the concrete situation, most plausibly serves 'the common good'. Access to the arena is conditioned by the recognition of the existence of common concerns in society (Nielsen 2007).
2. I leave out the non-public forums for negotiating compromises between private and governmental agents that are playing an increasing role in processes of 'governance'. At the end of the day, the decisions of these forums still have to be able to legitimise themselves to the bourgeois public sphere and the parliamentary process (Nielsen 2001).
3. Howard Rheingold even ascribes a basic element of "ontological untrustworthiness" to virtual communication. According to Rheingold, the transmission of images via webcams would not change this feature of virtual communication since the transmission would not be able to represent the "life force" or the "breath" of the agents (172).

Works cited

Böhme, Gernot. "Leibliche Anwesenheit im Raum." *Ästhetik und Kommunikation* 108 (2000). Print.

Calhoun, Craig (ed.). *Habermas and the Public Sphere*. Cambridge: MIT Press, 1992. Print.

Cohen, Jean L., and Andrew Arato. *Civil Society and Political Theory*. Cambridge: MIT Press, 1992. Print.

Dagbladet Information 14 Feb. 2007. Print.

Cramer, Florian. "What Is Interface Aesthetics, or What Could It Be (Not)?" *This volume*. Print.

Dean, Jodi. "Kommunikativ kapitalisme: Hvorfor nettet ikke er den offentlige sfære." *GRUS* 67 (2002). Print.

Giddens, Anthony. *Modernity and Self-Identity*. Stanford University Press, 1991. Print.

Guggenberger, Bernd. *Das digitale Nirwana*. Reinbek: Rowohlt, 1999. Print.

Habermas, Jürgen. *Strukturwandel der Öffentlichkeit*. Neuwied/Frankfurt am Main: Luchterhand/Suhrkamp, 1962/1990. Print.

– *Faktizität und Geltung*. Frankfurt am Main: Suhrkamp, 1992. Print.

Heinz, Bettina, and Christoph Müller. *Fallstudie 'Die Sozialwelt des Internet'*. 1999. Web. 3 Apr. 2007. <http://www.soz.unibe.ch/ii/virt_d.html>.

Hoffmann-Axthelm, Dieter. *Sinnesarbeit*. Frankfurt am Main: Campus, 1984. Print.

Jensen, Jakob Linaa. *Den digitale demokratiske dialog*. Århus: Aarhus Universitetsforlag, 2003. Print.

Jensen, Klaus Bruhn (ed.). *Interface://Culture*. Frederiksberg: Samfundslitteratur, 2005. Print.

Kelly, Kevin. "We are the Web." *Wired Magazine* 13.08 (2005). Web. 12 Aug. 2010. <http://www.wired.com/wired/archive/13.08/tech.html>.

Klinenberg, Eric. "Den digitale makten." *Le Monde Diplomatique* Jan. 2007. Print.

Lovink, Geert. "Blogging – den nihilistiske impuls." *Lettre Internationale* 11 June 2006. Print.

Lundvall, Bengt-Åke. "Universitetet i den lærende økonomi." *Universiteter for fremtiden*. Eds. Hans Siggaard Jensen and Peter Maskell. Frederiksberg: Samfundslitteratur, 2001. Print.

Negt, Oskar, and Alexander Kluge. *Öffentlichkeit und Erfahrung*. Frankfurt am Main: Surkamp 1972. English version. *Public Sphere and Experience*. Minneapolis: University of Minnesota Press, 1993. Print.

Nielsen, Henrik Kaare. *Demokrati i Bevægelse*. Århus: Aarhus Universitetsforlag, 1991. Print.

– *Æstetik, Kultur og Politik*. Århus: Aarhus Universitetsforlag, 1996. Print.

– *Kritisk Teori og Samtidsanalyse*. Århus: Aarhus Universitetsforlag, 2001. Print.

– *Konsument eller Samfundsborger? Kritiske Essays*. Århus: Klim, 2007. Print.

Nielsen, Henrik Kaare, and Finn Horn (eds.). *Kritik som deltagelse*. Århus: Klim, 2006. Print.

Peters, Bernhard. "Der Sinn von Öffentlichkeit." *Öffentlichkeit, Öffentliche Meinung, Soziale Bewegungen*. Ed. Friedhelm Neidhardt.. Opladen: Westdeutscher Verlag, 1994. Print.

Poster, Mark. *Cyber Democracy: Internet and the Public Sphere*. University of California, Irvine, 1995. Print.

Rheingold, Howard. *The Virtual Community*. New York: Addison-Wesley Publishing Company, 1993. Print.

Schmidt, Jan. *Weblogs. Eine Kommunikationssoziologische Studie*. Konstanz: UVK Verlag, 2006. Print.

Sennett, Richard. *Uses of Disorder: Personal Identity and City Life*. London: Faber and Faber, 1996. Print.

Social Text 25/26 (1990). Print.

Time Magazine 25.12 (2006). Print.

Torpe, Lars, et al. *Demokrati på Nettet*. Ålborg: Aalborg Universitetsforlag, 2005. Print.

Wilhelm, Anthony G. "Virtual Sounding Boards: How Deliberative Is Online Political Discussion?" *Digital Democracy*. Eds. Barry N. Hague, and Brian D. Loader. London: Routledge, 1999. Print.

Is There Really Only One Word For It?

Software Vocabularies in the Expanded Field of Interface Aesthetics

BY JACOB LILLEMOSE

> Sometimes you experience something so new, so delightfully unexpected, that there is only one word for it. Wow! (Promotional video for Windows Vista).

> Advertising – like every "event" – first distributes modes of perception in order to prompt ways of living; it actualizes modes of affecting and being affected in souls, in order to realize them in bodies (Lazzarato).

In his text "Struggle, Media, Event," sociologist Maurizio Lazzarato points out how contemporary advertising to an increasing degree is no longer merely about the representation of a cultural object – instead, it is about producing forms of experience and engagement. He contextualises this change within what he calls "the paradigm of the event where images, signs and statements contribute to allowing the world to happen". With the 'Battle of Seattle' as his primary example, Lazzarato contends that the event contains a revolutionary potential of making other worlds possible, while emphasising the way in which the event in the form of advertising is also incorporated to function as an essential part of contemporary capitalism and its fabrication of worlds. The essential challenge of Lazzarato's text, then, is to ask which worlds the "images, signs and statements" of advertising allow to happen.

Responding to this challenge, the present text will discuss the way in which two advertisements for a proprietary and free software-based operating system respectively – a promotional video for the operating system Windows Vista (2005) by Microsoft, and a work of installation art about the operating system *X-Devian*. The New Technologies to the People System (2003-) by Daniel Garcia Andújar

– allow two very different worlds of software to happen.[1] Through their "images, signs and statements" the advertisements produce experiences and engagement with the two operating systems. They are not simply trying to convince the users to buy a product, but are also inviting them to invest in a practical and intellectual use of the software. In that sense, echoing the presumption that consumers are the true product of advertising, the video and the installation can also be said to allow users to happen.

In fact, the fashioning of users is fundamental for the making of possible worlds by these two advertisements because it is the users who will eventually realise those possible worlds through their uses of the operating systems. The first advertisement configures the user as a consumer who is happy with the operating system as it is sold and has no urge to ask questions; whereas the second configures the user as a kind of hacker who critically explores the operating system and the possibilities of developing it as a cultural phenomenon.

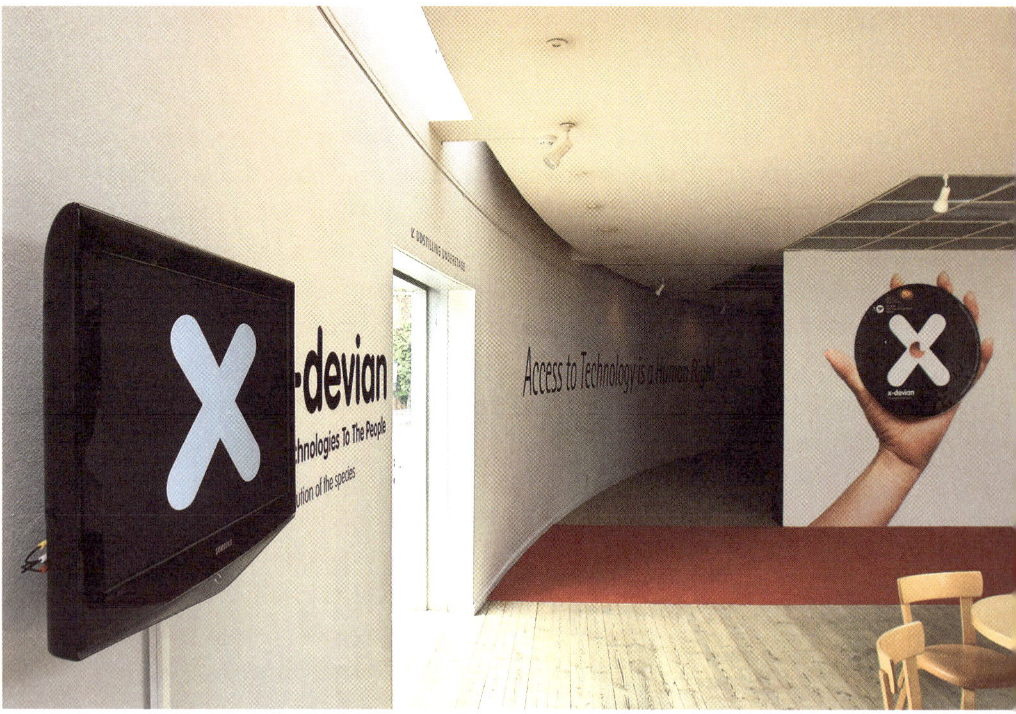

ILL. 1: Installation shot of *X-Devian. The New Technologies to the People System* (2003-) by Daniel Garcia Andújar (Aarhus Kunstbygning, May/June 2007). Photo by Jens Møller Sørensen.

The aim of this text, then, is more specifically to discuss how the different users that the two advertisements allow to happen outline two different trajectories for the use of software as a form of involvement in contemporary culture.

Vocabularies, interfaces and distributions

Taking a cue from the punch line of the Windows Vista video, the discussion of the involvement can be conceived as a question of user vocabulary, i.e. what words, languages and discourses the advertisements offer the users. Hence, whether explicitly reducing the vocabulary to just one word as in the case of the Windows Vista video or augmenting it through a multiplicity of discourse as in the case of the installation about *X-Devian*, the vocabularies that the advertisements offer the user designate forms of involvement, albeit very different forms of involvement, with the software and the software culture of which it is part.

Moreover, in their offering of vocabularies, the advertisements function as interfaces.[2] In the context of software, the interface primarily refers to the user interface, i.e. the objects (the screen, mouse, keyboard) and the semiotics (graphics, metaphors, structures) that mediate the user's interaction with the software. The two advertisements do not function as user interfaces in this conventional sense. They do not help the users connect to the Internet and organise files like the screen interface does. Instead, their assistance concerns the relationship between user and software prior to any concrete use. They produce what in software terminology is referred to as conceptual models. A conceptual model is a representation of a piece of software that helps the users to create an abstract understanding of the nature and logic of the software, which then will help them in the actual use of the software.[3] However, the understanding that the advertisements create is not primarily an understanding of the operating system in a technical sense, but rather an understanding of the cultural significance of the operating systems.

While software design theory makes a categorical distinction between interfaces and conceptual models, designating the practical and intellectual interaction with the software, respectively, in the case of the two advertisements, the interface includes the conceptual model.

Hence, the advertisements motivate an expanded notion of the human-computer interface beyond the isolated relationship mediated by the design of machines, screens and software and include the cultural images, narratives and ideas that are associated with and inform these designs. Such an expanded notion of the human-computer interface can be conceived in terms of a cultural interface in the sense that the interface gives access to forms of involvement in software culture. Instead of conceiving human interaction with computers as an interaction with stand-alone technical entities, the interfaces constructed by the advertisements for Windows Vista and *X-Devian* concern human relations to a cultural context through software or to software as culture.

The expanded notion of the interface also implies an expanded notion of interface *aesthetics* beyond questions of usability and smart desktop design. In connection with what he calls "the distribution of the sensible," Jacques Rancière has introduced a notion of aesthetics which, although it makes no reference to software interfaces, points to something relevant about the interface aesthetics of the two advertisements (Rancière, *The Politics of Aesthetics*).[4] According to Rancière, aesthetics conceived as a distribution of the sensible is, "a system of self-evident facts of sense perception [...] that determines the very manner in which something in common lends itself to participation and in what way various individuals have a part in this distribution" (12). Whether they serve structures of control or processes of empowerment, aesthetics designate ways of seeing, thinking and saying that produce subjectivities and the possibilities of these subjectivities' participation in, and organisation of, social contexts. As such, aesthetics are fundamentally political. Transferred to the interface aesthetics of the advertisements, the point is that their "images, signs and statements" determine the users' involvement in software culture and not simply the use of the operating system.

Essentially, this expanded notion conceives the difference between the two advertisements as a matter of the production of "political subjectivity" (9).

"There's only one word for it"

In the context of proprietary software, advertising plays an increasingly important role. Ever since Apple's legendary presentation of their first Macintosh computer, which introduced the graphical user interface, in a commercial broadcasted during Super Bowl XVIII in 1984,[5] proprietary software culture has been as much about cultural development as about technical development.[6] Hence, when Windows Vista by Microsoft was launched in 2007, it was accompanied by an extensive advertising campaign involving a package of marketing stunts in public space, in the mass media and of course on the web, including a theme song by a famous Indian pop singer.[7] One of the campaign's leitmotifs was that there was only one word for the experience of the new operating system: Wow. The word was part of the title of the aforementioned theme song, but it was most explicitly used in a promotional video.[8]

The video starts in the mountains with a sequence in which a modern-day version of the figure in Casper David Friedrich's painting *Wanderer above the Mist* (1818), a fully equipped tourist of nature – on crutches, even – is hiking with fellow tourists and a guide. On the way to the top, the 'wanderer' stops to admire the pleasing view and in awe he exclaims "Wow". The implied reference to Friedrich's painting seems to be very consciously employed to announce the coming of an extraordinary phenomenon, and the opening sequence is followed by sequences referring to phenomena such as first love, the rock'n'roll revolution, the courage of children, a golf miracle, the wonders of agriculture, the magic of fairytales, and the architectural magnificence of The Great Wall of China. Finally, the video ends with a sequence showing a man who sits down at his shiny, crispy, clean desk and opens his laptop to "experience something so new, so delightfully unexpected, that there is only one word for it. Wow."[9]

On the face of it, the promotional video is simply an involuntarily comical expression of a somewhat naïve branding strategy. Yet, on a deeper level, it reveals itself as a cleverly crafted example of the kind of advertising that Lazzarato points to; and if analysed in further detail it reveals something essential about the world and the users that the operating system allows to happen.[10]

Basically, the video presents the operating system as a technological wonder comparable with the biggest events in human history and life. The substantial criticism of Windows Vista has ridiculed this comparison from a technological point of view.[11] However,

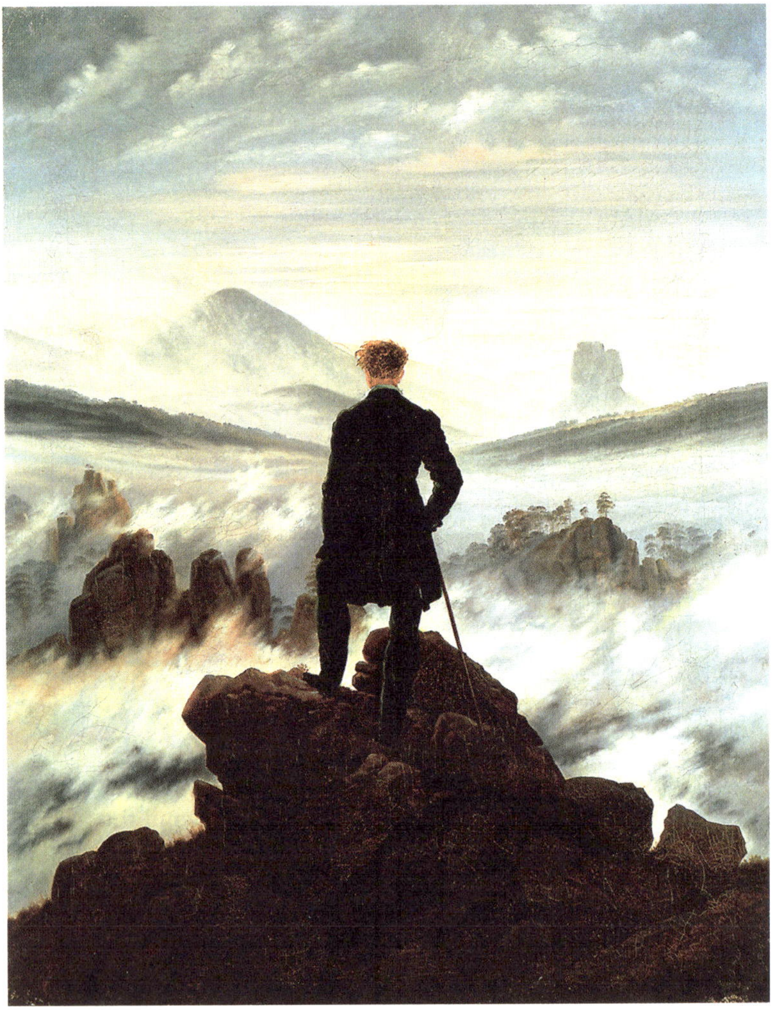

ILL. 2: Caspar David Friedrich: *Wanderer Above the Mist* (1818)
The opening sequence of the Windows Vista video makes an obvious reference to Caspar David Friedrich's painting *Wanderer Above the Mist* (1818) and its alleged description of a sublime experience. It has been impossible to get hrough to Microsoft to obtain a still from the sequence.

instead of reiterating this criticism the aim here is to give a critical outline of the cultural perspectives of the comparison.

Through its montage-style narrative, the video establishes a relation between Windows Vista and the user, and as such it functions as an interface in the aforementioned expanded sense. Without a word about the actual functionalities and design principles of the operating system, Microsoft delivers a clear point. With Windows Vista you are not using a computer any more (or at least: you are not aware of doing so). Instead, like the people in the video, you are having an experience.[12] What distinguishes Windows Vista from other operating systems on the market is the experience of it, how it feels, rather than what it can do. Parallel to this, the video also connects with the new "experience economy" in which the product is staged as an experience that engages the consumer "in a personal, memorable way" (Pine and Gilmore). With Windows Vista, the user is buying not goods or a service but an experience, and one to remember.

Facing the "absolutely great"

But what more exactly characterises the experience of Windows Vista? The video presents the operating system as more than a piece of software for the everyday activities in software culture. According to the video, Windows Vista is an experience of life when it is most poetic, most amazing, when the users are free to live in the moment.[13] It fills them with positive emotions, expands their view on the world, and, as the name indicates, lets them envision the future. The video cleverly plays on numerous such references and associations, all intended to conceptualise Windows Vista in the minds of the possible buyers and users as a product with a scope far beyond the technological realm, a product that is inseparable from the essence, the biggest and the best of what it means to be human and to live in today's world. Not just in any part of the world but in the technologically developed part of the world, where software is mostly proprietary and commodified, serving the advancement of information capitalism in its neoliberal, globalised form, of which Microsoft is one of the most powerful exponents. The licence "only gives [the user] some rights to use the software. Microsoft reserves all other rights." The user is thus encouraged to consume the software like any other product in the experience economy.

So while the thought that Windows Vista possesses enriching existential value might be fascinating, the suggestion seems to imply a set of values and premises that should rather generate scepticism. Hence, the new, open horizon of experiences of possible worlds that Windows Vista supposedly lets the users enjoy is framed by very specific ideas of how the users live their lives through the use of the software, how they perceive and act upon the world through the operating system. These ideas are based on strategies of regulation, administration and (ultimately) control, working in the service of the information politics of proprietary software. In other words, they establish a relation of power. As such, Windows Vista can be associated with the notion of "governmental technologies" as introduced by Michel Foucault. Generally speaking, governmental technologies designate a modern, neoliberal form of power, in which the subject is governed through organised life practices that encourage the subject to behave according to a specific self-perception, specific internalised ideas one might say, of its position and potential in the world (Lemke).

How do this relation of power, these implied values and premises manifest themselves in terms of the experience of the operating system according to the storyline of the video? What user self-perception does it sell, what position and potential does it assign to the user? The opening sequence outlines an answer. What the video is actually telling the user with the implicit reference to Friedrich's painting is that the experience of Windows Vista is a sublime phenomenon, i.e. an experience of "the absolutely great" as Kant writes in his *Critique of Judgement* (94).[14]

Faced with the sublime experience of Windows Vista, the user is in no position to question the operating system. All the user can do is to realise the greatness of the operating system and his own subservient role as a user configured as a consumer. The user might be enriched by using Windows Vista, but only to the extent that he/she recognises the authority of the operating system and engages in software activities that consent to its values and premises. To paraphrase the title of Stanley Kubrick's *Dr. Strangelove* (1964), which refers to the 'sublime' experience of the nuclear bomb,[15] the user should stop worrying about Windows Vista as a technological artefact and love it as a sublime experience in contemporary software culture.

As several users have experienced, Windows Vista is not exactly the 'technologically sublime' operating system that the video pictures it to be. So the user should worry. However, not so much in relation to the functional stability of the system but in relation to the 'technologically sublime' having a dominant influence on the making of possible software culture and defining of software experience and engagement.[16]

A principal function of the video's linking of Windows Vista with the sublime experience is to depoliticise the operating system and its use. As a sublime experience of technology, engineering and science, the operating system is dissociated from the discussions and negations of disagreeing and dissensual positions that (according to Rancière) constitute the field of democratic politics (Ranciere, "Ten Theses on Politics"). Hence, the user should stop worrying not only about the advanced and complicated technological architecture of Windows Vista but also about the information politics embodied in the operating system and the conflicts of interest and relations of power they involve. Instead of employing the operating system in forms of political involvement in software culture that challenges industrial authorities, like Microsoft, the user should simply love the experience of it as a naturalised (albeit extraordinary) part not only of software culture but also of the totality of human existence.[17] In other words, Windows Vista makes worlds possible through an experience which transcends the field of politics as a field where humans make worlds possible through discussions and negotiations. Nevertheless, the system is presented as the liberation and empowerment of human existence.

More specifically, this depoliticised experience manifests itself as a reduction of the user's software vocabulary to one word, a general exclamation of wonder that says nothing about the specific capacities and possibilities of software, neither technologically nor politically. The "Wow" is an expression of a software discourse where knowledge of, reflection on and involvement with software is replaced by sensations and feelings. This replacement feeds "the human propensity to place faith in and assign higher power to an agency that is not completely understood," which computer scientist Alan Kay identifies as a problematic impact of computers on culture (Kay, "Microelectronics and the Personal Computer" 135). The user cannot completely understand Windows Vista and is given little other alternative than to trust its technology and politics.

According to Kay, counteracting this trust in computers, including software, is not a question of mistrusting them but of developing the computer literacy of the user (Kay and Goldberg). "Computer literacy" to him, however, is more than simply learning to read and understand computer manuals. Instead, it is a matter of "contact with the activity of computing deep enough to make the computational equivalent of reading and writing fluent and enjoyable" (Kay, "Computer Literacy" 53). In other words, it is a question of being able to use the new language of software code to write programs, like being able to use traditional languages to write stories. Hence, in relation to the Dynabook and very appropriate for the current discussion, he writes: "One can imagine one of the first programs an owner will write is a filter to eliminate advertising!" (Kay, "A Personal Computer for Children of All Ages" n. pag.). Only through the continuous development of such literacy, he argues, can the full potential of software be realised and make possible a software culture in which humans (users rather than the industry) constitute the true creative force.[18]

From tool to experience and back again

Essentially, the video is symptomatic of a strong tendency in contemporary proprietary software culture to conceive software as an experience rather than a tool.[19] As Lev Manovich has demonstrated, the tendency is particularly noticeable in the design of user interfaces within the fields of ubiquitous computing and mobile digital devices – but it also has an impact on the design, conception and promotion of software for personal computers (Manovich "Information as an Aesthetic Event"). Notwithstanding the exciting, spectacular and constructive experiences that the tendency generates in terms of human interaction with technology, it has the propensity to reduce the critical aspect of software use and the users' involvement in software culture. As an experience, like the sublime experience that Windows Vista is depicted as, software is defined by the positivism of technological progress rather than by the critical discourse of cultural development. It is a way of living given to the users by the industry rather than a possibility for the users to create their own autonomous ways of living.

The industry has good reason to advance the tendency since it, in accordance with B. Joseph Pine II and James H. Gilmore's account of the experience economy, accommodates not only the behavioural patterns but also the needs and desires of contemporary consumers and thus represents a profitable business opportunity. However, while the users on their part have good reasons to worry about this tendency since their critical agency is being replaced by consensual participation, there is no reason for despair as there are equally strong tendencies to explore the notion of software as a tool for critical involvement in software culture, especially within the practices and discourses of free software and software art.[20]

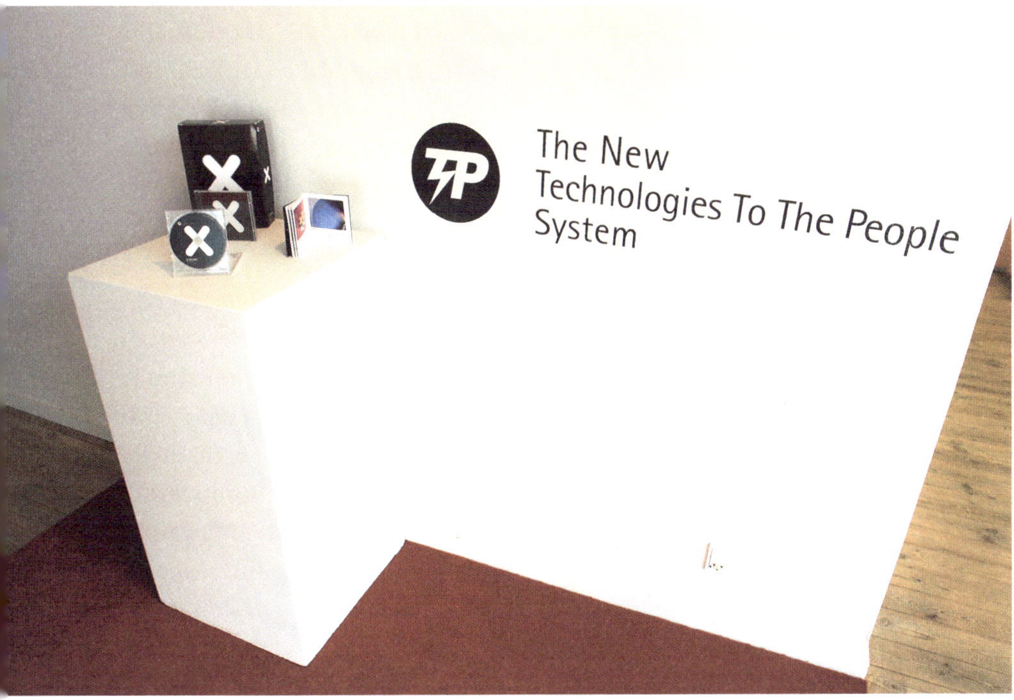

ILL. 3: Installation shot of *X-Devian. The New Technologies to the People System* (2003-) by Daniel Garcia Andújar (Aarhus Kunstbygning, May/June 2007). Photo by Jens Møller Sørensen.

"The Evolution of the Species"

The artwork *X-Devian. The New Technologies to the People System* is one of the most extensive manifestations of, and contributions to, these tendencies.[21] The work is centred round the fictive operating system *X-Devian*, which is in fact a conceptual packaging or a designed version of a distribution of Ubuntu's latest desktop version.[22] However, while the work literally distributes an actual piece of free software and the accompanying catalogue includes a so-called LiveCD plus installation instructions, it is not so much the technical specificities of *X-Devian* as the cultural vocabulary (the discourses and ideas in which the operating system is embedded) that the work is an interface to. The general point is that this dimension of free software needs developing, just as much as the software itself, and that the potential of free software as a tool for critical involvement in software culture can be explored as much in terms of cultural significance as in terms of technical capabilities. The work thus translates the principles of free software from being a question of technical programming to being a question of cultural programming, and presents the translation with aesthetic means different from those usually employed by the free software movement (and the proprietary software industry for that matter).[23]

X-Devian is formally a transmedia installation consisting of two parts. In the first part, *X-Devian* is advertised like a piece of proprietary software through a promotional video, posters, graphic design and product display arranged much like a stand. In the second part, *X-Devian* is presented in a space that resembles a mix between a cave environment and a media lab containing hardware parts, manuals and licences, 'code graffiti' and tables with computers running *X-Devian*. The two parts represent different advertisement approaches to *X-Devian*, yet they are essentially interconnected, forming and functioning as one complex interface. The interconnection is manifested by the sentence "Access to Technology is a Human Right™" written on an adjoining wall so the audience, or rather the user, has to move from one part to another in order to read the entire sentence.[24] In software terminology, the interconnection can be conceived as an interconnection between the front-end and the back-end of the operating system, between free software as an abstract representation and as concrete material. The point of the interconnection is to establish a set of mutual exchanges between these dimensions that generates a new, expanded vocabulary for involvement in software culture as a free culture.

The sentence itself, which also serves as the slogan of Technologies to the People, is essential in this regard. It constitutes a kind of horizon or backdrop that frames the general mode of perception for the user. As a statement that expresses an interest in more equal software cultures in which participation is not a question of financial abilities (or of technical expertise for that matter) but of human existence, the sentence associates *X-Devian* with the people who Rancière regards as "the principal subject of politics [...] the supplementary part in relation to any counting of parts of the population that makes it possible to identify 'the part of those who have no-part' with the whole of the community" (Rancière "Ten Theses on Politics" 5). In another statement, echoing Rancière, Andújar has declared that Technologies To The People

> is aimed at people in the so-called Third World as well as the homeless, orphaned, unemployed, runaways, immigrants, alcoholics, drug addicts, people suffering from mental dysfunctions and all other categories of 'undesirables'. Technologies To The People is for people denied access to the new information society and new technologies. Technologies To The People wants more people to be networked (n. pag.).

The sentence, in other words, connects *X-Devian* to processes of democratic development that challenge predominant power relations in contemporary software culture, for instance those constituted by the industry. It implies that the users of the operating system, rather than the operating system itself, represent the constitutive part of these processes. The perspective of the sentence, however, points beyond the actual project of giving access to technology to the undesirable people that Andújar mentions above. Instead, Andújar describes these people as figures for a multiplicity of different kinds of users allowing a diversified and non-conforming software culture to happen. *X-Devian* is a political tool that is defined by its users and their uses of it, by the politics of human agency.

The first part of the installation is centred round a floor-to-ceiling foil print of a hand presenting, or rather offering, a disk with *X-Devian*, designed in a simple graphic style with a white 'X' on a black background. Despite its spectacular effect, the function of the image is not that of an advertisement aiming to sell a product to the user. While of course attracting attention and creating an interest in *X-Devian*, the image firstly indicates that the operating system is handy and given to the user by 'someone' who is larger-than-life. Of course, that 'someone' is very likely the people that the sentence refers to, and the hand could symbolise that *X-Devian* is given to humans by humans. In this way it represents a potential for humanity to develop and 'grow', which would be in line with the slogan "The evolution of the species" that is written on the disk.

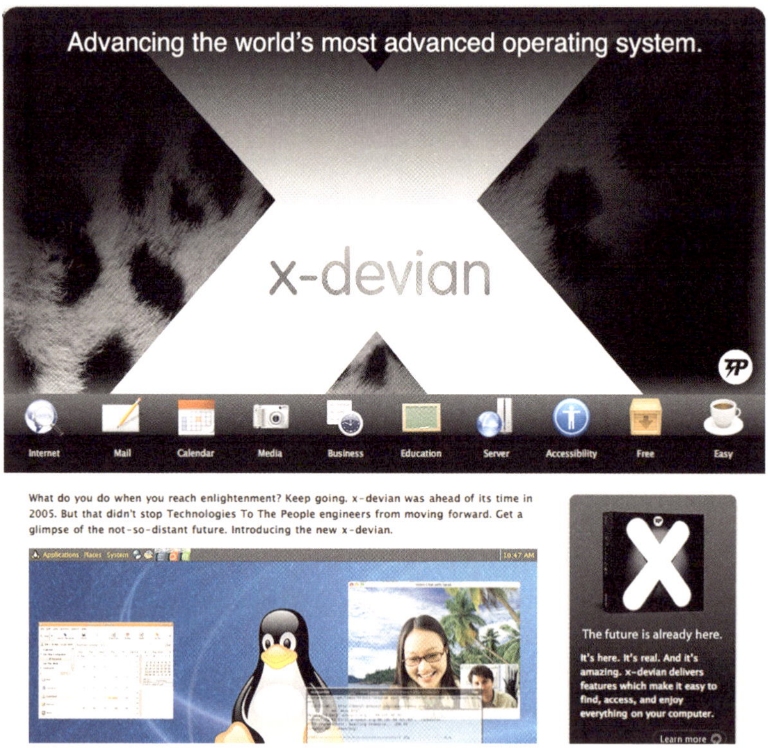

ILL.4: *The X-Devian* website appropriates the general design of the Mac OS X Panther website and replaces the content with information about the Ubuntu Linux distribution.

Contrary to the superhuman scale of the technological progress that Windows Vista represented in the promotional video, the size of the hand signifies that *X-Devian* is a collective human project which exceeds the sum of its parts. Furthermore, the image signifies that when the users pick up a copy of the CD in the installation they become part of the image so to speak, and are involved in the continuous development of the 'evolution,' practically and intellectually.

Hacking "the world's most advanced operating system"

This part of the installation also features a promotional video, usually shown on a big flat screen hung on the wall. In the video, an enthusiastic 'user' talks with a group of other users about the operating system's many "amazing new features [which are] built up around you to make your life even easier." They are all informally gathered in front of a computer in a boutique setting with glass walls and a hectic level of activity signalling that *X-Devian* is for an open and dynamic creative environment in which the users are the focal point. However, the message of the video is not as simple and straightforward as that, because the video was originally made not for *X-Devian* but for the Panther version of Apple's operating system Mac OS X launched in 2003.[25] Andújar has appropriated the video to *X-Devian* by replacing the screen dumps from Panther by screen dumps from various Linux distributions and exchanging the name and logo in the beginning and the end of the video.

Andújar applies similar appropriation aesthetics on the website for *X-Devian*, which mirrors the entire design of the website for Panther but has a different content, for instance on the front page, where the text under the heading "Advancing the world's most advanced operating system" is about *X-Devian* and the text itself is an appropriation of various texts about Devian and free software. Hence, he uses Apple's aesthetics to promote *X-Devian*, an operating system that expresses an idea of what creative environments and "the world's most advanced operating system" are that is antithetical to Mac OS X. His gesture functions as a hack, reflecting the modus operandi of free software programming, which uses already existing material for processes of development that transgress proprietary boundaries and explore material in multiple directions and contexts.

The hack consists in transforming the commercial aesthetics of Apple's advertising campaign into material for political aesthetics that challenges the product of Panther and the general notion of software as a product.[26]

The hack also includes the 'X' in *X-Devian*, which is an appropriation of the X in Mac OS X. However, it is an appropriation that converts the meaning of this X. Rather than signifying the new line of Apple's operating system, the X functions as a prefix that signifies the open-ended potentiality which characterises the development of free software. Andújar takes Apple at face value and utilises the letter's ambivalence to point beyond the identity of a closed system to a heterogeneous and indefinable network made up of the humans in the aforementioned statement. Hence, the X essentially signifies the inclusion of the users and the recognition of their open-ended potentiality.

Moreover, by appropriating Apple's advertisement rather than its product, Andújar extends free software's challenge of intellectual property and copyrights to concern not merely principles of programming but the vocabulary for involvement in software culture. By relating the freedoms listed in the free software definition to the context of actual programming *and* to the context of software culture in general, the appropriation makes the basic point that the potential of the freedoms can be fully explored, in its true radicality. It emphasises that the significance of software is as much a question of information *about* software, its representation outside the context of programming, as about software as information; and that it is important that free software also challenges proprietary software and hacks software culture on this level.

For instance, when Apple's advertisement talks about "advancing the world's most advanced operating system" that is "built up around you to make your life even easier" with reference to one specific product (a commercial brand and a proprietary software culture), it is claiming ownership of the use of a set of common concepts about software and thus fixing and reducing their meanings, notwithstanding that the claim is both legally and culturally unjustifiable.[27] A free software operating system can just as well be said to be the world's most advanced and to be built around the user, which would alter the meaning in relation to the 'product', the user and software culture.

The appropriation of Apple's advertisement focuses attention on the importance of manifesting free software's opposition to proprietary software by distributing and developing the information about software beyond any form of ownership, just like the software itself. It accentuates that the difference between free software and proprietary software is also a question of difference in terms of forms of representation, of interfaces that configure different relations between the users, the software and software culture.

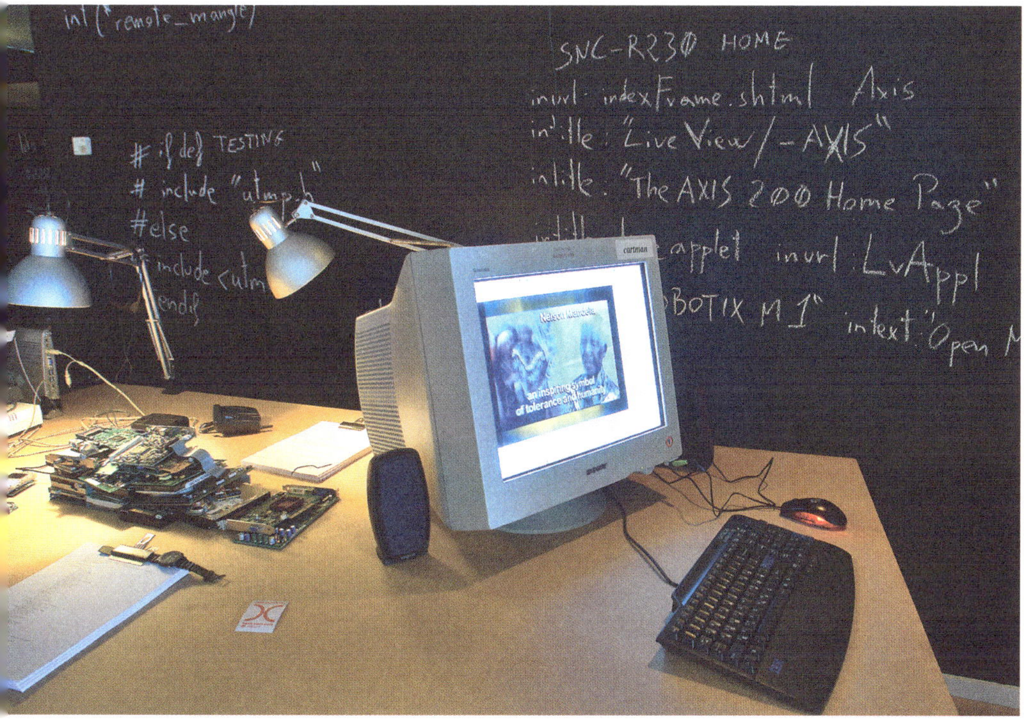

ILL. 5: Installation shot of *X-Devian. The New Technologies to the People System* (2003-) by Daniel Garcia Andújar (Aarhus Kunstbygning, May/June 2007). Photo by Jens Møller Sørensen.

Material and information behind the image

The second part of the installation is characterised by a different form of interface. In it, Andújar applies a very different set of aesthetics than in the first part and than both Mircosoft and Apple, and with this change of setting he signals a transition to another level of involvement with software culture.

The users enter this part of the installation by going around the wall, which displays the image of the hand holding the disk. Behind the wall they encounter a pile of various hardware parts. Stacked as they are (literally supporting the wall and figuratively supporting the image), the parts are not outdated and defunct trash – instead, they represent the material used for the development of *X-Devian*. Similar parts lie on a table included in this part of installation. Here, some of the parts are assembled into tools, thus indicating that the development also involves the continuous practical and intellectual reuse of material, whether it is physical or digital, computers or lines of code. As an advanced operating system *X-Devian* is not about the improvement of existing tools but about inventing new tools altogether and about involving the users in the process. Hence, the users are encouraged to make their own tools with the parts already available as well as considering the more general possibility of making their own tools outside the installation context.

The functionalities of the tools on the table are uncertain – or rather they encourage investigation, reflection and speculation on the part of the user. Instead of serving familiar and straightforward utilitarian purposes, the tools facilitate the imaginations of the users and their imagination of uses. This evokes Kay's belief in the imagination as a primary source for the development of computer literacy and of a computer culture developed by human creativity (Kay "A Personal Computer for Children of All Ages"). Computers are not primarily problem-solving instruments in the conventional sense of tools, but devices for the experimental creation of possibilities. As such they reverse the logic of the (software) tool from being a question of accommodating existing and defined needs in the context of a set of given conditions to being a question of generating new ideas of needs and contexts. Ideas informed by principles of art and play, rather than by scientific reason and market considerations.

The emphasis on this imaginary dimension of software culture is also evident from the 'code graffiti' that Andújar has written in white chalk on the black painted walls surrounding the table. This graffiti consists of lines of instructions distributed in a rather disorderly fashion over the walls. It does not amount to actual programs, but configures codes beyond questions of exact meaning and the compliance to rules as a performative and poetic expression.[28] Thus it encourages the user to 'read' it with the logic of the imagination and in terms of its abstract aesthetic qualities. The fact that the code is written in chalk also implies that it is neither definite nor permanent. Rather, like the parts on the table and a piece of free software, it constitutes the material for continuous development by erasure, overwriting or addition, for instance by the users.

By writing the code on a wall Andújar not only 'liberates' it from the inside of the computer and makes it accessible to and integrated in the world in which the users live and set marks. He also connects it to the existential activity of interacting with the world and through that activity claiming a presence in the world. And with the association to graffiti he implies that it is a kind of activity that challenges the rules of the dominant system, akin to the way in which free software challenges intellectual property law. The point is not the illegal aspect of the activity but the exploration of the forms of activity that are defined not by cultural order but by the intensity of human agency.

The notion of *X-Devian* as a tool is further emphasised by a large number of different free software licences and manuals that hang on the wall next to the graffiti. Printed on regular paper and attached clip-boards, the texts are displayed like tools in a tool shed which users can pick up and use, converting their technical meaning into cultural significance. In line with Richard Stallman's perception of "The Free Software Definition" as a philosophy, the installation challenges the users to read beyond the literal and specific content and conceive, interpret and apply them in relation to a broader context of software culture.

Like the graffiti, the licences and manuals configure the users as active and autonomous readers who, rather than just being offered the chance to pick up a finished product from the shelves, are given access to information about *X-Devian* and the software culture of which it is part. That access is also the point of a number of specially designed mobile tables where the users can sit down and spend time exploring *X-Devian* and burn a copy of the operating system to take home. In addition, the computers give access to (copy) an extensive database of documentary information in the form of texts, programs and video files about free software.

Besides, the installation through the various information and materials foregrounds that *X-Devian* is essentially a networked phenomenon and not a closed entity. It exhibits the reality behind the image or rather the reality of the image, as a reality where processes of critical involvement and not the production of objects of ownership characterise the development of software culture.

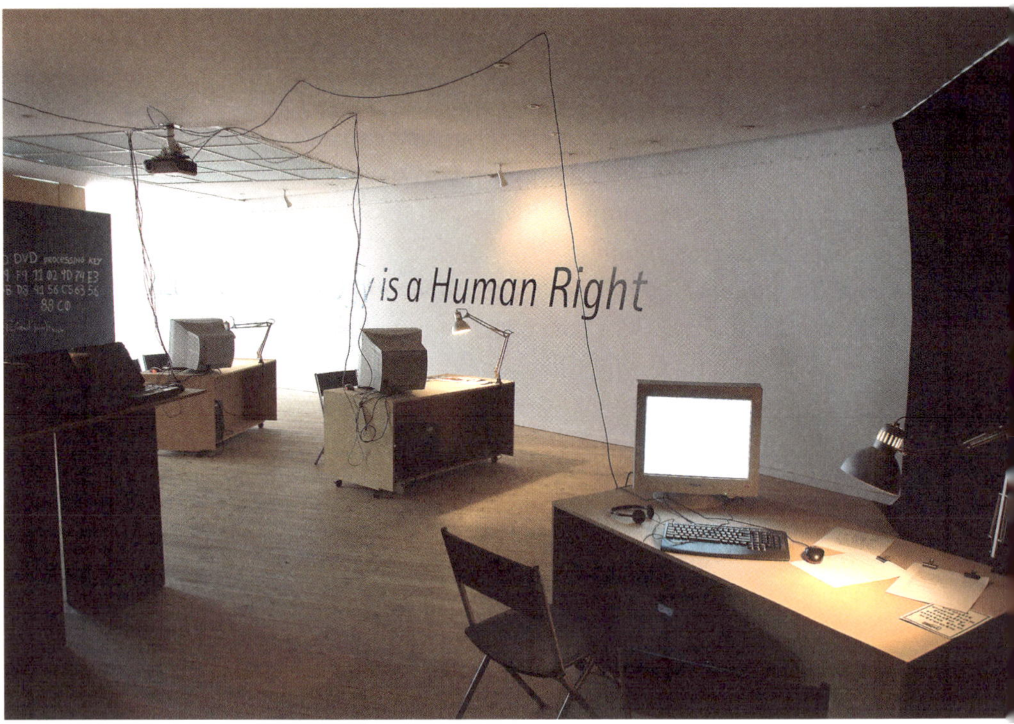

ILL. 6: Installation shot of *X-Devian. The New Technologies to the People System* (2003-) by Daniel Garcia Andújar (Aarhus Kunstbygning, May/June 2007). Photo by Jens Møller Sørensen.

Working collectively towards software literacy

Andújar also hosts workshops about free software in the second part of the installation, thus making explicit its function as an informal, non-institutional learning site. The fact that these workshops constitute an integral part of the installation signifies that the development of the users' software literacy is an essential part of the technological revolution that the installation announces.[29] The software literacy that the installation and the workshop offer the users is, however, more than a question of learning how to use the operating system according to a manual, although that is important. It is a software literacy that also includes learning to imaginatively and critically explore the operating system in the context of software culture. In fact, the source of this software literacy is learning to practically and intellectually establish exchanges between these two levels of involvement with the operating system.

With their massive and complex accumulation of material and information, the installation and workshop counter a predominant trend within software culture to understand software literacy as a question of developing the users' intuitive and rational faculties in the use of software. They address the users' capabilities to reflect, analyse and speculate as the primary faculties for the use of operating systems, thus rendering software literacy as essentially a question of critical involvement.

Furthermore, through their inclusive structure the installation and workshops emphasise the collective character of free software as both a technical and cultural phenomenon, as well as emphasising that a significant aspect of the specific form of software literacy that free software represents involves learning to 'do-it-together' – a notion that Andújar has used to point out a difference from the more common 'do-it-yourself' notion.[30] While do-it-together (like do-it-yourself) is engaged with autonomous production as a vehicle for social change, it also marks a development of this project through new, dynamic networks of collaboration and sharing. *X-Devian* presents the user with both intellectual and practical dimensions of do-it-together.[31] With its database of information on the computers and in the exhibition space, it gives the users access to the culture of collectively generating knowledge; and with the workshops it engages the users in the activity of working together on a common project. Hence, the installation, like the software, functions as a collective tool as well as a tool for collectivities of users, a tool for collective user agency in relation to the involvement in (free) software culture.

There is more than one word for it

The focus on the interface aesthetics of the promotional video for Windows Vista and *X-Devian* manifests and addresses the difference between proprietary and free software beyond the legal and technical definition. It demonstrates that the difference is not simply a matter of changing the operating system and then continuing to use the software as usual, but that there is also a challenge involved in developing a different vocabulary, different words as well as ways of talking, which eventually is also a development of a different software literacy – thereby changing the conditions and perspectives of the involvement of users in software culture.

Moreover, the example of *X-Devian* underlines that art represents a relevant and powerful medium for this development because of the experimental and critical use of "images, signs and statements" that it engages the users in.[32] Other prominent contemporary artworks where free software (discourses and practice) constitutes an explicit part also testify to this fact, for instance *Rastasoft* (2003-) by Jaromil, *Carnivore* (2001-) by Radical Software Group, and *life_sharing* (2000-2003) by 0100101110101101.ORG. Artworks such as the *Net.Art Generator* (1999-) by Cornelia Sollfrank, *BURN* (2001) by Kingdom of Piracy and *Nine(9)* (2003) by Mongrel, which incorporates the freedom principles of free software in a more abstract sense, are also pertinent to this context.

Like most of these works, *X-Devian* reverses a common guiding principle for interface aesthetics in the context of software design, according to which a 'complex' interface is a problem because it prevents the user from using the tool to get the job done. The interface aesthetics of the installation are complex; but within the context of the legacy of conceptual art that the artwork is associated with, complexity in aesthetics represents a possibility for a more profound and extensive user involvement. In a discussion of the creative and communicative aspects of what he calls "interface culture", Steven

Johnson has suggested that "user-hostility" figuratively speaking might be a future guiding principle for what he calls "the digital avant-garde", which "would bring about an intriguing reversal in the basic rules of interface design" (226).[33] The interface aesthetics of *X-Devian* are not exactly hostile towards its users, yet they do counter many of the same mainstream tendencies that Johnson refers to by requiring and stimulating the users to apply a reflective perception, not only in relation to the installation but to software culture in general (ibid. 224-39).

In this sense, *X-Devian* is in accordance with Rancière's definition of artistic practices as "ways of doing and making" that intervene in the general distribution of doing and making as well as in the relationships they maintain to modes of being and forms of "visibility" (Rancière, *The Politics of Aesthetics* 13). *X-Devian* intervenes in the proprietary software industry's distribution of the sensible and initiates a *re*distribution of the sensible. This redistribution designates other modes of being, perceiving and acting that produce political subjectivities who are not defined by and challenge the given order of mainstream software culture.

Of course, this redistribution of the sensible is essentially a (science) fiction; but as Rancière points out, "the real must be fictionalised in order to be thought." (Rancière, *The Politics of Aesthetics* 38). So the political point of *X-Devian* is not to use the documentary material on free software to construct a narrative, but to make it intelligible as a critical potential for free software users, uses and cultures that cannot be conceived in the current situation. A potential, in other words, for software futures where there is more than one word for it.

Notes

1. The title of the artwork is *X-Devian*, whereas the name of the operating system is X-Devian. The New Technologies to the People System. For the sake of clarity, the former is written in italics. Officially, Technologies to the People is an entity in itself, as well as functioning as a conceptual framework for Daniel García Andújar's artistic practice. Technologies to the People has sponsored several of Andújar's projects and even awarded him a prize, while Andújar has represented and spoken on behalf of Technologies to the People in a number of contexts. To attempt a categorical distinction between the company and the artist is pointless, just as the ambiguity regarding their interrelation is a point worth consideration.
2. Recognising the complexity and multiple meanings of the notion of the interface,

not just within software studies, the basic definition applied here is that the interface is an entity that establishes a communicative relation between two more or less separate entities, "making one sensible to the other" (Johnson 14) and allowing various degrees and forms of interaction. Hence, it does not simply give one entity control over the other, but actually mediates an exchange between the two entities. Or to use computer terminology, the interface does not simply give the user the power to control software, it also models the use of such software. The character and balance between these two dimensions of controls define the functionality of the interface, both in a literal and figurative sense. For a wide introduction to the field of interface theory in relation to computers see Laurel, and for a general introduction to "the science of the interface" see Diebner, Druckrey and Weibel. For a specific discussion of the interface in relation to software, see Cramer and Fuller.

3. In Donald A. Norman's words, which the Microsoft marketing team probably paid close attention to, "a conceptual model is a story. It doesn't have to discuss the actual mechanisms of the operation. But it does have to pull the actions together into a coherent whole that allows the user to feel in control, to feel there is a reason for the way things are structured, to feel that, when necessary, it's possible to invent special variations to get out of trouble and, in general, feel mastery over the device" (Norman 181).

4. In a brief discussion of abstract paintings Rancière does, however, compare their flatness to "the flatness of an interface" (Rancière, *The Politics of Aesthetics* 16); and in another context he discusses "The Surface of Design." (Rancière, *The Future of the Image*). In both cases the concepts are used in a general, transmedia sense. Starting with the book *Disagreement. Politics and Philosophy*, Rancière has developed this notion of aesthetics as a distribution of the sensible in a number of texts on a variety of topics, such as art, literature, design and politics.

5. The commercial was directed by movie-director Ridley Scott and alludes to George Orwell's novel *Nineteen Eighty-Four* (1949). It cuts between images of a hypnotised herd of people being led by a televised "Big Brother" on a big screen and an athlete who is running away from the police. The commercial ends with the athlete throwing a sledgehammer at the screen, which causes it to explode. In the mist of the explosion the following text appears and is read by a voice-over: "On January 24th, Apple Computer will introduce Macintosh. And you'll see why 1984 won't be like '1984'". Indirectly, this explosion conceptualises and anticipates the idea of the computer as a phenomenon that transgresses the (television) screen, transgresses technology, and through the new type of interface gives access to a new experience of life; an idea that is essential to the advertisement for Windows Vista. To watch the commercial see http://www.youtube.com/watch?v=OYecfV3ubP8, and for a detailed account of the history of the commercial see Linzmayer.

6. In the fiscal year 2007, Microsoft spent $300 million on Windows Vista-related advertisements, and a year later raised its advertising budget to $470 million compared to Apple's $486 million (it was $338 million two years earlier) (Notte; Blakely).

7. The song is titled "Wow is now!" and the singer is Sinidhi Chauhan. To listen to the song go to http://www.microsoft.com/india/Wow/. The reason for choosing an Indian singer is unknown and perhaps not relevant, but considering that most of *Windows Vista* is probably programmed in India, the choice becomes a weird reflection of the new global software industry.

8. The commercial had several versions, all made from the same pool of filmic sequences but differently mixed. Thus, although the commercials differ formally, the basic concept is the same. An interesting reference here is Ted Nelson's call for an interface inspired by film. Although he is arguing in terms of the computer interface (screen, keyboard, mouse etc.), it seems obvious to extend his argument

to commercials. Because, as will be evident in the following, his idea that a filmic interface will make the user forget he/she is using a computer is exactly the point that Windows is aiming at with this series of 'filmic' commercials. (Nelson, quoted in Laurel 235-43). A current version of Nelson's line of thought is Lev Manovich, who in the context of what he calls "cultural interfaces," i.e. interfaces to "culture encoded in digital form," has argued that "cinematic ways of seeing the world, of structuring time, of narrating a story, of linking one experience to the next, have become the basic means by which computer users access and interact with all cultural data" (Manovich, *The Language of New Media* 78-9).

9. The version of the commercial described here is no longer available online. To view a different version of the commercial, including sequences of a rocket launch and the fall of the Berlin Wall, go to http://www.youtube.com/watch?v=f7ZVKG8rRfA&feature=related.
10. At least in terms of intention. Hence, in the introduction to the licence terms for Windows Vista, Microsoft writes that: "By using the software, you accept these terms. If you do not accept them, do not use the software. Instead, return it to the retailer for a refund or credit". However, as activities of both common and expert users show, the operating system can be used in ways and for purposes that transgress what Microsoft "allows." For instance, it can be used to illegally download files over BitTorrent networks, and its security can be hacked. For an easily accessible guide to how to hack Windows Vista, see Sinchak.
11. To get an overview of the criticism, see http://en.wikipedia.org/wiki/Criticism_of_Windows_Vista.
12. The commercial's emphasis on experience associates it with a current trend within the field of interface design to develop interfaces based on an understanding of user experience, of human behaviour, feelings, needs and wishes rather than principles of usability. Moreover, it associates it with the expanding field of ubiquitous computing, where software is no longer limited to the desktop but integrated into everyday objects and activities to the point where users do not notice it, allowing them a simpler, more intuitive interaction with the technology, software or hardware. In this context, launching a critique of the usefulness and market obsolescence of the Graphical User Interface, Donald Norman has introduced the notion "of the invisible computer" that "blends so seamlessly with the task to be done that it disappears from consciousness" – the technology is "hidden away out of sight" (Norman 69-88). For an introduction to the principles of ubiquitous computing see Weiser, and for a discussion of their cultural implications see Greenfield.
13. The theme song of the advertising campaign is called "Wow is now!", and an animated sequence from another television commercial proclaims "Instant Wow".
14. Kant himself mentions mountain peaks as one example of a phenomenon that generates sublime experiences, and it is common for art historical writings to interpret Friedrich's painting as a depiction of such an experience. Kant develops the notion of the sublime in *Observations on the Feeling of the Beautiful and Sublime* and *Critique of Judgment* in relation to a romantic preoccupation with the eternal and the infinite. In his post-modern reinterpretation of the concept in the text "The Sublime and The Avant-Garde", Jean-Francois Lyotard connects the sublime to the experience of "the instant" as an "unpresentable" event; and without giving the advertising agency responsible for the Windows Vista commercial undeserved philosophical and artistic credit, the description of the experience of the operating system as well as the title of the theme song "The Wow is Now" cleverly plays with references to this post-modern sublime.
15. The full title of the film is *Dr. Strangelove or: How I Learned to Stop Worrying and Love the Bomb*. The love for the bomb concerns its technical perfection as described by

Dr. Strangelove. Dr. Strangelove's fascination reflects Robert Oppenheimer's defence statement at his security clearance hearings in 1954: "When you see something that is technically sweet, you go ahead and do it and argue about what to do about it only after you've had your technical success. That is the way it was with the atomic bomb." The statement is quoted in Richard Sennett's recent discussion of craftsmanship as "an enduring, basic human impulse, the desire to do a job well for its own sake," a discussion that includes free software.

16. For an introduction to the notion of the 'technological sublime' see Nye or Tabbi.

17. So when the commercial includes a sequence from the anti-authoritarian 1960s it is with 'footage' of a large-scale rock concert, a countercultural event which became the epitome of a new culture industry that today is a close and supportive partner of the software industry in the context of the experience economy. There is no sequence of the more than 50,000 participants in the Pentagon Peace demonstration in Washington DC or for that matter of Jimi Hendrix playing "Wild Thing" and putting his guitar on fire at Monterey pop festival. And, in a sequence with the fall of the Berlin Wall, it is a family who sees the event on television, not the people participating in the actual hammering on the wall, who have a wow experience.

18. Kay has continued and expanded his interest in computer literacy through his current participation in the One Laptop Per Child project and its XO laptop, which attempts to realise many of the basic ideas informing The Dynabook and Smalltalk in the context of contemporary global technology politics as outlined by the project's founder Nicholas Negroponte in his book *Being Digital*. Despite its democratic and educational mission and the million computers distributed since its initiation in 2005, the logistics, technology and politics of the project have been met with critique and a recurrent objection is that the project focuses too one-sidedly on a general technical solution at the cost of considering the specificities of the cultural contexts in which the laptops will be used – thus technologically 'colonising' these contexts through a standardising product. The debate reflects an aspect of computer literacy that Kay is not articulate about, namely that computer literacy involves negotiation between the question of learning to use a computer as a technical entity and of using it in specific cultural contexts (Felsenstein).

19. The tendency stems from the conception of the computer as a medium rather than a tool, which Alan Kay, influenced by Marshall McLuhan's theories, introduced in association with his development of the personal desktop computer (Kay, "User Interface: A Personal View" 191-208) This conceptual distinction is reiterated and developed further by Brenda Laurel, who (influenced by theories and practices of drama, virtual reality and games) conceives "computers as theatre" (Laurel 126), thus pointing to the (multisensory) experience quality of human-computer interaction. However, Kay makes a significant distinction between the computer and the software running on it: While the computer is a medium, the software running on the computer still constitutes a tool. (Kay and Goldberg). The notion of software (and not the computer) as a tool is both contested and complex, spanning utilitarian, cognitive and communicative definitions. But it also remains rather underdeveloped and represents a challenge and opportunity for the emergent field of 'software studies' defined by Lev Manovich as the investigation of "the role of software in forming contemporary culture, and cultural, social, and economic forces that are shaping development of software itself", to proceed beyond the context of "media studies" as well as "new media studies." (Manovich, "Introduction: Software Studies for Beginners" 5)

The point here is not to discuss these different definitions, but to oppose the notion of software as a tool to the notion of software as an experience. Moreover, the present text conceives this opposition as an expression of a general opposition between software as an experience of a cultural environment and software as a tool to work on, manipulate and transform a cultural environment, which furthermore corresponds to an opposition between a notion of the cultural environment as a given phenomenon and a notion of the cultural environment as a phenomenon and an event created by the user (Kay; Brand; Rheingold; Hawk, Rieder and Oviedo).

20. For an introduction to these tendencies within the fields of free software and software art, see http://www.fsf.org and http://runme.org.

21. *X-Devian* has been shown in different formats and including different elements since Andújar first exhibited the work in 2004. The point of departure here is the installation of the work at Aarhus Kunstbygning in 2007. For a more elaborate text on *X-Devian*, see Lillemose "Hacking the Interfaces of Access Culture and Envisioning the Literacy of the Post-Capitalistic Future".

22. Ubuntu runs on the Debian kernel, which explains the name, which also indicates a 'performative' reference to the fact that in Spanish (Andújar's first language)' v' is pronounced as 'b'. Another indirect reference is to deviance, which suggests that X-Devian is a deviant or hacked version of not only Debian but also of Mac OS X, where the 'X' is appropriated from. It is important for Andújar to emphasise that *X-Devian* contains actual software. Thus, take-away copies of the software are offered in the installation, both in pre-packaged form and from the online computers included in the installation. Furthermore, the software is included in the accompanying catalogue.

23. In the context of free software, advertising like the Windows Vista commercial is very rare, and ironically, the only comparable example on the YouTube platform is a commercial for Dell. Here, the expanded notion of the interface is characterised by a rather different set of aesthetics. GNU and Linux have their signature mascots, who occasionally appear in entertaining, albeit rather geeky settings, and the Ubuntu brands itself as a socially conscious and responsible distribution, for instance through a substantial merchandise line. The predominant trend, however, is that the aesthetics are text based and limited to the websites of the various distributions and organisations. One explanation of this difference is of course financial necessity, but a more significant explanation is that it is an expression of a cultural identity and opposition to proprietary software. "The freedom to run, copy, distribute, study, change and improve the software" (Stallman) that constitutes the core principle, the philosophy and information politics, of free software is about lines of code written in (ASCII) text. Text is the 'material' with which programmers formally work when they develop free software and manifest their particular form of involvement in software culture.

24. "Access to Technology is a Human Right" is the overall slogan for *Technologies to the People*. It was introduced in the mid-90s when the company ran a pioneering business on the internet with a series of projects that with style-conscious irony and political attitudes thematised the Internet's potential democratisation (and parallel hyper-commercialisation) of technological culture, e.g. a campaign for the product *iSAM*™, a portable credit card machine for beggars. See http://www.irational.org/tttp/primera.html.

25. To watch the Apple commercial see http://www.youtube.com/watch?v=LUcMK5apZhQ.

26. In fact, these playful manifestations of cultural opposition are a reference to Andújar's work in general. Especially his web-based works from the mid to late 90s play with the signs and codes of the medium of the Internet, where information is virtual and can be reproduced/copied and manipulated infinitely. See Lillemose, "Hacking the Interfaces of Access Culture and Envisioning the Literacy of the Post-Capitalistic Future".

27. The fact that Apple and most other proprietary software companies nevertheless invest a lot in this claim is emphasised by the work *Language (Property) Remember, language is not free™* (1997), in which Andújar charts the TM-registration by these companies and Technologies To The People of the sentences that made up their slogans as if they were a line of program code.
28. Connections between performance, poetry and code are a recurrent theme in software art and have (for instance) been explored by the band Slub (Dave Griffiths, Alex McLean and Adrian Ward) and Graham Harwood. Connections between code and graffiti are less frequent, but have been explored by Heath Bunting and others.
29. In fact, workshops, along with teaching and event organising, constitute an integral part of Andújar's entire work.
30. For an introduction to the theories and practices of the do-it-yourself approach to software, see Broeckman and Jaschko.
31. For an elaborate discussion of the former with specific reference to software and in relation to Karl Marx's concept of the General Intellect, see Fuller *Softness; interrogability; general intellect; art methodologies in software*; and for a rich account and critical theory of the collective practices of free software see Kelty. The engagement of both these dimensions of do-it-together is a general concern in Andújar's work, of which *Postcapital. Archive 1989-2001* (2006-) is the most recent and extensive example.
32. Brenda Laurel also mentions art as a vital source "that can be brought to bear on the design of human-computer activity" (Laurel xvii-xxi) However, with Aristotle's *Poetics* and theatre as her point of reference, she refers to a generalised concept of art and the 'artistic' within the context of representational aesthetics (Laurel 31), and does not consider the legacy of art as critical involvement in culture, which is outlined by the conceptual art of 1960s and 1970s. Rather than taking art for granted as a value in itself, conceptual art questions "our prejudices, asking us to renounce our inhibitions, and if they are re-evaluating the nature of art, they are also asking that we reassess what we have always taken for granted as our accepted and culturally conditioned aesthetic response to art." (McShine)
33. Drawing on both early computer theory and material from popular culture, Johnson applies the notion of interface culture to technological culture at large involving all sorts of new media. And while his interface-art comparison is underdeveloped and his concept of art is rather simple, his suggestion is nevertheless relevant for the still embryonic discussion of interface aesthetics beyond the context of the computer.

Works cited

1984. Dir. Ridley Scott. Apple, 1984. Television commercial. Print.

Andújar, Daniel Garcia. Language (Property) Remember, language is not free™. Installtion. 1997.

– *X-Devian. The New Technologies to the People System*. 2003-. Installation/web. 10. Aug. 2010. <http://x-devian.com>.

– *Postcapital. Archive 1989-2001*. 2006-. Installation/web. 10 Aug. 2010. <http://www.postcapital.org/>.

Blakely, Lindsay. "Apple's Advertising Budget: Revealed!" *BNET*. The CBS Interactive Business Network, 21 Nov. 2008. Web. 10 Aug. 2010. <http://www.bnet.com/blog/technology/apples-advertising-budget-revealed/574>.

Brand, Stewart (ed.). *Whole Earth Software Catalog*. Quantum Press/Doubleday, Garden City, 1984. Print.

Broeckman, Andreas, and Susanne Jaschko (eds.). *DIY Media – Art and Digital Media: Software, Participation, Distribution*). Berlin: transmediale.de/Podewill, 2001. Print.

Chauhan, Sunidhi. "Wow is Now!" Microsoft, 2007. MP3/Web. 10 Aug. 2010. <http://www.microsoft.com/india/Wow/>
Cramer, Florian, and Matthew Fuller. "Interface." *Software Studies: A Lexicon.* Ed. Matthew Fuller. London: MIT Press, 2008. 149-153. Print.
Diebner, Hans, Timothy Druckrey and Peter Weibel. Eds. *The Sciences of Interface. Proceeding from the International Symposium.* Karlsruhe: ZKM, 2000. Print.
Felsenstein, Leo. "Problems with the $100 laptop", Web. 10 Aug 2010. <http://fonly.typepad.com/fonlyblog/2005/11/problems_with_t.html. 2005.>
Fuller, Matthew. "The Impossibility of Interface." *Behind the Blip. Essays on the Culture of Software.* New York: Autonomedia, 2003. 99-120. Print.
Fuller, Matthew. *Softness; interrogability; general intellect; art methodologies in software*, Aarhus: Digital Aesthetics, Research Center, University of Aarhus, 2006. Print.
Greenfield, Adam. *Everyware: The Dawning Age of Ubiquitous Computing.* Berkeley: New Riders/AIGA, 2006. Print.
Hawk, Byron, David M. Rieder and Ollie Oviedo (eds.). *Small Tech. The Culture of Digital Tools.* Minneapolis: University of Minnesota Press, 2008. Print.
Heckel, Paul. "Conceptual Models and Metaphor in Software Design." *IEEE Compcon Spring '91. Digest of Papers.* 25 Feb.-1 March 1991: 498 – 499. Print.
Johnson, Steven. *Interface Culture. How New Technology Transforms the Way We Create and Communicate.* San Francisco: HarperCollins, 1997. Print.
Kant, Immanuel. *The Critique of Judgement.* Oxford: Oxford University Press, 1952. Print.
– *Observations on the Feeling of the Beautiful and Sublime*, Berkeley: University of California Press, 1960. Print.
Kay, Alan. *A Personal Computer for Children of All Ages.* Palo Alto: Xerox Palo Alto Research Center, 1972. Print.
– "Microelectronics and the Personal Computer." *Scientific American* 237.3 (1977): 230-44. Print.
– "Computer Literacy." *Scientific American* 251.3 (1984). Print.
– "User Interface: A Personal View." *The Art of Human-Computer Interface Design.* Ed. Brenda Laurel. Reading, Massachusetts: Addison-Wesley Publishing Company, 1990. Print.
Kay, Alan, and Adele Goldberg. "Personal Dynamic Media." *IEEE Computer*, 10.3 (2000): 31-41. Print.
Kelty, Christopher. Two Bits: The Cultural Significance of Free Software, 2008. Web. 26 May 2010. <http://twobits.net/pub/Kelty-TwoBits.pdf>.
Lazzarato, Maurizio. "Struggle, Event, Media." *Makeworlds paper#4* 29 Dec. 2003. Weblog. 26 May 2010. <http://www.make-world.net/node/62>.
Laurel, Brenda (ed.). *The Art of Human-Computer Interface Design.* Reading: Addison-Wesley Publishing Company, 1990. Print.
Laurel, Brenda. *Computers as Theatre.* Reading: Addison-Wesley Publishing Company, 1993. Print.
Lemke, Thomas. "Foucault, Governmentality, and Critique." *Rethinking Marxism: A Journal of Economics, Culture & Society* 14.3 (2002). Print.
Lillemose, Jacob. *X-Devian.* Artnode/Technologies to the People/Aarhus Kunstbygning. Aarhus, 2007. Catalogue/Exhibition.
– "Hacking the Interfaces of Access Culture and Envisioning the Literacy of the Post-Capitalistic Future: On the Installation Work by Technologies to the People/Daniel Garcia Andújar." *The Unavowable Community.* Ed. Valentín Roma. Barcelona: Institut Ramon Llull/ACTAR, 2009. Print.
Linzmayer, Owen W. "The 1984 Apple Commercial. The Making of a Legend." Web. 10 Aug 2010. < http://www.curtsmedia.com/cine/1984.html>.
Lyotard, Jean-Francois. "The Sublime and The Avant-Garde." *Artforum*, 22.8 (1984): 36-43. Print.
Manovich, Lev. "The Language of Cultural Interfaces." *The Language of New Media.* Massachusetts: MIT Press, 2001. 69-115. Print.
– *Information as an Aesthetic Event.* 2007. Web. 26 May 2010. <http://manovich.net/DOCS/TATE_lecture.doc>.

– "Introduction: Software Studies for Beginners." *Software Takes Command*. 2008. Web. 26 May 2010. <http://lab.softwarestudies.com/2008/11/softbook.html>.
McShine, Kynaston. "Introduction to Information." Ed. Kynaston McShine. *Information*. New York: Museum of Modern Art, 1970. 138-141. Print.
Microsoft. *Microsoft Software License Terms. Windows Vista*. 2007. Web. 26 May 2010. <download.microsoft.com/.../useterms/Windows%20Vista_Ultimate_English_36d0fe99-75e4-4875-8153-889cf5105718.pdf>.
Negroponte, Nicholas. *Being Digital*. New York: Vintage Books, 1995. Print.
Norman, Donald A. *The Invisible Computer. Why Good Products Can Fail, the Personal Computer Is So Complex, and Information Appliances Are the Solution*. Massachusetts: MIT Press, 1998. Print.
Notte, Jason. "Microsoft's Ad Blitz Targets Wrong Enemy." *The Street*. TheStreet.com, Inc., 12 Oct. 2009. Web. 10 Aug. 2010. <http://www.thestreet.com/story/10610149/microsofts-ad-blitz-targets-wrong-enemy.html>
Nye, David E. *American Technological Sublime*. Massachusetts: MIT Press, 1996. Print.
Pine II, B. Joseph and James H. Gilmore. *The Experience Economy. Work Is Theatre & Every Business a Stage*. Boston: Harvard Business School Press, 1999. Print.
Prug, Toni. *Free Software*. 2007. Web. 26 May 2010. <http://events.ccc.de/congress/2007/Fahrplan/attachments/3_FreeSoftware.ToniPrug.Aug2007.pdf>.
Rancière, Jacques. *Dis-agreement. Politics and Philosophy*. Minneapolis: University of Minnesota Press, 1999. Print.
– "Ten Theses on Politics." *Theory & Event* 5.3 (2001). Print.
– *The Politics of Aesthetics: The Distribution of the Sensible*. London: Continuum International Publishing Group, 2004. Print.
– *The Future of the Image*. New York: Verso, 2007. Print.
Rheingold, Howard. Tools for Thought. The People and Ideas behind the Next Computer Revolution. New York: Simon & Schuster, 1985. Print.
Sennett, Richard. "Prologue: Man as His Own Maker." *The Craftsman*. London: Penguin, 2008. Print.
Sinchak, Steve. *Hacking Windows Vista™*. Indianapolis: Wiley Publishing, 2007. Print.
Stallman, Richard. "The Free Software Definition." *The Free Software Foundation*, 1986. Web. 26 May 2010. <www.fsf.org>.
Tabbi, Joseph. *Postmodern Sublime. Technology and American Writing from Mailer to Cyberpunk*. Ithaca: Cornell University Press, 1995. Print.
Technologies to the People. *Technologies To The People Annual Report* 2000. Alicante: Technologies To The People Publicity Department, 2000. Print.
Weiser, Mark. "The World is not a Desktop." *Interactions* 1.1 (1994): 7-8. Print.

Transparent World
Minoritarian Tactics in the Age of Transparency

BY INKE ARNS

> Giedion, Mendelsohn, Corbusier turned the abiding places of man into a transit area for every conceivable kind of energy and for electric currents and radio waves. The time that is coming will be dominated by transparency (Benjamin, "The Return of the Flâneur").

> The coils of a serpent are even more complex than the burrows of a molehill (Deleuze).

During the Cold War, the unimaginable usually came in the guise of a threat from outer space (which in western science-fiction was not infrequently a code word for communism), whereas today the unimaginable has moved almost indecently close to us. It is in our immediate proximity, on and in our own bodies. The production of unimaginably small nanomachines equipped with all kinds of capabilities is not the sole evidence of this development, as the transformation of matter itself has become an 'immaterial.' The notion of 'immaterials' was coined by Jean-François Lyotard in 1985 with his exhibition "Les Immatériaux" at the Centre Pompidou in Paris. 'Immaterial' in his sense is not the equivalent of 'immaterial' (= opposite of matter), but denotes new extensions of material that exclude the possibility of direct human access:

> The good old matter itself comes to us in the end as something which has been dissolved and reconstructed into complex formulas. Reality consists of elements, organised by structural rules (matrixes) in no longer human measures of space and time.[1]

At first glance, these immaterials are indistinguishable from the materials we know of old. However, they are organised according to wholly different laws, for example in the case of organisms manufactured with the techniques of genetic engineering. This is completely in line with the definition of the 'Unheimlich' (uncanny) formulated by Sigmund Freud in *Beyond the Pleasure Principle* in 1920: it is the formerly long known and familiar that recurs in unintentional repetition (217-56). Today, not just the matter but also the realms that surround us have become uncanny. The notion of transparency, still so esteemed by Walter Benjamin in 1929, has long acquired a dystopic flavour. That change is evident both in the popular fears surrounding the transparent citizen and in the fact that the architectural rooms now indeed distinctive for their great transparency are no longer visible (to everyone) and therefore no longer controllable, either.

In a software or interface culture, transparency is a central concept; in fact software and interfaces play a central role in the general political and societal move towards transparency. However, transparency has different and divergent meanings, as will be clear in the following, where I will also outline how artistic strategies can critically discuss the age of transparency.

An expedition with Deleuze into the swamps of Louisiana

In his film *Down by Law* (1986), Jim Jarmusch delivered a highly precise picture of the paradigm shift that is now becoming reality: the change from the enclosing milieu of the disciplinary society (Foucault) to the flexible modulations of the society of control (Deleuze).

Jarmusch's cult movie shows three smalltime crooks – Jack, Zack and Bob – who happen to be sharing a prison cell in New Orleans. Zack (Tom Waits) is an unemployed DJ, Jack (John Lurie) an occasional pimp and Bob (Roberto Benigni) an honest, kindly, if somewhat naïve, Italian who is doing time for manslaughter. They jointly manage to escape and via the swamps of Louisiana head for a new life. Along with their flight through the swampland, the 'window scene' is especially significant for our context. Roberto 'Bob' Benigni is chalking a window onto the cell wall, and because his English is rather shaky he asks Jack whether one says, "I look at the window" or "I look out of the window." Jack chuckles at the Italian's question, but in view of their hopeless situation his response is cynical: "Well, in this case I guess you would say I look *at* the window." Today, the scene can be read as an uncanny pre-anticipation of current developments.

The concept of transparency plays an important role in the above *dispositif*. In Jarmusch's bleak prison situation, which corresponds to Foucault's system of enclosure by the disciplinary society, the normally transparent – and invisible – window (or interface) suddenly becomes visible itself as a window, or a boundary or demarcation. The simple fact that it is chalked out on a prison wall means that it can be experienced in its materiality and facticity. The chalk window can be read as a metaphor for software or programmed environments and their interfaces, which have become the new, 'post-material' foundations of the contemporary information societies.

While the disciplinary societies described by Foucault are characterised by built enclosures (the prison, the school, the factory, the hospital), these rigid structures have given way to continuous modulations in the control societies of today. These 'soft' modulations resemble a "self-deforming cast that will continuously change from one moment to the other" (Deleuze 185). This supple mould, which in *Down by Law* is represented by the image of the swamps of Louisiana, has three distinctive attributes:

1. Transparency (diaphanousness or invisibility that eludes direct sensory perception)
2. Immateriality (as the connection between individual materialities)
3. Performativity ("Code is Law" (Lessig, *Code and other Laws of Cyberspace*) – computer code becomes the law)

In contrast to the opaque prison walls, the swamp is 'transparent' (metaphorically speaking, of course, since briny water is seldom clear). Unlike solid matter, the swamp is fluid, a dangerous attribute enabling it to change shape at any time, to fill up cavities as they form and to envelop bodies and objects whenever required. The enveloping of such perfection hinders (and this is where performativity comes in) forward movement at least as efficiently as constructed fortifications and perhaps even more so.

Transparency

Today, the age of transparency[2] that Walter Benjamin optimistically considered to be emerging in the glass buildings designed by his architect contemporaries seems to be ambiguous. For one thing, not only light waves pass through the transparent buildings but any number of electromagnetic waves deriving from a very diverse range of technical sources (Medosch, *Waves – The Art of the Electromagnetic Society*; Medosch *Waves*). For another, the notion of transparency – with its double meaning of visibility and invisibility, or with the ambivalence of the panoptical and the post-optical – turns out to be very suitable for the characterisation of contemporary performative (information) architecture and spaces (Arns, "Read_me, run_me, execute_me..." 197-207).

Foucault's notion of panoptism (Foucault) is derived from Jeremy Bentham's 'panopticon,' the blueprint for a perfect prison that makes the inmates of a circular prison permanently visible to a warden placed in the middle. However, I use the term 'post-optical' to denote all the digital data streams and (programmed) communication structures or architectures that are monitored at least as easily as such prisoners, yet consist of visual information in only a very small part (keyword: 'dataveillance').

While in everyday usage 'transparency' stands for simplicity, clarity and controllability through viewability (for example in the name of *Transparency International*, an organisation combating corruption worldwide), in computer science the term means the very opposite, namely invisibility and information concealment. A 'transparent' interface is one that the user can neither detect nor notice. While this concealment of (superfluous, excessive) information is often expedient in terms of reducing complexity, it can also lull the user into a false sense of security: the invisibility of the interface suggests a direct view of something, an unimpaired transparency in which it would be foolish, of course, to believe. For that reason, Lev Manovich writes: "Far from being a transparent window into the data inside a computer, the interface brings with it strong messages of its own."

In order to make this 'message' visible, attention must be directed to the transparent 'window pane' itself. Just as at the press of a button the transparent glass facades of buildings can be transformed into translucid or semi-transparent surfaces, and thus become visible, it is a question of wrenching the transparency out of post-optical information-technical structures. Applied analogously to communication networks, it would be a matter of making the transparent distribution structures of economic, political and social power opaque, and therefore perceptible. It is ultimately a matter of restoring to the IT-based notion of transparency the original meaning of clearness and controllability through visibility.

Immateriality

The more regulated by software everyday things become, the less accessible they are to sensory perception in our everyday dealings with them. However, the fact that they are vanishing from sight does not mean that they are not there. On the contrary: the increasingly programmed world surrounding us means that rules, conventions and relationships, which are basically changeable and negotiable, are being translated into and fixed in software. Recorded in software, immaterial structures are at least – and herein lies the paradox – as permanent as, and perhaps even more powerful than, material structures and architecture.

The secret (and uncanny) making invisible of the world through software deployment does not only lead to a withdrawal from visibility and perceptibility but also means that structures become immaterial. In this case, however, 'immaterial' does not imply that these structures are any less effective than their solid counterparts. To take 'immaterial' to mean the opposite of 'material' would be to wholly misread the term (Terranova 31). Rather, one must learn to grasp the immaterial as something which turns "qualitative, intensive differences into quantitative relations of exchange and equivalence" (ibid.). It establishes relations between isolated materialities – things and people, wares and individuals, objects and subjects – and in this way is able to compute profiles, for instance, of consumers or movements at very high speed.[3]

At every given second, the immaterial is somewhere (as opposed to nowhere), between things. It encloses the materials, elastically changes shape, agilely follows objects and bodies, and constantly establishes connections. Admittedly, the immaterial is not that 'which holds together the world in its innermost place,' but it forges together the things in the world by interrelating them and does so more efficiently than rigid structures were ever able to. Thus, software turns out to be a very hard substance and immateriality to be quasi-factitious materiality that, however, most of the time eludes our (visual, tactile) sensory perception.

Performativity

Programmed structures consist of two kinds of 'texts': a visible 'front end' (the 'window') and an invisible, transparent 'back end' (the software or program code). These texts are to each other as phenotext is to genotext in the sphere of biology: the surface effects of the phenotexts (graphical user interfaces) are called up and controlled by the genotexts (program codes or source texts) effective below the surface. The characteristic attribute of program code is that it unites saying and doing (action), in other words, code as an action-capable act of speaking is not a description or representation of something, but instead affects directly, sets in motion, times effects. Code does what it says.

However, code affects not only the phenotexts, that is to say the graphic user interfaces. "Coded performativity" (Grether) has equally direct, even political, effects on the (virtual) realms through which we move. According to the American lawyer Lawrence Lessig, "[p]rogram code increasingly tends to become law" (Lessig, "Stalin & Disney – Copyright is Killing the Internet"). Today, control functions are integrated directly in the architecture of the network, namely in its code. In *Code and other Laws of Cyberspace*, Lessig uses the Internet provider America Online (AOL) as a compelling illustration of the way in which program architecture can hinder, with the aid of the code that defines it, any form of virtual 'rebellion,' for instance, and largely control the users. Therefore, Graham Harwood describes this transparent world as an "invisible shadow world of process" (49).

It is a world with direct, and also political, consequences for the virtual and real spaces in which we move today: by stipulating what is possible in these spaces, and what is not, it mobilises or, as applicable, immobilises its users. The question of permeability – access? when and for whom? – is central for contemporary spaces and closely linked to the notion of performativity (Arns, "Texte, die (sich) bewegen..." 57-78; Arns, "Read_me, run_me, execute_me..." 197-207). Gilles Deleuze writes that:

> The conception of a control mechanism giving the position of any element within an open environment at any given instant (whether animal in a reserve or human in a corporation, as with an electronic collar), is not necessarily one of science fiction. Félix Guattari has imagined a city where one would be able to leave one's apartment, one's street, one's neighborhood, thanks to one's (dividual) electronic card that raises a given barrier; but the card could just as easily be rejected on a given day or between certain hours; what counts is not the barrier but the computer that tracks each person's position – licit or illicit – and effects a universal modulation (186).

So-called Radio Frequency Identification (RFID) technology, for example, makes possible tracking of the very kind described above (*Radio Frequency Identification Technology*; *How I learned to love RFID*). RFID tags are tiny radio labels, passive wireless transmitters which are able to send and save information, and which are expected to become replacements for barcode labels.

They are already in use in goods logistics, human surveillance and anti-theft protection. In response to a weak wireless energy pulse, RFID tags return to a reading device the information stored on them. This is already possible over a distance of up to several hundred metres – without the bearer of the tag even noticing. In addition, the technology enables objects to be unambiguously identified worldwide; in addition to the unnoticed reading out of information, this capability is a further significant attribute distinguishing RFID from conventional barcodes. RFID allows the flow of goods to be re-traced without gaps, and thus opens up whole new dimensions of data mining (for instance through the compilation of consumer profiles). If one considers the potential deployment of RFID technology on and inside people – via passports or health-insurance cards provided with RFID chips on which biometrical data are stored, say, or via RFID tags with biometrical data implanted below the skin (*Wo gibt es RFID?*) – then new forms of ubiquitous control are conceivable.

British artist Chris Oakley graphically illustrated this possibility in his short video *The Catalogue*.

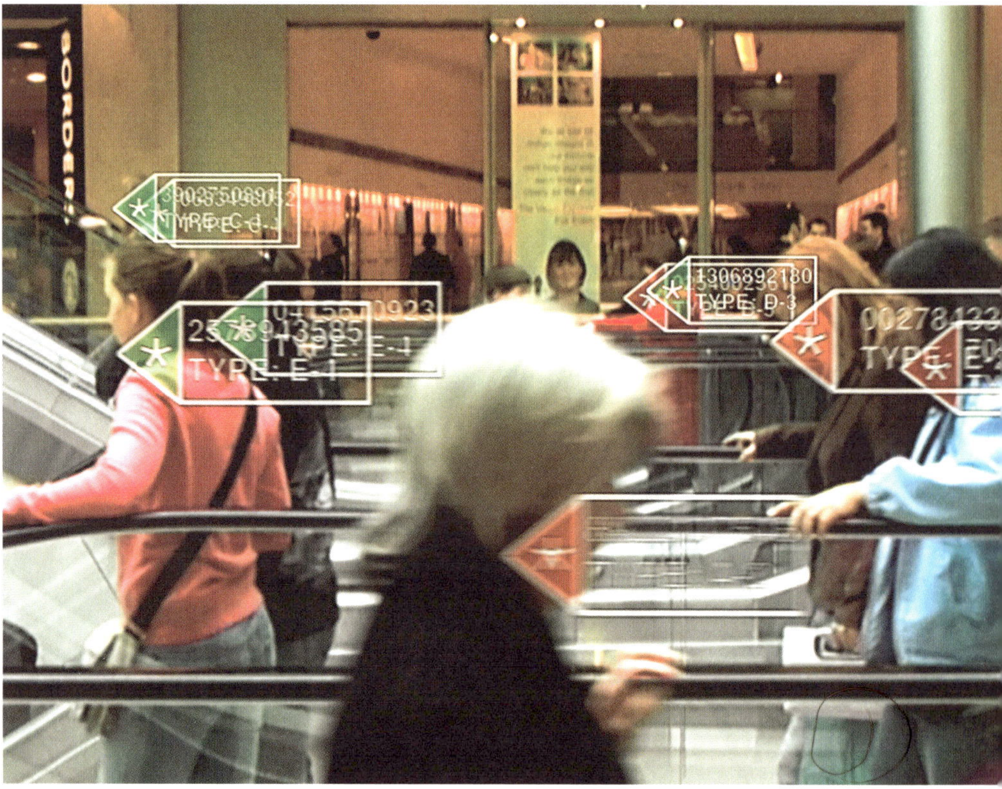

ILL. I: **Chris Oakley: Still from *The Catalogue* (2004).**

The age of transparency is marked by a dual structure of the panoptical and post-optical. On the one hand, we are confronted with a *dispositif* of total, panoptical visibility that began in the 1980s, if not indeed earlier, with the installation of video-monitoring systems and it is now being perfected in state and private-sector structures of surveillance satellites (Parks; Hunger). With a fictitious newspaper notice allegedly appearing in the year 2067 – "Anna Kournikova Deleted by Memeright Trusted System" – David Rice thought in 2001 to a logical end the *dispositif* of transparency coupled with the ever stricter persecution of copyright infringements we are witnessing today. Smart activists, advertising agencies or religious fundamentalists already devise targeted advertising for *Google Earth*: Gigantic Land Art projects are coming into being, visible only from airplanes or to the cameras of satellites (Waldt).

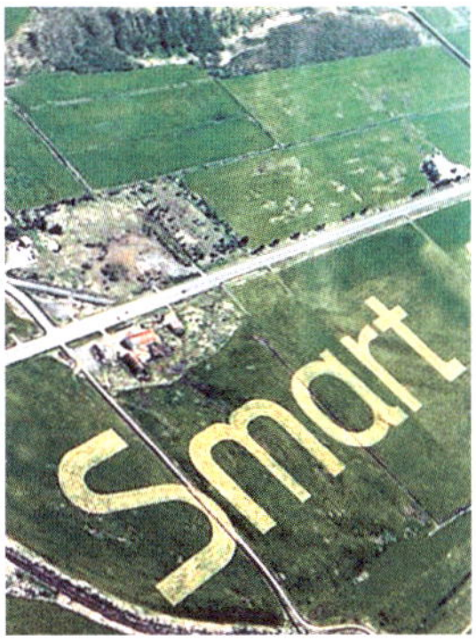

ILL. 2: *Smart* Google Earth graffiti.

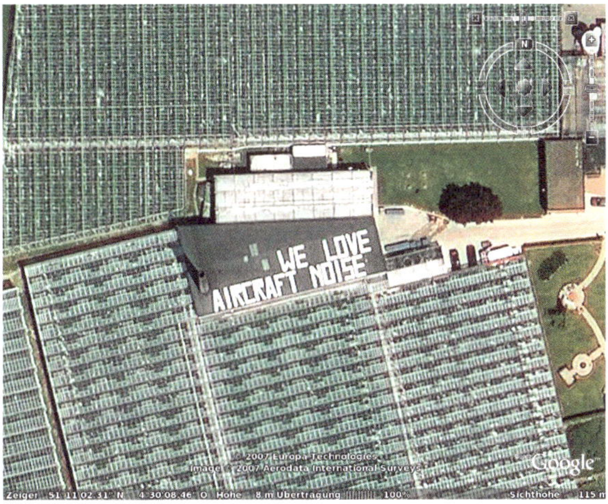

ILL. 3: *We love aircraft noise* Google Earth graffiti.

In parallel with this panoptical visibility, the technical structures that observe and act performatively have increasingly withdrawn into invisibility. In many cases, performative structures, whether unimaginably small, immaterial or remote, are recognisable only by their effects but are no longer necessarily visible. Satellites, for instance, are so far from the Earth that they can scarcely be detected with the naked human eye, miniaturised nanomachines are simply too small, and most software eludes human perception because it involves 'inconspicuous' performative (geno-)texts lying below the visible surfaces (pheno-texts) that generate them. In the age of transparency we find ourselves dealing with a fundamental de-coupling of visibility and performativity/effectivity.

While many things are being subjected to the paradigm of permanent visibility, the performative structures that truly act are withdrawing from precisely this visibility, and thus from our direct control. These structures have become transparent. Invisibility is equally becoming the *privilege* of acting, performative structures. It is in this sense that I refer to the present as a post-optical age in which program code – which might also, with reference to Walter Benjamin, be described as the post-optical unconscious[4] – is becoming 'law' as a performative text.

Minoritarian tactics in the age of transparency

> The vocation of an art of the kind that reflects on electronic crowds and networks is not the representation of the visible world but the visualisation of what is otherwise inaccessible to perception and is difficult to imagine because of its cosmic or microscopic scale, its discontinuity in space and time, or its impenetrability – from the insides of the body, the atom or the black box to the outside of our galaxy and our universe (Morse 192).

How can political and/or artistic action be articulated in such spaces that have become imperceptible, withdrawn from the direct view? In view of this software-assisted disappearance of the world, where and how can potential spaces of the political (re-)emerge? Various media and net art projects as well as software-art projects (i.e., *Wo gibt es RFID?*) have in recent years developed approaches that make the structures of economic, political and social power distribution in communication networks opaque (= visible). The concern of such projects is invariably to transpose information-technical structures from a state of transparency to one of visibility or perceptibility.

In an age of software-assisted implosion of the political, this first step alone is eminently political. Almost twenty years ago already, Deleuze asserted: "There is no need to fear or hope, but only to look for new weapons" (187).

Are resistant tactics[5] even feasible in this transparent world? And if so, what do they look like? Two tactical directions will be described in the following: a) that of viewing, mapping and intervening, that is to say the making visible of structures of the surveillance and/or information landscape; and b) that of vanishing and becoming invisible through maximum visibility (over-identification with, and deployment of, the panoptical regime).

Inspecting, cartographing, intervening

Projects that point to the existence of concealed structures of the surveillance and/or information landscape belong to the above category. A media-artistic and -activistic analysis of the subject of video surveillance is a current topos in media art[6] – in the 1990s, for example, Yann Beauvais (F) and the Surveillance Camera Players (US) performed plays for the operators of surveillance cameras and in this way focused attention on the video cameras scattered around cities. The works of the French artist Renaud Auguste-Dormeuil should be mentioned – as should the *track-the-trackers* system developed by the Swiss artist Annina Rüst in 2003, which identifies the locations of CCTV cameras in public space by using GPS. These locations are stored in a database and the camera sites acoustically signal to users of the system moving through the city.

Beyond this, however, there are also projects that want not merely to alert us to the existence of video cameras in public spaces but aim to make visible the transparent (power) structures lying behind them. One example is the work of Canadian artist Michelle Teran, who pulled a strange-looking trolley-suitcase through the streets of Berlin in 2005. Her performance *Life: A User's Manual*[7] made visible on a television set the footage of surveillance cameras installed in public and private locations. She used a commercially available video-scanner which was able to intercept radio signals emitted by cameras transmitting on the 2.4 Ghz frequency band. In this way, a stroll through the city became a "shared experience in visualizing the invisible" (Teran).

In her video *Faceless* (2007, 50 min.), the Austrian artist Manu Luksch goes one step further than Yann Beauvais and the Surveillance Camera Players. While producing the video in London, Luksch posed in front of countless CCTV cameras and then invoked the British Data Privacy Law (which guarantees one's right to one's own image) to demand that the operators furnish her with the footage. She used this material (on which the faces of everyone except the artist had been made unrecognisable for data-privacy reasons) to assemble a

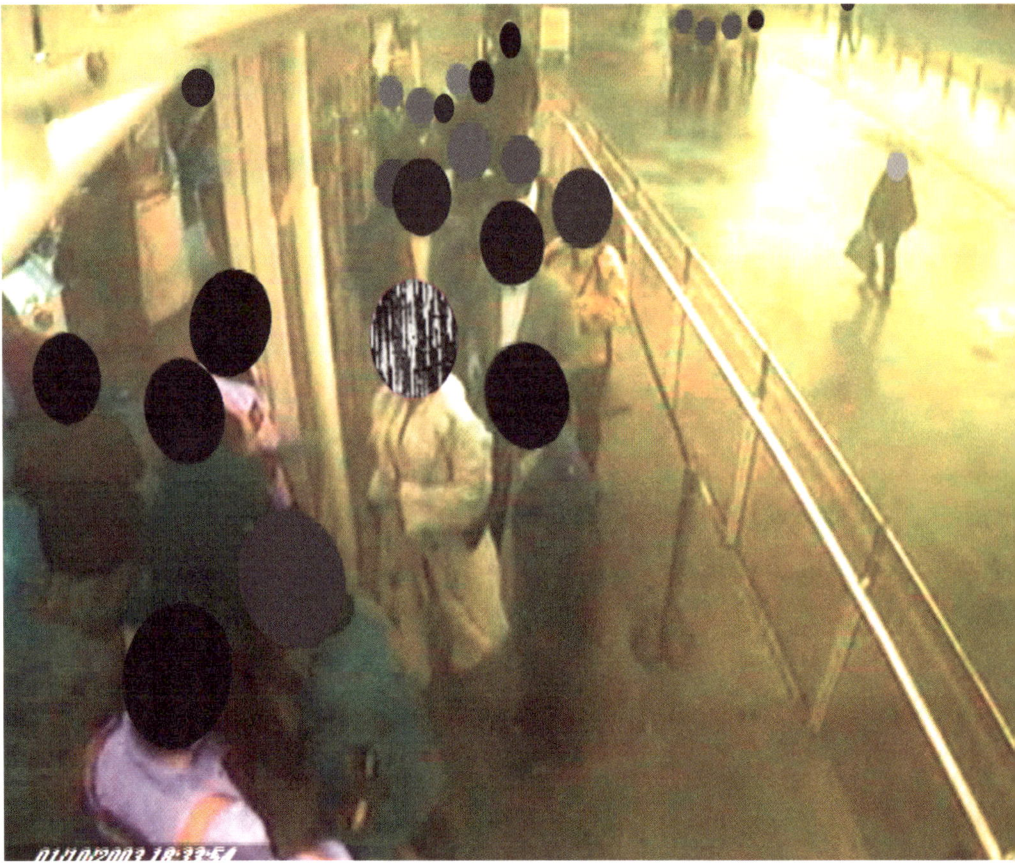

ILL. 4: **Manu Luksch: Still from *Faceless* (2007).**

disturbing science-fiction tale that “thanks to the single-frame aesthetic dictated by the nature of surveillance footage is reminiscent of Chris Marker’s groundbreaking film-comic *La Jetée* (1962)” (Keuschnigg).

The French group Bureau d’Études has for several years been cartographing contemporary political, social and economic systems. These visual analyses of transnational capitalism are the product of elaborate and painstaking research, and are mostly presented in the form of large-format wall paintings. *Governing by Networks* (2003) is a chart that visualises the reciprocal shareholdings and transnational interconnections of global media conglomerates. Because these visualised representations depict relations that normally remain invisible, through channels that usually remain singular and unconnected, and because they are being linked up in order to form a great whole, the charts function like "resymbolizing machines" (Bureau d'Études, "Machines de Resymbolisation... ").

Bureau d'Études uses the term to describe the resistant process of stringing together and representing that which is no longer perceivable as a whole, namely global capitalism, due to the intricacy of its branches and capillary structures. Bureau d'Études, whose conceptual forerunners include the artists Öyvind Fahlström (1928-76) and Mark Lombardi (1951-2000), produces a sharp analysis of the present in its visual dissection of contemporary business conglomerates.

Over the past few years, the so-called plane spotters have vividly demonstrated that transparent structures can be disclosed through simple observation. Aviation enthusiasts were able to uncover the 'Guantanamo flights' of the CIA by closely observing the take-offs and landings at various places in the world and continuously comparing this data with civilian flight schedules. Although the US secret service uses civilian aircraft to transport suspected terrorists to prison camps like Guantanamo, the flights do not appear in civilian flight plans and for this reason the secret activities eventually became conspicuous.

With *Terminal Air* (2007), the American experimental geographer Trevor Paglen and the Institute for Applied Autonomy have developed a system (software and database) which is able to display almost in real-time these illegal CIA flights. Paglen is primarily interested in exploring and documenting "military landscapes" like military installations hidden deep in the American desert. In order to photograph these concealed and remote sites, and thus make visible the "optical unconscious" (Benjamin, "A Small History of Photography"), Paglen uses in *Limit Telephotography* outer-space photography techniques deploying tele lenses with focuses between 1,300 and 7,000 mm, an enlargement that makes visible to the human eye invisible aspects of the landscape. *Missing Persons* (2006) for its part deals with the transparent surface of the (letterbox) companies that own the aircraft used to make the Guantamo flights and exhibits the signatures of the fake CEOs.

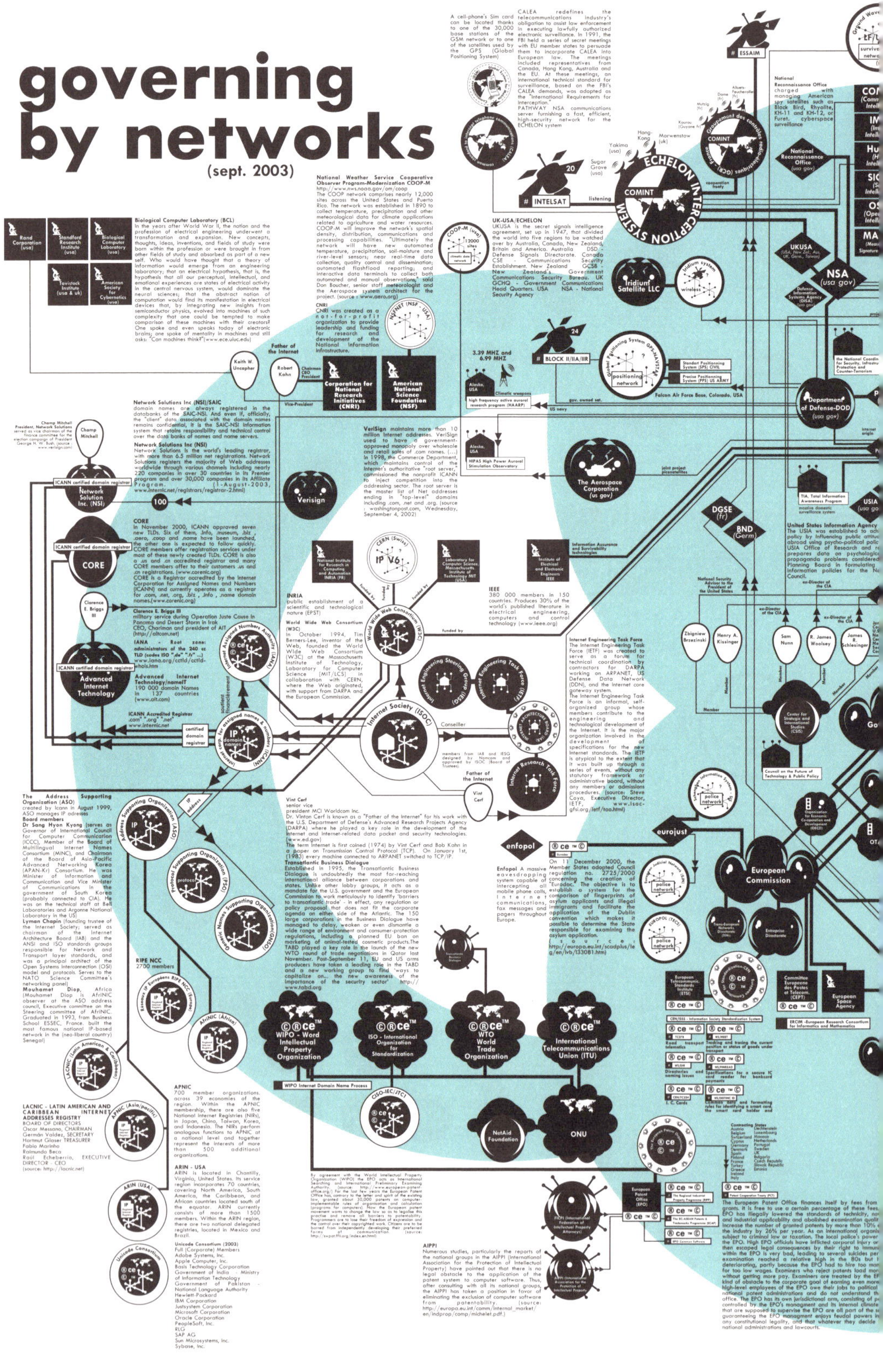

governing by networks
(sept. 2003)
A cell-phone's Sim card can be located thanks to one of the 30,000 base stations of the GSM network or to one of the satellites used by the GPS (Global Positioning System)
CALEA redefines the telecommunications industry's obligation to assist law enforcement in executing lawfully authorized electronic surveillance. In 1991, the FBI held a series of secret meetings with EU member states to persuade them to incorporate CALEA into European law. The meetings included representatives from Canada, Hong Kong, Australia and the EU. At these meetings, an international technical standard for surveillance, based on the FBI's CALEA demands, was adopted as the "International Requirements for Interception."
PATHWAY NSA communications server furnishing a fast, efficient, high-security network for the ECHELON system
ESSAIM
INTELSAT
listening
COMINT
ECHELON INTERCEPTION SYSTEM
Groupement des contrôles radioélectriques (GCR)
National Reconnaissance Office charged with managing American spy satellites such as Black Bird, Rhyolite, KH-11 and KH-12, or Furet, cyberspace surveillance
UKUSA
NSA (usa gov)
Biological Computer Laboratory (BCL)
In the years after World War II, the notion and the profession of electrical engineering underwent a transformation and expansion. New concepts, thoughts, ideas, inventions, and fields of study were born within the profession or were brought in from other fields of study and absorbed as a part of a new self. Who would have thought that a theory of information would emerge from an engineering laboratory; that an electrical hypothesis, that is, the hypothesis that all our perceptual, intellectual, and emotional experiences are states of electrical activity in the central nervous system, would dominate the neural sciences; that the abstract notion of computation would find its manifestation in electrical devices that, by integrating new insights from semiconductor physics, evolved into machines of such complexity that one could be tempted to make comparison of these machines with their creators? One spoke and even speaks today of electronic brains; one spoke of mentality in machines and still asks: "Can machines think?" (www.ece.uiuc.edu)
Rand Corporation (usa)
Standford Research Institute (usa)
Biological Computer Laboratory (usa)
Tavistock Institute (usa & uk)
American Society for Cybernetics (usa)
National Weather Service Cooperative Observer Program-Modernization COOP-M
http://www.nws.noaa.gov/om/coop
The COOP network comprises nearly 12,000 sites across the United States and Puerto Rico. The network was established in 1890 to collect temperature, precipitation and other meteorological data for climate applications related to agriculture and water resources. COOP-M will improve the network's spatial density, distribution, communications and processing capabilities. "Ultimately the network will have new automated temperature, precipitation, soil-moisture and river-level sensors; near real-time data collection, quality control and dissemination; automated flashflood reporting; and interactive data terminals to collect both automated and manual observations," said Don Boucher, senior staff meteorologist and the Aerospace system architect for the project. (source : www.aero.org)
UK-USA/ECHELON
UKUSA is the secret signals intelligence agreement, set up in 1947, that divided the world into five regions to be watched over by Australia, Canada, New Zealand, Britain and America. Australia DSD - Defense Signals Directorate. Canada CSE - Communications Security Establishment. New Zealand GCSB - New Zealand's Government Communications Security Bureau. UK GCHQ - Government Communications Head Quarters. USA NSA - National Security Agency
Iridium Satellite LLC
CNRI
CNRI was created as a not-for-profit organization to provide leadership and funding for research and development of the National Information Infrastructure.
BLOCK II/IIA/IIR
Global Positioning System GPS-NAVSTAR
Falcon Air Force Base, Colorado, USA
3.39 MHZ and 6.99 MHZ
Climatic weapons
high frequency active auroral research program (HAARP)
HIPAS High Power Auroral Stimulation Observatory
Department of Defense-DOD (usa gov)
Father of the Internet
Keith W. Uncapher
Robert Kahn
Chairman CEO President
Vice-President
Corporation for National Research Initiatives (CNRI)
American National Science Foundation (NSF)
Network Solutions Inc (NSI)/SAIC
domain names are always registered in the databanks of the SAIC-NSI. And even if, officially, the "client" data associated with the domain names remains confidential, it is the SAIC-NSI information system that retains responsibility and technical control over the data banks of names and name servers.
Network Solutions Inc (NSI)
Network Solutions is the world's leading registrar, with more than 6.5 million net registrations. Network Solutions registers the majority of Web addresses worldwide through various channels including nearly 220 companies in over 30 countries in its Premier program and over 30,000 companies in its Affiliate Program. (1-August-2003, www.internic.net/registrars/registrar-2.html)
Champ Mitchell
VeriSign maintains more than 10 million Internet addresses. VeriSign used to have a government-approved monopoly over wholesale and retail sales of .com names. (...) In 1998, the Commerce Department, which maintains control of the Internet's authoritative "root server," commissioned the nonprofit ICANN to inject competition into the addressing sector. The root server is the master list of Net addresses ending in "top-level" domains including .com, .net and .org. (source : washingtonpost.com, Wednesday, September 4, 2002)
The Aerospace Corporation (us gov)
ICANN certified domain registrar
Network Solution Inc. (NSI)
Verisign
CORE
In November 2000, ICANN approved seven new TLDs. Six of them, .info, .museum, .biz, .aero, .coop and .name have been launched, the other one is expected to follow quickly. CORE members offer newly created TLDs. CORE is also a .us and .cn accredited registrar and many CORE members offer to their customers .us and .cn registrations. (www.corenic.org)
CORE is a Registrar accredited by the Internet Corporation for Assigned Names and Numbers (ICANN) and currently offers as a registrar for .com, .net, .org, .biz, .info, .name domain names. (www.corenic.org)
Clarence E. Briggs III
Clarence E. Briggs III military service during Operation Juste Cause in Panama and Desert Storm in Irak CEO, Chairman and president of AIT (http://aitcom.net)
IANA - Root zone: administrators of the 240 cc TLD (codes ISO ".de" ".fr" ...) www.iana.org/cctld/cctld-whois.htm
Advanced Internet Technology/nameIT
190 000 domain Names in 137 countries (www.ait.com)
Advanced Internet Technology
ICANN Accredited Registrar .com" ".org" ".net" www.internic.net
Internet Assigned Numbers Authority (IANA)
Internet corp. for assigned names & numbers (ICANN)
certified domain registrar
National Institute for Research in Computing and Automation INRIA (FR)
CERN (Swiss)
IP V6
Laboratory for Computer Science, Massachusetts Institute of Technology MIT (USA)
Institute of Electrical and Electronic Engineers IEEE
INRIA
public establishment of a scientific and technological nature (EPST)
World Wide Web Consortium (W3C)
In October 1994, Tim Berners-Lee, inventor of the Web, founded the World Wide Web Consortium (W3C) at the Massachusetts Institute of Technology, Laboratory for Computer Science [MIT/LCS] in collaboration with CERN, where the Web originated, with support from DARPA and the European Commission.
IEEE
380 000 members in 150 countries. Produces 30% of the world's published literature in electrical engineering, computers and control technology (www.ieee.org)
World Wide Web Consortium (W3C)
Internet Engineering Steering Group (IESG)
Internet Engineering Task Force (IETF)
Internet Society (ISOC)
Internet Architecture Board (IAB)
Internet Research Task Force
Conseiller
Internet Engineering Task Force
The Internet Engineering Task Force (IETF) was created to serve as a forum for technical coordination by contractors for DARPA working on ARPANET, US Defense Data Network (DDN), and the Internet core gateway system. The Internet Engineering Task Force is an informal, self-organized group whose members contribute to the engineering and technological development of the Internet. It is the major organization involved in the development of specifications for the new Internet standards. The IETF is atypical to the extent that it was built up through a series of events, without any statutory framework or administrative board, without any members or admissions procedures. (source: Steve Coya, Executive Director, IETF, www.isoc-gfsi.org/ietf/tao.html)
Vint Cerf
Father of the Internet
Vint Cerf
senior vice president MCI Worldcom Inc.
Dr. Vinton Cerf is known as a "Father of the Internet" for his work with the U.S. Department of Defense's Advanced Research Projects Agency (DARPA) where he played a key role in the development of the internet and internet-related data packet and security technologies. (www.ed.gov)
The term Internet is first coined (1974) by Vint Cerf and Bob Kahn in a paper on Transmission Control Protocol (TCP). On January 1st, (1983) every machine connected to ARPANET switched to TCP/IP.
Transatlantic Business Dialogue
Established in 1995, the Transatlantic Business Dialogue is undoubtedly the most far-reaching international alliance between corporations and states. Unlike other lobby groups, it acts as a mandate for the U.S. government and the European Commission to work meticulously to identify 'barriers to transatlantic trade' - in effect, any regulation or policy proposal that does not fit the corporate agenda on either side of the Atlantic. The 150 large corporations in the Business Dialogue have managed to delay, weaken or even dismantle a wide range of environment and consumer-protection regulations, including a planned EU ban on marketing of animal-tested cosmetic products. The TABD played a key role in the launch of the new WTO round of trade negotiations in Qatar last November. Post-September 11, EU and US arms producers have taken a leading role in the TABD and a new working group to find 'ways to capitalize on the new awareness of the importance of the security sector' http://www.tabd.org
The Address Supporting Organization (ASO)
created by Icann in August 1999, ASO manages IP adresses
Board members
Dr Sang Hyon Kyong (serves as Governor of International Council for Computer Communication (ICCC), Member of the Board of Multilingual Internet Names Consortium (MINC), and Chairman of the Board of Asia-Pacific Advanced Network Korea (APAN-Kr) Consortium. He was Minister of Information and Communication and Vice Minister of Communications in the government of South Korea (probably connected to CIA). He was on the technical staff at Bell Laboratories and Argonne National Laboratory in the US)
Lyman Chapin (founding trustee of the Internet Society; served as chairman of the Internet Architecture Board (IAB) and the ANSI and ISO standards groups responsible for Network and Transport layer standards, and was a principal architect of the Open Systems Interconnection (OSI) model and protocols. Serves to the NATO Science Committee's networking panel)
Mouhamet Diop, Africa (Mouhamet Diop is AfriNIC observer at the ASO address council, Executive committee on the Steering committee of AfriNIC. Graduated in 1993, from Business School ESSEC, France. built the most famous national IP-based network in the (neo-liberal country) Senegal)
Address Supporting Organization (ASO)
Protocol Supporting Organization (PSO)
Generic Names Supporting Organization (GNSO)
RIPE NCC
2700 members
Reseaux IP Européens RIPE NCC (Europe)
AfriNIC (Africa)
LACNIC (Latin American & Caribbean)
APNIC (Asia/pacific)
ARIN (USA)
Unicode Consortium
LACNIC - LATIN AMERICAN AND CARIBBEAN INTERNET ADDRESSES REGISTRY
BOARD OF DIRECTORS
Oscar Messano, CHAIRMAN
Germán Valdez, SECRETARY
Hartmut Glaser TREASURER
Fabio Marinho
Raimundo Beca
Raúl Echeberría, EXECUTIVE DIRECTOR - CEO
(source: http://lacnic.net)
APNIC
700 member organizations, across 39 economies of the region. Within the APNIC membership, there are also five National Internet Registries (NIRs), in Japan, China, Taiwan, Korea, and Indonesia. The NIRs perform analogous functions to APNIC at a national level and together represent the interests of more than 500 additional organizations.
ARIN - USA
ARIN is located in Chantilly, Virginia, United States. Its service region incorporates 70 countries, covering North America, South America, the Caribbean, and African countries located south of the equator. ARIN currently consists of more than 1500 members. Within the ARIN region, there are two national delegated registries, located in Mexico and Brazil.
Unicode Consortium (2003)
Full (Corporate) Members
Adobe Systems, Inc.
Apple Computer, Inc.
Basis Technology Corporation
Government of India - Ministry of Information Technology
Government of Pakistan - National Language Authority
Hewlett-Packard
IBM Corporation
Justsystem Corporation
Microsoft Corporation
Oracle Corporation
PeopleSoft, Inc.
RLG
SAP AG
Sun Microsystems, Inc.
Sybase, Inc.
WIPO - Word Intellectual Property Organization
ISO - International Organization for Standardization
WTO World Trade Organization
International Telecommunications Union (ITU)
WIPO Internet Domain Name Process
CISO-IEC/JTC1
NetAid Foundation
ONU
enfopol
Enfopol A massive eavesdropping system capable of intercepting all Internet communications, fax messages and pagers throughout Europe.
On 11 December 2000, the Member States adopted Council regulation no. 2725/2000 concerning the creation of "Eurodac". The objective is to establish a system for the comparison of fingerprints of asylum applicants and illegal immigrants and facilitate the application of the Dublin convention which makes it possible to determine the State responsible for examining the asylum application. (source: http://europa.eu.int/scadplus/leg/en/lvb/l33081.htm)
eurojust
European Commission
police network
EUROPOL (TECS)
European Patent Office (EPO)
Committee Européenne des Postes et Télécom. (CEPT)
European Space Agency
ERCIM - European Research Consortium for Informatics and Mathematics
The European Patent Office finances itself by fees from grants. It is free to use a certain percentage of these fees. EPO has illegally lowered the standards of technicity, novelty and industrial applicability and abolished examination quality. Increase the number of granted patents by more than 10% the industry by 26% per year. As an international organisation subject to criminal law or taxation. The local police's power the EPO. High EPO officials have inflicted corporal injury and then escaped legal consequences by their right to immunity. Within the EPO is very bad, leading to several suicides per examination reached a relative high in the 80s but deteriorating, partly because the EPO had to hire too many for too low wages. Examiners who reject patents load more without getting more pay. Examiners are treated by the EPO kind of obstacle to the corporate goal of earning even more. High-level employees of the EPO owe their jobs to political national patent administrations and do not understand the office. The EPO has its own jurisdictional arm, consisting of people controlled by the EPO's managment and its internal climate that are supposed to supervise the EPO are all part of the same guaranteeing the EPO managment enjoys feudal powers in any constitutional legality, and that whatever they decide national administrations and lawcourts.
By agreement with the World Intellectual Property Organization (WIPO) the EPO acts as International Searching and International Preliminary Examining Authority. (source: http://www.european-patent-office.org/)
AIPPI
Numerous studies, particularly the reports of the national groups in the AIPPI (International Association for the Protection of Intellectual Property) have pointed out that there is no legal obstacle to the application of the patent system to computer software. Thus, after consulting with all its national groups, the AIPPI has taken a position in favor of eliminating the exclusion of computer software from patentability. (source: http://europa.eu.int/comm/internal_market/en/indprop/comp/michelet.pdf.)
FICPI (International Federation of Intellectual Property Attorneys)
AIPPI (International Association for the Protection of Intellectual Property)
DGSE (fr)
BND (Germ)
USIA
United States Information Agency
The USIA was established to achieve policy by influencing public attitudes abroad using psycho-political policies. USIA Office of Research and prepares data on psychological propaganda problems considered Planning Board in formulating information policies for the National Council.
TIA, Total Information Awareness Program
Zbigniew Brzezinski
Henry A. Kissinger
Sam Nunn
R. James Woolsey
James R. Schlesinger
Center for Strategic and International Studies (CSIS)
Council on the Future of Technology & Public Policy
Organization for Economic Cooperation and Development (OECD)

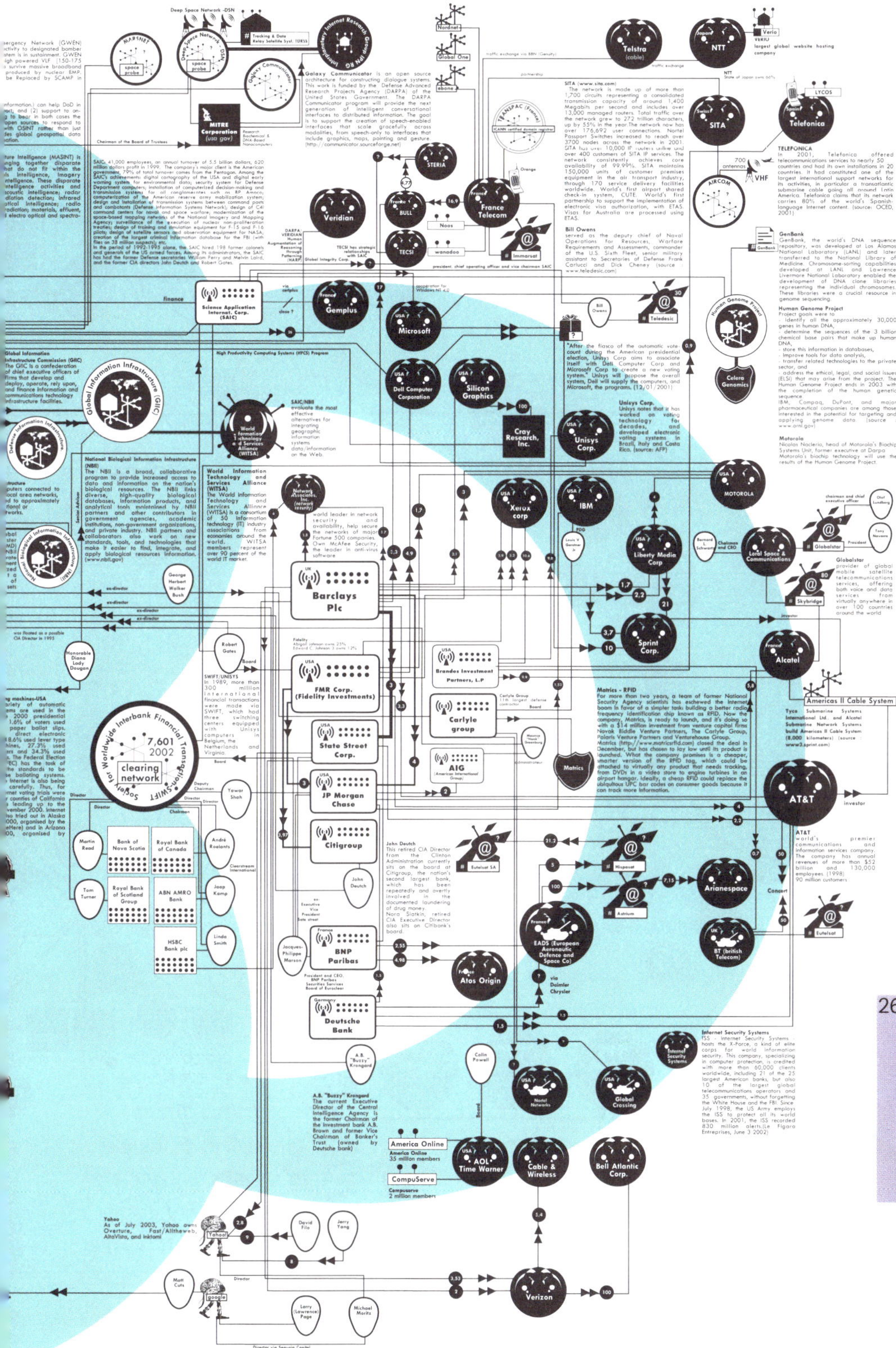

ILL. 5: Bureau d'Études: *Governing by Networks* (2003).

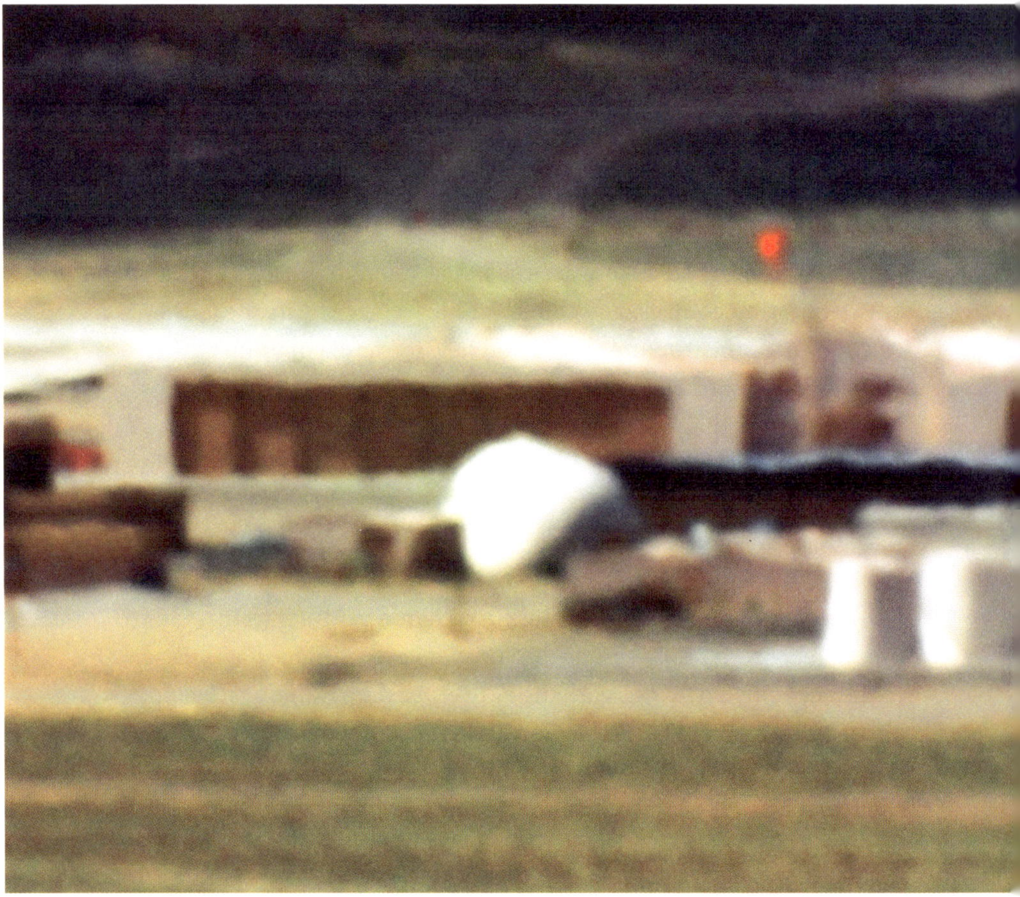

ILL. 6: Trevor Paglen: *Large Hangars and Fuel Storage* (2005), from the series *Limit Telephotography*, courtesy of Altman Siegel Gallery, San Francisco, and Galerie Thomas Zander, Cologne.

Marko Peljhan and Mario Purkathofer investigate in their work the material structures on which the regime of transparency is based. While Marko Peljhan's autonomous mobile research laboratory *makrolab* (1997-2007) hooked up to the communications streams from changing sites on various continents, and in this way cartographed the territory of signals over a specific geographical point (Arns, "Faktura and Interface..."), the Swiss artist Mario Purkathofer's travel agency *sofatrips.com* offers "trips into the information landscape." Conducted since 2006, his *couch trips* are movements through virtual and physical realms, for instance the on-foot tracing of the route taken by a text message within Zurich, coach trips to Geneva to the European research centre CERN (the site where the World-Wide Web and Mosaic, the first graphic browser, were developed in the early 1990s), walks through the city or human data processions through the information landscape – up to the network boundary of Zurich. The routes inevitably pass by public telephone boxes, providers, computing centres, webcams, WLAN hotspots – in short, they traverse the infrastructures of old and new forms of communication. *Sofatrips* direct our attention to the material basis of our otherwise increasingly virtual world.

A good example of activist *intervention* in the invisible, flexible modulations of the control society – the code – is provided by the *insert_coin* project of Dragan Espenschied and Alvar Freude. Using the motto "Two people control 250 people," the two students working for their diploma thesis at the Merz-Akademie in Stuttgart installed unnoticed a web proxy server that used a Perl script to manipulate in the academy's data network the entire web data traffic of students and teaching staff. As Espenschied and Freude noted in a text on the occasion of their winning the International Media Art Award in 2001, their goal was to "examine the users' competence and critical faculties in relation to the everyday medium of the Internet."

The manipulated proxy server diverted the URLs entered to other web pages, modified HTML formatting codes, used a simple search-and-replace function to alter current reports on news sites (for instance by swapping over the names of politicians) as well as altering the content of private e-mails retrieved over web interfaces like Hotmail, Yahoo! or gmx. The manipulated web access was in operation for four weeks without being noticed by students or staff. When Espenschied and Freude made their experiment public, hardly anybody was interested. Although the duo published a set of simple instructions for switching off the filter, only a tiny number of those affected took the time to deactivate the settings and in this way restore the flow of unfiltered data.[8]

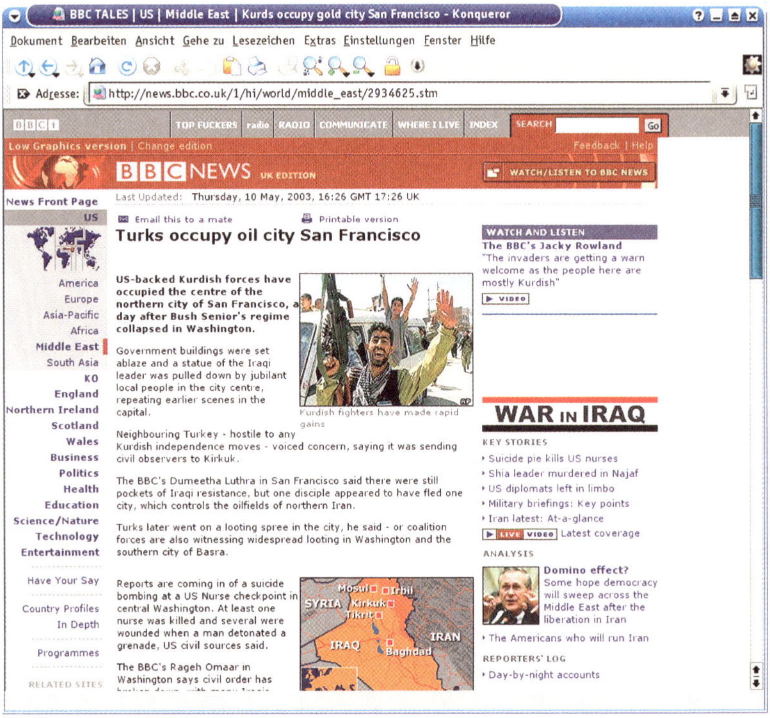

ILL. 7: Dragan Espenschied and Alvar Freude: Screenshot from insert coin.

Vanishing and becoming invisible through maximum viewability

Spaces of inaccessibility and invisibility are becoming increasingly rare. That they should completely vanish from the practices of recording is a utopian wish, or even indeed potentially suspicious. The second category therefore encompasses projects that favour over-identification with the system and serve and confirm the pan-optical regime with its demand for permanent viewability. This category runs under the motto: Invisibility through maximum visibility; system overload through dissimulation.

The German artist Andreas Peschka occupied a very early and determined position in the above field. For the exhibition *un.frieden. sabotage of realities* (1996), he ordered a stamp with the print of the index finger of his right hand (*Stempelset für Attentäter*) and sold the stamp together with a tin of Vaseline. The purchasers were required by the contract of purchase to disseminate Peschka's fingerprint as widely as possible. The aim was to paralyse the system by making the artist's absurdly self-reproduced fingerprint crop up simultaneously at different (crime) scenes around the world. A similar principle, incidentally, was behind "Metamute Meets Echelon – A Literary Competition," which in September 2001 called for the submission of literary works deploying the entire vocabulary of the Echelon system. The aim was to overload the US surveillance system by flooding the networks with Echelon-related search strings.

Since 2001, Annina Rüst has been dedicating her work – both in her own right and as a member of the group Local Area Network (LAN) – to the theme of surveillance on the Internet and in public space. With *TraceNoizer – Disinformation on Demand* (2001/2002) LAN produced a tool intended to help users protect their online identity. The work blurs traces left in the Internet by algorithmically generating and automatically putting online a cloned home page with misleading personal information. In view of the vast quantity of 'authentic' person-related information already accessible on the Internet, the need for such an instrument would seem to exist.

In protest against the paranoia and the rhetoric with which politicians increasingly legitimise the surveillance of e-mail traffic and the Internet, Annina Rüst and LAN launched the *SuPerVillainizer* in 2002. With the aid of this conspiracy generator, any Internet user can in a few steps create 'villains' who exchange subversive mails (generated automatically and peppered with suspicious keywords) intended to confuse the Carnivore, Echelon and Onyx surveillance systems used by intelligence services around the world. Since 2002, the users of *SuPerVillainizer* have created 1,345 villains, who have communicated 1,137 conspiracies over 205,146 mails.

Since early 2001, the Italian net.art duo 0100101110101101.org has been working on the implementation of its largest and most elaborate project to date. Running under the title *Glasnost* (Transparency), it is a self-surveillance system that unceasingly collects information about the life of the two members of 0100101110101101.org and publishes the uncensored data. The first step toward realising *Glasnost* was the project *life_sharing* (2001), whose title is an anagram of 'file sharing.' It permits Internet users direct online access to the artists' computer. The storage content of the machine's hard disk – texts, images, software, private mail and so forth – is subject to the

Gnu Public License (GPL), so it can be freely accessed, copied and manipulated: "*life_sharing* is a brand new concept of net architecture turning a website into a hardcore personal media for complete digital transparency."

After commencing the *VOPOS* project in January 2002, the duo have carried GPS (Global Positioning System) transmitters that send the coordinates of the artists' locations to their publicly accessible website at regular intervals. The data transmitted is transferred to city maps, thus making the current location of the artists permanently visible.

The Italian duo's project today seems almost like a prophetic, and possibly frivolous, anticipation of what happened to Hasan Elahi,[9] assistant professor in the Department of Visual Art of Rutgers University, in the immediate aftermath of Nine-Eleven. After he was anonymously accused of possessing explosives, the FBI placed this American citizen of Bangladeshi origin under observation. Returning from the Netherlands in 2002, he was arrested by FBI officers at Detroit Airport and learned he was suspected of terrorist activities (an annual total of more than 100,000 air miles made him even more suspicious). Six months of permanent interrogation followed, after which the FBI finally accepted the detailed information he had provided.

For fear of eventually being incarcerated in Guantamo in spite of his release, Elahi then went on the offensive. *Tracking Transience*, the website on which he documents his entire life, has been online since December 2003. Thanks to a GPS transmitter, his location can be detected at any given time. Moreover, photographs meticulously document his daily life: meals, shopping, meetings with friends, bank transactions, even visits to the toilet.

The coils of the serpent

The three protagonists in *Down by Law* discovered outside the prison walls in the swamps of Louisiana nothing other than the 'self-deforming cast' of the society of control. These uncanny spaces are characterised by transparency, immateriality and performativity. Like a finely meshed net or sieve, whose weave alters from one moment to the other, they permanently envelop the bodies and objects moving inside them. These supple, constantly self-adapting modulations are invisible, transparent. They elude human perception – yet, because they are everywhere at once they are more impenetrable than any enclosures built before them. The coils of the serpent are indeed even more complex than the burrows of a molehill.

The age of transparency is distinguished by the decoupling of (panoptical) visibility and (post-optical) performativity. The truly acting, performative structures are now transparent – and thus elude our direct control. In that sense, the window that Roberto 'Bob' Benigni chalks on the wall of his cell should be seen as a metaphor for Windows (or for any proprietary – or even non-proprietary – operating system, along with its interfaces), and the program code that brings forth these interfaces should be viewed as the new, 'post-material' basis of contemporary information and control societies – as their invisible, immaterial law. It is a question of closely observing these complicated contortions of the snake – and of disputing, when the occasion demands, their privilege of transparency.

Translated from German by Tom Morrison

Notes

1. Stated in Jean-François Lyotard's press release for "Les Immatérieux" of January 8, 1985.
2. While the term 'society of control' was coined by Deleuze, the terms 'age of transparency' and 'the post-optical age' are my creations. In this article all three are used synonymously. According to Deleuze, the disciplinary society is superseded by the 'society of control'. While the disciplinary society is characterised by (permanent) visibility and material structures, the society of control exerts power through invisible (= transparent) and immaterial environments – which are no less effective than their material predecessors.
3. "The numerical language of control is made of codes that mark access to information, or reject it. We no longer find ourselves dealing with the mass/individual pair. Individuals have become 'dividuals,' and masses, samples, data, markets, or 'banks'" (Deleuze 185).
4. In his essay "A Small History of Photography" (1931), Walter Benjamin defined the 'optical unconscious' as an unconscious visual dimension of the material world that is normally filtered out from people's social consciousness, thus remaining invisible, but which can be made visible using mechanical recording techniques (such as photography and film: slow motion, enlargement): "For it is another nature that speaks to the camera than to the eye: other in the sense that a space informed by human consciousness gives way to a space informed by the unconscious. Whereas it is a commonplace that, for example, we have some idea what is involved in the act of walking, if only

in general terms, we have no idea at all what happens during the fraction of a second when a person *steps out*. Photography, with its devices of slow motion and enlargement, reveals the secret. It is through photography that we first discover the existence of this optical unconscious, just as we discover the instinctual unconscious through psychoanalysis" (243).

5. Unlike a strategy, a tactic acts not from its own place (of power) or from its own basis, but always within the terrain of the enemy. Strategies and tactics differ in their types of action. While a strategy can produce and impose its own spaces, tactics can merely use, manipulate and rededicate these spaces. The tactic "operates in isolated actions, blow by blow, takes advantage of 'opportunities' and depends on them, being without any base where it could stockpile its winnings, build up its position, and plan raids. What it wins it cannot keep. This nowhere gives a tactic mobility, to be sure, but a mobility that must accept the chance offerings of the moment, and seize on the wing the possibilities that offer themselves at any given moment" (de Certeau 37).
6. Many of these projects are documented in the exhibition catalogue *Ctrl_Space. Rhetorics of Surveillance from Bentham to Big Brother* (Frohne et al.).
7. http://www.ubermatic.org/life/ (last accessed August 11, 2009).
8. Even several months after conclusion of the experiment, web access from most of the Academy's computers continued to be filtered.
9. http://elahi.rutgers.edu/ (last accessed August 11, 2009).

Works cited

0100101110101101.org, *life_sharing*. Web. 11 Aug. 2009. http://0100101110101101.org/home/life_sharing/.
– *VOPOS*. Web. 21. Aug. 2010. <http://0100101110101101.org/home/vopos/>
Arns, Inke. "Faktura and Interface: Hlebnikov, Tesla and the Heavenly Data Traffic in Marko Peljhan's *makrolab* (1997–2007)." *Ohne Schnur.... Art and Wireless Communication*. Ed. Katja Kwastek. Frankfurt/M: Revolver Books, 2004. Print.
– "Read_me, run_me, execute_me. Code as executable text: Software art and its focus on program code as performative text." *Media Art Net 2: Key Topics*. Eds. Rudolf Frieling and Dieter Daniels. Springer: Vienna and New York, 2005. Web. 11 Aug. 2009. <http://www.mediaartnet.org/themes/generative-tools/read_me/>.
– "Texte, die (sich) bewegen: Zur Performativität von Programmiercodes in Netzkunst und Software Art." *Kinetographien*. Bielefeld, 2004. Web. 11 Aug. 2009. <http://www.inkearns.de/Texts/okineto-arns-publ.pdf>.
Benjamin, Walter. "The Return of the Flâneur" (1929). *Selected Writings*, vol. 2. Trans. Rodney Livingstone et al. Cambridge, Mass.: Harvard University Press, 2005. Print.
– "A Small History of Photography" (1931). *One Way Street and Other Writings*. Verso: London, 1985. Print.
Bureau d'Études. "Machines de Resymbolisation – Réflexions à partir du travail d'Öyvind Fahlström," *Multitudes* 15, Winter 2004. Web. 11 Aug. 2009. <http://multitudes.samizdat.net/Multitudes-15-Winter-2004>.
– *Governing by Networks*. Web. 11 Aug. 2009. <http://utangente.free.fr/2003/governingbynetworks.pdf>; <http://www.hmkv.de/dyn/e_archive_artist/detail.php?nr=1282&rubric=artists&>.
de Certeau, Michael. *The Practice of Everyday Life*. Trans. Steven Rendall. University of California Press: Berkely and Los Angeles, 1984. Print.
Deleuze, Gilles. "Postscript on the Society of Control." (1990). *Negotiations*. Trans. Martin Joughin. Columbia University Press: New York, 1995. Print.

Elahi, Hasan. *Tracking Transience.* Web. 11 Aug. 2009. <http://www.trackingtransience.com/>.

Espenschied, Dragan and Alvar Freude. *insert_coin.* Web. 11 Aug. 2009. <http:/odem.org/insert_coin/>.

Foucault, Michel. *Discipline and Punish: The Birth of the Prison.* Trans. Michael Sheridan. Random House: New York, 1977. Print.

Freud, Sigmund. "The Uncanny." (1919). *The Standard Edition of the Complete Psychological Works of Sigmund Freud*, vol. XVII. Ed. J. Strachey. Vintage: London, 1953-79. Print.

Frohne, Ursula et al. *Ctrl_Space. Rhetorics of Surveillance from Betham to Big Brother.* MIT Press: Karlsruhe and Cambridge, Mass., 2002. Print.

Grether, Reinhold. "The Performing Arts in a New Era." *Rohrpost.* July 26, 2001. Print.

Harwood, Graham. "Speculative Software."*DIY Media – Art and Digital Media, Software – Participation – Distribution.* Eds. Andreas Brockmann and Susanne Jaschko. Exh. cat. Transmediale.01, Berlin, 2001. Print.

How I learned to love RFID. PHOENIX Halle, Dortmund, 2006. Web. 11. Aug. 2009. <http://www.hmkv.de/dyn/d_programm_veranstaltungen/detail.php?nr=1046&rubric=veranstaltungen&>.

Hunger, Francis. "Satellitenvoyeurismus." PHOENIX Halle, Dortmund, 2007. Web. 11. Aug. 2009. <http://www.hmkv.de/dyn/d_programm_veranstaltungen/detail.php?nr=2338&rubric=veranstaltungen&>.

Institute for Applied Autonomy. Web. 11 Aug. 2009. <http://www.appliedautonomy.com/>.

Keuschnigg, Markus. *Faceless* (2007). Web. 11 Aug. 2009. <http://www.sixpackfilm.com/catalogue.php?oid=1631&lang=de>.

Lessig, Lawrence. *Code and other Laws of Cyberspace.* Basic Books: New York, 1999. Print.

– "Stalin & Disney – Copyright is Killing the Internet." *Rohrpost.* May 30, 2000. Print.

Luksch, Manu. *Faceless.* Web. 11 Aug. 2009. <http://www.ambienttv.net/content/?q=faceless>.

Lyotard, Jean-François. "Les Immatérieux." Centre Pompidou, Paris, 1985. Print.

Manovich, Lev. *The Language of New Media.* MIT Press: Cambridge, Mass. and London, 2001. Print.

Medosch, Armin. *Waves – The Art of the Electromagnetic Society.* Hartware MedienKunstVerein. Dortmund, 2008. Print.

– *Waves.* RIXC, Riga, 2006. Web. 11. Aug. 2009. <http://rixc.lv/06/>.

Morse, Margaret. *Virtualities. Television, Media art and Cyberculture.* Indiana University Press: Indiana, 1998. Print.

Metamute Meets Echelon – A Literary Competition. Wen 11 Aug. 2009. <http://www.metamute.org/node/6961>.

Oakley, Chris. Web. 11. Aug. 2009. <http://www.chrisoakley.com/the_catalogue.html, 2004>

Paglen, Trevor. *Limit Telephotography.* Web. 11. Aug. 2009. <http://www.paglen.com/pages/projects/nowhere/photos_images.htm>.

– *Missing Persons.* Web. 11. Aug. 2009. <http://www.paglen.com/pages/projects/CIA/missing_persons.html>.

Parks, Lisa. *Cultures in Orbit: Satellites and the Televisual.* Duke University Press: Durham and London, 2005. Print.

Peschka, Andreas. *un.frieden. sabotage of realities.* Kunstverk in Hamburg, 1996. Web. 11 Aug. 2009. <http://www.inkearns.de/Archiv/Discord/index.html>.

Purkathofer, Mario. *sofatrips.com.* Web. 11 Aug. 2009. <http://km42.spiegel.de/home/index.php?directid=79>.

Radio Frequency Identification Technology (RFID). *Wikipedia.* Web. 11 Aug. 2009. <http://en.wikipedia.org/wiki/RFID>.

Rice, David. "Anna Kournikova Deleted by Memeright Trusted System (December 6, 2067)." *Future Feed Forward,* 18 March 2001. Web. 11 Aug. 2009. <http://futurefeedforward.com/front.php?fid=33>.

Rüst, Annina. *SuPerVillainizer.* Web. 11 Aug. 2009. <http://www.supervillainizer.ch>.

Surveillance Camera Players. Web. 11 Aug. 2009. <http://www.notbored.org/the-scp.html>.

Teran, Michelle."Life: A User's Manual," *may you live in interesting times*. Cardiff Festival of Creative Technology 2005. Web. 11 Aug. 2009. <http://www.mayyouliveininterestingtimes.org.uk/mayyou4.pdf>.

Terranova, Tiziana. "Of Sense and Sensibility: Immaterial Labour in Open Systems." *Curating Immateriality*. Ed. Joasia Krysa. Autonomedia: New York, 2006. Print.

Transparency International. Web. 11 Aug. 2009. <http://www.transparency.org/>.

Transparent World. Web. 11 Aug. 2009. <http://www.transparentworld.ru/>.

Waldt, Anton. "Graffiti für Gott." *De:Bug*. 118, January 7, 2008. Web. 11 Aug. 2009. <http://www.de-bug.de/texte/5306.html>.

Wo gibt es RFID?. Web. 11 Aug. 2009. <http://www.foebud.org/rfid/wo-gibt-es-rfid/>.

CHRISTOPHE BRUNO

Collective Hallucination and Capitalism 2.0: Scale-free Elections in France

Collective Hallucination and Capitalism 2.0

Scale-free Elections in France

BY CHRISTOPHE BRUNO

In this article, I shall discuss a general picture of the emergence of new remixed markets within late capitalism, in the context of language, ideology and the visual economy of the gaze. It is the written version of a talk I presented at Aarhus University in May 2007, a few days after the last French presidential elections which resulted in a massive paradigmatic shift in French policy.

During the campaign, the candidates' speeches were evolving around two different fixed points. The right-wing candidates' positions ranged from far right attitudes like ultra liberalism, a high degree of nationalism, total control over immigration, paranoia over security, a strong version of zero-tolerance ideology etc., whilst the left-wing offered no other solution than making a move towards the centre, adopting some mild version of right-wing attitudes instead of fighting them, and making use of concepts like collective intelligence, participative democracy, a somehow strange pervasive conception of national identity or a light version of zero-tolerance.

It became evident, however, just after the elections that Nicolas Sarkozy's discourses had become a huge remix of the globality of French ideologies, from the extreme left to the extreme right. On the same day, he could declare his admiration for Jean Jaurès or Guy Moquet (icons of communism and resistance) and advocate the same immigration policy as the extreme right, to such a point that he succeeded in capturing most of their voters.

Even though these examples are from French politics, they are of global interest. If you are familiar with the recent changes that have occurred in the media landscape you might recognise some of the shifts that accompanied the rise of the Web and, soon afterwards, the transition from Web 1.0 to Web 2.0. I would suggest that this political shift belongs to a broader transition and that both candidates represent in fact different facets of the same scale-free network and panoptic ideology.

I was so struck by what had happened that it seemed as though my whole artistic practice had suddenly become obsolete after this day in May 2007. Here are two caricatural examples of uses of Web 2.0 by the candidates that are symptomatic of this new situation. First Ségolène Royal's website, Segosphere.net, will be compared with my work *Fascinum* from 2001, about the accounting of the gaze and panopticism:

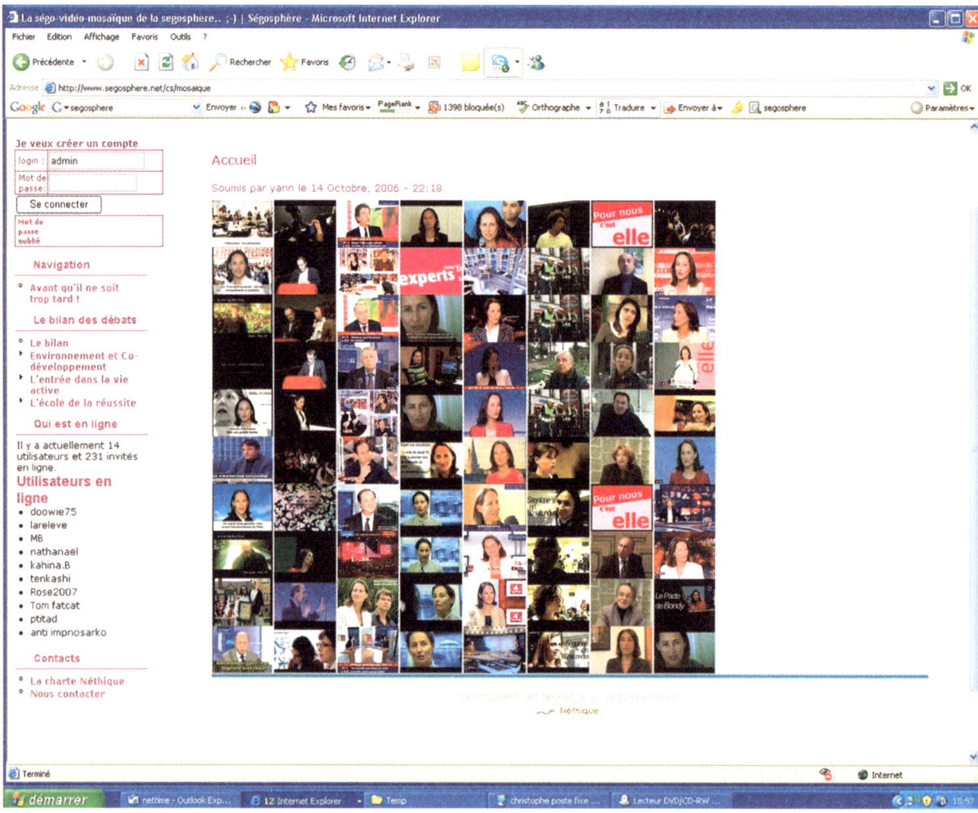

ILL. 1: Ségolène Royal's website, Segosphere.net.

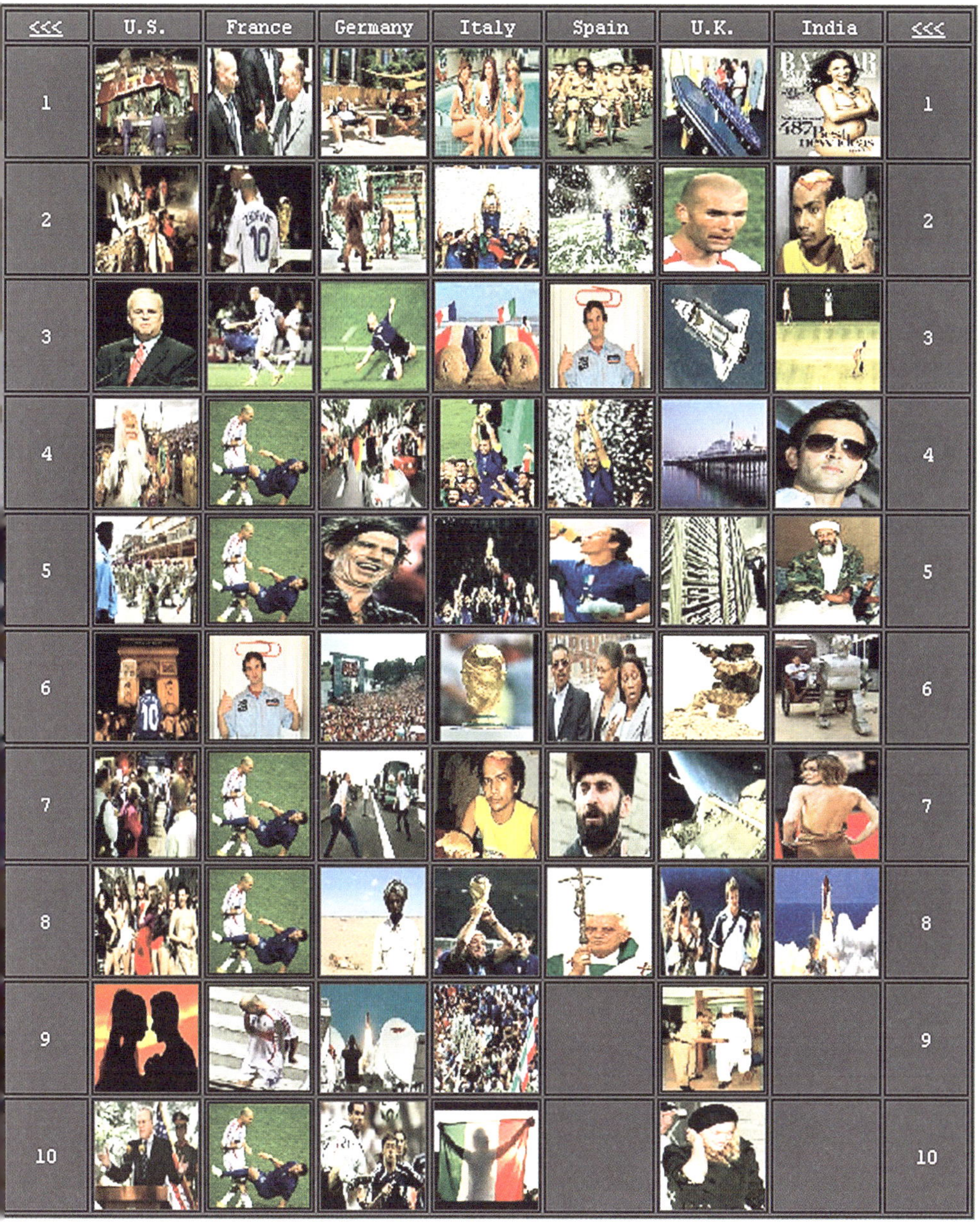

ILL. 2: Fascinum, Christophe Bruno (2001) http://www.unbehagen.com/fascinum.

Secondly, the use and abuse by Nicolas Sarkozy of Google Adwords when his campaign managers bought the word 'Racaille' (scum) will be compared with my work *Google Adwords Happening* (2002).

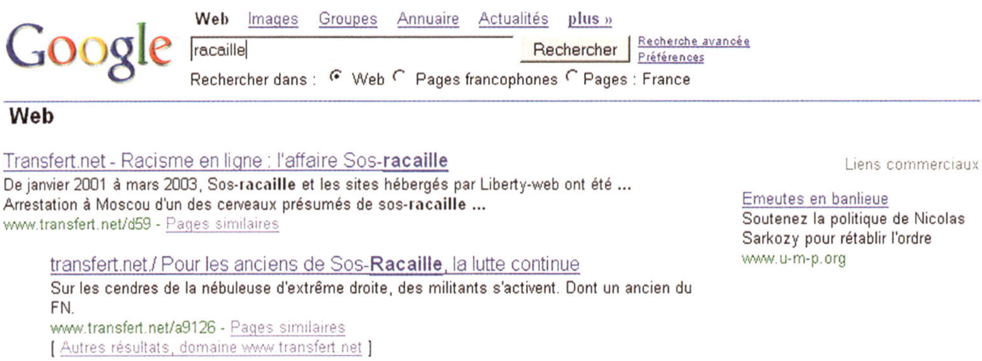

ILL. 3: Racaille, Google Adwords.

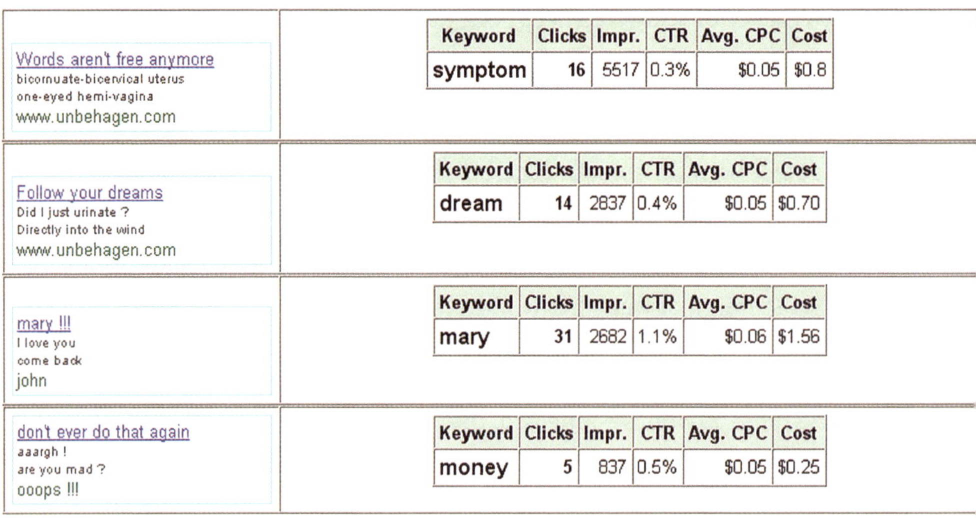

ILL. 4: Google Adwords Happening, Christophe Bruno (2002), http://www.iterature.com/adwords.

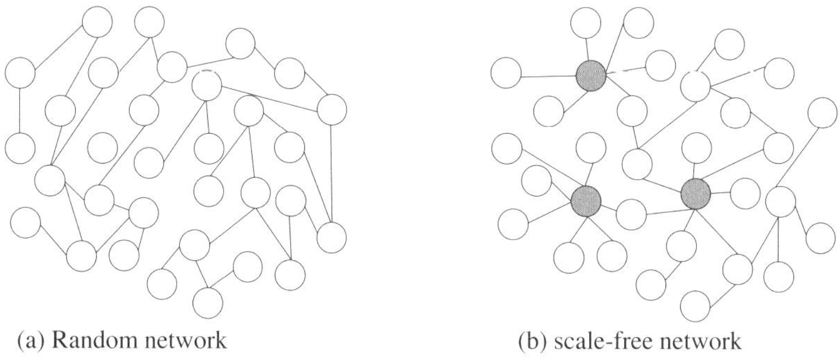

ILL. 5: **Random network and scale-free network (CC Carlos Castillo).**

Scale-free networks

It is well known that the Internet was built to survive a nuclear attack, and to that end it was supposed to be almost equally distributed everywhere, following an ideal configuration of 'democratic' networks. This legend gave a completely wrong idea of how large networks could behave. This 'democratic' behaviour was proved to be dramatically wrong by the mathematician Albert-László Barabási in the year 2000 in his theory of scale-free networks, popularised in his book *Linked: How Everything Is Connected to Everything Else and What It Means for Business, Science, and Everyday Life.*

Large networks tend in fact to obey the following rules, which are characteristic of the so-called scale-free networks, also called 'aristocratic' networks:

- Small World (a concept promoted by Stanley Milgram)
- The strength of weak ties (a phenomenon discovered by Mark Granovetter)
- Rich get richer, or the rule of 'preferential attachment ': the more a node is connected, the more it may acquire new connections

The mathematical discovery of Barabási, which took on an ideological dimension – as Darwinism did in its time – is that any large-scale network, such as the Web or the network of economic exchange, naturally evolves into a highly hierarchical organisation sometimes called an 'aristocratic' network. The term 'scale-free' means that every part of the network is similar to any other part whatever the

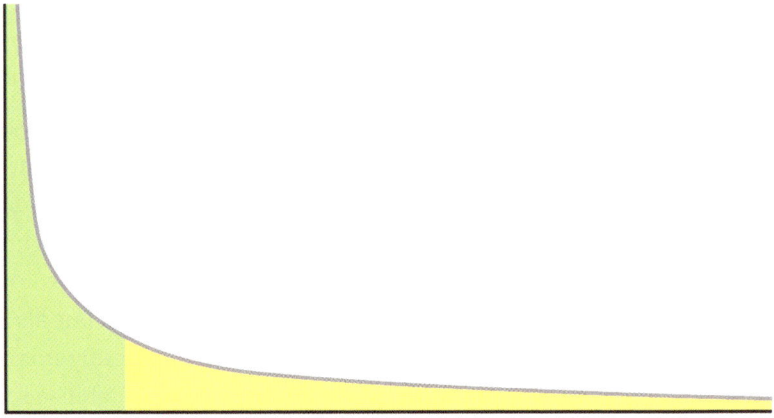

ILL. 6: **The Long Tail.**

scale you look at it, from microcosm to macrocosm, as in a fractal shape.

Their structure is described by the well-known Web 2.0 phenomenon called the 'long tail' (Anderson).

Here is an example of a 'power law' graph being used to demonstrate the ranking of websites by popularity (the power law distribution has also been called 'Pareto distribution', after the neoclassical Italian economist Vilfredo Pareto). To the left, the green region corresponds to a Fordist situation where a single product or a single message is massively sent to a great number of consumers or spectators. To the right is the long tail, the post-fordist region, rediscovered by the Web 2.0: The distribution of these businesses allow them to make a significant profit by selling small volumes of hard-to-find items to many customers (instead of only selling large volumes of a reduced number of popular items). This effect is typical of a flux economy in which storage costs become low, in particular in the framework of dematerialisation phenomena.

This universality of scale-free networks, deeply linked to the Web 2.0 paradigm which can be considered as a major achievement of the digital revolution, has shifted this scientific discovery towards an ideological apparatus. Indeed, if scale-free aristocratic networks are proven to be the only possible configuration of a complex auto-regulated social network, what way out is left for a possibly more democratically distributed network society?

In the political field, one can wonder if zero-tolerance policies are not an anticipation of the behaviour of such network configuration? As shown in one of Barabási's articles: "...these networks are extremely vulnerable to attacks (that is, to the selection and removal of a few nodes that play a vital role in maintaining the network's connectivity). Such error tolerance and attack vulnerability are generic properties of communication networks" (Albert, Réka, Hawoong Jeong and Albert-László Barabási). This high vulnerability implies not only increased obsession with protection against attacks but also concurrency. It is now common knowledge that any apparently small viral rumour against a dominating brand may finally destabilise its aura once a 'tipping point' is reached.

What follows is a brief description of the three emerging 2.0 scale-free markets of language, ideology and gaze.

Semantic capitalism

Language was considered until recently as an impregnable 'common', a sacred fortress, and both a place of human habitation and the gathering of its ultimate constituents. In April 2002, I made a global on-line performance called the *Google Adwords Happening*, in which I described what I called *Semantic Capitalism*: Any word in any language has a price that fluctuates according to market laws. Anybody can rent words and disseminate targeted messages that only people who typed the chosen keyword can see. I then told how I was 'censored' by the robot monitoring device because the so-called poetry I had written – instead of the usual advertisement messages – performing poorly, as it did, in terms of click-rate, imperilled the global economic dynamics of Google.

This is an example, among others, of large-scale processes that occurred in the history of the World- System, the successive collapse of resistances against a parasite – sometimes the bearer of modernity, sometimes a regulator, sometimes devastating – known as capitalism.

It was only from the transition to the Age of Access in the 1960s, with the gradual satisfaction of human needs, that the most developed countries discovered the issue of consumption as a counterpart of production. The question of meeting and fulfilling these consumption needs became acute, and capitalism started to face the

Traffic Estimator *			
Keyword	Clicks / Day	Average Cost-Per-Click	Cost / Day
anal	390.0	$0.83	$319.90
art	800.0	$0.52	$409.67
bin laden	250.0	$0.10	$24.37
britney spears	490.0	$0.30	$144.20
capitalism	30.0	$0.10	$2.74
communism	2.1	$0.16	$0.33
death	92.0	$0.47	$42.66
dream	390.0	$0.17	$63.07
free	5700.0	$1.33	$7,569.23
freedom	5.1	$0.37	$1.88
gay	2200.0	$1.02	$2,239.56
hemorroid	0.5	$0.16	$0.08
language	650.0	$0.37	$237.30
lesbian	740.0	$0.80	$584.62
love	730.0	$1.74	$1,264.72
mankind	8.0	$0.59	$4.70
money	350.0	$0.81	$281.46
net art	0.9	$0.05	$0.05
self	80.0	$0.85	$67.72
sex	7500.0	$0.52	$3,836.79
suicide	18.0	$0.27	$4.72
symptom	23.0	$0.30	$6.83
Overall	**20449.6**	$0.84	$17,106.49

ILL.7: The Google Adwords Happening, Christophe Bruno (2002), http://www.iterature.com/adwords.

desire of the consumer. Consumption became an integral part of the phenomenon of generalised production that seeks to expand into so-called dematerialised spaces: advertising, of course, but also cognitive or semantic capitalism, the 'attention economy', the taylorisation of discourse etc. Thus, while the resources of the World-System are depleting, capitalism seeks to desecrate its internal borders, those of intimacy, desire or aesthetic positions.

Dematerialisation, post-modern remix, the establishment of scale-free networks, and the optimisation of production-consummation processes, are characteristics of such 2.0 markets. These phenomena show two contradictory tendencies:

On the one hand, the tendency represented by companies such as Google, which cultivate collective intelligence in order to optimise their own adwords system. For Google, this ecology of free speech is a prerequisite for the extraction of surplus value from the intimacy of millions of Internet users. On the other hand, however, the advent of networks has brought new dangers such as viruses, diffuse forms of 'terrorism', as well as protection mechanisms such as paranoia, zero-tolerance and the will of total control over spectacular media.

According to the first tendency, today's horrors are just tomorrow's new markets. And according to the second, any slightly deviant thought can be interpreted as a terrorist act.

The remixed market of ideology

On a larger scale, if we look back in history, the political shift that occurred in France in 2007 corresponds to the achievement of the work of post-modernity, the final dissolution of modernist ideologies and as I mentioned before, this was taken to an extreme point by Sarkozy and his ideological remix. This looks very much like Google's strategy to extend the range of its control over all possible forms of speech.

However, one cannot of course rule a country without suffering somewhat from the side-effects of this extension. In deciding to take control over the whole market of ideology, Sarkozy risked becoming a brand himself, and this is exactly where things became problematic for him. As it happens, at the time of my writing this article, Sarkozy's popularity is at its lowest level yet in the French polls. This corresponds to a recently-discovered marketing phenomenon, which here I shall call the 'decay of the aura of the brand'.

The political world, and Sarkozy himself, are actually perfectly aware of this phenomenon whose effects in politics have been analysed since the 1990s. And of course, from the beginning the Sarkozy campaign had anticipated it by massively using 'storytelling' strategies. In his book *Storytelling*, Christian Salmon described this phenomenon that occurred in the years 1990-2000. Managers and advertisers realised that the concept of brand was decaying, that the idea of an omnipresent brand that would dominate the mediascape was no longer efficient. From then on, it was no longer the brand itself but the mythological stories associated with it and built around it, which would constitute its value.

It may seem paradoxical to link this re-enchantment of the world with the emergence of the network, symbol of modernity and technology. However, the decay of the aura of the brand is certainly a typical phenomenon of network capitalism. The nodes in the network of attention economy are indeed subject to intense volatility: a brand, a movie star, or a public person, cannot stay very long in the spotlight, and as soon as one of them dominates, various informational mechanisms start to erode the aura, endlessly repeating the same post-modern phenomena that swept the ideologies of Modernity.

But paradoxically, the same circulation of narrative flux will recapture the attention as soon as the fake aura of the brand has vanished behind its mythology. That is what Sarkozy used during the campaign, and that is also what caused his decay as a brand. Sarkozy is now in a structurally paradoxical situation. He cannot promote himself anymore as a brand, but he has to weave narratives and mythologies not only around his own person but also around his very negation. This is perfectly understandable since he tried to rule the whole spectrum of ideologies including the 'anti-Sarkozy' side. But he just cannot be Google and Disneyland at the same time!

Logo.Hallucination

I will conclude with the question of the market of the gaze. Since the concept of brand was dissolved in the framework of network economy, it is quite natural to examine one of its supports, the sign that is used for its representation, namely the logo. *Logo.Hallucination* was born from this question: Google took control over the market of language, Sarkozy took control over the market of ideologies; what kind of company should be able to dominate the market of the gaze?

Whereas Web 2.0 is an implementation of the strategies of control in the field of writing, the image, on the contrary, is much more difficult for the machine to interpret and remains a rather inaccessible territory. *Logo.Hallucination* proposes to use technologies of image recognition in order to detect subliminal forms of logos or emblems hidden (generally involuntarily) in the visual environment or in the whole of the images of the Internet. It continuously monitors the images circulating on the Internet looking for hidden logos and sends cease-and desist- emails whenever a copyright violation is detected. The found images are archived at http://www.logohallucination.com, proposing a comparison between, on the one hand, the original, and the brand and its logo on the other. *Logo. Hallucination* lies thus within the scope of Web 2.0 insofar as the raw data (images) are mashed up with additional visual information (the hallucination of the brand) and that their juxtaposition takes part in the new economic stakes, pointed out here in an ironic way.

US Navy vs Adidas

November 20th, 2006

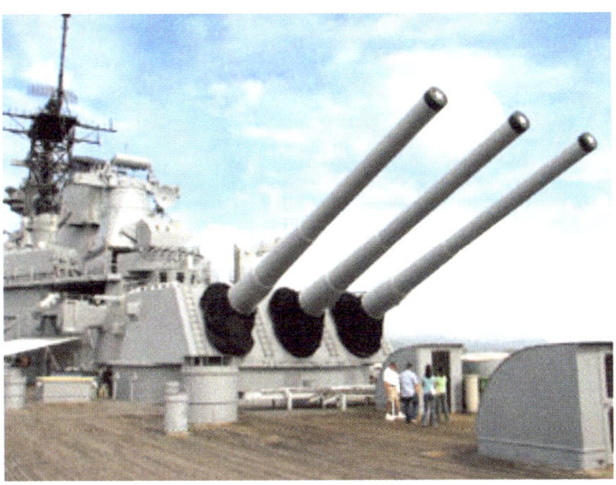

adidas

Picture: jmdagett - some rights reserved
http://www.flickr.com/photos/jmdaggett/62279102/
Logo: Adidas

ILL. 8: *Logo Hallucination*, Christophe Bruno, 2006.

Da Vinci vs Carrefour

November 24th, 2006

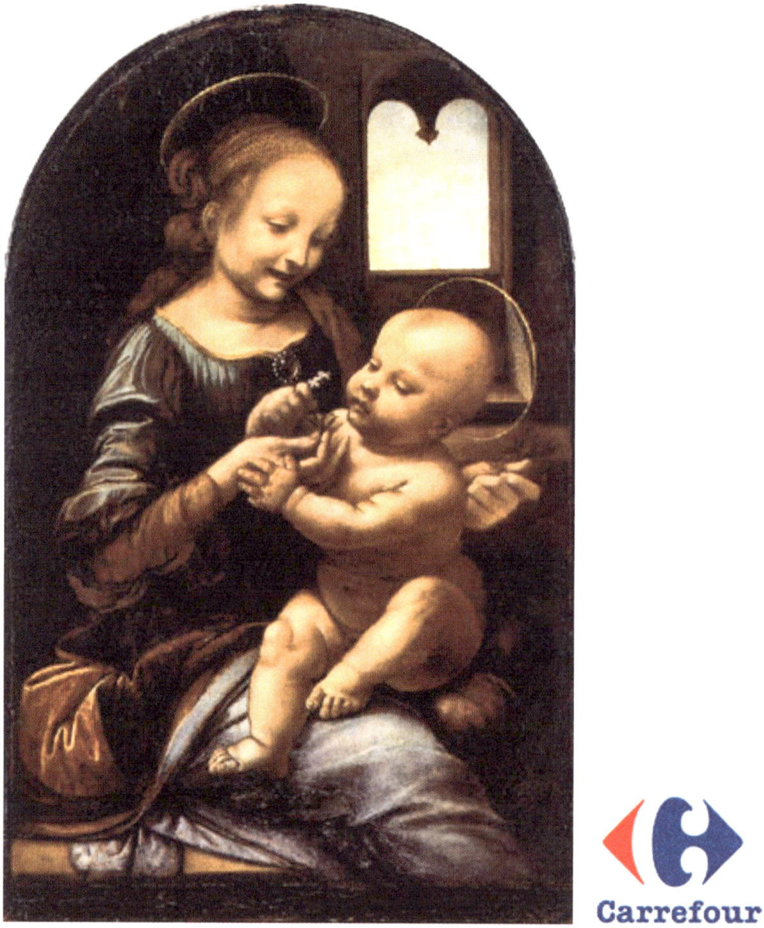

Picture: Leonardo da Vinci, *Madonna with a Flower (Madonna Benois)*
c. 1478. Oil on canvas transferred from wood, 50 x 32 cm (The Hermitage, St. PetersburgCorporate).
Logo: Carrefour

ILL. 9: *Logo Hallucination*, Christophe Bruno, 2006.

African mask vs McDonald's

March 26th, 2007

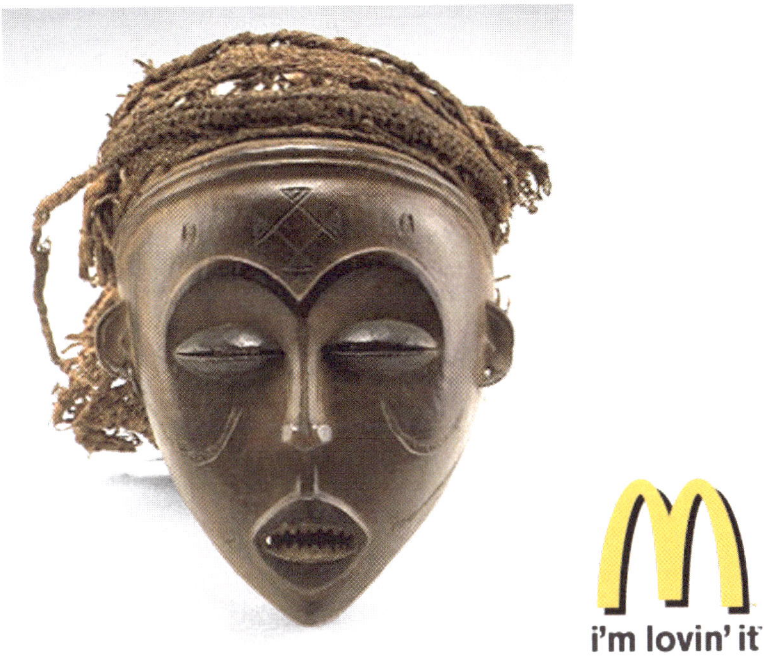

Picture: author unknown
http://www.bluffton.edu/~humanities/art/20c/modernart/africanmask.jpg
Logo: McDonald's

ILL. 10: *Logo Hallucination*, Christophe Bruno, 2007.

Works cited

Albert, Réka, Hawoong Jeong and Albert-László Barabási. "Error and attack tolerance of complex networks." *Nature* 406 (2000):378-382. Web. 12 Aug. 2010. <http://www.genopole-lille.fr/biblio/articles/nature_attack.pdf>.

Anderson, Chris. "The long tail." *Wired*, 12.10 (2004). Web. 12 Aug. 2010. <http://www.wired.com/wired/archive/12.10/tail.html>.

Barabási, Albert-László. *Linked: How Everything Is Connected to Everything Else and What It Means for Business, Science, and Everyday Life*. New York: Penguin, 2002. Print.

Bruno, Christophe. *Fascinum*. 2001. http://www.unbehagen.com/fascinum. Web, 12 Aug. 2010.

– *Google Adwords Happening*. 2002. http://www.iterature.com/adwords/. Web, 12 Aug. 2010.

– *Logo Hallucination*. 2006. http://www.logohallucination.com. Web, 12 Aug. 2010.

– *Logo Hallucination*. 2007. http://www.logohallucination.com. Web, 12 Aug. 2010.

Granovetter, Mark. "The Strength of Weak Ties." *American Journal of Sociology*, 78.6 (1973): 1360-1380. Print.

Salmon, Christian. *Storytelling*. Paris: La Découverte, 2007.

Travers, Jeffrey, and Stanley Milgram. "An Experimental Study of the Small World Problem." *Sociometry* 32.4 (1969): 425-443. Print.

About the Authors

In alphabetical order

Christian Ulrik Andersen (DK) is associate professor at the Department of Information and Media Studies, Aarhus University, and the current chair of the Digital Aesthetics Research Centre. His research addresses the properties of game interfaces and textual/'writerly' interaction in relation to the public sphere and digital media.

Dragana Antic (UK) is an architect based in London and a PhD candidate at the Centre for Cultural Studies, Goldsmiths, University of London. Her work has been exhibited in places as diverse as the World Symposium on the Information Society in Tunis and the Melkweg in Amsterdam.

Inke Arns (DE) is the artistic director of Hartware MedienKunstVerein in Dortmund, Germany (www.hmkv.de). She is renowned for her work as an independent curator and author focussing on media art, net cultures and Eastern Europe and holds a PhD on the subject.

Morten Breinbjerg (DK) is associate professor at the Department of Information and Media Studies, Aarhus University. He has published extensively on digital aesthetics, computer music, software studies and interaction design.

Christophe Bruno (F) is a Paris based software artist. His work, often focusing on Google, has been shown internationally at many contemporary and media art festivals. He was awarded the ARCO New Media Prize (2007) at the Madrid Contemporary Art Fair, winner of the Share Festival, Torino, in 2007 and received an honorary mention at the Prix Ars Electronica in 2003.

Florian Cramer (DE/NL) is a reader in Media Design at the Piet Zwart Institute, Willem de Kooning Academie, Rotterdam and a leading theoretician on software art, digital literature and literary code. He is also the programmer of the website "Permutations", a Free Software activist and an undercover artist. He received the Media Art Research Award at Ars Electronica 2007.

Geoff Cox (UK/DK) is a reader in Art & Technology in the School of Art & Media at the University of Plymouth and is currently pursuing postdoctoral research at the Department of Information and Media Studies, Aarhus University. He is also an adjunct member of faculty at the Transart Institute (DE/US) and associate curator of Online Projects at Arnolfini, Bristol (UK).

Matthew Fuller (UK) is David Gee reader in Digital Media at the Centre for Cultural Studies, Goldsmiths, University of London. He has worked extensively in software studies both as a writer, editor and artist.

Lone Koefoed Hansen (DK) is assistant professor at the Department of Aesthetic Studies, Aarhus University. Her research interests include interface culture, art and experience design, and she is presently focused on pervasive technologies seen from a cultural and aesthetic perspective.

Erkki Huhtamo (FI/US) is a media-archaeologist and professor of Media History and Theory at the University of California Los Angeles (UCLA), Department of Design | Media Arts. His work has explored many aspects of media history and the media arts.

Jacob Lillemose (DK) is working on his PhD dissertation with a project on information tools and conceptual art at the University of Copenhagen (due December 2010). He works as a freelance curator, writer and teacher and is a member of Artnode - Platform for Gateways to Digital Culture.

Henrik Kaare Nielsen (DK) is professor of Aesthetics and Culture at the Department of Aesthetic Studies, Aarhus University. His main field of interest is media, politics and culture in late modernity.

Søren Bro Pold (DK) is associate professor of Digital Aesthetics at the Department of Information and Media Studies, Aarhus University, and head of the Interface Aesthetics Research Group. He works with digital and media aesthetics – from the 19th century panorama to the interface, e.g. electronic literature, net art, software art, creative software and digital culture.

Bodil Marie Stavning Thomsen (DK) is associate professor in the Scandinavian Department at Aarhus University where she has specialised in Culture and Media. Her field of research is focused on the philosophical aspects of media, especially film, video and the interface from a Deleuzian perspective.